Professor Vere Gordon Childe was born in Sydney, New South Wales, in 1892. He graduated in Classics from Sydney University and studied at The Queen's College, Oxford, under Sir Arthur Evans and J. L. Myers. In 1927 he was appointed to the newly founded Abercromby Chair of Prehistoric Archaeology at the University of Edinburgh, and directed many excavations in Scotland and Northern Ireland. From 1946 to 1956 he was Professor of Prehistoric Archaeology and Director of the Institute of Archaeology in the University of London. He died in Australia in 1957.

Internationally recognized as the most outstanding figure in contemporary world archaeology, he received honorary degrees from European and American universities. Childe wrote nearly twenty books including *New Light on the Most Ancient Near East*; *The Prehistory of Scotland*; *Man Makes Himself*; *Prehistoric Communities in the British Isles*; *What Happened in History*; and *Piecing Together the Past*.

The Dawn of European Civilization is published in an archaeology series under the general editorship of Barry Cunliffe.

V. Gordon Childe

Dawn of European Civilization

Paladin

Granada Publishing Limited
Published in 1973 by Paladin
Frogmore, St Albans, Herts AL2 2NF

First published in 1925 by Routledge & Kegan Paul Ltd
Sixth edition (revised) published in 1957
Copyright © V. Gordon Childe 1957
Made and printed in Great Britain by Richard Clay
(The Chaucer Press), Ltd, Bungay, Suffolk
Set in Monotype Ehrhardt

Contents

List of Illustrations

Introduction

Gordon Childe, an ugly unknown Australian, arrived in London in 1922. Three years later he was to astound the scholarly world with the first edition of *The Dawn of European Civilization*, reprinted here in its final sixth edition which appeared in 1957, the year of his death. For 35 years *The Dawn* remained a standard textbook: now it takes its place as a classic in the history of archaeological thought.

To understand the book, it is necessary to know something of its author. He was a loner, dedicated to the pursuit of archaeology above all else. Brought up in the rigorous, dreary atmosphere of late Victorian Sydney and dominated by his strict clergyman father, the Rev. S. H. Childe, he was soon to rebel. In 1914, at the age of 22, he escaped to Oxford, where having obtained a First in Greats, he began to work on a B.Litt., influenced and guided by two of the greatest scholars of the time, John Linton Myres and Sir Arthur Evans. His views of Oxford archaeology were summed up many years later in a characteristically terse but not unkind reflection: 'My Oxford training was in the Classical tradition to which bronzes, terracottas and pottery (at least if painted) were respectable while stone and bone tools were banausic.'

After Oxford, he returned briefly to Australia to serve as secretary to the Labour premier of New South Wales, publishing his first book *How Labour Governs*, an episode he was later to describe as 'a sentimental excursion into Australian politics'. But archaeology was his first love and after a short while he returned to Europe – a Europe shattered by the effects of the First World War, where all was in flux and fears of a Bolshevik revolution were everywhere apparent.

His wanderings through eastern Europe clearly had a considerable effect on him. Not only did he study most of the major museum collections and meet the leading authorities, but he absorbed something of the pervading atmosphere of political ferment. Thus when he arrived back in England in 1922 at the age of thirty, the influences that were to condition his later concepts were already present. On an archaeological level he had absorbed the flavour of diffusionist thinking, and had also mastered a great mass of technical detail which enabled him to test his theories and those of others against hard facts; on the personal level, his natural disenchantment with his childhood environment had led him to become a confirmed atheist and to flirt with Marxist (or more correctly Marrist) political theory.

It was fortunate that on his arrival he was able to find employment as librarian to the Royal Anthropological Institute. Five years later, after the appearance of the first edition of *The Dawn*, he became the first Abercromby Professor of Prehistoric Archaeology at Edinburgh, a post which he held until he was appointed Professor of European Archaeology and Director of the Institute of Archaeology in the University of London in 1946. In 1957 he retired at the age of sixty-five, and returned to Australia, where he died within a few weeks. Thus his life was uneventful, but his intellectual achievements, communicated through his numerous books and articles, have had a dramatic and lasting effect on the archaeological world.

Just before his sudden death he wrote a remarkable autobiographical note which was published posthumously under the title of 'Retrospect' in volume 32 of *Antiquity*. In it he describes how his life's work followed a logical pattern of research and discovery which gradually unfolded, the results of which were presented in a series of books culminating in the last edition of *The Dawn* and its more popular counterpart *The Prehistory of European Society*.

To begin with, he saw himself as the link between the great Aegean archaeologists and their rapidly accumulating, sometimes sensational, discoveries, on the one hand, and the parochial developments in Britain on the other. By travelling widely in the intervening areas of Europe, he

accumulated a volume of facts and numbers of notions that were unfamiliar to English prehistorians . . . I absorbed the German concept of a culture, defined but not constituted by distinctive pottery and representing a people . . . at that time the significance of the löss for Neolithic settlement and of forest as a barrier thereto were strangely unfamiliar in Britain, though Myres had long been preaching a geographical approach. Eventually I stumbled upon Gams and Nordhagen and so introduced the idea of post-glacial climatic changes to English readers. . .

Childe had in fact laid the basis for much future archaeological thought by emphasizing the dynamic relationship between the changing environment and prehistoric communities, which he characterized using his own elaboration of the culture concept: 'The Dawn aimed at distilling from archaeological remains a preliterate substitute for the conventional politico-military history with cultures, instead of statesmen, as actors, and migrations in place of battles.'

Childe was always a diffusionist, but of a moderate kind. He believed in the 'irradiation of European barbarism by Oriental civilization' but he could not follow the extreme views of people like Perry and Eliot Smith, whose faith in ex oriente lux caused them to postulate the mythical Children of the Sun (a concept still surprisingly adhered to in some fringe quarters even today). Childe admits that his reliance on a diffusionist model was to some extent conditioned by a reaction against the theory of indigenous development put forward by Schmidt and Kossinna and distorted by politicians to prop up the edifice of German nationalism. Although throughout subsequent editions of The Dawn he came to rely less and less on a diffusionist explanation, he was still using phrases like 'the missionaries of megalithic religion' in his last book, The Prehistory of European Society, to explain the widespread phenomenon of megalith tombs distributed from the Mediterranean and the Atlantic sea coasts to as far north as Denmark. The western sea-ways and the Danubian valley were to him the corridors through which the 'irradiation' of barbarian Europe took place. Even though he firmly rejected the idea that the people responsible for the spreading of this oriental influence were Egyptians, the influence of the diffusionists remained apparent in his work throughout his life.

In 1926, the year after the publication of The Dawn, his second major archaeological work, The Aryans, appeared. Here he was returning to his first interests. He had come to archaeology through a study of Comparative Philology:

I began the study of European archaeology in the hope of finding the cradle of the Indo-Europeans and of identifying their primitive culture ... I hoped to find archaeological links between (Thessaly) and some tract of the north Balkans whence similar links might lead also to Iran and India. This search – naturally fruitless – was the theme of my B.Litt. thesis at Oxford.

None the less *The Aryans* summed up the situation as it was then known, and it has remained a valuable source until quite recently, when a resurgence of interest in the subject has led to rapid new developments.

The Aryans was essentially a consolidating operation; so too was *The Danube in Prehistory* (1929), a massive work expanding and documenting the cultural development in the Danube corridor. *The Danube* was compiled in parallel with another book, *The Most Ancient East*, sub-titled 'The Oriental Prelude to European Prehistory', and published in 1928. The creative output of these years was incredible: *The Dawn* (1st edn) 1925, *The Aryans* 1926, *The Dawn* (2nd edn) 1927, *The Most Ancient East* 1928, and *The Danube* 1929. The groundwork had now been laid.

In 1930 Childe published *The Bronze Age*, which he quite clearly regarded as a turning point in his own thinking. Here he was to emphasize the importance of regular trade, particularly in copper, in allowing for the emergence of a class of specialists. This for him marked the first significant step towards the social division of labour. Later, in *The Prehistory of European Society*, he elaborated the point, describing the complex politico-economic structure of temperate Europe in *c*. 1500 B.C., composed of tiny independent warring units linked together by a common technology practised by a specialist élite.

Whoever had the perseverance to earn initiation into the appropriate mysteries of technique and the courage to face the enormous risks and severe hardships involved, could escape the necessity of growing his own food and shake off the bonds of allegiance to an overlord or the more rigid fetters of tribal custom.

He saw these men as the first of the great tradition of free crafts-men–scientists–philosophers: 'The metics at Athens, the way-faring journeymen of the Middle Ages, and the migrant craft unionist of the nineteenth century are the lineal descendants of the itinerants just described.' This is indeed bold evocative stuff – perhaps a little difficult to accept in all its implications today. Nevertheless by viewing the Bronze Age in this way, he was, he says, 'finally committed to an economic interpretation of the archaeological data'.

From this new viewpoint he was able to look afresh at the discoveries being made in the Near East, and when in 1934 he came to republish *The Most Ancient East*, under the title of *New Light on the Most Ancient East*, he found it helpful to introduce the concepts of 'Neolithic Revolution' and 'Urban Revolution' to explain what at the time appeared to be the sudden development of agriculture followed by an upsurge of city life. These two great 'events', one following closely upon the other, were seen to pave the way for the 'Industrial Revolution' of the eighteenth century. Soon, after a visit to Russia, he began to adopt Marxist terminology, integrating the stages of 'savagery', 'barbarism', and 'civilization' used by Morgan, with his 'revolutions'. Thus before the Neolithic revolution, communities were in a stage of savagery; between the Neolithic and Urban revolutions there was barbarism, while civilization went hand in hand with the emergence of towns. This simple socio-economic model was produced as an alternative to the more commonly adopted technological model or Three Age System, first propounded early in the nineteenth century.

If the period 1925–30 had been for Childe a time for collecting and ordering data, 1930–40 was the period during which his ideological approach matured. He found in Marxism (or what he referred to as the Marrist perversion) an acceptable intellectual framework for understanding prehistory which was in sympathy with his political leanings. 'I suppose,' he wrote, 'most prehistorians are inclined to be so far Marxist as to wish to assign (means of production) a determining role among the behaviour patterns that have fossilized.' This, indeed, was one of the themes of his little book *Man Makes Himself* (1936).

Thus when he came to revise *The Dawn* for its third edition, published in 1939, his view had developed so far as to demand a thorough revision of the text: he explains 'I paid lip service to "Marxism" in a standardized scheme for the description of cultures: first the food quest, then secondary industries and trade, only thereafter social and religious institutions, insofar as they can be inferred or deduced.' A few years later he used the Marxist model to provide the interpretative structure for his *Scotland before the Scots* (1946), a book which covered the same ground as his earlier work *The Prehistory of Scotland* (1935). In spite of the views of many of his colleagues, he remained convinced that the later approach was the better, being 'far more realistic and far more historical than had been achieved with migrationist hypotheses'.

He was to produce two other major works of synthesis, a text book on British prehistory entitled *Prehistoric Communities of the British Isles* (1940) and *Prehistoric Migrations* (1950), based on a series of lectures delivered at Oslo, in which he returned once more to his first love – the search for the cradle of Indo-European culture – only to admit later that he had completely failed to locate it.

Alongside these works of high technical quality he wrote a series of slighter books designed to communicate the essence of his views and methods to a wider audience. *Man Makes Himself* (1936) represents the first exercise in this field. Then in the depths of the war he published *What Happened in History* (1942). 'I wrote it,' he says, 'to convince myself that a Dark Age was not a bottomless cleft in which all traditions of culture were finally engulfed.' He was evidently well-pleased with the public's response to this bookstall work. Next came *Progress in Archaeology* (1944), *History* (1947), *Social Evolution* (1951), *Piecing Together the Past* (1956), and finally the culminating summary of his life's work, *The Prehistory of European Society*, published posthumously in 1958.

By the time he began to prepare the last editions of *New Light* in 1954 and *The Dawn* in 1956, he had come to believe not only in the uniqueness of the status which European culture had achieved in the Bronze Age but he also felt that he at last understood the processes by which this had come about. This was the underlying theme in the final edition of *The Dawn*. He was evidently triumphant at this new insight, and not content to bury it in the rigid descriptive format of *The Dawn* he characteristically created a new vehicle to display its elegant simplicity – his last book, *The Prehistory of European Society*.

Towards the end of 'Retrospect' he sets out, with simple pride, his personal rules of scholarship.

I invoke no agencies external to the observed data, no eternal laws transcending the process as empirically given, but historical conjectures of well-established environmental circumstances and equally well-known patterns of human behaviour legitimately inferred from their archaeological results. The archaeological data are interpreted as the fossilized remnants of behaviour patterns repeatedly illustrated in ethnography and written records.

This single quotation is a firm reminder of where Childe saw himself within the wide spectrum of archaeological scholarship: he was a conceptualist and a synthesizer. At no time did he show any inclination to create neat itemized typologies or to define cultures in the rigorous way demanded by scholarship. Nor was he at all happy with fieldwork. Admittedly while professor at Edinburgh he did carry out a few excavations in Scotland, at Castle Law and Finavon, for example, two Iron Age hillforts, and at the Neolithic settlement of Skara Brae on Orkney, but his work was, to put it kindly, undistinguished, undertaken more from a sense of duty than from any deeply motivated desire to answer questions relevant to his research. Inexperience of excavation and reluctance to embark upon detailed studies based on the production of definitive *corpora* may well have stemmed from a lack of patience with trivia. Time spent excavating or writing reports would be seen to conflict with time devoted to working in libraries. This was unfortunate, for it meant that he could not fully appreciate the intricate subtleties of excavation evidence – it is an understanding which does not come from books. In consequence he sometimes tended to accept apparent evidence with less criticism than might otherwise have been applied to it.

Childe recognized full well his place in archaeology, even if he greatly underestimated his own dramatic impact on the discipline. At the beginning of 'Retrospect' he wrote:

The most original and useful contributions that I may have made to prehistory are certainly not novel data rescued by brilliant excavation from the soil, or by patient research from dusty museum cases, nor yet well founded chronological schemes nor freshly defined cultures, but rather interpretative concepts and methods of explanation.

He understood, too, the frailty of the evidence. In the last paragraph he was to write for publication he concluded:

Now I confess that my whole account may prove to be erroneous; my formulae may be inadequate; my interpretations are perhaps ill-founded; my chronological framework – and without such one cannot speak of conjectures – is frankly shaky. Yet I submit the result was worth publishing.

Now, sixteen years after the appearance of the last edition of *The Dawn*, how well have Childe's interpretations stood the test of time? There have undoubtedly been staggering changes brought about by the enormous volumes of new material, published annually in every country in Europe, not only new artifacts but new data derived from associations, settlement excavation, scientific analysis, and sophisticated techniques for producing and testing typologies. But outstripping all this in importance has been the establishment of a totally independent chronological framework based on radiocarbon dating. Radiocarbon dating was still in its infancy when Childe wrote his last preface to *The Dawn*, but he readily embraced its potential even if remaining wary of putting too much reliance on the few individual dates then available. His caution has since proved to be well justified.

Before we can assess the impact of radiocarbon dating on *The Dawn* it is necessary to see how Childe built up his chronological framework for barbarian Europe. His fixed points were the absolute chronologies of Egypt and Mesopotamia. By establishing synchronisms between these areas and the city of Troy in north-western Turkey it was possible to calibrate the successive levels of build-up at Troy; thus the change from Troy II to Troy III was usually put at about 2300 B.C. For earlier periods, dating was a matter of guesswork based largely on the assessment of how long individual archaeologists considered was necessary for the deposits representing Troy II and Troy I to accumulate. At one time it was believed that Troy I began about 2700 and Troy II about 2500, although Blegen proposed a longer chronology with *c*. 3000 for the beginning of Troy I and 2600 for Troy II. The next step in the chain was to link the sequence of cultures in the Troad to the developments in Eastern Europe. This was done by defining similarities between the beginning of the Vinča culture and the beginning of Troy I, thus allowing cross datings to be applied. Using the short Troy chronology which Childe accepted, the Vinča culture was thought to begin about 2700, and since the Vinča culture could be directly correlated with the Larisa, Gumelniţa, and Cucuteni cultures the basis for the chronological development of Europe was regarded as established.

A second link was forged by establishing synchronisms between the independent Aegean sequence and the cultures of the Iberian peninsula. Briefly stated, Childe firmly maintained that certain characteristics of the Almerian culture of Southern Iberia, notably tomb architecture, the appearance of fortified settlements, certain types of figurines, and the development of metallurgy, were introduced by 'sea voyagers' from the Aegean, arriving at the time of the Aegean Early Bronze Age which was contemporaneous to well-dated Early Dynastic Egypt.

In the total absence of independent chronologies for barbarian Europe, this kind of argument – constructing calibrated sequences by cross dating to historical sources and then establishing synchronisms with European cultures – was totally acceptable: indeed it was the only method available for arriving at a chronological framework, and without one, however shaky (as Childe said), one could not go on to make further conjectures.

Now if closely similar culture traits appeared in an eastern territory and a western, there were three possible explanations: that they resulted from independent invention; that the west 'influenced' the east; or that the east 'influenced' the west. Childe by inclination rejected the first, since independent invention seemed to him to be inherently unlikely and anyway involved a multiplication of hypotheses, and since he believed that 'the sole unifying theme was the irradiation of European barbarism by Oriental civilization', he would naturally suppose that influences spread from the civilized areas of the east to the barbarian west. Within the framework of the data then available such an hypothesis was wholly acceptable, but it should be stressed, as Childe indeed was at pains to do, that his moderate diffusionist views were hypotheses not conclusions.

The impact of radiocarbon dating first began to make itself felt in 1960 as dates for the cultures in the Balkans started to appear. With dates of between 4000 and 3300 for the various phases of the Vinča culture and of between 5000 and 4000 for the preceding Starčevo culture, it was clear that something was basically wrong. On this showing Vinča began about 4100 instead of the 2700 required by the old 'synchronisms' with Troy! Either one rejected radiocarbon dating altogether or one was forced to examine again the entire basis of European chronology. Although a small minority of archaeologists still reject the radiocarbon method, its validity is now widely accepted.

Gradually the wider implications began to be realized: not only was barbarian Europe now provided with its own chronological framework, independent of flimsy and often dubious cross datings with civilized areas, but many of the cultural attributes thought to derive from the east were found to have existed in Europe many centuries earlier. The way was at last open for a fresh examination of the processes of European cultural development, unhampered by the constraints of diffusionist hypotheses.

Before looking at some of the directions in which this new thought is leading, something must be said regarding the accuracy of the radiocarbon method. Briefly, the earliest dates were calculated on the twin assumptions that the amount of C14 in the atmosphere had remained constant and that the half-life was 5,568, but it soon became apparent that something was wrong when radiocarbon dates for Egyptian material were compared with reliable historical dates for the same objects. In 1961 the half-life was recalculated on physical grounds, but while the new figure of 5730 made all dates a little older, it still did not overcome all the discrepancies. The next stage was for tests to be carried out comparing radiocarbon age determination for the annual growth rings of trees with the real ages assigned to those rings by dendrochronological methods. The first of these tests, for samples dating to between A.D. 659 and 1859, showed that, in spite of minor fluctuation, there was a good general agreement. These studies were then extended back in time by the use of an extremely long-lived tree, the bristlecone pine which still grows at high altitudes in California today. Working back by linking the tree rings of living trees to those of a series of dead trunks, it was possible to produce a continuous tree ring sequence extending back 7,100 years, which could then be cross correlated to radiocarbon determination for the independently dated tree rings. This preliminary work has shown a marked divergence between real date and radiocarbon date, particularly after about 1500 B.C.; for example a date of 3500 B.C. in radiocarbon years when recalibrated using the bristlecone pine data would be a thousand years earlier.

A great deal more work still remains to be done in cross checking the reliability of the tree ring sequences as well as in examining the physical assumptions behind the radiocarbon method, but it is now generally agreed that conventional radiocarbon dates based on the 5,568 half-life and quoted in years bc, or radiocarbon years, can be reasonably used to construct a new *relative* chronology for prehistoric Europe. The further implications of the corrected or calibrated dates, which are believed to approximate to real years (or years B.C.), are only just beginning to be worked out; until the botanical and physical basis for their reliability has been finally established, it is advisable to use them with restraint, since further corrections may well be required.

Let us now return to look briefly at some of the implications of conventional radiocarbon dating on our understanding of European prehistory. Recent work has shown that techniques of food production were introduced into Europe probably from Anatolia in the seventh millennium as is shown by early dates in this range from Knossos (Crete) and on mainland Greece at Neo Nicomedia. Thence neolithic economy spread into the Balkans, where a number of closely related groups developed from about 5500 bc: the earliest of these are generally known after a range of individual site names such as *Starčevo, Körös, Criş, Karanovo I*. Between 4400 and 4200 bc certain typological changes occurred, particularly in the pottery styles, which used to be thought to represent a wave of immigrants spreading into Europe from Anatolia. Nowadays there is a tendency to explain such changes as the result of local development rather than outside contact. The resulting cultures, variously known as Veselinovo, Vinča-Tordoš, Vădastra I, Turdaş, etc. are best regarded as a loosely knit continuum of well-established farming communities spanning the period c. 4400–3800 bc.

In parallel with this development, techniques of neolithic agriculture spread west along the löss lands of central Europe. These were the Early Danubian Cultures so beloved of Childe, which are now more generally known as *Linearbandkeramic* since their settlements are no longer seen to be restricted to the Danube basin. The spread was not only remarkably extensive; it was also rapid, the distribution of the highly distinctive culture extending from Hungary to France and the Low Countries within the period 4500–3900 bc.

A second line of penetration, by way of the Mediterranean, introduced farming economies together with characteristic Impressed or Cardial wares into Italy, Southern France, and Iberia. The only reasonable series of radiocarbon dates at present available for impressed wares come from Southern France where it is now clear that the culture should be assigned to the period 5500–4000 bc. Thus by about 4000 bc much of Europe was occupied by farming communities and within the next 1,000 years even the outlying areas such as Britain and Denmark were colonized.

Little of what has been said above would have surprised Childe; he would merely have adjusted his chronologies to suit the new evidence – the main structure of his hypothesis remaining unchanged. But what is of vital importance is that the new long chronology allows ample time for the development of well established innovating cultures in south and east Europe before the appearance of metal technology.

A view which Childe would have found more difficult to accept is that the smelting of copper may well have been developed independently in more than one area of the Old World. On present showing copper smelting is thought to have originated in the Near East by 6000 bc, by 4000 an industry had been established in the Balkans and by 2500 bc new production centres had developed in the Aegean and in southern Iberia. Only by 3000–2500 did a knowledge of metallurgy spread over the areas between the Near Eastern centres and the Balkans, and it was not until just after *c.* 1500 bc that copper became commonly used in the rest of Europe. Although these facts could be explained in terms of 'influences' emanating from the east with 'prospectors and traders' moving first into the Balkans and later into

Southern Iberia and the Aegean, the simplest explanation of the observed data, taking into account both the new chronology and the cultural evidence, would be that copper smelting emerged independently in the Balkans and in Iberia at times when the communities of these areas were in vigorous innovating stages of their development. Independent invention may strike some as unlikely on theoretical grounds, but since it is now established beyond reasonable doubt that cultivation and domestication developed in isolation in several parts of the world there should be no logical barrier to our acceptance of the concept of more than one discovery of the smelting process. The general picture that has now emerged may be grasped more readily in the accompanying maps (see pp. 29, 30).

While archaeologists were looking to the east as the centre of inspiration for all skills and expertise, it was natural to believe in the spread of tomb architecture, characterized by the great megalithic monuments of western Europe, from a point of origin in the Aegean to Iberia, western France, and ultimately Britain and perhaps even Denmark. Maps were produced with thick black arrows marking the passage of these megalithic 'saints' or 'missionaries'. But radiocarbon dates have shown how wrong all this really was. It is now abundantly clear that the earliest megalithic tombs of Western Europe wholly predate those of the Aegean, the earliest so far known occurring in Brittany (although it must be admitted that no satisfactory dates have yet been produced for early Iberian tombs). On this showing the complex architecture of passage grave construction, the coerced communal activity which it implies and the religious motivation which lay behind it were phenomena which developed in Western Europe, originating before 4000 B.C. and covering most of the Atlantic sea board from Iberia to Scotland by 3000 B.C. Far from being a pale and somewhat barbarous reflection of the civilized East, the communities occupying the western extremes of Europe in the third millennium demonstrated a staggering degree of skill and sophisticated organization. In this context the claims made by Professor Thom, that in these areas some members of the community were not only highly numerate but were also carrying out complex astronomical observations, need occasion no surprise.

European prehistory has developed far and fast since 1957; it is still changing. Much of the old order has gone, but new configurations are appearing. Simple explanations of culture change based on migration and invasion are now giving way to a deeper understanding of cultural dynamics which admits that at certain times and in certain places people can be immensely creative. Childe would have enjoyed it all. He would have savoured the evidence, gladly abandoned outdated concepts, and produced an updated edition of *The Dawn*. At the end of his life he believed with evident satisfaction that he could see a stage about 1500 B.C. when a truly European culture had emerged. Had he been alive today, he would probably have reduced the date to 3000 or even 4000 B.C. and been equally delighted with the result.

BARRY CUNLIFFE

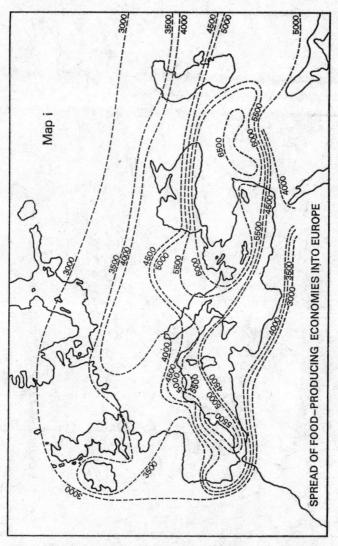

Map i: Isochronic map showing the spread of farming economies into Europe. The isochrons enclose areas within which farming was practised by the stated date. The isochrons are based on radiocarbon assessments in years bc (i.e. uncorrected and uncalibrated).

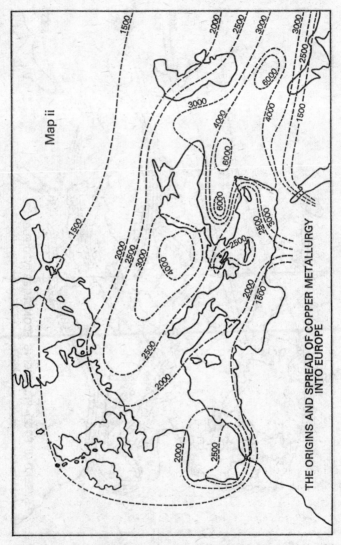

Map ii: Isochronic map showing the origin and development of early metallurgy in Europe. (After Renfrew 1970 modified to years bc).

Select Bibliography

Works discussing Childe's life and thought

Allen, J. 1967: Aspects of Vere Gordon Childe, *Labour History* XII, 52–9.

Childe, V. G. 1958: Retrospect, *Antiquity*, XXXII, 69–74.

Gathercole, P. 1971: Patterns in Prehistory: an examination of the later thinking of V. Gordon Childe, *World Archaeology*, III, 225–32.

Piggott, S. 1958: Vere Gordon Childe, *Proc. British Academy*, XLIV (1958) 305–12.

Ravetz, A. 1959: Notes on the work of V. Gordon Childe, *The New Reasoner*, no. 10, 56–66.

A selection of the principal works reflecting new thought since 1957

Bender, B. and Phillips, P. 1972: The Early Farmers of France, *Antiquity*, XLVI, 97–104.

Clarke, J. G. D. 1965: Radiocarbon Dating and the expansion of farming culture from the Near East over Europe: *Proc. Prehist. Soc.* XXI, 58–73.

Gimbutas, M. 1965: *Bronze Age Cultures in Central and Eastern Europe* (The Hague).

Giot, P. R. 1971: The impact of radiocarbon dating on the establishment of the prehistoric chronology of Brittany. *Proc. Prehist. Soc.* XXXVII, 208–12.

Kutzian, I. B. 1971: *The Copper Age of the Great Hungarian Plain* (Budapest).

Mellaart, J. 1960: Anatolia and the Balkans, *Antiquity*, XXXIV, 270–78.

Nandris, J. 1970: The Development and Relationship of the Earlier Greek Neolithic. *Journ. Royal Anthrop. Inst.* V, 2, 192–213.

Neustupny, E. 1969: Absolute Chronology of the Neolithic and Aeneolithic periods in Central and South-east Europe, *Arch. Rozh.* XXI, 6, 783–810.

Piggott, S. 1965: *Ancient Europe* (Edinburgh).

Quitta, H. 1967: The C14 Chronology of the Central and South-east European Neolithic, *Antiquity* XLI, 263–70.

Renfrew, C. 1969: The Autonomy of the South-east European Copper Age, *Proc. Prehist. Soc.* XXXV, 12–47.

Renfrew, C. 1970: The Tree Ring Calibration of Radiocarbon, an Archaeological Evaluation: *Proc. Prehist. Soc.* XXXVI, 280–311.

Renfrew, C. 1972: *The Emergence of Civilization* (London).

Soudsky, B. and Pavlu, I. 1971: The Linear Pottery Culture Settlement Patterns of Central Europe, in Ucko, P., Tringham, R., and Dimbleby, G. (eds) *Settlement Patterns and Urbanization* (London).

Srejović, D. 1972: *New Discoveries at Lepenski Vir* (London).

Tringham, R. 1971: *Hunters, Fishers and Farmers of Eastern Europe 6000–3000 B.C.* (London).

Preface to the Sixth Edition

When the First Edition was written as a pioneer attempt at a comprehensive survey of European prehistory, the archaeological record was so fragmentary that a pattern could only be extracted by filling up the gaps with undemonstrable guesses. A spate of excavations, investigations, and publications in the next twenty years rendered obsolete some of those speculations, enriched the record with a wealth of often quite unexpected facts, but actually complicated the picture. Since 1945 still more intense activity has doubled the available data, but in some points has simplified the scene; several formerly discrete assemblages now appear as aspects of a very few widespread cultures. Moreover, the new technique of radiocarbon dating, though still very much in the experimental stage, offers at least the hope of an independent time-scale against which archaeological events in several regions can be compared chronologically. These advances allow and demand drastic revision and rearrangement of my text. At the same time the fresh data, as much as Mongaït's pertinent criticisms in his Introduction to the Russian translation, have induced a less dogmatically 'Orientalist' attitude than I adopted in 1925. In particular the discovery that not all farmers were potters has entailed a complete revaluation of the ceramic evidence! Radiocarbon dating has indeed vindicated the Orient's priority over Europe in farming and metallurgy. But the speed and originality of Europe's adaptation of Oriental traditions can now be better appreciated; it should be clear why, as well as that, a distinctively European culture had dawned by our Bronze Age! Two more points should be noted. The radiocarbon dates here given, many of them unofficial, are all subject to a margin of error of several centuries and must be regarded as tentative and provisional! Secondly, to me the Near East still means what it meant in English before 1940 and still means in American, Dutch, French, and Russian.

For opportunities of studying at first hand the latest finds from Eastern Europe I wish to thank the Academies of Sciences of Bulgaria, Czechoslovakia, Hungary, Roumania, the U.S.S.R., and Yugoslavia, and to colleagues in those countries as well as in Austria, Belgium, the British Isles, Denmark, Germany, Greece, Holland, Italy, Poland, Sweden, Turkey, and the U.S.A. I am grateful for information on unpublished finds, for reprints, drawings, and photographs. Dr Isobel Smith has very kindly read the proofs.

March 1957   V.G.C.

1 Survivals of Food-Gatherers

Despite a startling refinement of industrial equipment and a masterly graphic art, Pleistocene Europe altogether lacked civilization in the economic sense. During the last Ice Age collective hunts on open steppes and tundras in South Russia, Moravia, and France yielded such plenteous and reliable supplies of mammoth, reindeer, bison, and horse flesh, that the hunters could establish relatively permanent camps and enjoy leisure to cultivate art. But they remained, nonetheless, pure food-gatherers, dependent on what the environment offered them. With the passing of glacial conditions, the old herds vanished; forest, invading the open lands, rendered obsolete the familiar technique of communal hunting, and so the culture based thereon shrivelled and decayed. Indeed, last century it appeared that Europe, abandoned by reindeer- and mammoth-hunters, was left an empty wilderness for neolithic immigrants to subdue to pasturage and tillage.

Forty years' researches have erased the last outlines of that picture. Archaeologists have discovered the remains left by various communities occupying Europe continuously since the close of the Ice Age, but still lacking the hallmarks of neolithic civilization. Their remains constitute cultures that are termed mesolithic, because in time – but only in time – they occupy a place between the latest palaeolithic and the oldest neolithic cultures. At the same time botanists and geologists have defined more precisely the changes in environment to which the mesolithic cultures were adaptations. Modern vegetation was only slowly established in the glacial landscape; a temperate climate did not abruptly replace an arctic one.

In Northern Europe phases in the colonization of the once frozen plains by forest trees have been determined with great precision by pollen-analysis (i.e. a quantitative study of the pollen grains preserved principally in peat mosses).[1] The first immigrants were birches and willows, then come pines, later the hazel, soon followed by elms, limes, and oaks – the mixed oak woods – lastly, in Denmark, the beech. But of course the composition of a forest is profoundly affected by topographical and geological as well as climatic factors so that even on the North European plain itself the local variations are large and significant. Stages in the gradual amelioration of climate can also be distinguished, largely on the basis of the same botanical evidence. In North Europe the long late glacial phase passed over eventually into a cold continental 'Pre-Boreal phase' when birches and a few pines began to colonize the tundra. This in turn gave place to a Boreal period, still continental but characterized by summers longer and warmer than today, but severe snowy winters. Next a relatively abrupt increase of rainfall and westerly winds affected North-Western Europe without reducing the average annual temperature, so that the climate of Denmark was really Atlantic, and mixed oak woods attained a maximum extension at the cost of pine woods. In Britain, on the contrary, excessive rain and wind caused deforestation in exposed areas. Gradually the course of the Atlantic storms shifted again, allowing a second period of forest growth in England but inducing some contraction on the Continent. This phase, still warmer than today, is termed the Sub-Boreal. It ultimately ended with the onset of modern cold wet weather in an exaggerated form in the so-called Sub-Atlantic phase. Of course, the terms Boreal, Atlantic, and so on are not strictly applicable to Switzerland or South Germany and are meaningless in Mediterranean lands: they were devised in Denmark and Sweden, where alone they are accurately descriptive.

In the meanwhile the distribution of land and water was also changing. The release of the vast volumes of water locked up in glaciers during the Ice Age produced a general, if gradual, rise in sea-level or *marine transgression*, but this was offset in the north, where the accumulations of ice had been deepest and heaviest, by an 'isostatic' re-elevation of the earth's crust that had been depressed by their weight. While much of the North Sea basin was still dry land, or at least fen (Northsealand!), uniting England to the Continent, Scotland and Scandinavia were thus depressed by the weight of the Ice masses. The Baltic depression was occupied by a frozen sea, communicating with the Arctic Ocean and termed the *Yoldia Sea*. The rebound of the earth's crust on the melting of the superincumbent ice raised strips of the Scottish coast above their present relative level and isolated the Baltic depression; it was occupied by the *Ancylus Lake*, rendered slightly brackish by a small inflow of salt water across Central Sweden. At the end of Boreal times the continued rise of sea-level flooded the North Sea basin and salt water poured into the Baltic depression, forming the *Litorina Sea*, larger and salter than the modern Baltic. England was completely separated from the Continent, while in Scotland whales could swim up the enlarged Forth estuary to above Stirling. The resultant extension of the area occupied by warm salt water was perhaps the cause of the shift in storm tracks that brought about the Atlantic phase of climate in the North. But north of a line that runs through Southern Zealand and County Durham the isostatic re-elevation of the land has continued so that the shore line of Atlantic times is now represented by the '25 ft raised beach' in North Britain and corresponding raised strands round the Baltic. Nevertheless some time elapsed before this local re-elevation of the land overtook the general rise in sea-level, so that in marginal areas like Denmark and East Anglia several local transgressions can be distinguished. In Denmark and Southern Sweden, in fact, four have to be admitted – the first at the beginning of the Atlantic phase, the last, and sometimes the greatest, during early Sub-Boreal times,[2] coinciding with Northern Neolithic III *a* and *b* (p. 222).

This changing environment constitutes for the archaeologist a provisional chronological framework, but contemporary men had to adjust their cultures to it. To small groups of food-gatherers the temperate forests offered greater facilities for picking up a bare livelihood without intensive social cooperation or a highly specialized kit-bag than had the bleak hunting-grounds of the Ice Age. Mesolithic groups appear in general isolated and poorly equipped in contrast to Magdalenians or Předmostians. But all had acquired, or themselves domesticated, dogs whose coopera-tion would be of greatest assistance to man precisely in the pursuit of the smaller, less gregarious game of the new woodland. Everywhere the collection of nuts, snails, and shell-fish played a conspicuous part in the new economy. Several of the mesolithic cultures are clearly just the responses of palaeolithic survivors to the new environment.

The *Swiderian* culture,[3] represented by assemblages of small flint tools collected from sand-dunes in Russia and Poland, sometimes under fossil turf-lines of Atlantic age, is characterized by small asymmetrically tanged-points (Fig. 1) used presumably

Fig. 1. Swiderian flint implements, Poland. After Kozłowski ($\frac{2}{3}$).

as arrow-heads, but morphologically descended from the large dart-heads used by the South Russian mammoth-hunters. Such was their ultimate response to the extinction of the mammoth.

Descendants of the Franco-Cantabrian Magdalenians, who combined with hunting and collecting fishing with the harpoon in the ancestral manner, created the *Azilian* culture.[4] The Azilians, like their ancestors, lived by preference in caves where they buried their dead too.[5] The famous cave of Ofnet in Bavaria contained a nest of twenty-one skulls, buried without the trunks, but not belonging certainly to Azilians. Because eight of the skulls were brachycranial, anthropologists used to think that the burial indicated the immigration of a new race into Europe, but now admit that at least a tendency to round-headedness existed among Upper Palaeolothic Europeans.[6] The Azilians' equipment seems poor. The type fossil is the harpoon of red-deer's antler (Fig. 2), flat and clumsy in comparison with the ancestral Magdalenian instrument of reindeer antler. Flint blades and gravers persist, but tend to be diminutive. The cores could be used for wood-working, but were not specialized into axes. However, some heavy wedge-like tools from the cave of Bize (Aude) may denote responses to the needs of primitive carpentry. And in the Falkenstein cave, Hohenzollern, a ground stone celt was found mounted in an antler sleeve with seemingly typical Azilian harpoons.[7] But now similar harpoons[8] have turned up with geometric microliths in a Tardenoisian layer in the Birsmatten cave in the Swiss Jura so that all the Alpine-Jura 'Azilian' may really be Tardenoisian and so at best 'late mesolithic'. The only reminiscences of Magdalenian art are highly conventionalized figures painted on pebbles.

The cave deposits suggest that the Azilians lived in very small and generally isolated communities; their isolation was not,

Fig. 2. Magdalenian harpoon from Cantabria and Azilian harpoons and painted pebbles from Ariège ($\frac{2}{3}$).

however, complete, since shells of *Columbella rusticana*, imported from the Mediterranean, reached the Falkenstein cave. Some sort of boat must have been available, since Azilians encamped on small islands. Azilian encampments are found on the slopes of the Cantabrian mountains and the Pyrenees, of the Massif Central, the Jura, Vosges, Black Forest, the Alpine foothills, and finally on the south-west coast of Scotland. But the industry here is distinctive enough to be regarded as a new culture, 'the Obanian',[9] not certainly descended from the French Azilian. In South France the Azilian succeeds the Magdalenian almost immediately, presumably in Boreal times; the Scottish sites are situated above the 25-ft beach and must be Atlantic in age. The discrepancy might indicate the slow rate of migration by short stages presumably along tracts of coast now submerged.

Descendants of the local Aurignacians created a very similar culture in early post-glacial times in the Crimea[10] and Transcaucasia. They too lived in caves and buried the dead therein either in the contracted position or extended. They had tamed a local wolf or jackal to help them in the chase. In the Crimea harpoons of bone, but of Azilian form, and slotted points armed with flints as in the Forest cultures, appear late. Geometric microliths, at first triangles and lunates, later also trapezes, were made and that even in layers that contain pottery and polished celts and so look formally neolithic.[11]

The *Tardenoisian culture* survives in the archaeological record almost entirely in the form of pigmy flints or microliths, ingeniously worked into regular geometrical shapes – triangles, rhombs, trapezes, and crescents – or into microgravers (Fig. 3)

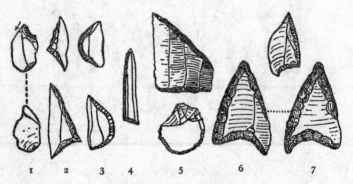

Fig. 3. Geometric microliths (2–5) and microgravers (1) from Franconia. After Gumpert ($\frac{1}{1}$).

that may be a by-product in their manufacture.[12] These do not really define a single culture, but represent several disparate industries.[13] As the latter can only be distinguished statistically, all will here be grouped together under the rather misleading term Tardenoisian. All microliths were presumably parts of composite tools of wood or bone, but no one knows why the little blades should be so carefully trimmed. Their makers camped exclusively on sandy soils[14] that would be lightly wooded, and sheltered at first often in caves, but also in flimsy huts[15] partly sunk into the sandy soil. At Muge[16] on the Tagus and on Teviec and Hoëdic, two tiny islets off the coast of Morbihan,[17] Tardenoisians settled on the open shore, hunting and collecting shell-fish and leaving mounds composed of the debris of their repasts. Skeletons, some brachycranial, were buried in these midden heaps in the contracted attitude. On Teviec and Hoëdic a little cairn was heaped over each of the corpses, which were sprinkled with ochre; some were covered with a sort of crown of stags' antlers. In the Ligurian cave of Arene Candide,[18] too, was a mesolithic – perhaps more Azilian than Tardenoisian – cemetery of ten graves, each containing an extended adult, twice accompanied by an infant, lying on a bed of ochre.

A tendency to reduce the size of flint blades was common to most Upper Palaeolithic industries. It led to the production of geometric forms already in the Gravettian of France and Italy,[19] while at Parpalló in Eastern Spain[20] even microburins occur from the Solutrian layers upward. This tendency was perhaps more marked in the Mediterranean environment than on the steppes

Fig. 4. Microliths from Muge, Portugal, and transverse arrowhead shafted from Denmark ($\frac{1}{1}$).

and tundras of periglacial Europe and strongest in North Africa. There a profusion of geometric microliths characterizes the middens and other deposits of the later Capsian culture. Moreover, these Capsians buried their dead in the middens. Some Tardenoisians may then be immigrants, driven north by the incipient desiccation of the Sahara at the close of the European Ice Age. The flints from such sites as the cave of La Cocina in Eastern Spain are indeed virtually identical with the late Capsian.[21] The topmost layers of this cave yielded 'Almerian' pottery which we shall see (p. 318) represents a neolithic of Capsian tradition. It does not follow that all makers of 'Tardenoisian microliths' were recent immigrants from Africa. Such microliths are found in most parts of France, Britain, Belgium, South Germany, Poland, and the Pontic Steppes; most are derivatives of local Upper

Palaeolithic industries, and had emerged in Britain, France, Belgium, and Germany by Boreal times.[22] But in both Britain[23] and France,[24] and probably too in south-west Germany[25] and Portugal,[26] Tardenoisians still survived, retaining their primitive economy and microlithic traditions in industry, when a neolithic or even a Bronze Age economy had already been established among neighbouring groups. And certain Tardenoisian types – trapezes and lunates – used by later communities in the Peninsula, France, and South Russia, may denote the absorption of Tardenoisian hunters by food-producing peoples. Microlithic must not be mistaken for mesolithic. On the other hand, isolated bones of sheep, reported exceptionally from pure Tardenoisian layers, otherwise pre-neolithic,[27] suggest the possibility that the term Tardenoisian may include some early immigrant sheep-breeders who made no pots nor ground stone celts.

Asturian[28] is the term applied to the culture of strandloopers who succeeded the Azilians on the coasts of North Spain and appear in Portugal too. They lived very largely on shell-fish during a period of greater rainfall than the present and are characterized in the archaeological record by a pick-like tool formed by chipping a beach pebble to a rough point.

Though inhabiting wooded countries, none of the communities so far described give any sign of a sustained effort to master this element in their environment by the elaboration of specialized carpenter's tools. Peoples occupying the forested plain of North Europe, on the contrary, did develop adzes and axes for dealing with timber. To emphasize this adaptation to their environment they may be grouped together as the Forest folk. Their ancestors had advanced as far north as Jutland before the end of Pre-Boreal times. The pioneers in the colonization were known down till 1936 only by stray discoveries of 'Lyngby axes' – reindeer antlers on which the brow tine has been trimmed to form an adze or an axe edge, or the socket for a flint blade (Fig. 5), which, however, are ill-adapted for chopping and were doubtless used as clubs. In 1936 a camp of reindeer-hunters who used them was located on the banks of a shallow mere at Stellmoor near Hamburg and revealed the content of the *Ahrensburg* culture.[29] The reindeer were killed with wooden arrows smoothed on grooved stone straighteners (like Fig. 113) and tipped with asymmetrically tanged flint points; game or fish were speared with barbed harpoons made on strips roughly wrenched from reindeers' antlers.

A reindeer's skull, mounted on a post, was planted on the shore like a totem pole.

Stellmoor was just a temporary camp where the Ahrensburg hunters spent summer and autumn, retreating presumably farther south to winter. Their ancestors should doubtless be sought among the Eastern Gravettians; 'Lyngby axes' had in fact been used in late pleistocene times in Moravia,[30] Hungary, and Romania.[31] At the same time flint axes were already being used in South Russia.[32]

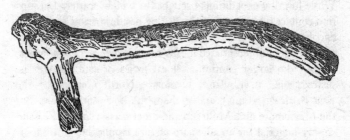

Fig. 5. 'Lyngby axe' of reindeer antler, Holstein ($\frac{1}{4}$).

The Ahrensburg folk were, however, not the direct or sole ancestors of the Forest tribes who did develop an effective wood-working equipment. These can most clearly be recognized at Star Carr in Yorkshire near Scarborough.[33] There in Pre-Boreal times about 7500 B.C. (according to a radiocarbon estimate) used to winter a band of four 'households' of hunter-fishers on the banks of an extinct lake. They fished from a rough platform of birch trunks sloping down into the mere. They had felled the trees with chipped flint celts, edged by a tranchet blow – i.e. a blow at right angles to the main axis of the flint; both the celts and the flakes detached in resharpening them were found lying between the logs.

Game – elk, red deer, and wild ox – and the birds were slain with arrows or darts tipped with geometric microliths; fish speared with leisters. The barbed prongs of the latter, usually called harpoons, were fashioned on strips neatly carved from stags' antlers by the groove-and-splinter technique inherited from the Aurignacian,[34] but in form foreshadow the classical Maglemosian bone points of the Boreal period. To aid them in the chase as disguises or to ensure an ampler supply of game in magic ceremonies the hunters wore frontlets carrying the antlers cut from stags' skulls. Similar Forest folk must have been spread all over Northsealand and perhaps farther east, but are directly attested only in Denmark by distinctive flints.

Certainly by Boreal times the Forest folk had spread all over the still unbroken North European plain from Southern England to Finland, and had achieved a very nice adjustment to their environment of pine woods, interrupted only by lakes and rivers. While hunting expeditions brought the widely scattered groups into contact from time to time, fishing beside streams and meres encouraged more permanent encampment so that equipment was already being differentiated locally to meet divergent conditions. Within the larger continuum local facies or cultures can be distinguished in England, Denmark, North Germany,[35] the East Baltic[36] (Kunda), and perhaps the Norwegian coast. But the Maglemose near Mullerup and other classic sites in Zealand supply material for an adequate picture, applicable with modifications to the rest.

These were summer-camps, submerged each winter, whither men repaired for hunting, fowling, fishing, and nut-gathering. To secure food they had devised or perfected a highly efficient equipment – for hunting, bows[37] of elm wood reinforced with sinews from which were shot wooden arrows armed with geometric microliths inserted into grooves on the shaft or merely gummed on with birch-pitch,[38] slotted bone points, also armed with small flints (Fig. 6, 3), and clubs with spheroid or spiked stone heads perforated by percussion. Their still more specialized fishing tackle:[39] leisters with several kinds of barbed bone prongs (Fig. 6, 1–2; cf. Fig. 105, 6), bone fish-hooks, nets of lime bast with pine bark floats and ingenious wicker weels (traps). For killing fur-bearing animals with minimum damage to the pelts they employed conical wooden arrow-heads which east of the Baltic were translated into bone (Fig. 105); there an antler pick had been specialized for breaking the ice. Bone needles were made for netting, flint gravers for cutting bone, small disc scrapers

(Fig. 6, 4) for dressing skins, and split boars' tusks for knives. The wood-worker was now provided with chisels of antler, socketed chisels made from marrow bones of large game (Fig. 6, 8), perforated antler adzes, and flint core-axes (Fig. 6, 5) or exceptionally flake-axes (Fig. 6, 6) mounted as adze-blades in

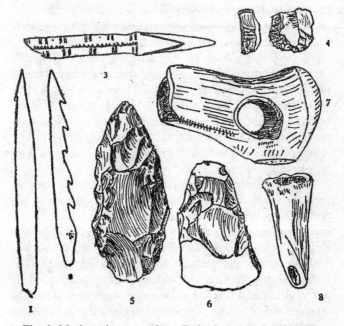

Fig. 6. Maglemosian types from Zealand. 1–3, 7–8 ($\frac{1}{2}$); 4 ($\frac{2}{3}$); 5–6 ($\frac{4}{5}$).

perforated antler sleeves (Fig. 6, 7). East of the Baltic, where flint was scarce, the adze-blades were pebbles sharpened, like the antler tools, by grinding. In England the flake-axe was still unknown.

Communications were maintained most easily by water in boats, presumably of skins, which have not survived, though the paddles that propelled them are extant. For land transport over the winter snows sledges were available east of the Baltic.[40] Dogs of a wolfish type were everywhere domesticated and may be the ancestors of modern sledge-dog breeds. The electrical properties of amber had already been recognized as a magic virtue so that the substance was collected in Denmark. Aesthetic satisfaction was obtained by decorating bone implements with geometric patterns, generally outlined by a series of points in the so-called drill-technique.

Remarkably exact replicas of the Maglemosian bone equipment have been recovered from undated levels of peat bogs in the Urals, but these can hardly be used to document an eastern origin for the Maglemosians; Briusov[41] suggests that a common southern origin for both the Baltic and Uralian groups would adequately explain the agreements. An eastward spread would seem more likely; for the Maglemosian is a natural development of the Pre-Boreal cultures of Northsealand. So too the Komsa and Fosna cultures, represented by assemblages of stone tools (including tranchet celts) from high strands on the Norwegian coasts,[42] must be due to a simultaneous coastwise spread from the same region.[43]

The marine transgression that ushered in the Atlantic phase broke up the unity of the Forest cultures and offered new opportunities to certain groups. Rich oyster banks combined with sealing and sea-fishing allowed communities to settle down at sheltered spots along the Danish and South Swedish coasts. The *Ertebølle culture* represents an appropriate adjustment.[44] The sites are marked by huge shell-heaps (that may be 100 yds long and 30 yds wide), the refuse of a more sedentary population. The exposure of new deposits of superior flint resulted in an increasing substitution of flint for bone in making heavy tools. Flake-axes were preferred to picks, plump green-stone axes were sometimes made by grinding, as earlier in the East Baltic, but perforated antler axes[45] – no longer adzes – and sleeves for axes were still made. The only microliths manufactured were transverse arrowheads. Fish were not speared with harpoons but caught with hook and line. The sedentary life permitted the manufacture of pottery in the form of large jars with pointed bases and troughs that may have been used as blubber lamps. A taste for personal adornment is indicated by bone combs and armlets. The dead were buried extended in the middens,[46] generally without grave goods, occasionally wrapped in a birch-bark shroud[47] and laid upon a bier, or once apparently cremated.[48] On the other hand, human bones, broken up just like those of game, afford good evidence for cannibalism.[49]

Now a local invention of pottery cannot be *a priori* ruled out and ground stone adzes had been made in Boreal times (p. 46). So the Ertebølle culture as just described could be regarded as an autochthonous adjustment of the native culture of the Boreal phase – if not of the classical Maglemosian as illustrated in the lakeside camps, at least of its hypothetical counterpart as developed on the now submerged coasts of Northsealand. However, in

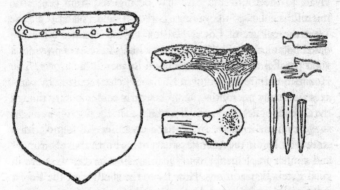

Fig. 7. Ertebølle pot, antler axes and bone combs, Denmark (⅙).

1953 Troels-Smith[50] showed that bones of domestic cattle and sheep or goats, and sherds bearing imprints of naked barley and of emmer and hexaploid wheats, do occur in several Ertebølle middens in Denmark that are dated by pollen-analysis to the Atlantic phase, while weeds of cultivation were already growing in their vicinity. Accordingly some Ertebølle folk were not mere food-gatherers, but farmers cultivating the soil and keeping domestic animals, tethered and stalled and not allowed to graze freely. Moreover, the earliest 'neolithic' pots – Becker's A funnel-beakers – were made by the same technique and found on the same sites as the coarse 'mesolithic' jars and troughs.

As there were no wild sheep or goats to tame in Denmark nor wild cereals to cultivate, an actual infiltration of neolithic farmers must be admitted in Denmark already. Their stock and grains point unambiguously to the south-east, their diffusion forms a major theme in subsequent chapters. Meanwhile a pure continuation of the old gathering economy can be traced round the North Sea and the Baltic.

While the coastal populations thus took advantage of a new environment, the communities inhabiting Norway, Central Sweden, the East Baltic lands, and even the interior of Jutland and Schleswig-Holstein remained true to the Boreal way of life and preserved much of the old equipment – particularly harpoons or, as in the *Gudenaa culture* of Jutland,[51] geometric microliths – throughout the greater part of the Atlantic phase. Similar survivals to the south and east may be inferred from geometric microliths collected in Southern Sweden[52] and Poland.[53] To the West the culture of Lower Halstow on the Thames estuary,[54] dated botanically to Atlantic times, with its flake-axes provides a good parallel to Danish Ertebølle in its mesolithic aspect. The Horsham culture of Southern England[55] characterized by core-axes and many microliths should be partly contemporary though the absence of flake-axes and the archaism of the microliths might suggest an earlier date. In Scotland an antler axe found with a stranded whale in the Atlantic estuary of the Forth above Stirling[56] and similar implements from Obanian sites farther west are in good Ertebølle traditions. How far to the south-west the Forest culture had spread in Atlantic times before it was overlaid or transformed by immigrant neolithic farmers cannot yet be determined. The famous site of Le Campigny, Seine Inferieure, once the patent station of a mesolithic culture, now proves to be the hilltop settlement of fully neolithic Western farmers (p. 356).[57]

The mesolithic cultures just described prove the continued occupation of large tracts of Europe from the glorious days of mammoth-hunting and the existence there of sparse but vigorous populations that could expand when the introduction of cereals and domestic stock offered an enlarged food supply. They may, moreover, be credited with positive contributions to later cultures that must be adapted to a like environment. Most conspicuously had the Forest folk perfected an apparatus for exploiting the natural resources of their habitat, items of which survive to the present day where the environment has persisted. Fish-traps and leisters, structurally identical with those devised in Boreal times, are still used by fishermen round the Baltic – a striking example of a craft tradition persisting locally for some eight thousand years. So they had discovered the process of making birch-pitch, an artificial material still used by the peasants of the region.[58] Forest folk had perfected an efficient kit of woodworking tools and in particular the ingenious tranchet technique for edging flint chopping-tools. That is not to say that this technique was diffused from Northern Europe to Italy, Egypt, Palestine, and the Solomon Islands, where it was certainly applied. It had in fact been anticipated in the late Acheulian cleavers of the Lower Palaeolithic and in the rare Moustierian *coupoirs* of the last Ice Age.[59] The positive contributions made by Swiderians, Azilians, Asturians, and the diverse groups here termed Tardenoisian are less well documented, but surely not altogether negligible. But by themselves none of the food-gatherers of temperate Europe could turn into food-producers. Is it not significant that mesolithic cultures are most richly represented in regions remote from the oldest historical centres of civilization and the native habitat of wild cereals and wild sheep? Whatever part mesolithic folk may have formed in neolithic populations, the flocks of sheep and the seeds of grain on which the new economy was based were not carried by wind or intertribal barter, but brought by actual immigrant shepherds and cultivators.

2 The Orient and Crete

The now desiccated zone of North Africa and Hither Asia had been grassy prairie when Northern Europe was tundra or ice-sheet. On the upland steppes of South-West Asia grew wild grasses which under cultivation became barleys and wheats – the ancestor of one-corn wheat (*Triticum monococcum*) from the southern Balkans to Armenia and wild emmer (*Triticum dicoccoides*) from Palestine to Iran.[1] Sheep and cattle fit for domestication were roving there too. In such an environment human societies could successfully adopt an aggressive attitude to surrounding nature and proceed to the active exploitation of the organic world.

At Jarmo in Kurdistan[2] the inhabitants of a little hilltop village were cultivating emmer and barley that already exhibit some effects of domestication as early as 4750 B.C. In Palestine where the mesolithic Natufians had been reaping annual grasses,[3] farming may have started before 6000 B.C. at Jericho.[4] But neither at Jarmo nor at Jericho did the first farmers make pottery.

Stock-breeding and the cultivation of cereals were revolutionary steps in man's emancipation from dependence on the external environment. They put man in control of his own food-supply so far that population could – and did – expand beyond the narrow limits imposed by the naturally available supply of wild fruits and game. But the expansion of population led by its very conditions to the expansion of the revolutionaries themselves – the primitive half-sedentary farmers – or their transmutation by a second revolution into a settled peasantry producing surplus food-stuffs for its own surplus offspring who had become artisans and traders, priests and kings, officials and soldiers in an urban population.

The second revolution was accomplished first in the valleys of the Nile, the Euphrates, and the Indus. There irrigation cultivation had produced a surplus vast enough to support the whole superstructure of literate civilization. By 3000 B.C. archaeology and written history reveal Mesopotamians and Egyptians already grouped in vast cities any one of which might, like Erech, measure two square miles in area, and in which secondary industry and trade offered an outlet for the surplus rural population.

In *New Light on the Most Ancient East* I have tried to sketch in some details in that prehistoric background of Oriental history. And I have tried to show too how the first revolution that precedes it had to spread, and how the growing demands of the new urban centres of population and wealth must involve the propagation both of the arts and crafts on which the second revolution rested and of the economy that sustained it. To find food for rising generations, the simplest step was to bring fresh land under cultivation and annex new pastures. That meant a continuous expansion of colonization and the progressive multiplication of farming villages. But the surplus accumulated in Egyptian and Mesopotamian cities could serve as capital for the promotion of trading expeditions through which the villages thus founded could share in the surplus and use it in their turn for the development of secondary industries. To obtain this share by supplying the effective demands of civilized societies, the Anatolian or Syrian villages must turn themselves into towns producing a surplus of farm-produce to support industrial workers and traders. And villages, thus urbanized, must become secondary centres of demand and for diffusion; they must in turn repeat the process of propagation, generating thereby tertiary centres to carry on the work. We should thus expect a hierarchy of urban or semi-urban communities, zoned, not only in space but also in time and in cultural level around the metropoles of Egypt, Mesopotamia, and India. How far does prehistoric Europe confirm such anticipation?

Farming must of course have started in South-West Asia. But in tracing its primary expansion thence, it must now be remembered that the first farmers were not necessarily also potters; the first peasant colonists to reach Europe may not have left a trail of potsherds to mark their tracks! And those tracks were not necessarily on land. Fishing communities along the Levant coasts could perfectly well have learned to supplement the produce of food-gathering by cultivating cereals and breeding stock. Such incipient food-producers, forced to colonize fresh territories, might perfectly well have taken to their boats and paddled or sailed on the alluring waters of the Mediterranean to the next landfall – and then the next.

By its spatial position and by special favours of the winds and currents the great island of Crete is easily accessible from the Nile, from Syria, from Anatolia, and from peninsular Greece. Its fertile lowlands guarantee a living to farmers and orchardists; its resources in timber, copper, and other raw materials can supply the needs of secondary industry; its natural harbours are not only bases for fishermen but havens for merchants who can transport Cretan produce to urban centres and bring back in return the manufactures and also the science of older cities.

The ruins of neolithic villages have formed a tell, 6·5 m high, beneath the oldest Minoan levels at Knossos in Central Crete, where the Minoan civilization was first identified. But trial pits have revealed but little of the neolithic culture.[5] It was formally neolithic in that pebbles were ground and polished to make plump celts (axes and chisels). But obsidian was imported from Melos and from Yali so that the farmers were hardly self-sufficing. For the later levels indeed the term neolithic is not even formally correct, since a copper flat axe was found on a house floor with stone celts. Stone was also drilled to make spheroid and pear-shaped mace-heads and worked into studs and even vases. The latest houses consisted of agglomerations of small chambers with fixed hearths and stone foundations for their walls.

Pottery,[6] though hand made, was of fine quality, self-coloured grey-black or red-brown according as to whether it were fired in a reducing or an oxidizing atmosphere; the surface was often burnished, sometimes so as to produce a decorative rippled effect. The forms cannot be called primitive: the vases may be provided with genuine handles (including wish-bone, nose-bridge, and flanged ribbon handles) as well as simple and trumpet lugs; some vases have short spouts, most flat bases. Goblets on tall half-hollow pedestals and fruit-stands with hollow feet appear before the period ends. Ladles are common, as in neolithic Egypt and Western Europe. Some middle neolithic vessels have club rims, as in Portugal and Britain. The potter decorated her products with incised patterns, including triangles and ribbons filled with punctuations. In the transitional pottery of the Trapeza cave [7] in the mountainous interior a schematized human face was modelled on the vase rim.

For their fertility rituals the farmers modelled in clay or carved in soft stone highly conventionalized figurines of the 'Mother Goddess', seated or squatting (Fig. 8). As amulets they wore miniature stone axes pierced for suspension (axe-amulets). Caves were used for burials but for individual interments, not as ossuaries. [8]

Since palaeolithic food-gatherers have left no relics on the island, we may assume that the earliest Cretan farmers were immigrants who brought their neolithic equipment with them. 'Neolithic Crete', writes Evans, 'may be regarded as an insular offshoot of an extensive Anatolian province.' His table (Fig. 8) shows many Asiatic relatives to the squatting figurines. The self-coloured pots, with handles and spouts, have a general Anatolian aspect, the fine grey wares can be paralleled in the 'Chalcolithic levels' of Megiddo [9] and in the deepest layers of many Asiatic tells. [10] The mace-heads too belong to an Asiatic family but recur, like the axe-amulet, in the neolithic village of Merimde [11] in Lower Egypt, which also yielded plump axes and clay ladles. But punctured ribbon decoration and pedestalled goblets have analogies also in the Balkans (p. 132), and the wish-bone handle is typical of the Macedonian Bronze Age, while Trapeza ware is still more reminiscent of Balkan and Apennine fabrics.

The 'neolithic' phase was ended by a 'quickening impulse from the Nile, which permeated the rude island culture and transformed it' into the Minoan civilization. Evans suspects an actual immigration of predynastic Egyptians, perhaps refugees from the Delta fleeing from Menes' conquest. At least on the Mesará, the great plain of Southern Crete facing Africa, Minoan Crete's indebtedness to the Nile is disclosed in the most intimate aspects of its culture. Not only do the forms of Early Minoan stone vases, the precision of the lapidaries' technique and the aesthetic selection of variegated stones as his materials carry on

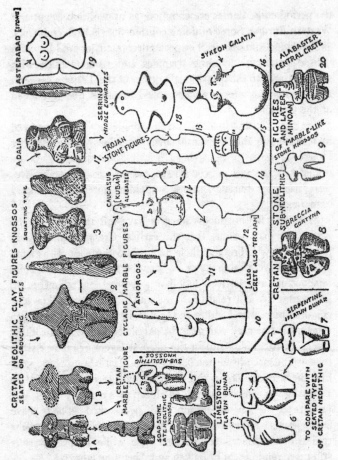

Fig. 8. Neolithic figurines from Crete and their relatives. After Evans.

the predynastic tradition: but also Nilotic religious customs such as the use of the sistrum, the wearing of amulets in the forms of legs, mummies and monkeys, and statuettes plainly derived from Gerzean 'block figures',[12] and personal habits revealed by depilatory tweezers of Egyptian shape, and stone unguent palettes from the early tombs and, later, details of costume such as the penis-sheath and the loin-cloth betoken something deeper than the external relations of commerce.

At the same time even more explicitly Asiatic traits can be detected among the innovations distinguishing the 'Metal Age' from the 'Neolithic' civilization. Some might indeed have been transmitted via Egypt: block-vases – paint-pots consisting of two or more compartments hollowed out of a stone parallelepiped with perforated corners – which were especially favoured in the Mesará, are common to Sumer and Egypt in Early Dynastic times.[13] But Minoan metallurgy is based entirely on Asiatic traditions; the coppersmith cast axe-heads with a hole through the

Fig. 9. Early Minoan III 'teapots' and button seal. After Evans.

head for shafting in the Mesopotamian manner, the artists treated rosettes and similar figures in the Asiatic, not the Egyptian style.[14] The most striking Minoan pot-forms – the pyxis with cylindrical neck and string-hole lid, the jug with cut-away neck and the side-spouted jar have parallels on the Anatolian, not on the African side; the so-called teapot with curious spout (Fig. 9) recurs without the handle – as far away as Tepe Hissar near Damghan[15] and even Anau in Turkestan. The technique of glaze paint that distinguishes Minoan pottery had been earlier employed by the Tel Halaf potters of North Syria. So in religion the cult of the Double-Axe is foreshadowed by Tel Halaf amulets.[16] The use of engraved bead and button seals as contrasted with carved amulets is a very ancient North Syrian–Iranian practice later adopted in Egypt as in Crete.

How far fresh Anatolian or Syrian colonists – merchants or artisans – joined with Egyptian refugees in founding the Minoan cities is for us a secondary question. Minoan civilization was not brought ready made from Asia nor from Africa, but was an original native creation wherein Sumerian and Egyptian techniques and ideas were blended to form a novel and essentially European whole. The admittedly Nilotic and Oriental elements that we see superadded to the Cretan neolithic culture may be treated as concrete expressions of the transformation of the island's economy with the support of capital accumulated in the great consuming centres that arose, round about 3000 B.C., on the Nile and the Euphrates. In supplying their needs the Cretan farmer's sons might find a livelihood in trade and industry; their self-sufficing villages would become commercial cities.

On the basis of the stratigraphical sequence, best preserved at Knossos, Sir Arthur Evans divided the Cretan Bronze Age into the famous 'nine Minoan periods' to which he attributed absolute dates on the strength of contacts with the literate centres of civilization. His scheme, columns I and II below, needs some revision after fifty-five years. Firstly, the chronologies of Egypt and Mesopotamia[17] have been deflated since then. Secondly, Evans's division was based mainly on the sequence of ceramic styles observed at Knossos. This turns out to be applicable to other parts of the island only with drastic modifications. The ceramic art, defining Evans's L.M.II, was a 'palace style', in vogue only at Knossos. The same thing had happened before. Once it looked as if East Crete had been deserted in M.M.II, since the eggshell-fine polychrome pottery defining that phase was lacking. In reality this style too was confined to the palaces of Knossos and Phaestos in Central Crete.[18] Even in the Mesará, *a fortiori* in East Crete, the M.M.I style was still in fashion as late as 1790 B.C.[19] Moreover, at Knossos the Early Minoan period is poorly represented owing to the levelling carried out by later builders; Evans's account had to be filled out by large drafts on material from East Crete and the Mesará. But during E.M. Minoan culture was by no means uniform so that there is a real danger of inflating the sequence by using local styles to represent chronological periods. Thirdly, the first reliable synchronisms based on an actual and dated interchange of products are afforded by M.M.II vases in Middle Kingdom Egypt securely dated about 1850 B.C. We have no Early Minoan imports in dated contexts in Egypt or Hither Asia, and, though actual Egyptian manufactures of Old Kingdom and even predynastic type were imported into the island, hardly any come from closed finds. One Egyptian jar from a Late Neolithic deposit is considered by Reisner to be no earlier than Dynasty I. If he be right, E.M.I must begin after 2830 or 3188 B.C. whichever date for that dynasty's beginning be accepted. Another imported vase from an E.M.I context, however, cannot be later than Dynasty III, some four centuries later. Further Egyptian imports imply an overlap between E.M.III – in the Mesará and East Crete – and the rise of Dynasty XII about 2000 B.C.[20] We thus have the following scheme:

Period	Abbreviation and Subdivision		Absolute Date B.C.
	Knossos	East Crete	
Early Minoan	E.M.I		
	E.M.II		
	E.M.III	E.M.III ?	? 2000
Middle Minoan	M.M.I		1850
	M.M.II	M.M.I	
	M.M.III	M.M.III	1700
Late Minoan	L.M.I		1550
		L.M.I	
	L.M.II[21]		1450
	L.M.III(A)	L.M.III(A)	1400
	L.H.III(B)		1300
	L.H.III(C)		1200

No attempt can be made here to evoke in a few pages an adequate picture of Minoan civilization. We must content ourselves with a brief outline of the economic development and some reference to the industrial products that are relevant for comparative purposes.

As in neolithic times the foundations of Minoan economy were fishing, the breeding of cattle, goats, and pigs (sheep are not osteologically attested till Late Minoan times) [22] and the cultivation of unidentified cereals together with olives and other fruits. But now specialized craftsmen – jewellers, coppersmiths, lapidaries – must have been supported by the surplus produce of the peasantry. And so in addition to rural hamlets, larger agglomerations of population must be assumed though no Early Minoan township has been fully excavated. Soundings at Vasiliki [23] in East Crete and beneath the palace of Knossos give hints of the existence of complexes of rectangular houses of brick and timber on stone foundations, like the contemporary towns of Anatolia and Mainland Greece. But even as late as M.M.I we find the rural population living in isolated house-complexes more reminiscent of a big farm than even a village. A dwelling of that period at Chamaizi [24] was an oval walled enclosure, measuring 20 m by 12 m and divided by radial walls into eleven compartments – exactly like the Iron Age courtyard houses and wheel dwellings of Western Britain!

Similar conclusions might be drawn from the graves. The standard Minoan burial practice at all periods was collective interment in a family or communal ossuary used for many generations. This practice, foreign to Egypt, Sumer, and the Anatolian plateau, was current all round the Mediterranean, going back to 'Mesolithic' times among the troglodyte Natufians of Palestine. [25] In the Minoan ossuaries the bones are generally lying in the utmost disorder. The dislocated condition of the skeletons, which has been observed in collective tombs farther west too, has been taken as evidence of secondary burial; the remains would have been deposited in a temporary resting-place until the flesh had decayed. Xanthudides' [26] careful studies of the Mesará burials have, however, shown that the disordered condition of the bones was due in the main to disturbances by those undertaking later interments who showed little respect to the former occupants of the tomb in making room for a fresh interment. The bodies had generally been placed on the floor of the tomb in the contracted attitude. Similarly traces of fire, sometimes noted on the bones, are due to ritual or purificatory fires kindled within the ossuary rather than to cremation.

The ossuaries themselves may be natural caves (E.M.I to M.M.I), rectangular stone chambers, imitating two-roomed houses, or circular enclosures commonly termed tholoi. In the Mesará the tholoi vary in internal diameter from 4·10 to 13 m, and are entered through a low doorway, formed of two megalithic uprights supporting a massive lintel and often entered from a small walled enclosure. The walls are from 1·8 to 2·5 m thick and the inner courses oversail one another as if the whole had been roofed with a corbelled vault on the principle employed in the Cycladic tomb illustrated in Fig. 25, 1. While it is hard to believe that a space 30 or 40 feet across could really have been spanned by a false dome, the smaller chambers certainly do deserve the name of tholoi, or 'vaulted tombs'. In an early example at Krazi[27] in East Crete, 4·2 m in diameter, the corpses must, as in the Cyclades and Attica (pp. 89, 111), have been introduced through the roof, since the door, only 0·5 m high, was completely blocked by an accumulation of bones and offerings; the 'door' would in fact be purely symbolic as in Egyptian *mastabas* and some British long barrows.

Evans has compared the Cretan tholoi to Libyan and Nubian closed tombs of later date, but Mallowan, followed by Peake, would find the prototypes of the Minoan tholoi in circular brick constructions of unknown, but certainly non-sepulchral, use which he had discovered in the chalcolithic Tel Halaf township at Arpachiya in Assyria that goes back at least far into the fourth millennium B.C.[28] By that date the device of corbelling was certainly well understood in Hither Asia, but it is not attested in Egypt before the Second or Third Dynasty. In fact, the Minoan tholoi, like the contemporary rectangular ossuaries, may be just imitations in permanent material of dwellings for the living, since round houses are attested by a model from Phaestos. As the tholos tomb was current also in the Cyclades, pottery and ornaments of Cycladic character were abundant in the early tholos at Krazi, and Cycladic idols occur even in the Mesará tombs, Marinatos seems inclined to think that the type of sepulchre may have been introduced by families from the small islands.

In East Crete (for instance at Mochlos) the house-tombs may be grouped to form small cemeteries such as should correspond to a township where several lineages lived together. Tholoi are more often isolated as if the territorial unit corresponded to a single clan or lineage. But in the Mesará small cemeteries are known – three tholoi and a rectangular ossuary at Koumása, three tholoi at Platanos, etc. Such aggregations imply the association of several kinship groups in a single village, but no actual settlements anterior to Middle Minoan have been yet identified in the vicinity. Both in the Mesará and at Krasi, when the tholoi had become congested, accessory chambers were built on to the original mausoleum to receive subsequent interments, mostly of Middle Minoan date. And by M.M.II there developed the practice of excavating in the soft rock sepulchres designed for a single small family – irregular chambers entered by a short passage or ante-chamber – as attested by the Mavro Speleo cemetery near Knossos.[29] Cases of cremation occur among the latest interments in an adjacent cemetery.[30] A small tholos seems to have been built in an excavation in a hillside in the same period. Subterranean chambers became the standard form of tomb in Late Minoan times in Crete as in Mycenaean Greece. But even before the end of Early Minoan, individual burial in small stone cists, in clay coffins (larnakes), and in jars (pithoi) grouped in cemeteries as contrasted with ossuaries was beginning to compete with ossuary practice, and steadily increased in popularity during later periods. The clay coffins[31] have early parallels both in Mesopotamia and Egypt, whereas jar burial is a specifically Anatolian–Syrian rite.

The variety of burial practices coexistent in Early Minoan times, like the variety of ceramic traditions, suggests that the island had been colonized by distinct communities which had not yet fused to form a single people with an homogeneous culture. But they seem to have lived together peaceably, as no fortifications have been found, and as members of a single economic system in view of the uniformities in types of metal tools, stone vases, jewellery, and seals. This system secured and distributed foreign materials, gold, silver, lead, obsidian, marble, and perhaps amber (from the tholos of Porti), Egyptian and Asiatic manufactures such as fayence beads and stone vases that were copied locally, and perhaps Cycladic figurines. Individual artisans needed seals (buttons, beads, and prisms) that might bear scenes symbolic of their craft; merchants stamped therewith bales of goods exported to Asine and other mainland ports. But no regular system of writing and ciphering was yet needed nor publicly sanctioned for correspondence or accounts. Though sepulchral furniture discloses considerable personal wealth, neither monumental private tombs, palaces, nor temples indicate concentration of wealth in the hands of capitalists human or divine. Cult was conducted in rustic sanctuaries and grottoes. Its symbols – stone figurines imported from the Cyclades or imitating predynastic Egyptian block figures, phalli[32] and model horns of consecration[33]

Fig. 10. The Minoan 'Mother Goddess' and (left) Horns of Consecration, from a sealing. After Evans.

as in Anatolia, dove-pendants[34] as in the Cyclades and Assyria, and votive double-axes[35] of copper and lead – while foreshadowing the distinctive apparatus of later Minoan ritual, still appear in forms appropriate to domestic worship.

In Middle Minoan times power and wealth began to be concentrated in the hands of dynasts residing in Central Crete and combining political and religious authority. Palaces that were also temples, factories, and warehouses were erected at Mallia, Knossos, and other sites. Specialization invades the domain of domestic industry. The potters' wheel, symbolizing the industrialization of the ceramic art, is attested from M.M.I. The wheel itself was a large clay disc which itinerant potters could carry about with them as they do today.[36] Wheeled vehicles are first represented at the same period by a model four-wheeled cart from Palaikastro.[37] They could hardly be serviceable without roads maintained by some authority with more than local jurisdiction. And in fact during Middle Minoan times the divergent local traditions that had persisted throughout the preceding period were gradually fused until Crete came to enjoy a single civilization. But the distinction between province and metropolis becomes prominent. The provincial potters of Eastern Crete could not compete with the experts employed in the palaces of Knossos or Phaestos in turning out polychrome ware of eggshell thinness.

The priest-kings organized more effectively trade with Egypt, Melos, peninsular Greece, and other foreign lands where even the eggshell pottery has been discovered – in Egypt in a Twelfth Dynasty tomb sealed some time after 1850 B.C. And this commerce must have substantially augmented their real wealth. For its administration a civil service would be required. And the perpetual corporation thus instituted needed a socially sanctioned system of keeping records and accounts. In fact a conventional script of an ideographic type was developed during M.M.I and used for accountancy. The idea was presumably borrowed from the Minoans' correspondents in Egypt or Syria, where writing had been in use for a thousand years. The actual conventions were local, though several signs have Egyptian analogues and the numeral forms are reminiscent of early Sumerian, while the use of a clay tablet as a vehicle of writing is an Asiatic habit.

Increase of wealth is usually accompanied by increase of population. The palace of Knossos was surrounded with an extensive town of two-storeyed houses, known not from actual excavation so much as from a mosaic attributed to M.M.IIb. The native population would be swelled by the immigration of craftsmen attracted by the wealth of Minoan courts and towns. So professional potters from Asia may have introduced the potters' wheel and trained native apprentices in its use. And other specialists such as fresco-painters may have arrived to minister to courtly desires for refinement. But if new arts were introduced by immigrants, the Minoan schools these founded were original and creative both in devising fresh techniques and in creating a new naturalistic style that owed little to Oriental models. In beholding the charming scenes of games and processions, animals and fishes, flowers, and trees that adorned the Middle Minoan II and III palaces and houses we breathe already a European atmosphere.

The development of Minoan civilization was interrupted by catastrophes which may be taken to mark the end of the phases termed M.M.II, M.M.III, and L.M.I. The disasters are usually attributed to earthquakes and were followed by reconstructions of the ruined palaces without any break in the continuity of architectural, artistic, and technical traditions. But after the last a new and simplified script – Linear B – was introduced at Knossos, and with it apparently a new language; for while the older, Linear A writings still defy decipherment in 1956, Ventris and Chadwick have read the L.M.II tablets as documents in an early Greek dialect identical with that current in Mycenaean Greece. Thus it looks as if Knossos had become the capital of a conquering dynast from the Mainland who established over the whole island a regular empire of the Oriental pattern. His empire did not last. About 1400 B.C. hostile forces razed the palace of Minos to the ground. The hegemony in the Aegean had passed to Mycenae on the Mainland (p. 121). But urban civilization still flourished in Crete for two centuries. Gournia, for instance, in East Crete, now covered six acres and comprised some sixty houses. And the richly furnished Late Minoan cemeteries comprising corbelled tombs (partially subterranean), rock-hewn chamber tombs, pit-caves, and shaft graves as well as larnax burials, remained in use in places even into the Iron Age.[38]

This inadequate sketch must be supplemented by a brief reference to certain industrial products that will be cited in later chapters dealing with less progressive parts of Europe. Tools and weapons are particularly relevant in this context. Obsidian was used for knives, sickle-teeth, and arrow-heads (including the transverse type). Fine hollow-based specimens are found even in Late Minoan tombs. At least in Early Minoan times stone was used even for axe-heads; notable is a 'jadeite' celt from the tholos of Kalathiana in the Mesará. But copper was being used for celts even in the latest 'neolithic' phase[39] and soon ousted stone. Copper ore exists in East Crete[40] and may have been exploited in Early Minoan times. The addition of tin to copper to facilitate casting is attested as early as M.M.I, though the standard alloy containing

10 per cent of tin was not firmly established till M.M.III. Bronze was known to the Sumerians before 2500 B.C. and knowledge of its qualities was probably transmitted thence to the Aegean via Anatolia (p. 75). But the Minoans' demand for tin may ultimately have been supplied from lodes in Etruria, Cornwall, or Bohemia, since in each country we shall encounter ambiguous hints of contact with the Aegean world (pp. 171, 289, 388). Iron is represented by a ring from a Middle Minoan tomb in the Mavro Speleo cemetery, but was not used industrially before 1200 B.C.

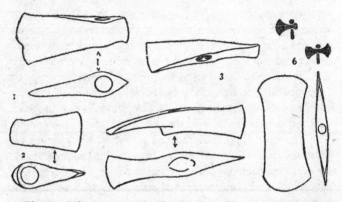

Fig. 11. Minoan axes, axe-adzes, and double axe ($\frac{1}{8}$), and seal impressions ($\frac{3}{2}$). After Evans and MA.

For axes the flat celt of the copper age did not lead, as in Cisalpine Europe, to flanged and socketed forms, but was superseded by the shaft-hole axe (Fig. 11, 1) that had been current from prehistoric times in Mesopotamia. After Middle Minoan III the single-bladed axe was ousted in Crete by the two-edged variety – the Double Axe – known also to the Sumerians and elevated to become a fetish or symbol of divine power by E.M.II. Double adzes too were used by the Knossian workmen by the beginning of L.M.I.[41] Finally, the axe-adze that may be regarded as a combination of two types of axe used by the Sumerians is represented by a gold model attributed to E.M.II[42] and actual specimens from the farmhouse at Chamaizi (Fig. 11, 3) attributed to M.M.I and then the standard Minoan form (Fig. 11, 4) from M.M.II on. Heavy perforated hammers of metal rectangular in cross-section are reported as early as M.M.II [43] and carpenters' saws are attested as early as wheeled vehicles, by M.M.I. [44] But elongated flat celts served as chisels and no sickles older than L.M.III [45] survive.

Early Minoan daggers are triangular or provided with a very short wide tang (Fig. 12, 1), and sometimes given longitudinal

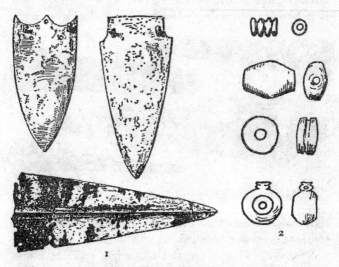

Fig. 12. 1, Early Minoan daggers ($\frac{1}{3}$); 2, Stone beads ($\frac{2}{3}$). After Evans.

rigidity by means of a midrib cast on both faces. They were attached with small rivets, sometimes of silver, to their bone or wooden hilts that were surmounted by globular or hemispherical pommels [46] of stone or ivory, laterally perforated for transverse rivets to hold them in position. During Middle Minoan times the blades, still either flat or strengthened with a midrib, were elongated and assume an ogival form (Fig. 13). Some have a flat tang, like Asiatic daggers, and the rivets are large. But the palace of Mallia has yielded a genuine rapier, attributed to M.M.I, [47] which is shown by its elongated pommel and its attachment to the hilt to be a development of the Sumerian series illustrated in the Royal Tombs of Ur. And in M.M.III the great rapiers from the Shaft Graves of Mycenae (Fig. 14, 1–3) are clearly elongations, to the surprising length of 93 cm, of the native types of Fig. 13. The pommels are improvements on the Early Minoan form approximating to Fig. 21, 3, while the hilt-plate of type 1 preserves a reminiscence of the distinctively Egyptian crescentic gap. In L.M.Ib type 2 develops into the rapier with horned guards (Fig. 14, 4), and then in L.M.III into a short sword with flanges carried right round the hilt (Fig. 15, 1).[48] But towards the close of the period a new type, adapted for cutting as well as thrusting and

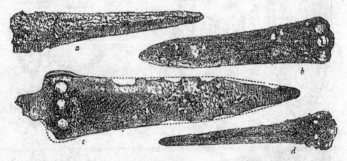

Fig. 13. Middle Minoan I–II daggers ($\frac{1}{4}$). After Evans.

apparently evolved beyond the Balkans, appears to herald the collapse of Aegean civilization.

Some Early Minoan dagger-blades might really have been mounted as spear-heads – that must be the case with a two-pronged weapon[49] from Mochlos. But the classical Minoan spear-head, going back to M.M.III, was provided with a socket, once formed by folding a wide, flat tang into a tube (Fig. 15). This device had been employed by the Sumerians from the middle of the third millennium, but was replaced by a cast socket, sometimes split to reproduce the effect of the fold, even in M.M.III.

Minoan warriors carried armour too. Helmets,[50] consisting of rows of boars' tusks sewn round a leather cap as described in Homer, were worn from M.M.III on. In L.M.II a bronze bell helmet, surmounted by a knob carrying a plume, was in use.[51] The type was popular in Central Europe from the Unětician phase on throughout the Bronze Age; it may have originated there or been inspired from Crete.

For removing facial hair Minoans used, in addition to tweezers, razors, generally leaf-shaped in Late Minoan times.[52]

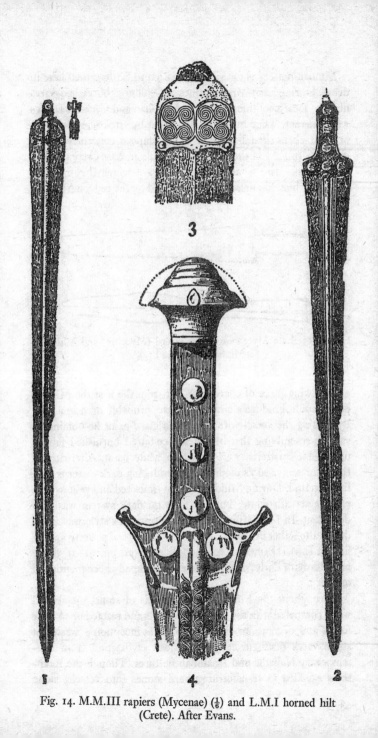

Fig. 14. M.M.III rapiers (Mycenae) (⅙) and L.M.I horned hilt
(Crete). After Evans.

Minoan pottery is too rich and varied to be described here in detail. During Early Minoan times self-coloured burnished wares like the local neolithic and Early Anatolian and Cycladic fabrics were current. They might be decorated by stroke-burnishing[53] or with channelled lines that may compose concentric semi-circles.[54] In E.M.II the potters of Vasiliki in East Crete covered their vessels with a red ferruginous wash which they relieved with dark blotches deliberately produced by the reducing agency

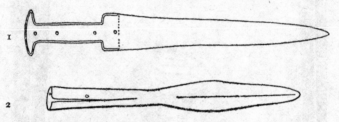

Fig. 15. Late Mycenaean short sword (Mycenae) and Middle Minoan spear-head ($\frac{1}{4}$).

of a glowing piece of charcoal.[55] But from the first the Minoan potter could produce a clear buff ware, probably fired in a kiln. By coating the vessel with a lustrous glaze paint he obtained a surface resembling that of the self-coloured burnished fabrics upon which patterns were drawn in white paint. Alternatively the paint was used as medium for producing dark patterns on a light ground. During Middle Minoan times red and yellow were combined with white, but the light on dark system was predominant. In Late Minoan on the contrary this style was abandoned altogether in favour of dark on light. Spiral patterns appear first in E.M.III under Cycladic influence (cf. pp. 91–2). Some main forms of Early Minoan pottery have already been mentioned on p. 55.

Throughout the Minoan epoch vessels of stone, metal, and wood competed with the potters' products and reacted upon their forms and decorations. Indeed, from its inception a wealth of stone vases distinguishes the Minoan civilization from contemporary Helladic and Anatolian cultures. Though the Egyptians excelled in transforming hard stones into vessels, stone vases had been used in Mesopotamia and Syria too since the fourth millennium and were made in Cyrpus before the oldest pots.[56] Of importance for comparison are the block-vases already mentioned that may have been copied in clay in the Danube valley and the birds'-nest vases that might be the prototypes for certain Almerian pots; both forms are Early Minoan.

Metal vessels may have been in use even in Early Minoan times and were undoubtedly quite common in later periods. But the competition of plate on the tables of the rich did not involve any degradation of the ceramic art in Crete as it did in Mesopotamia and Egypt. Two shapes are noteworthy – a two-handled tankard or cantharos with quatrefoil lip (represented by a silver specimen from Mochlos allegedly M.M.I)[57] which is known in pottery from Hittite times in Anatolia and the Middle Bronze Age of

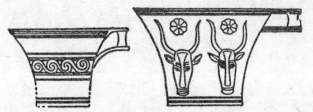

Fig. 16. Egyptian representations of Vapheio cups.

Hungary and in alabaster from Shaft Grave IV at Mycenae, and the so-called Vapheio cup of M.M.III to L.M.II (Fig. 16),[58] the curious handle of which may after all be inspired by a wooden model; a clay cup with a rather similar handle turned up at Nienhagen in Saxo-Thuringia apparently in an Early Bronze Age cemetery.

Minoan costume, like the Egyptian, did not require fastening with pins, so that, apart from a few hairpins, these toilet accessories, so common in Mesopotamian, Anatolian, and Central European graves, are missing in Bronze Age Crete. On the other hand, the Minoans, like the Egyptians, Sumerians, and Indians, were skilled at shaping and perforating hard stones for beads. Rock crystal and carnelian were used from Early Minoan times as well as ivory and fayence. Two amorphous lumps from the tholos of Porti have been identified as amber, but Evans has questioned

3 Anatolia the Royal Road to the Aegean

In the fifth century the Royal Road from Mesopotamia to the Aegean led not to the Levantine coasts alone but on across the plateau of Anatolia – a promontory of Asia thrust out towards Europe. Here ran the route along which Persian armies marched to impose Oriental culture on Greece, along which diplomatists, scientists, and merchants travelled to transmit more peacefully and successfully Babylonian ideas to the young Ionian states. More than a millennium earlier the plateau was a bridge along which merchant caravans could travel to transport westward a share of Mesopotamian capital. Between 2000 and 1800 B.C. the region's wealth in ores had induced a colony[1] of Assyrian merchants to settle at Kanes (Kültepe) in Cappadocia; they maintained continuous intercourse with the cities on the Tigris and Euphrates, illustrated by their business archives, the so-called Cappadocian tablets. They may have had earlier precursors. In any case they found, if not a literate civilization, at least some degree of urbanization and an incipient state organization. Rich 'royal tombs' at Alaca Hüyük[2] illustrate the wealth amassed by local princes, several specialized crafts, and trade that secured a variety of raw materials. Unfortunately these tombs contain no undoubted imports nor even types that can be dated by reference to Mesopotamian literature. The culture of the princes' subjects is reduplicated in many little hüyüks (tells), too small to represent anything but modest villages. In them, copper was already competing with stone and bone as an industrial material but without in the least replacing them. This 'Copper Age' culture, as Turkish archaeologists label it, is fairly uniform all over the plateau; judged by its pottery – self-coloured dark-faced wares, jugs and cups with true handles and side spouts, corrugated ornament – its preference for the sling, the multiplicity of female figurines – it is allied to the Early Troadic to be described below. It differs sharply from the latter in burial practice; the dead were regularly interred under the house floors as in Syria, Assyria, and Iran, and not in distinct cemeteries.

Many of these peculiarities seem to have been inherited from a previous phase, termed by Turkish archaeologists Chalcolithic because copper was already in use if mainly for ornaments. It is very imperfectly known from the deeper levels of Alişar in the Halys[3] basin, and perhaps from Büyük Güllücek[4] and Maltepe near Sivas[5] farther north.

As compared to the Early Aegean Bronze Age, the Anatolian Copper Age does not seem early, though the discrepancy may be due to the more modest guesses of its investigators.[6] A seal of Jemdet Nasr type from the Copper Age strata and a radiocarbon date of 2500±250 B.C.[7] for layer 14 at Alişar might justify more generous estimates. It does not seem an apt vehicle for the transmission westward of the cultural achievements of the Tigris-Euphrates at an early date. Nor does the so-called Chalcolithic disclose earlier Oriental advances on their way westward. There are indeed stamp seals and figurines, but painted sherds are exceptional, the pottery being mostly self-coloured though comprising fruitstands. Nothing approaching the precocious neolithic of Kurdistan and Palestine nor yet mesolithic remains have been found on the plateau so far, but though unrepresented in the tells, they may still come to light on other sites. Until they do, no recognizable archaeological milestones mark an ancient route across Anatolia from the Orient to Europe. Nor do the available data disclose there an ancient cultural centre nor yet a human reservoir from which the Aegean coastlands could have been populated.

On the other hand, at least in the north-western extremity of Asia Minor, a vigorous and original culture is documented quite early. The first settlement in the area is represented by pottery found in the lowest levels of Kum Tepe, a tell in the Troad.[8] Notable are fruitstands with profiled pedestals, as in Fig. 86, and stroke-burnished ware which recurs on Samos as well as in Europe.

In the sequel develops a culture which may conveniently be called Early Troadic, though it is not strictly confined to the Troad. The same culture is represented at Poliochni on Lemnos,[9] Thermi on Lesbos,[10] at Yortan in Mysia and elsewhere. But the classic site remains Hissarlik, the ancient Troy, a key position on the Hellespont commanding at once sea-traffic up the straits and a land route's crossing to Europe. There Heinrich Schliemann last century distinguished seven superimposed prehistoric cities, but left a multitude of crucial issues. Re-excavation of the site by an expedition under C. W. Blegen,[11] supplemented by the stratigraphy of Thermi and Poliochni, has yielded the following scheme as the standard for the culture sequence in North-Western Anatolia:

Troad		Greece	Lesbos	Lemnos	Absolute Dates
Troy VIIa		L.H.IIIb	Thermi	Poliochni	1275–1200
Troy VI	Late	L.H.IIIa and b	—	—	1400–1300
	Middle	L.H.I and II	—	VII	1550–1400
	Early	M.M.III, M.H.	—		? –1550
Troy V		—	—	VI	
Troy IV		E.H.III	—		
Troy III		E.H.	—	V	
Troy IIg to a		E.H.	—		
			Thermi V	IV	
Troy I	Late	E.H.	Thermi		
	Middle	E.H.	I to		
	Early	—	IV	II–III	

All 'cities' can be dated in terms of Aegean chronology by sherds of actually imported Aegean vases found in the several levels at Troy.

Troy I and the contemporary settlements on Lesbos and Lemnos consisted of clusters of two-roomed houses (often of the long rectangular plan), closely juxtaposed along well-defined but crooked and narrow streets. The mud-brick walls rested on foundations of stones, sometimes (in Thermi I and IV and Troy I) laid not horizontally but obliquely in herring-bone formation, an arrangement often employed in the brick architecture of Early Dynastic Sumer. And as in Mesopotamia the doors were pivoted on stone sockets. Some houses in Thermi were provided with low domed ovens of clay only 3 ft high. Especially in Thermi III pits (bothroi) were often dug in the house floors and carefully lined with clay.[12]

But Troy I comprised also a 'palace' – a rectangular hall 12·8 m long by 5·4 m wide, entered through a porch at the west end. So Troy was already ruled by a chief, an institution not yet attested in other Early Troadic settlements. Moreover, Troy I, at least by the Middle phase, was girt with a massive stone rampart enclosing some $1\frac{1}{4}$ acres; Poliochni was probably fortified at the same time.

Anatolian economy rested on the cultivation of wheats,[13] barley, millet, and presumably vegetables, perhaps also of vines and fruit-trees, the breeding of cattle, sheep, goats, and pigs, and fishing with hook and line or with nets. Axes and rare adzes were made from pebbles ground and polished and also from stags' antlers pierced for a shaft-hole, knives, and sickle-teeth from flint blades simply trimmed. But stone battle-axes with drooping blade, precursors of ceremonial weapons like Fig. 21, 1, must immediately be copies of metal weapons. In fact, copper battle-axes of the same pattern have been found at Yortan as at Polatli on the plateau and in the Royal Tombs of Alaca.[14] Bone splinters, pointed at both ends, served as arrow-heads, while the armoury comprised also sling-stones and maces with spheroid stone heads.

But trade already brought metal even to Lesbos, and at Thermi I and Troy I there were specialized smiths available to work it. A crucible was found on virgin soil at Thermi, and small metal pins and trinkets were comparatively common at all levels. Most were made from unalloyed copper, but a pin from Thermi II contained as much as 13 per cent of tin, and a bracelet of this rare metal was found in town IV. Indeed, by the time of Thermi II and III metal was common enough for large implements to be left lying about for modern excavators to find, while at Troy lead rivets were employed for repairing pots. The smiths produced flat chisels with rounded butts, as in Egypt and protoliterate Sumer, flat axes and axes with the sides hammered up to produce low flanges[15] – implying that celts were mounted as axes in knee-shafts as in Central Europe – and as weapons flat-tanged daggers like Fig. 20, 2–4, cast in two-piece valve moulds of stone.

The types of metal daggers and pins suffice to show that Troadic metal-workers followed Asiatic rather than Egyptian traditions. Though shaft-hole axes of the normal Mesopotamian pattern were not manufactured, the earliest dated battle-axes are represented by clay models from al'Ubaid levels in Babylonia.[16]

But the most distinctive types and actual imports point explicitly to intercourse with Greece, the Cyclades, and the Levant coasts. Emery and marble vases were imported from the Cyclades; bird-headed pins are common to Thermi I and Syros; polished bone tubes like Fig. 27, 1, from Thermi III–IV and Troy I recur not only on the Aegean islands but also in Syria and Palestine – in the last-named area in an E.B.III context (after 2500 B.C.).[17]

Despite the specialization of the metallurgical industry and the ramifications of commerce, pot-making was not sufficiently industrialized for the use of the wheel. The self-coloured, burnished vases, varying in hue from deep black to brick red and often copying gourd or leather vessels, are representative of a tradition common to the whole of Anatolia. A conspicuous peculiarity throughout the province is the popularity of genuine handles in addition to simple lugs. The handles are often of the 'thrust' type – the lower ends being inserted into a hole at the side of the vessels[18] – a trick popular in later periods too and in other parts of Anatolia. Forms distinctive of West Anatolia are bowls with lugs growing from the inverted rims (Fig. 17, column 1), jugs with cutaway necks (Fig. 17, columns 2–3), tripod vessels, and collared pyxides with string-hole lugs and lids (Fig. 17, column 4). Significant changes in form, documented by the stratigraphy of Thermi, are the expansion of the ends of the tubular lugs on the bowls to 'trumpet lugs' in town III and the contemporary transformation of tripod legs into model human feet. At Troy the trumpet legs grew into regular handles, flanged and angled, quite reminiscent of Cretan neolithic types. Decoration was effected by bosses, ribs, corrugations, and incisions forming rectilinear patterns. White paint on the dark ground, quite exceptional at Thermi and Troy, was very popular at Yortan. The patterns were always rectilinear.

Spinning and weaving would be domestic arts too. Their importance is attested by the numbers of spindle-whorls, and clay spools. The weaver may have used perforated arcs of clay up to 9 cm in length, represented in Thermi III, that seem to be forerunners of the narrower crescentic loom-weights so common in the Hittite levels of Kusura and Aliṣar.[19]

The domestic fertility cults of a superstitious peasantry may be illustrated by numerous female figurines of stone and clay, the former always highly conventionalized in the manner of Fig. 8,

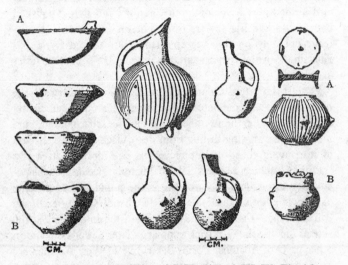

Fig. 17. Pottery from Thermi I–II (A) and III–IV (B). After W. Lamb, *BSA.*, XXX.

13–16[20]; clay figurines begin later at Thermi and sometimes indicate the division between the legs. But at Troy itself the 'Mother Goddess' (if such she be) was represented on a more monumental scale: an owl-like visage had been carved in low relief on a stone slab, 1·27 m high, that was found standing just outside the city gate. But to domestic cult again belong clay phalli from Thermi and perhaps a horned clay spit-support (? altar) rather like Cretan horns of consecration. The dead were apparently buried, if adults, outside the town in regular cemeteries – enclosed in jars, judging by the case of Yortan.

After the long period of relatively peaceful development represented by the 4 metres of 'Troy I' and the four successive townships at Thermi, unrest led to a concentration of power and wealth. Though its population was already dwindling, Thermi V was fortified with a stout stone wall supplemented by complicated outworks. Even so, the site was soon deserted; it has yielded vases imported from Troy IIa, but none of those proper to the later phases of that city. Poliochni in Lemnos likewise declined. But at Troy potent chieftains had arisen who exploited to the full the

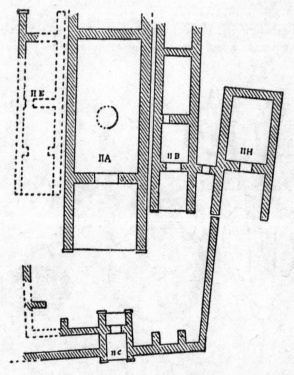

Fig. 18. 'Megaron' palace, Troy II.

strategic advantages of their site and concentrated in the city West Anatolian trade to the ruin of their rivals. Troy II was now encircled with a new stone wall, surmounted with a parapet of mud-brick. But, though larger than Troy I, the circuit of Troy II still enclosed only some 7850 sq metres, or less than two acres. Its ruler built himself a palace of the 'megaron' plan – a hall with central hearth, 66 feet long by 33 feet, preceded by a porch 33 feet long and wide (Fig. 18). The citadel had reached the apex of its glory in phase IIc, but underwent four further reconstructions before it was taken by hostile assault and burnt. But before the final catastrophe the defenders had hidden many of their valuables. Our knowledge of Trojan metal-work and jewellery is mainly derived from these hoards that the plunderers had missed.

Ere its destruction Troy II had become economically, if not physically, a city. Through its monopoly of Hellespontine trade, its citizens amassed wealth to support an industrial population

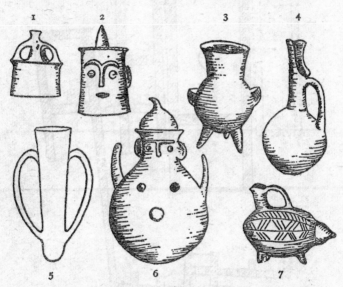

Fig. 19. Pottery from Troy II (⅛).

and pay for imported goods. Tin was obtainable in such abundance that bronze containing the standard proportion of 10 per cent tin and 90 per cent copper was in general use. Gold, silver, lead, obsidian were also imported; lapis lazuli from Iran and amber from the Baltic are also represented in hoard L, the date of which is not, however, quite certain. Specialist jewellers, potters, and other craftsmen, trained in Asiatic schools, settled in the rich city. The jewellers introduced solder, filagree work, and the trick of making beads from two discs of gold soldered together or from two folded tubes each ending in spirals – all devices employed by Mesopotamian goldsmiths in the third millennium.[21]

The potters' wheel, indicating a further advance in urbanization, was introduced in the time of Troy IIc, but the products, turned out *en masse* by the new specialist craftsmen, carry on the native traditions in form and surface treatment and did not replace handmade vessels. Shapes easily recognized as emerging during the lifetime of Troy II are anthropomorphic lids and

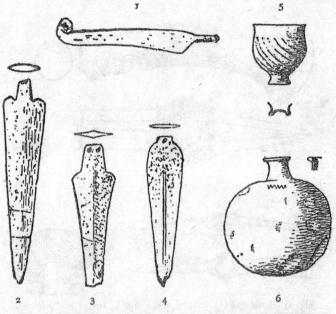

Fig. 20. Knife (½) and daggers (½) and gold vessels (¼), Troy II. 2–6 from Treasure A. Museum f. Vorgeschichte, Berlin.

jars ('face-urns', Fig. 19, 2 and 6), jugs with flaring mouths (Fig. 19, 4), and curious two-handled *depas* (Fig. 19, 5). But these appear already hand-made in phase IIc and are merely exaggerated expressions of tendencies inherent in the earlier and more generalized Anatolian tradition. The representation of the 'Mother Goddess' on the face-urns is significantly like that on the handles of early Sumerian funerary jars[22]; but the convention is already foreshadowed in the stele from Troy I. Side-spouted jugs, multiple vessels, jugs with double necks, zoomorphic vases are essentially Anatolian and not confined to Troy II. Improvements in the preparation of the clay and firing, probably introduced at the same time as the wheel, allowed the potter to produce harder, paler, and less porous vessels. But to preserve the effect of the old-self-coloured vases, their surfaces were normally covered with a ferruginous wash that turns red on firing (red wash ware) – a device popular at Alişar and farther east, and employed even in the Middle Danube basin.

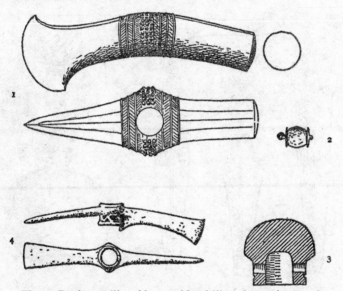

Fig. 21. Battle-axe ($\frac{1}{4}$), gold-capped bead ($\frac{1}{4}$), and crystal pommel ($\frac{1}{2}$) from Treasure L, and stray axe-adze ($\frac{1}{4}$). Museum f. Vorgeschichte, Berlin.

Despite the abundance of metal, stone, flint, obsidian, bone, and antler were still freely and almost predominantly employed for axes, battle-axes, agricultural implements, knives, awls, pins, and combs. The battle-axes carry on the tradition of Troy I, but include some superbly polished weapons of semi-precious stones (Fig. 21, 1) (from Treasure L) that must be ceremonial.

The jewellery from the hoards not only demonstrates the wealth of Troy but the divergent ramifications of its commerce.

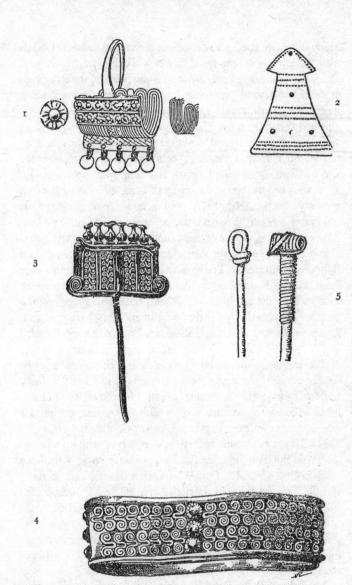

Fig. 22. 1–2, Gold earring and pendant from Treasure A, 3, pin from Treasure D, 4, bracelet from Treasure F, and 5, knot-headed pins ($\frac{1}{1}$). Museum f. Vorgeschichte, Berlin.

Many items are specifically Eastern; the earrings and lock-rings with flattened ends, the spiral filigree work (Fig. 22, 3), the gold disc beads, etc., may be regarded as Sumerian and the technique of the knot-headed pin[23] was known there as in predynastic Egypt. Pins with double spiral heads (of which Fig. 22, 3, is a glorified version) are found all across Anatolia and Iran to India and Anau.[24] A 'spearhead' identical with the Cycladic specimen of Fig. 23, 1, from Treasure A, belongs to a family represented also in Central Anatolia, Cyprus, and Iran.[25] Earrings like Fig. 22, 1, are worn by foreign dancing girls depicted in an Eighteenth Dynasty tomb-painting.[26] A gold hammer pin from 2g[27] is ultimately a South Russian type, but was familiar also at Alaca. At the same time, so many types common at Troy recur in Central Europe as to prompt the suspicion that Trojan tin came from Bohemia, copper from Transylvania or the Balkans. On the other hand, bossed bone plaques, like Fig. 115, indicate connections westward as far as Sicily and Malta, but their stratigraphical position at Hissarlik is a little doubtful and they have gold analogues to the east at Alaca.[28] Ring pendants of stone, paralleled in gold in Wallachia and Transylvania, might disclose one source of Trojan gold while copies in Sweden and Sammland may be counterparts of the amber beads from Treasure L. If Troadic trade were founded on Oriental demand for metal, Troy II was itself a centre of accumulated wealth, providing capital for development of industry and trade in our Continent.

Yet Trojan merchants seem to have managed without writing. They did not even, like the Minoans, engrave stone seals. Two cylinders were found at Troy,[29] but their attribution is uncertain. But the Trojans did copy Asiatic seals in clay while an imported sherd from IIb bears the imprint of an Early Minoan seal.

The old native fertility cult continued without any notable changes, but the figurines, now predominantly of stone, are all highly conventionalized (Fig. 8, 15), and the phalli are made of stone.

After the sack of Troy II a reoccupation of Hissarlik on a smaller scale is represented by the ruins of towns III, IV, and V,[30] each fortified and each reconstructed several times. All were urban in the sense that they comprised specialized potters and smiths and relied upon trade, though a marked increase in the proportion of game bones in the food refuse from town III may denote a temporary decline in farming. Throughout the pottery attests unbroken continuity of tradition. But face-urns are commoner in Troy III than in II. Pots found on Euboea and at Orchomenos look like exports from Troy III, while a copper pin from that town is taken for a Cycladic manufacture.[31] Domed ovens,[32] taller than those from Thermi, appear at Troy for the first time in IV. In town V Aegean imports are rare. But bowls adorned with a red cross in the interior that are characteristic of Troy V have close parallels on E.H.III sites in Greece, while analogous vessels are found at Gözlü Kale, Tarsus, together with Cappadocian tablets.[33]

With the sixth settlement[34] Troy approximates more closely than ever before to the dignity of a city. It was girt with a new and more formidable stone rampart enclosing an area of over five acres. But revival seems due to the advent of a new people who introduced pottery foreign to the native tradition, novel domestic architecture, the practice of cremation and probably the horse, whose presence is osteologically attested first in Troy VI. The new pottery is termed Minyan ware – a fine grey ware, owing its colour to the reduction of the iron oxides in well-selected clay by controlled firing in a kiln – and accompanied by a red oxidized variant. These are the characteristic native wares of Troy VII too. The houses no longer conform to the megaron plan, but are entered through doors in their long sides. No cemeteries of Troy I to V, nor even of Early and Middle VI, have been located, but that of Late VI was an urnfield in which the cremated bones were enclosed in cinerary urns. The first Indo-European Hittites at Boğaz Köy had likewise laid out an urnfield and deposited remains of horses with the urns, while burial in urnfields was characteristic of Period VI in Central Europe and began in Hungary even in Period IV.

Under the new rulers trade and industry flourished luxuriantly once more. Middle III, Late Helladic I, II, and IIIa – but hardly any IIIb – vases were imported from the Aegean, white-slipped ware from Cyprus, ivory from Syria or Egypt through the Aegean, but not a single Hittite manufacture. Bronze sickles, of Asiatic looped type,[35] show that metal was now cheap enough for use in rough agricultural work. Smiths produced a chisel provided with a socket formed not by casting but by hammering a projecting tang of metal round a mandril as in Hittite cities.[36]

Judged by the imported Aegean vases, Troy VI should have lasted from about 1700 to 1300 B.C. Then it fell, overthrown perhaps by an earthquake, perhaps by the Homeric Achaeans under Agamemnon. In any case the site was reoccupied and Troy VIIa – a rather poorer city – survived for another century, only to be destroyed with obvious violence. For the last twenty years it has been held that Troy VIIa was Homer's Ilion, but that view was plausibly challenged in 1955. In any case, after its destruction barbarians settled at Hissarlik and introduced a coarse wart-ornamented pottery without, however, exterminating the older population or suppressing the old ceramic tradition; for grey wares, like Minyan, were still manufactured in Troy VIIb. On the other hand, socketed bronze celts cast on the spot by the usual Central European method leave no doubt as to the origin of these invaders.

4   Maritime Civilization in the Cyclades

The Cyclades are scattered across the Aegean, remnants of a land-bridge between Anatolia and Greece affording a passage for cultural ideas from Asia to Europe. To mere food-gatherers or self-sufficing peasants, the islands, often small and barren, offered no attractions. But to mariners crossing from Asia to Europe they offer convenient halting places and lairs to any pirates who might wish to prey on more peaceful voyagers. Moreover, they contain raw materials of the sort needed by urban civilizations – copper (Paros and Siphnos), obsidian (Melos), marble (Paros and others), emery (Naxos). Accordingly, while larger islands like Chios and Samos seem to have been settled by neolithic peasants, the little Cyclades were at first passed by, but early colonized by communities that could find a livelihood in commerce and perhaps in piracy too. Such communities must have lived near the shore and presumably in townships. But only at Phylakopi in Melos[1] has a Cycladic settlement been fully explored. There, three consecutive townships could be distinguished, preceded by some earlier occupation represented by sherds collected beneath the oldest house-floors. The city has been partially engulfed by the sea, but must have extended well over four acres. The first town was apparently unfortified, the second and third girt with strong stone walls, 20 feet thick in the latest phase. Fortified settlements are also known at Chalandriani[2] on Syros, on Paros,[3] and elsewhere. But these fortifications seem relatively late. Soon after the foundation of Phylakopi II, M.M.Ib polychrome vases were imported from Crete; the city is accordingly hardly older than the twentieth century B.C.; it is frankly Middle Cycladic.

For the remaining islands and for earlier periods we are reduced to estimating the size and stability of the settlements from the cemeteries. Few have been fully explored, but they were admittedly extensive. Three on Despotikon comprised fifty to sixty graves each; on Syros one cemetery at Chalandriani was composed of nearly 500 graves, a second of more than fifty; on Paros, Tsountas mentions nine cemeteries of from ten to sixty

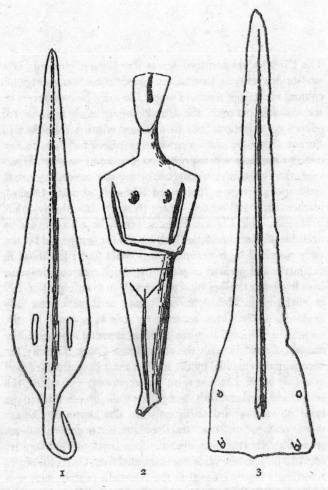

Fig. 23. Tomb-group. Amorgos (⅓).

graves. Of course, all these burials are not contemporary. While it has been customary to assign most cemeteries to the Early Cycladic period (before 2000 B.C.), Åberg[4] has shown that some graves must be Middle or even Late Cycladic. Fortunately Cycladic imports in Egypt, in Crete, at Thermi and Troy, and on Mainland Greece suffice to show that the islands' culture reached its zenith in the third millennium. Marble idols like Fig. 23, 2, were imported into Crete chiefly during E.M.III, a blade like 23, 1, from the same tomb on Amorgos, was included in Treasure A of Troy II; Cycladic marble vases were used in Thermi I–III, and the bird pins of Thermi I recur on Syros; a pin with double spiral wire head like Fig. 27, 9, was found in an Early Helladic tomb at Zygouries; 'frying-pans' with spiral decoration like Fig. 24 were found in the oldest Early Helladic township at H. Kosmas in Attica, and in the E.H.III level at Asine; duck vases (like Fig. 28, 2) were imported into Aegina in Early Helladic times though they continued to reach Eutresis in Boeotia during Middle Helladic I (pp. 108 ff.).

Finally, a zoomorphic vase of Parian marble was recovered from a predynastic grave in Egypt[5] while a cylinder seal of Jemdet Nasr style[6] had been buried in a tomb of the Pelos group on Amorgos.

The inference that the density of population on the islands was made possible by trade and manufacture is confirmed by the list of exports just given. And of course that list is by no means exhaustive. Obsidian was quarried on Melos and exported as nuclei or blades to Crete, Mainland Greece, and the other islands. The Cycladic grave goods comprise the products of specialized craftsmen – smiths, jewellers, lapidaries – and prove the use of copper, tin,[7] lead, silver, and other materials which in some cases must have been imported. The role of maritime intercourse is further emphasized by the frequent representation of boats on the vases (Fig. 24).[8] But the islanders do not seem to have needed writing for their business transactions and did not even make regular use of seals like the Minoans. The prominence of weapons in the tombs (especially of Amorgos) and the fortification of the settlements may indicate that piracy was already combined with legitimate trade. In any case, being dependent on overseas trade, the prosperity of the islands might be expected to

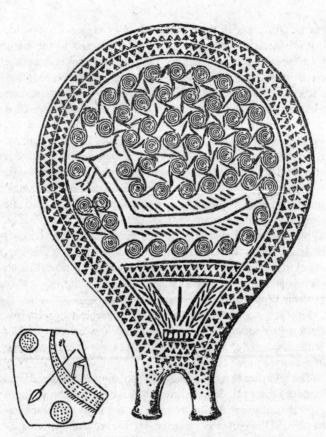

Fig. 24. Cycladic 'frying-pan' and sherd showing boat.

decline when that trade was 'cornered' by monopolistic princes in Crete and the Troad. A real contraction of population during Middle Minoan II–III and Late Minoan I–II would be perfectly comprehensible. In that case the bulk of our material would really be Early Cycladic.

But this Early Cycladic culture was by no means homogeneous. Culturally the islands fall into a southern and a northern group overlapping only on Naxos.[9] To the former belong Melos, Amorgos, Despotikon, Paros, and Antiparos; to the northern Syros, Siphnos, Andros, and also Euboea. The contrast is revealed in burial practices as well as in grave goods. In the southern group, though shaft graves and chamber tombs of uncertain age are plentiful near Phylakopi,[10] the early graves were normally trapezoid cists. In the oldest cemeteries[11] (the Pelos group), definitely antedating Phylakopi I, the cists served as ossuaries and contain several skeletons together with vases like Fig. 28, 1, and 'fiddle idols' like Fig. 8, 10-12. The later tombs were individual graves; they contain idols like Fig. 23, 2, marble vases and weapons. On Syros[12] in the northern group rectangular or oval tombs were built in excavations in the hillside and roofed by corbelling (Fig. 25). But these too served as individual graves, and

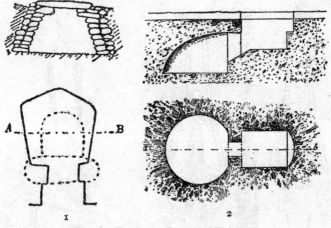

Fig. 25. Tombs on Syros and Euboea.

the single body was introduced through the roof. As at Krazi in Crete, the door (only ·50 m square) was merely a ritual element. In Euboea[13] the tomb was a pit-cave, excavated in the ground and containing only a single corpse (Fig. 25). The earliest vases of the Pelos group are mud-coloured, imitating the shape of marble vessels and are decorated with simple basketry patterns (Fig. 28, 1). Late pottery from the northern isles includes dark-faced fabrics often decorated with running spirals and excised triangles (Fig. 24). Technically it corresponds to the Early Helladic I of the Mainland, though Cycladic imports at Eutresis[14] prove that on the islands this fabric remained current in Middle Helladic times. Favourite forms are the so-called frying-pans and globular or cylindrical pyxides with lids. In some graves on Syros pottery of this class is associated with marble idols like Fig. 23, 2, which are common to both groups of islands.[15] Other graves on Syros and Naxos[16] contain sauce-boats, jugs with cut-away necks and other vessels decorated in lustrous glaze paint in the style of Early Helladic III (p. 108). Finally, Anatolian forms are common in the northern isles, and one tomb group on Euboea contained exclusively Troadic vases (like Fig. 19, 3-4) and daggers (like Fig. 20, 2).

The fish emblem carried by (Northern) Cycladic boats had been the standard of a predynastic parish in the Delta that did not

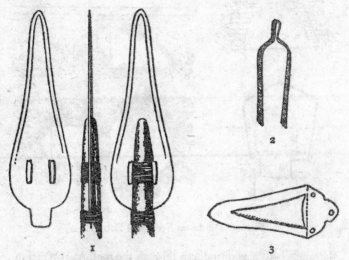

Fig. 26. Slotted spear-head (showing method of mounting), halberd, and tweezers. Amorgos (⅓).

survive into historic times in Egypt.[17] So Fish-folk from the Nile may have fled to the Cyclades when Menes conquered the Delta. Other Cycladic traits – the tweezers (Fig. 26, 2), the popularity of stone amulets and particularly the type represented in Fig. 27, 4; the use of palettes (though the Cycladic specimens are generally more trough-like than the Egyptian and Minoan[18]) and the preference for stone vases may also be Nilotic traits.

Metal-work, pottery, and dress, on the contrary, are rather Asiatic than African. Broad flat celts were used as axe-heads.

Shaft-hole axes are represented only by an axe-hammer and an axe-adge from a hoard on Cythnos.[19] Daggers with a stout midrib and rivets, sometimes of silver as in Crete, are common chiefly on Amorgos. Spear-heads were slotted for mounting as shown in Fig. 26; the type with hooked-tang, shown in Fig. 23, 1, has already been connected with Asiatic models on p. 82.

At least in the northern islands clothing had to be fastened with pins, as in Anatolia, and the types with double-spiral and bird heads have already been encountered in that area. Rings, bracelets, and diadems of copper or silver were also worn as in Asia.

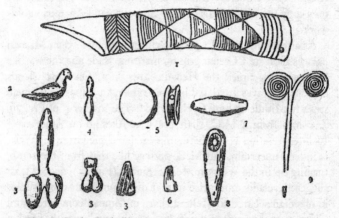

Fig. 27. Early Cycladic ornaments: 2–8 Paros; 1, 9, Syros ($\frac{2}{3}$).

The silver diadems resemble gold ornaments from an E.M.II tomb at Mochlos in Crete and from the Royal Tombs of Ur.[20] Some of the beads and amulets may be Asiatic, notably the dove-pendants that are found even in the early tombs of the Pelos class.[21] The so-called phallic (or winged) beads (Fig. 27, 3) might be compared with the fly-amulets of Egypt and Mesopotamia,[22] but probably derive from a form fashioned of deers' teeth by the mesolithic Natufians of Palestine.[23] A speciality of the northern isles was the decorated bone tube designed to contain pigments (Fig. 27, 1). But similar tubes have been found in Troy IV and Va, and at Byblos in Syria[24] as well as on Levkas in Western Greece.

The self-coloured sepulchral pottery belongs in a general way to the same Anatolian tradition as the early Cretan, and some vase forms such as the pyxides are in the same vague way Anatolian. Even the curious frying-pan form so common in the northern graves recurs, in copper, in a 'royal tomb' at Alaca Höyük in Central Anatolia.[25] (The excised decoration and the form of the handles show that these odd utensils are copied from wooden originals.) On the other hand, the running spiral design on North Cycladic pottery has generally been considered a Danubian motive. Weinberg,[26] however, suspects inspiration from the disconnected impressions of spiral shells such as appear on the early Ghassulian pottery of the Jordan valley while Kaschnitz-Weinberg[27] considers that the incised spirals on the pots copy the wire spirals of early Sumerian and Anatolian goldwork.

As already indicated, Cycladic culture declined when Minoan palaces indicate a Cretan grip on maritime trade and the warlike 'Minyans' occupied the Helladic townships. On most islands only a few graves are dated by long rapiers or imported Minyan vases to Middle or Late Cycladic I-II. The 'halberd' of Fig. 26, 3, comes from a M.C. shaft grave at Akesine on Amorgos.[28] Its interpretation as a halberd, imported or copied from the West, is indeed uncertain, but M.C. pottery like that from the tomb, turning up in the Western Mediterranean (Fig. 41), does at least suggest Cycladic enterprise in that direction. But her resources in obsidian secured to Melos a share in Minoan commerce, and Thera[29] too benefited from her neighbours' wealth until a volcanic convulsion overwhelmed her inhabitants. Phylakopi II was a fenced city with regular streets. Imported M.M.I–II polychrome pottery and Minyan vases from Greece found together on the earliest house floors show how close was the island's connection both with Crete and with the Mainland. Conversely, the matt-painted Middle Cycladic I pottery of Melos is significantly like the Early Bronze Age or Cappadocian ware of Alişar, in Central Anatolia, as if the island had also connections with the East. At a later stage in Phylakopi II a large building equipped with pillar-rooms like a Cretan palace and decorated with a fresco of flying fishes in M.M.III technique might be the residence of a Minoan governor or consul. The potters' craft was industrialized, but the wheelmade vases were decorated with lovely naturalistic patterns in matt paint imitating the Minoan

Fig. 28. Cycladic pottery: 1, Pelos; 2, Phylakopi I, 3, Phylakopi II (L.C.).

style of M.M.III–L.M.I (Fig. 28, 3). But though ceramic technique and style changed, there is no break in the tradition; matt paint had replaced the glaze medium at the beginning of Phylakopi II or even earlier though the patterns at first were geometric, as in Early Cycladic. In Late Mycenaean–L.M.III times the fortifications of Phylakopi were strengthened; the walls were now 20 feet thick, and near the gate a staircase led up to a tower or rampart-walk. Most of the other islands have yielded traces of occupation at this time, but their culture now was just a variant of the Mycenaean 'koine' described on p. 121.

5 From Village to City in Greece

The southern extremity of the Balkan peninsula, though intersected by jagged mountain ranges, chasms, and gulfs, yet displayed as much cultural unity during the prehistoric Bronze Age as it did during the historical Iron Age. In the Stone Age, though peninsular Greece fell for a time into two divisions, Macedonia and even Southern Thrace belonged to the same cultural province. Hence the stratigraphy, observed at citadels, continuously occupied, and in rural tells, provides a chronological frame applicable to the whole region with certain reservations. In Classical times Thessaly, Arcadia, and the mountainous country of North-West Greece and still more Macedonia were culturally backward as compared with Boeotia, Attica, and Laconia, while Thrace was frankly barbarian. A similar retardation can be observed in the Bronze Age. Then from the beginning of the Bronze Age Macedonian culture diverged so far from that of peninsular Greece as to deserve a different name – Macednic – that may be applied to Thessaly too.

Subject to these limitations, the Mainland Bronze Age has been divided into three main periods termed, on the analogy of the Cretan, 'Early', 'Middle', and 'Late Helladic', and each subdivided. The preceding Neolithic is similarly subdivided; but Early Neolithic is still very shadowy, and Middle corresponds to the first or 'A' phase in the old sequence. Absolute dates can confidently be assigned to the Late Helladic or Mycenaean period by interchanges of goods with Crete and the literate countries of the East Mediterranean: L.H.I began no later than 1500 B.C., L.H.IIIb ended just after 1200. The beginning of Middle Helladic about 1800 B.C. is deduced from the association of M.H.

and M.M.II pottery at Phylakopi on Melos (p. 85). Finally, Minoan seals and sealings from E.H.III layers demonstrate a parallelism with E.M.III Crete and Egypt between Dynasties VI–XI. For estimating the antiquity of earlier periods the relative depths of deposits are at least suggestive: at Eutresis 4 m out of 6·5 are composed of E.H. ruins, at Korakou 2 m out of 4·5 m. But in the Thessalian tell at Tsangli, occupied in Early and perhaps Middle Aegean times, 5 m out of a total height of 10 m is attributable to Middle Neolithic debris. In conclusion, it must be recalled that the Helladic and Neolithic periods are generally defined by pottery styles and are in fact usually treated as the period when pottery of the distinctive style was being manufactured at a particular site. Now on Levkas, in the backward north-west, rapiers of L.H. or at least M.M.III type were apparently associated with good E.H. pottery.[1] Hence the absolute dates for Early and Middle Helladic given above are valid only for the Aegean coasts and their immediate hinterland. In peripheral regions a retardation of several centuries must be allowed for! Moreover, the distinction between Late Neolithic and Early Helladic I is nowhere very sharp. In fact, a substantial overlap between some Late Neolithic and E.H.I is generally admitted. Weinberg[2] equates Late Neolithic in Thessaly with E.H.I in the Peloponnese.

Early and Middle Neolithic

While palaeolithic food-gathers had reached peninsular Greece, no remains have yet been found of any mesolithic successors, perhaps merely because no systematic search for such remains has been made. In 1956 the archaeological record begins with mature neolithic cultures characterized by well-made pottery and little else. From Corinthia to Thessaly 'variegated ware', part pink, part grey,[3] seems to characterize the earliest levels. But from the next level at Otzaki magoula[4] in Thessaly as from the cave of Khirospilia on Levkas[5] come sherds ornamented with the edge of a *Cardium* shell or by rustication that we shall find are the symbols of the earliest neolithic farmer-colonists throughout the Balkans and round the Western Mediterranean too. With them are associated distinctive female figurines. From the figurines and from the incipient tell formation it may be inferred that the rural economy and ideology of these early colonists coincided with those of still earlier cultivators in South-Western Asia, some of whom did decorate their pottery with *Cardium* impressions,[6] as of their better-known kinsmen farther north (p. 127) and of their successors in the Middle Neolithic phase.[7]

By the latter a rich culture already ruled throughout the mountain-ridged peninsula from Servia in Western Macedonia to Asea in Arcadia and from Levkas on the west to the coasts of Attica. It is best illustrated in the fertile valleys of Thessaly and Central Greece and is usually named after the Thessalian site of

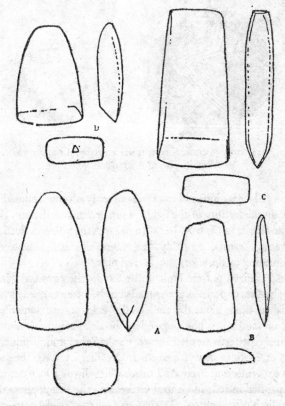

Fig. 29. Thessalian stone axes (A–C) and adzes (B–D). After Tsountas ($\frac{1}{2}$).

Sesklo on the Gulf of Volo. In Thessaly and Central Greece the peasants found an environment that they could exploit from self-sufficing hamlets, continuously occupied. They lived in modest round or rectangular huts of wattle and daub or of mud-brick on stone foundations. A model from Sesklo shows a house with gabled roof. The repeated reconstruction of such dwellings has converted the settlements into little tells (toumba or magoula). Such mounds are very numerous but generally small: 100 by 75 m is an average area for a Thessalian tell, but at Hagia Marina in Phocis the mound covered 300 by 200 m.

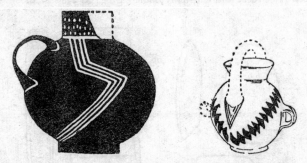

Fig. 30. Pottery of Sesklo style, white on red and red on white. After Wace and Thompson ($\frac{1}{4}$).

Now tell formation implies a rural economy advanced enough to maintain the fertility of the fields, if not orchard husbandry that ties the farmer to his fruit-trees. In phase A the villagers lived by cultivating cereals, probably also vegetables and fruit-trees[8] and breeding cattle, sheep, goats, and pigs.[9]

Unspecialized potters built up by hand delicate vessels, imitating baskets or perhaps even metal vessels[10] in an extremely fine burnished ware, generally red, in the Peloponnese sometimes black or mottled.[11] The pots might be decorated with simple rectilinear patterns formed by wedge-shaped or round punctuations or by lines in white paint. In Northern Greece the vase surface was more often covered with a white slip on which designs were painted in red; in Central Greece and the Peloponnese the white slip is often omitted. The patterns, often very elaborate, are clearly derived from basketry originals, but each hamlet developed its own distinctive style of painting. Ring bases and genuine handles betoken an unusual degree of sophistication, while an imitation of a leather bottle from Nemea approximates to the Early Helladic askos (like Fig. 36, 2).

Simple stone vases too were found at Sesklo, but a bone spatula like Fig. 45 must come from an unrecognized Early Neolithic settlement.

Though self-sufficing communities, the neolithic hamlets were not mutually isolated; they exchanged pots [12] and doubtless other commodities. War is not attested; the only definite weapons found were sling-stones, probably used by hunters. Peaceful commerce outside the province is disclosed by the general use of obsidian. At Tsani a stone button seal bearing a cruciform design was found, and clay models of seals are reported from Sesklo, Hagia Marina, and from Nemea in the Peloponnese. The type is certainly at home in Hither Asia [13] and there generally occurs in a 'chalcolithic' milieu, and copper may well have been known to the 'neolithic' Greeks. Some of their pots seem to imitate the shape and even the rivets of metal vases, and at Hagia Marina Soteriadhes [14] claims to have found riveted copper daggers on virgin soil in a Sesklo settlement. Still, no sustained effort was made to secure regular supplies of metal.

Surplus energies were devoted rather to domestic fertility cults. For these figurines (Fig. 31) were modelled in clay, depicting, often with considerable verisimilitude, a female personage, standing or seated, or, in one example from Chaeroneia, nursing an infant (the 'kourotrophos'). Model thrones or altars (Fig. 32) were also manufactured. As ornaments and charms the peasants wore bracelets of stone or *Spondylus* shells (as on the Danube), and stone nose-plugs as in the al'Ubaid culture of Sumer.

In its rural economy and ideology and in more specific items of equipment – mud-brick architecture, use of the sling instead of the bow as well as the shape of the clay missiles, familiarity with stamp seals, the decoration of kiln-fired pots with basketry designs in dark paint – the Sesklo culture reveals just the westernmost outpost of the South-West Asiatic province, extending from the Mediterranean coasts to Iran and Turkmenia. Peculiarities of the pottery alone connect it more specifically with Syria than with the

Anatolian plateau. Technically the chalcolithic pottery of Cyprus[15] is very like the red-on-white ware described above and may constitute a link with the Hassuna-Halaf complex farther

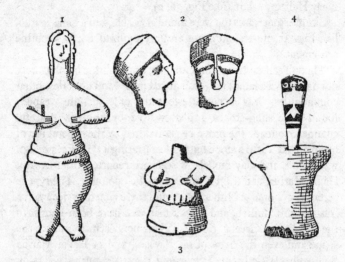

Fig. 31. Neolithic figurines, Thessaly. After Wace and Thompson. (1, $\frac{2}{3}$, 3–4, $\frac{1}{2}$; 2, $\frac{1}{1}$.)

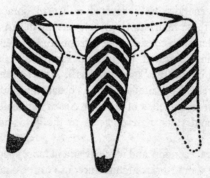

Fig. 32. Miniature altar or throne. After Wace and Thompson ($\frac{1}{2}$).

east. At the same time connections with the cultures of the Lower and Middle Danube valley are already discernible; significant common elements are shoe-last adzes, triangular altars, and shell bracelets.[16]

The Sesklo culture endured for a long time: at Tsangli five out of ten metres of settlement debris are attributed to it, and four out of eight occupational levels at Zerelia. But eventually the continuity of tradition was interrupted. Changes in ceramic technique, in art, in architecture, and even in economy not only define a new period, the Late Neolithic, but also may betoken an infiltration of new colonists. Among these two groups at least may be distinguished – Dimini folk in Eastern Thessaly and Corinthia, and Larisa people in Western Macedonia and Thessaly, Central Greece, and Corinthia. But the break is nowhere complete. Thus female figurines were still modelled in clay; in Eastern Thessaly the kourotrophos survived, painted in Dimini style, and later a very schematized type emerged in which the head is a stumpy cylinder of stone or clay, fitted into a legless torso (Fig. 31, 4) – a type that recurs beyond the Danube in the Gumelnița culture.[17] Hence it may be assumed that the old population absorbed, or was subjugated by, the new settlers. The latter's cultural affinities seem to lie in the Balkans, but the manifestations of their advent differ in different regions.

Late Neolithic

At Dimini near the Gulf of Volvo a completely new settlement was founded. In contrast to the earlier open hamlets it was defended by a complex of stone walls (Fig. 33). Sesklo was probably fortified at the same time.[18] In both citadels houses of the megaron type with porch and central hearth were erected. At Dimini and Sesklo the bevelled adze (D) went out of use, and axes (Fig. 29, C) were employed for the first time. Adzes were hafted at Dimini with the aid of perforated antler sleeves. Copper and gold were now imported; they are represented respectively by two flat celts and a ring-pendant (Fig. 34, 2), all from Dimini. In East Thessaly the vases were now decorated with spirals and maeanders normally combined with the older basketry patterns; the designs may be incised or painted in white or warm black on a buff, red, or brown ground, and may then be outlined with a second colour – black or white; the fruitstand – a dish on a high pedestal – is an important innovation. Similar pottery turns up in Corinthia and the Argolid, again in a Late Neolithic context.[19]

Technically Dimini pottery is inferior to that of Sesklo; ring-bases were abandoned, true handles give place to pierced lugs, though some of these are horned or elaborated into animal heads. So Dimini ware cannot be treated as an autochthonous development of the native Middle Neolithic tradition. It was surely

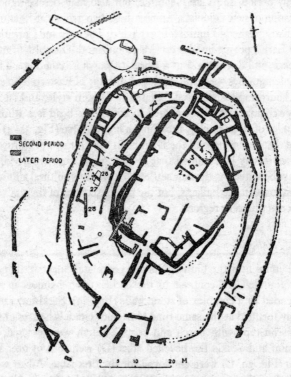

Fig. 33. Plan of fortified village of Dimini. After Tsountas.

introduced by a new people, come most probably from the Danube valley; for there spiral and maeander patterns were always popular and antler was extensively used in industry. Technically Dimini ware is identical with the painted ware of the Balkan Starčevo culture, where, however, it is associated with rusticated ware such as we have already met in Early Neolithic Greece. The patterns, however, whether painted or incised, can best be matched in the Tisza-Maros region.[20]

In Thessaly the Dimini culture is confined to the east. To the west its place is taken by the Larisa culture, found also in Central Greece and Western Macedonia. In the latter region the Late Neolithic phase began with the violent destruction of the Sesklo village of Servia. The site was reoccupied by a new people whose Larisa culture is as different from that of Sesklo as is Dimini, at least judged by its pottery. The commonest ware is self-coloured, generally black and highly burnished, but sometimes at least in Macedonia parti-coloured – black inside and round the rim,

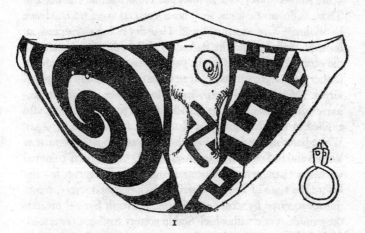

I

Fig. 34. Dimini bowl ($\frac{1}{4}$) and gold-ring pendant ($\frac{2}{3}$). After Tsountas.

elsewhere red like the grey and pink variegated pottery of the Early Neolithic. Vessels no longer stand on ring bases, handles are replaced by lugs that may be horned.[21] Decoration is effected by stroke-burnishing, shallow fluting or channelling, incisions, or rarely by thin lines of white paint. (Crusted ware occurs in Eastern Thessaly, but in a later horizon.) The patterns are generally rectilinear, but include occasional spirals. Besides self-coloured wares a light fabric was made and covered all over with shiny brown or black paint. This ware, termed 'neolithic urfirnis', looks like an attempt to reproduce the appearance of black burnished ware in kiln-fired bases, but is said to begin in Middle Neolithic times in Corinthia.[22]

As at Dimini, adzes were mounted in perforated antler sleeves, the sling was still preferred to the bow, but an arrow-head was found at Servia. Personal ornaments include bracelets of *Spondylus* shell and of marble and bone combs rather like those of the Danubian Vinča culture (Fig. 47).

Larisan ideology was still expressed in the production of female figurines, now very conventional, but one burial was found in the settlement at Servia.

All the new ceramic fabrics and shapes found at Servia (except white painted ware) recur in the Vinča culture on the Danube and Tisza, as do bone combs, shell bracelets, and other traits. Hence Frankfort,[23] Grundmann,[24] and Heurtley[25] have deduced an invasion from beyond the Balkans. On the other hand, many of the ceramic innovations can be paralleled equally in Crete and in Hither Asia. Agreements between Cretan neolithic and Mainland Greek black-polished wares have already been noted. Stroke-burnishing decorated one E.M.I fabric (p. 68) but was also applied in the chalcolithic of Kum Tepe in the Troad (p. 72). White painting on polished black ware was also later popular at Yortan and in South-Western Asia Minor,[26] while parti-coloured wares are characteristic of central Anatolia and Cyprus, but not before the time of Troy I. Finally, black polished wares, sometimes decorated by stroke-burnishing, in North Syria[27] precede the painted fabric with which Sesklo pottery has been compared. If the inference drawn from this comparison be correct, it would be chronologically impossible to attribute this Syrian neolithic to any Danubian inspiration. Hence, as Milojčic has argued most cogently, the Larisa culture should mark not a transplantation of the Vinča culture from north of the Balkans but a stage in the spread of an Asiatic-Aegean culture thither or at least a parallel emanation of the latter. That would further accord with Weinberg's[28] equation of the Late Neolithic of Thessaly and Macedonia with Troy I and E.H.I. Nevertheless, these archaeological arguments are not so conclusive as to exclude absolutely the idea of an invasion from the Danube valley, should other, e.g. philological, considerations make that imperative.

The Early Aegean Bronze Age

The influx of new settlers in Late Neolithic times had not involved an immediate transformation of the economic structure of Hellas; despite its copper axes, the Dimini culture can be termed neolithic as legitimately as its Sesklo precursor. The succeeding period witnessed a real advance towards the Urban Revolution and the nuclei of the classical City States were founded in peninsular Greece.

Not only there, but also in Macedonia and even in Thrace (at least at Mikhalic[29] on the Maritsa close to its junction with the Tundja), the Mainland Bronze Age is marked by innovations in domestic architecture and in pottery that find precise parallels on the eastern coast of the Aegean. Architectural tricks such as herring-bone masonry (in Boeotia and Attica, cf. p. 73) and bothroi in house floors (in Macedonia and, by E.H.III, in peninsular Greece) and ceramic novelties – 'thrust handles', pyxides, jugs with cut-away necks, bowls with tubular or trumpet lugs growing from the inverted rims – suggest a transfer of Anatolian culture across the Aegean and the Dardanelles. A closer study of the pottery, however, shows that no one known Anatolian culture was reproduced on the European shores. If a migration from Asia Minor be assumed, it will be necessary to postulate several streams with different starting-points. Only the Early Aegean pottery from Thrace and Macedonia is explicitly Troadic, while the local post-neolithic Thessalian pottery seems derived from the Early Macednic. In Macedonia and Thrace stone battle-axes occur at the same time, but they are not distinctively Troadic. In the Peloponnese and Attica Cycladic features in pottery and burial rites are prominent, as if the islands had been at least stepping-stones on the way from Asia. At Asine the best analogy to one of the earliest E.H. pots is to be found in the Copper Age of Ali̇şar in Central Anatolia.[30] On the West Coast Ithaka seems to have been colonized from Corinthia.[31] Even in Thrace and Macedonia horses' bones occur on Early Aegean sites, while on the Troad that animal appears first in Troy VI.

Perhaps, then, the striking agreements could be explained as parallel adjustments of related cultures when visiting merchants and prospectors from the Levant and the Nile introduced metallurgical and other techniques and opened up opportunities for securing a share in the surplus accumulated in Sumerian and Egyptian cities.

All Early Helladic, Macednic, and Thracic societies of course still lived mainly by farming, though viticulture is now deducible from grape seeds at H. Kosmas in Attica, while in Thrace and Macedonia horses' bones occur. The early Aegean settlements in Thrace and Macedonia indeed remained simple villages, as did those at most inland sites in Central Greece and the Peloponnese (e.g. Asea in Arcadia). Many had already been occupied by neolithic peasants. Both in Macedonia and peninsular Greece Late Neolithic sherds are found on the oldest Bronze Age floors. But at least in peninsular Greece new settlements were established on sites chosen with a view to trade or piracy rather than agriculture. These, though often of no larger size physically, approximate to fenced cities in their location on naturally defensible sites and their protection by ramparts of stones, combined on Aegina with timber beams as at Troy.

The townsmen lived in long two-roomed houses, closely grouped along narrow lanes, as at Troy and Thermi. But in the more rustic villages houses were oval or apsidal and more scattered. At Tiryns and Orchomenos monumental circular structures were built, probably to serve as granaries.[32] By E.H.III tiles were already used for roofing. Finally, by that phase the town of Lerna[33] at least comprised a regular palace of several rooms grouped about a spacious court or hall and roofed with tiles and slates. So in at least one Mainland centre the social surplus was being concentrated and communal activity directed by a chief as at Troy.

Stone was still employed for axes, adzes, and knives even in the Peloponnese, and so extensively farther north that Thessalian and Thracian villages look positively neolithic. Obsidian was used for knives, sickle teeth, and hollow-based arrow-heads; for the bow is now attested for the first time, without, however, ousting the sling. In Thrace and Macedonia, but not in pensinsular Greece, stone battle-axes were now being made as in the Troad; one from H. Mamas in Macedonia (Fig. 35), though in course of local manufacture, reproduces a South Russian type. At Mikhalic in Thrace miniature battle-axes were modelled in clay as toys or votives.

But copper, tin, lead, silver, and gold were everywhere imported or distributed and worked. Close to the shore at Rafina in Attica, a convenient port for Cycladic or Cypriote ores, were found two large furnaces for smelting copper surrounded by quantities of slag and broken moulds. At Cirrha on the Gulf of Corinth, Davies[34] reported a crucible with tin oxide adhering to it in an open working from which all ore had been extracted, but tin ore in this context is almost inconceivable. Even in Macedonia[35] gold slag and a crucible have been described.

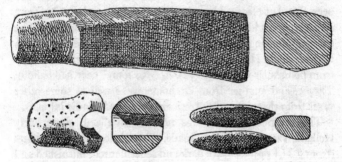

Fig. 35. Axe and battle-axes from H. Mamas. After Heurtley, *BSA.*, XXIX ($\frac{2}{5}$).

At least south of Thessaly the distribution of metal was so well organized that copper could be freely used for craftsmen's tools. Though most have been melted down in prehistoric times, an axe-adze and a flame-shaped knife like Fig. 20, 1, survived in the E.H.II level at Eutresis.[36]

Whether or not the techniques of metallurgy were implanted by immigrant prospectors or itinerant artificers from Asia, the capital for industrial development was secured in the last resort by supplying the demand of cities on the Nile and the Euphrates. As in Crete and the Cyclades, the coastal populations of peninsular Greece had now turned to trading. Perhaps they colonized the Ionian Islands and the west coasts to extend their commerce as the Dorians colonized Corfu in historical times.

The importance and wide ramifications of Early Helladic commerce are illustrated not only by the materials used but by actual foreign manufactures imported or copied locally: leg amulets as in Crete and Egypt (Zygouries,[37] Hagios Kosmas[38]), Cycladic bone tubes (Hagios Kosmas and Levkas), frying-pans (Hagios Kosmas, Eutresis,[39] Asine), marble idols and palettes (Hagios Kosmas), and a double-spiral pin like Fig. 27, 9 (Zygouries). From Asia came an arm-cylinder of twisted silver wire (like a gold one from Troy II) found in a grave on Levkas. In the E.H.III level at Asine lumps of clay stamped with E.M.III–M.M.I seal-impressions must have sealed bales of merchandise or jars of oil brought from Crete. And the Early Helladic merchants themselves felt the need of seals; seals, probably imported, have been found at Hagios Kosmas, Asine, and other sites. One from Asine is almost identical with a Sixth Dynasty Egyptian seal. The counterbalancing exports may possibly have included tin from Cirrha. Early Helladic vases were certainly exported to Troy from peninsular Greece (p. 74). A *depas* found near Mikhalic in Thrace, and another from Orchomenos as well as some other vases from that site and Eutresis may well be Troadic imports.

The ceramic industry was not industrialized, since Early Helladic vases are all handmade. The fabrics that appear first (from E.H.I onwards) are dark and self-coloured, burnished and decorated with incised and excised patterns. In a later phase (E.H.II) begins in peninsular Greece a buff ware which is covered with a dark glaze paint to reproduce the effects of the old burnished fabric. It is generally known as *Urfirnis* and probably denotes Cretan influence[40] though red wares had been coated with a rather similar 'glaze' in Late Neolithic times. In E.H.III the glaze paint is used as the medium for producing dark geometric patterns on a light ground – chiefly in the Peloponnese – or as a ground on which similar patterns are drawn in white – in Central Greece. The rectilinear light-on-dark designs recall Cretan E.M.II–III patterns, but are also foreshadowed on the black neolithic B vases of the Mainland. Distinctive Early Helladic II–III shapes are sauce-boats (also manufactured in gold[41]), hour-glass tankards, askoi and globular water-jars, at first with ring-handles,[42] later with flat vertically pierced lugs, on the belly (Fig. 36).

North of Othrys in Thessaly, Macedonia, and Thrace, Early Aegean potters did not use a kiln that would produce clear ware and so did not manufacture *Urfirnis* ware. Its place was taken by self-coloured wares as in Early Helladic I and Early Troadic. Save for 'sauce-boats', most of the forms popular in peninsular Greece were reproduced in local variations looking rather more

Fig. 36. Early Helladic sauce-boat (1), askos (2), tankard (3), and jar (4) (⅙).

Fig. 37. Early Macednic pot-forms. After Heurtley, *BSA.*, XXVIII.

Troadic than the latter (Fig. 37, 1, 2, 6). Even horned handles had been current at Troy, but in Macedonia a distinctive development was the wish-bone handle (Fig. 37, 3, 5), analogies to which have met us in neolithic Crete. In Thrace the vases from Mikhalic, where askoi are missing, look more Troadic still. But here, as in Chalcidice, trumpet lugs grow out of the inverted rims of bowls. Now in Lesbos this type of lug appeared first in Thermi III, having grown up out of the simpler tubular lugs of Thermi I (Fig. 17). For once pottery discloses an irreversible relation. Finally, a few sherds from Mikhalic in Thrace, from H. Mamas in Macedonia, and from E.H.III levels at Eutresis and H. Marina in Central Greece are decorated with cord imprints. This 'corded ware' has usually been connected with the battle-axes and horses' bones from the Thracic and Macednic sites as evidence for an invasion from Saxo-Thuringia[43] or at least from somewhere north of the Balkans. The forms of most vases have however nothing in common with Saxo-Thuringian corded ware,[44] while the similarities of the amphorae are due at most to a common pre-ceramic prototype (p. 220).

Fig. 38. E. H. Anchor ornament, Kritsana ($\frac{1}{4}$).

Imported marble figurines of Cycladic type may have been used in domestic fertility rites, but clay figurines do not seem to have been manufactured unless the 'anchor ornaments' (Fig. 38) be really ultra-conventionalized versions of such. They constitute one of the most distinctive type fossils of the Early Aegean Bronze Age, being found – in E.H.II–III layers – from Asea in Arcadia to Servia in Macedonia and Mikhalic in Thrace, and from Rafina and Asine on the east to Levkas and Ithaka on the west.[45] Really they are no more likely to be ritual than the clay hooks common to Early Thracic, Macednic, and Troadic. Clay horns of consecration from Asine on the other hand point to rites like the Minoan and Anatolian. But the principal superstitious impulse to accumulation of wealth was supplied by the desire for a good burial. In the Peloponnese and Attica the dead were buried in family vaults outside the settlements. At Zygouries the tombs were pit-caves or shafts cut in the rock, one of which contained fourteen skeletons. At Hagios Kosmas in Attica, the earlier ossuaries were cists with a false door facing the township. The cists were later replaced by built ossuaries like Fig. 25, 1, but still used as collective tombs; in each case the bodies, in the contracted attitude, had been introduced through the roof. Such cemeteries of family vaults show that in peninsular Greece quite a number of lineages or clans lived together in a single township. Out of six skulls measured from H. Kosmas three were long-headed, but two round-headed.[46]

In the north-west quite different burial practices prevailed. On Levkas Dörpfeld described a so-called royal cemetery of thirty-three round tombs. Each 'tomb' was a circular platform of stones defined by a built wall and suggesting a denuded cairn, in or on which were burial pithoi, cists, or shaft-graves – each containing a single corpse (allegedly roasted) – and the ashes of a 'pyre'. Among these lay burnt human and animal bones and remains of metal ornaments and weapons. The pottery from the graves is typically Early Helladic, but the metal gear from the 'pyres' includes besides good Early Aegean types a couple of rapiers and gold hilt mounts[47] that elsewhere would be Mycenaean or at least M.M.III. The cemetery must be a whole period, perhaps four centuries, later than that of H. Kosmas in Attica. The burial rites are equally abnormal. Cremation *in situ* must have taken place on the pyres, a rite otherwise unknown in Bronze Age Greece. The platforms sound like cairns, and in 1955 a cairn with pithos burials very like our round tombs was found in Messenia, but was M.H. in date. So the warriors and rich women buried on Levkas did not possess the standard Early Helladic culture though they used Early Helladic pots and Early Aegean weapons and ornaments.

The standard Early Helladic burial practices are in sharp contrast to the Troadic, but conform rather to Cycladic, Minoan, Cypriote and Levantine traditions. They cannot have been introduced from the Troad. But no Early Aegean burials have been recognized where Troadic parallels are clearest – north of Attica and Euboea or in Macedonia and Thrace.

In peninsular Greece, Early Helladic societies had created a polity and an economy under which some at least of the peasant's younger sons might find a livelihood in industry or commerce, but only in reliance on Oriental markets opened up by maritime transport. Remote from access thereto, the contemporary inhabitants of Macedonia had no alternative but to occupy fresh land. So they filtered southward into Thessaly. The culture that used to be attributed to Neolithic III and IV there was in fact basically Early Macednic.[48] But local Late Neolithic traditions were blended with the Anatolian. So clay figurines were still manufactured, but now male as well as female. At Rakhmani in Eastern Thessaly spiral patterns were applied in crusted technique.

Middle Helladic

The Middle Helladic period is ushered in by the violent destruction of Orchomenos and other sites. Many were reoccupied. But abrupt changes in architecture, pottery, burial rites, and general economy indicate the dominance of new and warlike settlers. The latter can be most easily recognized by their pottery – the reduced grey ware described on p. 83 and unhappily termed Minyan by archaeologists – and by the practice of burying the dead contracted in small cists or in jars among the houses. The martial

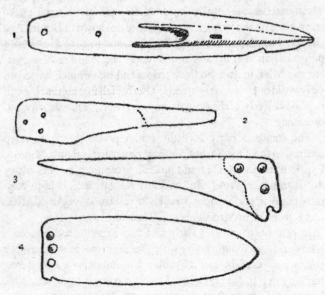

Fig. 39. Spearhead, knives, and dagger from M.H. graves in Thessaly. After Tsountas (½).

character of the invaders is disclosed by the deposition in the graves of metal weapons (Fig. 39) – knives, ogival daggers, and spear-heads with a socket, cast like a shoe on one or both faces of the blade (Sesklo, Levkas, Mycenae). Hollow-based obsidian arrow-heads were still used, but now the archer used also grooved stone arrow-straighteners like Fig. 113 (Asine, Levkas, Mycenae). Perforated stone axes appear for the first time at Eutresis and Asine and antler axes and sleeves at Asine. On the other hand, such craft tools as saws and gouges are first found in a Middle Helladic grave (on Levkas).

The Minyan invaders did not exterminate the older inhabitants or destroy their economy, but added to the population and accelerated the accumulation of wealth. Malthi now attained its maximum population; the walls comprised, within an area of $3\frac{2}{3}$ acres, 305 rooms, while the citadel was supplied with spring water by an aqueduct. The houses are more often agglomerations of rooms than long rectangular halls.[49] Tin-bronze was now worked by the smiths, and stone moulds for casting spear-heads like Fig. 39, 1, and Minoan double-axes were found even at Dimini in Thessaly.

The potters' craft was soon industrialized. The grey-ware vases were fired in a closed kiln and either formed in a mould or thrown on the wheel. A family of Minoan potters settled on Aegina, bringing with them their clay wheel as used in Crete.[50] Perhaps such immigrant craftsmen were responsible for introducing the wheel from Crete everywhere, but there is nothing Minoan about their products. The favourite 'Minyan' forms are ring-stemmed goblets, high-handled cups (Fig. 40), craters, and amphorae. Both in hue and form such Minyan vases imitate silver models. Indeed, in one Late Helladic grave the silver originals were actually found together with the clay skeuomorphs.[51] On the other hand, the influence of woodwork is patent – notably in the horned handles from Aetolia (Fig. 40, 3), which are repeated in good Minyan ware at Troy but have a long Balkan ancestry. But grey Minyan vases had to compete with hand-made vessels of the same shapes in polished brown or black and vitreous red wares.

Perhaps later, pithoi, bowls, and other shapes were built up by hand in clear wares and decorated with geometric patterns in matt paint (Fig. 41). In form and decoration these matt-painted vessels agree precisely with Middle Cycladic pots from Melos and show the same Central Anatolian affinities (p. 92). A M.H.III beaked jug from Asine[52] looks like an imported 'Early Hittite' manufacture. On the other hand, at Lianokladhi in the Spercheios valley the Macedonians, who had occupied the site in Early Aegean times, now learned to make in matt-painted ware jars, tankards,

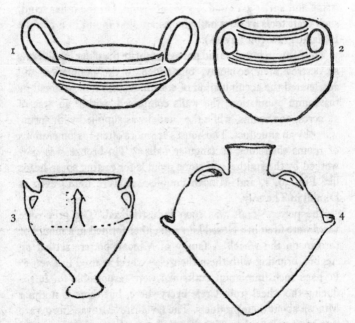

Fig. 40. Minyan pottery from Thessaly ($\frac{1}{5}$), and imitations from Thermon, Aetolia ($\frac{1}{15}$).

and bowls with wish-bone handles of good Macednic or Early Helladic shape, and decorate them with Macednic patterns, including pot-hook spirals, in Middle Helladic technique (Fig. 42). A similar fabric appears at Thermon in Aetolia together with 'imitation Minyan' vases, but not before L.H.II (fifteenth century) and also in Levkas. This Lianokladhi painted ware thus illustrates people of Macednic–Middle Helladic traditions surviving into Late Helladic times whom Heurtley plausibly identifies with the Dorians' ancestors.[53]

In peninsular Greece trade with Crete was at first interrupted by the invasion, but obsidian was still secured from Melos and the metal trade was unimpaired. Soon Middle Minoan II polychrome pottery was being imported into Aegina and imitated at Eutresis. A bossed bone plaque like Fig. 115 and a hammer pin,[54] from M.H. layers at Lerna, illustrate connections at once with Anatolia and with Sicily.

Fig. 41. Matt-painted bowl and pithos, Aegina ($\frac{1}{10}$); and Middle Cycladic jugs from Marseilles harbour and Phylakopi ($\frac{1}{5}$).

The dead were generally interred in cists or jars under or between the houses within the settlements. But on Levkas ten or twelve such burials might be grouped together in rectangular or circular 'platforms' (cf. p. 111). In Messenia [55] Middle Helladic pithos burials lay on the periphery of a regular cairn 14 m in diameter.

The instrusive culture typified by grey Minyan ware is found all over Greece to the Ionian Islands, Levkas, Thessaly, and even Chalcidice. Only in inland Macedonia did the native culture persist quite unaffected by it. Now most authorities agree that the

Minyan invaders were the first Greek speakers in the peninsula. From them should have sprung the new dynasty that began to write Indo-European Greek at Knossos in L.M.II (p. 63). If so, the origin of the invaders becomes a major issue for European prehistory. In 1914 Forsdyke suggested a Troadic origin for the invaders.[56] But, though Minyan ware was the normal pottery of Troy VI, it did not begin demonstrably earlier there than in

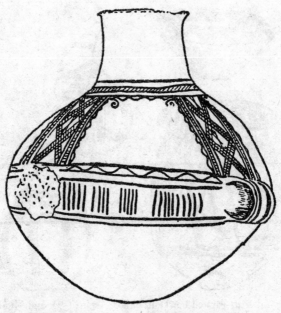

Fig. 42. Matt-painted jar, Lianokladhi III. After Wace and Thompson ($\frac{1}{4}$).

Greece. Burial among the houses contrasts as much with Troadic as with Minoan and Early Helladic practice, but was normal in Central Anatolia and farther east. Now grey vases, technically allied to Minyan and including pedestalled goblets, are characteristic of Hissar II in North-Eastern Iran and allied sites in Turkmenia,[57] where again the dead were buried among the houses. On the other hand, Persson insists on Northern features in the intrusive culture.[58] None is really convincing, and the most significant can already be found south of the Balkans in Thrace and Macedonia in Early Aegean times. If fresh 'Northern' elements entered peninsular Greece and the Troad at the beginning of Middle Helladic there is no evidence for bringing them from beyond the Balkans.

Mycenaean Civilization

The martial prowess of the Minyan invaders eventually allowed them to win by force of arms a share in the wealth accumulated in Minoan and Oriental cities while their war-chiefs, becoming kings, concentrated some of it for use as capital in the development of a Mainland civilization. The kings attracted or compelled Minoan craftsmen to settle at their courts while merchants brought regular supplies of raw materials and luxury goods. By Late Helladic times the Middle Helladic townships had grown into little cities.

The urban revolution was apparently first consummated at Mycenae, a citadel that commands a main artery of communications between the south-east and the north-west. The old settlement, founded in Early Helladic times, became the capital of a potent dynasty. The kings with their families were buried with regal wealth in two Shaft Grave cemeteries, each enclosed by a circle of upright slabs. Schliemann discovered a circle of six tombs, numbered I to VI, that had subsequently been incorporated in the walls of the Late Mycenaean citadel. A second circle comprising fourteen shaft graves (designated by Greek letters) farther out and disturbed by the erection of the 'Treasury of Clytemnaestra', came to light in 1951.[59] In both, the shafts, cut 10 to 15 feet into the rock and provided with a ledge 4 or 3 feet above the floor to support a wooden roof, normally contained several skeletons lying on their backs with the legs extended or drawn up; one skull had been trepanned. These may have been buried in wooden coffins, but at the bottom of the latest and largest shaft in the new circle had been built a stone mortuary house, divided into chamber and ante-chamber and roofed with a corbelled barrel vault. Stelae, carved in low relief with spiral patterns framing scenes of war and of the chase, once marked each grave. Now they provide the earliest evidence for the use of horse-drawn war-chariots in the Aegean. A little imported

M.M.IIIb pottery together with native matt-painted and Minyan vases suggest that the earliest interments in some graves go back into the sixteenth century; the latest dateable sherds from any shaft grave are L.M.II. The Shaft Grave period covered roughly the century 1600 to 1450 B.C.

The equipment acquired by the Shaft Grave kings is largely of Minoan inspiration. Their palace was equipped with a light-well, like those of Knossos, and decorated with frescoes in Minoan technique. Most vessels and ornaments are evidently products of Minoan craftsmen. On figured documents men wear the Minoan drawers and women the flounced skirt of the island. Minoan signets were adopted for official business. The cult of the Mother Goddess, associated, as in Crete, with the symbols of the dove, the double-axe, the sacred pillar and horns of consecration, was practised with Minoan rites at Mycenae, and draughts were played as in Crete. No one denies that craftsmen trained in Cretan schools produced the objects in question though many must have been executed at Mycenae itself to the order of the local king. An immigration of Cretan potters seems to have initiated the local manufacture of Mycenaean vases, decorated with shiny paint in the best Minoan tradition. It no longer seems likely, as it did thirty years ago, that Mycenaean civilization was founded by Minoan princes carving out for themselves kingdoms on the Greek Mainland. The martial character of Early Mycenaean culture, as revealed in the fortification of the citadel, the abundance of weapons, and the popularity of battle scenes in art, is quite foreign to the Minoan spirit. The kings of Mycenae wore beards; the Minoans generally shaved their faces. In their tombs native Minyan and matt-painted vases are juxtaposed to vessels painted in Cretan style and technique. An arrow-shaft-straightener in Shaft Grave VI and a Mainland spearhead like Fig. 39, 1 (Grave IV), occur side by side with arms in Minoan tradition. Though the terrible rapiers, nearly a metre long, like Fig. 14, 1, may be Middle Minoan types, the flange-hilted variant of Fig. 14, 2, is Mainland rather than Cretan. A round-heeled dagger from Shaft Grave VI would seem more at home in Central and Western Europe [60] than round the Aegean. Mycenaean warriors wore helmets plated with boars' tusk laminae, but so did Minoans (p. 66). Amber for beads found in several shaft graves must have been imported from the Baltic, a newly found crescentic necklace with pattern-bored spacers[61] (Fig. 43) of that material is likely to be of English manufacture.

Finally, the horse-drawn war-chariots, at once the symbols and the decisive instruments of Mycenaean kingship, are certainly not Minoan. The horses that drew them point north of the Aegean basin. That is not to say that Minyan invaders had brought chariots and horses with them into Greece in the eighteenth century. A small group of charioteers could easily seize power and maintain authority with this new and potent weapon. Structurally the Mycenaean shaft graves agree closely with the 'yamno' graves of the Pontic steppes, which do contain wheeled ox-carts and hammer pins (p. 196). Whatever the ancestry of the Shaft Grave rulers, by concentrating wealth, won by pillage, mercenary service in Egypt[62] or more peaceful trade, and so attracting or compelling expert craftsmen to settle on the Mainland, they prepared the way for an urban civilization.

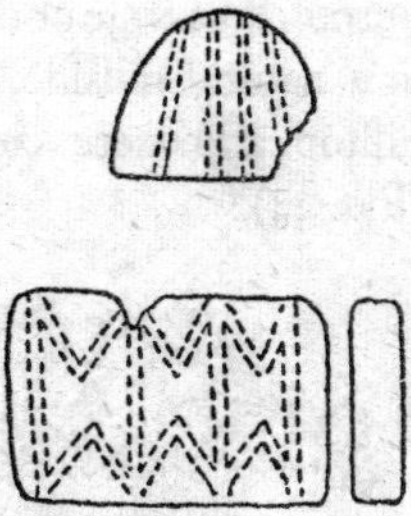

Fig. 43. Terminal and pattern-bored spacer-bead from amber necklace. Shaft grave at Mycenae ($\frac{1}{2}$).

Between 1500 and 1400 B.C. the same process of acculturation was accomplished at other sites which had remained rural townships during the Early Mycenaean Shaft Grave epoch. Here again the change coincided with the rise in the townships of chieftains, concentrating the local wealth for expenditure on the products of secondary industry and trade. These celebrated their elevation by erecting stately beehive tombs or tholoi. Such tombs are significantly located near the heads of southward-facing gulfs and along natural trade-routes by sea or land. On the east coast these Middle Mycenaean tholoi extend as far north as the Gulf of Volo, on the west to Cakovatos in Elis. At Mycenae itself, rulers, perhaps of a new dynasty, erected a series of tholoi in which Wace traced the typological development from earlier and ruder vaults to the celebrated 'Treasuries' of 'Clytemnaestra' and 'Atreus', built in ashlar masonry and provided with richly sculptured portals.[63]

The oldest dated tholos, one at Navarino,[64] contained only matt-painted and (a minority of) Cretanizing L.H.I vases, so should have been built in the sixteenth century. Kakovatos[65] and a few other tholoi yielded good L.H.I pottery pointing to a foundation before 1450 B.C., a larger number at L.H.II, the rest, including the finest 'treasuries' at Mycenae, were Late Mycenaean. A very rich tholos, found intact at Dendra,[66] contained no pottery earlier than L.H.III, but the gold and silver vessels are L.M.I in style and illustrate a survival of heirlooms for half a century at least!

Mycenaean tholoi are corbelled chambers entered by a long unroofed passage or dromos. Many were erected in an excavation in a natural hillside, but others stood on level ground or on a hilltop and were covered by an artificial mound or cairn[67] (Fig. 44).

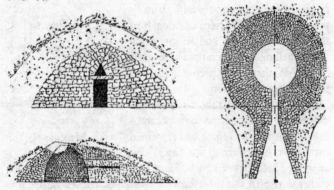

Fig. 44. Mycenaean tholos tomb in Euboea. After Papavasileiou.

Much of the grave goods from the Middle Mycenaean tholoi are either imports from Crete or products of craftsmen trained in the Minoan schools. So too the contemporary palaces at Tiryns and Thebes, neither a megaron, were decorated with frescoes in Minoan technique.

But the idea of the tholos tomb can hardly have been introduced from Crete; in that island no tholoi are known to bridge the five centuries between the building of the Early Minoan ossuaries and the erection of the Mainland vaults. On the other hand, the architectural similarities between the Mycenaean tholoi and the corbelled passage graves of Southern Spain and Portugal are familiar, and there typological series can be produced to illustrate the development of the tholos from simpler forms.[68] So if the idea of the tholos were introduced into Greece, it may have come from the Iberian Peninsula.

In any case connections with the West are conspicuous in Mycenaean culture. L.M.I (or L.H.I) pots were exported to the Aeolian islands, L.H.I metal-types were copied in Sicily (p. 287). The colonization of Kakovatos and the wealth of its ruler must be connected with the amber trade. His treasures included a crescentic amber necklace with pattern-bored spacer plates (Fig. 43), reputedly made in England.

Burial in a tholos must have been the prerogative of kings and their families. But even in the fifteenth century some of their urban subjects began to prepare for themselves family vaults. Villagers, however, were still buried singly in cists or pithoi. Similarly throughout L.H.II native potters continued to turn out Minyan and hand-made matt-painted vases.

But by 1400 B.C. the Mainland had thoroughly mastered Minoan techniques and assimilated the Cretan industrial system. Native workers, having been apprenticed to Minoan craftsmen, could turn out *en masse* rather shoddy articles that satisfied the less refined tastes of the Mainlanders and gradually ousted the products of household industry. Thus equipped, the Mainland took over from Crete the political and economic hegemony in the Aegean. Knossos was sacked; the Continental megaron replaced the Aegean palaces at Phaestos and Phylakopi. The Mycenaean cities were more numerous and perhaps more populous than the Cretan; the acropolis of Mycenae alone, not to mention unwalled suburbs, covered about 11 acres, that of Asine nearly 9, Gla in L. Copaïs no less than 24 acres. The immense cemeteries of rock-cut chamber tombs adjacent to each city are even more convincing than the areas. Each tomb, an irregular chamber entered by a narrow passage or *dromos*, was a family vault. Some contain as many as twenty-seven corpses. Though carefully sealed up after each interment, such tombs were in fact reopened periodically and used over several generations; vases of L.H.II, L.H.IIIa, and L.H.IIIb styles were found in one and the same tomb at Mycenae, showing its use for burial for at least two centuries (1450-1250 B.C.).[69] And a family likeness could be detected on the skeletons from the same tomb. This collective burial practice, though deeply rooted in the Aegean and still current in Crete in Middle Minoan times, is in sharp contrast to the 'Minyan' usage and looks like a reversion to Early Helladic customs or an imitation of the royal practice

The populous cities sought an outlet for their goods and overflowing population in trade and colonization. Mycenaean pottery and other products were exported in quantities to Troy, Palestine, Syria, Egypt, and Sicily, rapiers to Bulgaria and perhaps the Caucasus. The Aegean and Ionian islands and even the coastal tracts of Macedonia received contingents of Mycenaean traders, potters, and metal-workers and were incorporated in the Mycenaean economic system. Mycenaean colonies denoted by tholos tombs were planted even on the coasts of Asia Minor and Syria.[70] In the fourteenth and thirteenth centuries a complete cultural uniformity prevailed over the whole Aegean world – a uniformity that embraced the political diversity reflected in the *Iliad*.

The zenith of Late Mycenaean civilization, as fixed by Mycenaean imports in Egypt and Syria and Egyptian imports in Greece, was reached in the fourteenth century. After 1300 B.C. trade with Egypt declined, wealth diminished, art decayed as piracy and militarism took the place of peaceful commerce. Only the armament industry expanded; commerce with the barbarous West alone was intensified.

The fortifications of Mycenae, Tiryns, and Athens were extended.[71] Greaves [72] and probably corselets were worn as well as helmets. A new type of flange-hilted sword was introduced in which the flange is carried right round the pommel [73] (Fig. 15). Swordsmen were mounted on horseback to become the first cavalrymen of antiquity.[74] The supplies of amber, copper, and tin from the north and west were maintained. As a consequence, a flange-hilted sword of the new type was exported to Cornwall,[75] there to be buried with the chief of a tribe that controlled access to the tin lodes (p. 388). Relations with the West were more intimate than a mere interchange of goods. An Italian smith came to the court of Mycenae and there cast in a stone mould [76] Continental winged axes like Fig 119, 2. Peschiera daggers (like

Fig. 119, 4), cut-and-thrust swords,[77] and fibulae (both like Fig. 122, and with flattened leaf-shaped bow)[78] appear in such numbers as to imply changes in ways of fighting and in fashions of dress, if not in population. They herald the cataclysm that submerged the Mycenaean civilization – the 'Dorian Invasion' dated by Classical tradition about 1100 B.C.

6 Farming Villages in the Balkans

The rugged peninsular between the Black Sea and the Adriatic, despite the severity of the winters and the retardation of spring, enjoys, owing to its latitude and the prolongation of autumnal warmth, a climate intermediate between the Mediterranean and the Temperate. So the adaptation of an Asiatic rural economy would be less difficult there than in the rest of the European woodland zone. And incidentally the ancestors of one-corn wheat (*Triticum monococcum*) and several fruit-trees grew wild there. So the fertile valleys intersecting the Balkan ranges are, like Thessaly and South-West Asia, studded with tells representing the sites of permanent, though formally neolithic, villages. Their stratification should provide a reliable record of the process of adaptation. But in Bulgaria the latest accounts of the culture-sequence at Banyata[1] and Karanovo[2] are in flat contradiction with earlier accounts of the succession at Kyrollovo,[3] Veselinovo,[4] and Karanovo itself.[5] So too at Vinča on the Middle Danube the divisions of the material excavated by Vassits[6] from the 10 m deep deposit proposed respectively by Holste,[7] Milojčić,[8] and Garašanin[9] are equally discrepant.

In the peninsula and along the Lower Danube a mesolithic population, allied to the Northern Forest-folk, might be postulated to explain peculiarities in the local neolithic culture, but is not documented by any certified finds. In the caves so far explored no occupation layers intervene between strata containing Upper Palaeolithic (Aurignacian) implements and a pleistocene fauna and those yielding remains of developed neolithic cultures. The continuous record recommences with farmers whose cultures in general for all their local divergences are not only based on the same cereals and domestic stock as those of peninsular Greece and Hither Asia, but also reproduce the latter's rural economy and ideology expressed in female figurines and even their preferences for adzes and slings.

The Starčevo-Körös Culture[10]

Throughout the Balkan peninsula and on both sides of the Carpathians, north of the Danube, the continuous record of food-production begins in settlements of the Starčevo culture. This assemblage, only in the last ten years clearly distinguished from its successors, extends from the Aegean coasts in Thessaly and Gallipoli across the main Balkan range and the Danube to the Körös and the headwaters of the Pruth (Map I, crosses). In such a vast and diversified region the material remains of the culture are surprisingly uniform, though local divergences are of course recognizable, especially in pottery; we could easily distinguish a Maritza or Thracian, a Drave-Morava, and a Maros-Körös aspect.

Though occurring at the base of several tells both in Bulgaria and in Yugoslavia, the Starčevo layers seem to represent rather temporary settlements, and similar material has been collected from caves and from unstratified camp sites along streams and lake shores. On the Maros and Körös the latter consisted of groups of trapeze-shaped huts of wattle-and-daub with lean-to walls that formed also the roof,[11] but on the Maritza more commodious houses were built in the later phase of the culture. In the economy, hunting played a prominent role; bones of game animals are common in all settlements. But the hunters did not use flint-tipped arrows, but relied on traps and slings.[12] Fishing may be deduced from the location of the encampments along the banks of streams and lakes and from clay net-sinkers which in the Körös aspect assume the ornate form of Fig. 45. But Starčevo folk were always farmers even though their rural economy may have been incompatible with durable settlement in one place.

Actual cereals – so far only one-corn wheat in Bulgaria; millet in Yugoslavia! – have been identified; they were stored in clay-lined pits; sickle flints were found mounted in a curved horn-handle at Karanovo[13]; saddle querns and rubbers are found everywhere. Beside the querns in Bulgaria are regularly found bone spatulae (Fig. 45) that must have been used to scoop up the flour. Such spatulae recur on practically every Starčevo site throughout the province, but in no other context, so that they can be used as a diagnostic type of the culture as confidently as pots. Bread was probably already baked in low clay ovens. Finally, cattle, goats, sheep, and pigs were bred for food. But in general the rural economy must have been one of shifting agriculture and pastoralism combined with hunting and collecting. That will

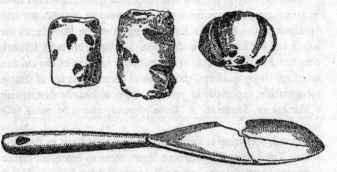

Fig. 45. Clay loom-weights or net-sinkers ($\frac{1}{4}$) and bone spatula of Starčevo Körös culture, ($\frac{1}{2}$).

account for the relatively rapid spread of such a homogeneous culture over so vast a province.

In industry carpenters used exclusively adzes (like Fig. 29, B and D) and chisels mounted in antler sleeves. In the Körös aspect at least celts were sometimes drilled with a hollow-borer and antler beams were perforated – and sometimes armed with stone blades – to serve as adzes or mattocks. Textiles may be inferred from spindle-whorls, spools, and loom-weights of baked clay.

The potters, though not full-time specialists, had complete mastery over their material. The universal and perhaps earliest Starčevo ware is indeed coarse and chaff-tempered. But the shapes are highly sophisticated. The vases, some 21 inches high, are all provided with flat bases or even stand-rings though not with true handles. North of the Balkan range the stand-rings may be quatrefoil or cruciform (Fig. 46) or replaced by four nipples that farther south have grown into four solid legs. These vessels were elaborately decorated by rustication (often called barbotine), which in the Körös aspect is combined with conventional figures of goats, stags, or men in relief. This coarse ware, save perhaps in the Körös aspect, was generally accompanied by finer fabrics, also chaff-tempered, with a well-smoothed or even burnished surface, grey, buff, or red in colour. The fine grey wares may be decorated with narrow flutings or channellings that both at Starčevo and on the Maritza may form spiraliform patterns.

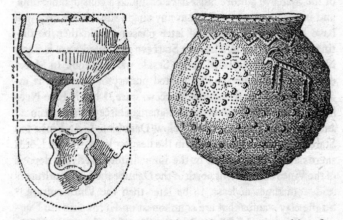

Fig. 46. Cruciform-footed bowl in fine Starčevo ware and jar of rusticated Körös style ($\frac{1}{12}$).

Finally, small vases, especially goblets on a low foot, may be painted in white or black on a red ground or – in Yugoslavia – in dark brown on buff, in fact just like Dimini ware (pp. 101–2). The lines of paint form simple designs among which spirals occur only rarely and, according to Milojčić, late. Neither the rusticated nor the painted designs were blended into harmonious compositions as in Thessaly. At Karanovo fluted ware seems to appear later than painted; both appear later than rusticated ware at Starčevo according to Fewkes,[14] Milojčić,[15] and Mrs Garašanin,[16] but Ehrich[17] denies this. Both Milojčić and Mrs Garašanin agree that the rusticated Körös ware represents a still later phase of the culture.

Trade brought obsidian to the encampments on the Pruth and along the Tisza and Körös, and *Spondylus* shells to the latter region from the Mediterranean.

Clay stamps, as in neolithic Byblos, are common on the Körös sites, at Starčevo itself and along the Pruth, but have not yet been reported south of the Balkans. Similarly figurines, well-modelled and markedly steatopygous, are common in the Körös group but rare and rude at Starčevo and on the Maritza. Burials were unceremonious, being represented by skeletons without grave goods, interred contracted in pits in the encampments. The expansion of the Starčevo culture must have occupied a considerable time, and in each area, though not at any single site, its life may well have been long. Earlier and later phases should then be distinguishable. Now in Thessaly Starčevo rusticated ware is Early Neolithic, being stratified below Sesklo wares (p. 96). In Macedonia, on the contrary, the painted pottery of Olynthus is indistinguishable from painted Starčevo ware,[18] but is Late Neolithic. On the Pruth in Northern Romania Starčevo wares (painted and rusticated) are stratified below Danubian I. At Vinča too Starčevo culture appears pure in the deepest level, though Körös sherds at least are mixed in the immediately overlying deposit of the Vinča culture. But north of the Danube the Körös culture is said, sometimes at least, to be later than the Vinča culture.[19] So the clay stamps that are commonest on Körös sites are Danubian II on the Middle and Upper Danube. Hence the Körös aspect is probably a late phase of the Starčevo culture as Garašanin and Milojčić contend, and painting may be a secondary feature in the pottery.

If this be correct, antler sleeves and mattocks and the spiral motive may be accretions developed or borrowed by Starčevo farmers from hypothetical hunter-fishers of Forest traditions along the Danube. Similarly vase painting, the manufacture of the more realistic figurines and of the stamps, that look most like Asiatic seals, and perhaps the improvement in rural economy, suggested by the more permanent settlements on the Maritsa, may be additions to the original culture inspired by fresh immigrants from Hither Asia. The hypothetical 'pure Starčevo culture', left by the abstraction of the foregoing accretions, could quite well have arisen in the Balkans, since the only directly attested cereals cultivated and animals[20] bred may be native there. It may, on the other hand, be due to immigrants from South-Western Asia related to the farmers who made unpainted pots in North Syria and Cilicia, or, if rusticated Starčevo ware seems too unlike the recognized incised fabrics of the area, to farmers who made no pots at all.[21]

The relatively homogeneous Starčevo culture was in the sequel replaced by – or by divergent adjustments to the environment grew into – distinct local cultures in the several natural subdivisions of the province. Divergent development would be quite natural if a sparse population of herdsmen and shifting cultivators that had maintained communication between dispersed bands as a consequence of transhumance, hunting expeditions, and the search for fresh soil to till, settled down in permanent villages; for owing to their neolithic self-sufficiency these could remain isolated.

The Vardar-Morava or Vinča Culture

In Western Macedonia, along the Vardar and Morava, on the Danube above the Iron Gates, and thence across the Banat and up the Maros, permanent villages growing into tells begin with the Vinča culture.

In the great tell of Vinča itself above the Starčevo levels appear fabrics and ceramic forms that are not found in pure sites of the Starčevo culture but do occur at sites where Starčevo types are totally absent. These ceramic features Milojčić[22] and Garašanin[23] have isolated from the Starčevo assemblage and used to define a distinct Vinča culture to which other traits may be attributed by association. As thus defined, the culture is represented at a series of sites from the Vardar-Morava watershed down the latter river, along the Save[24] and the Danube, and then beyond the river[25] as far as Tordos on the Maros[26] in Transylvania. The stratification at Vinča allows of the definition of phases in the development of those data susceptible of statistical treatment, but not of the determination of the relative age of isolated objects. Milojčić distinguishes five main phases, but Garašanin can recognize only two. He will be followed here.

The basis of life was still mixed farming combined with hunting, fishing, and collecting. But the rural economy had been adjusted to maintain permanent villages on one site. To catch the large fish of the Danube, the Tisza, and the Maros, antler harpoons or leister-prongs (Fig. 47) were employed as well as nets and hook-and-line (by Vinča II the hooks were barbed). Flint arrow-heads were only exceptionally used, but no clay slingbolts have been found either. The houses of wattle and daub were rectilinear but rather irregular in plan, divided into two or three rooms and furnished with low-vaulted ovens. Adzes were still preferred to axes. Perforated stone hammer-axes appeared

Fig. 47. Bone combs and ring-pendant, Tordos, and 'harpoon', Vinča ($\frac{1}{2}$).

first in Vinča II, but antlers were perforated for mattocks as in the Starčevo culture.

The pottery was of high quality. The commonest fabric at all levels and sites was black burnished ware. A red-surfaced version (erroneously termed 'red-slipped') was also made. Black and red part-coloured vases, as described on p. 103, are confined to the first phase. To the same phase belongs what Milojčić calls *urfirnis* and compares to the Late Neolithic ware of Greece (p. 104). Vases were flat-based. Handles were foreign to the pure Vinča tradition, but at Ploćnik[27] and other late sites in the Morava valley appear handled tankards and mugs resembling the Early Macednic. Instead, vases were provided with lugs that even in phase I may be hornlike and are provided with button-like projections in phase II. Tubular spouts may go back to phase I, but are commoner in II. Carinated bowls and dishes with flaring or vertical rims were popular throughout. Chalices on tall solid feet occur already in the first phase, tripod vases only in the second. Curious bottles, designed for carrying on the back, flat on one side and provided with looped lugs on the other, are assigned to Vinča I. The same type occurs in the Körös and Romanian variants of the Starčevo culture, but in Bulgaria is also post-Starčevo. Distinctive of both phases of the Vinča culture and found equally on the Save, the Morava, and the Maros are anthropomorphic lids (Fig. 48), traditionally compared to Trojan

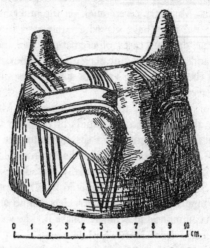

Fig. 48. 'Face urn' lid from Vinča. After Vassits.

face-urns and really like some from Troy III. Anthropomorphic and zoomorphic vases were likewise manufactured, presumably for ritual use.

Decoration was effected by stroke-burnishing, narrow flutings or corrugations, and incisions combined with punctuations; rouletting was introduced in phase II. White, red, or yellow colours were applied after firing to decorate altars and figurines in phase I, but crusted on the vase surface mainly in phase II. The motives in phase I include triangles, filled with punctuations, and punctured ribbons or corrugations, forming simple rectilinear patterns. Maeanders, spirals, and repetition patterns, derived therefrom, are reputedly confined to phase II.

In addition to pots, white limestone dishes were used at Vinča. Toilet articles include a comb from Tordos (Fig. 47), resembling that from Late Neolithic Macedonia, and ring pendants.

Ritual equipment was as rich in the Vinča culture as in other

Balkan, Greek, and South-West Asiatic cultures and implies a similar ideology. The earliest figurines are more schematic than those from Körös sites, but some were already seated on thrones. Later details of the visage were more carefully modelled; the face became pentagonal instead of triangular, the hands rest on the stomach, clasp the breasts or carry a suckling, but the legs fuse into pedestals. Mortuary ceremonial, on the other hand, is not well attested and must have played a minor part in ideological activity. Some dubious cases of cremation have indeed been mentioned, and at Vinča[28] nine skeletons were buried in a 'pit cave' cut in the löss, but at Vučedol similar 'chamber tombs' contained Slavonian pottery.

The site of Vinča, close to the junction of the Morava with the Danube above the perilous rapids of the Iron Gates, was well-adapted for trade. Indeed, Vassits attributed the settlement to a colony of Aegean merchants whom he eventually identified as Ionians of the seventh century. Actually the adjacent cinnabar deposits of Suplja Stena were exploited by Vinča people. Un-ambiguous imports are *Spondylus* bracelets, found at all levels, and obsidian commonest in Milojčić, phase B. The volcanic glass presumably came from North-East Hungary down the Tisza. With it came pots such as were being made along that river, first Körös types of Starčevo pottery, then numerous complete Tisza vases. Small scraps of copper are reported from all levels at Vinča, but the abundance of stone adzes and other tools at all levels and all sites implies that no regular supplies were organized. But at Pločnik in phase II was found a hoard of thirteen copper adzes and a hammer-axe like Fig. 64, 1, together with five stone adzes. Many similar Hungarian-Transylvanian types are scattered about throughout the Vinča province, all presumably imports from beyond the Danube. At Kladova on the Save[29] a typical Hungarian axe-adze was found with thirty-nine long flint blades such as are proper to the Bodrogkeresztur culture of Danubian III.

Such imports establish good synchronisms with the Danubian sequence: Vinča I overlaps with the Körös phase of Starčevo, but its later subdivisions (Milojčić B and C) are frankly contemporary with the Tisza culture. The latter should be Danubian II though direct links with the Lengyel culture, typical of that period, are lacking at Vinča.[30] The succeeding Vinča II phase is in turn contemporary with, or replaced locally by, the Baden and Bodrogkeresztur cultures of Danubian III. Correlations with the East Balkan sequence are equally explicit. On the Romanian bank of the Lower Danube, Vinča I remains at Verbicoara are stratified below those of the Salcuţa culture while Boian pottery is found at Tordos,[31] presumably with the Vinča I material from the site. Conversely the Vinča II relics from the upper Morava valley are hardly distinguishable from those proper to the Salcuţa culture. In other words, Vinča I and II are respectively homotaxial with Boian and Salcuţa.[32]

Chronological relations with the Aegean are much harder to determine. Relations are plain enough, but not in the form of direct imports across the Balkans or local reproductions of ephemeral types. The Vinča I culture on the Danube is so nearly identical with that of Late Neolithic Servia in Macedonia that we may say that this culture, like that of Starčevo, crossed the frontier between the Mediterranean and the Temperate zones intact. Most Vinča I pot-fabrics and forms recur also in Late Neolithic Central Greece, some even at Kum Tepe in the Troad. All that does not prove contemporaneity. Indeed, the priority of one region over the other would decide several crucial issues in European and Indo-European prehistory. Now Milojčić[33] has indeed claimed a pedestalled pyxis from his Vinča B2 as an Early Cycladic import, and it might well be a copy of an imported marble vase. An unstratified fragment from Vinča may again imitate an Early Helladic askoid jug,[34] while a vase from Bubanj II (i.e. Vinča II) may imitate a metal sauce-boat like those from Troy and the Peloponnese. The Vinča II handled jugs and tankards from the Morava sites must be related to the corresponding Early Aegean forms, but might be earlier as well as later.

Yugoslavian prehistorians are agreed that the Vinča culture did not develop out of the local Starčevo culture, but must be attributed to fresh colonists from the south-east. It would be these, then, who introduced into temperate Europe the form of sedentary life, the rural economy that supported it, and the ideology that held society together as they had been developed in South-Western Asia. On the other hand, as pointed out on p. 104, there may be archaeological and other grounds for believing that the Late Neolithic culture of Western Macedonia and Central Greece now identified as the Vinča I culture, was introduced by an incursion from beyond the Balkans. If no development of the Starčevo culture in that direction can be observed on the Morava, it may conceivably be traceable on the Maritza when the varied material from Karanovo I and Banyata I has been exhaustively studied and published.

During phase I, the Vinča culture exhibited remarkable uniformity from Servia on the Haliakmon, or at least from Pavlovce on the Vardar-Morava divide, to Tordos on the Maros, from Ostrul Corbului below the Iron Gates westward to Sarvas on the Drave. In phase II this unity dissolved, as had that of the Starčevo.

North of the Danube the permanent villages of Vinča type give place to more temporary hamlets, probably based on shifting cultivation. In the Balkans, however, many tells were still occupied and the ideology appropriate to settled agriculture everywhere continued to find expression in the production of female figurines. But in the Niš basin on the upper Morava the culture of Bubanj II is a sort of hybrid between Vinča and Salcuţa. About the same time arose on the Bosna the remarkable Butmir[35] culture. At the eponymous site, a low tell, adzes, figurines, and much of the pottery carry on the Vinča tradition. But the exuberant development of spiral ribbons and mouldings, sometimes forming a net pattern as on Early Cycladic vases, and the multiplication of tanged flint arrow-heads is quite novel. Finally, at Vinča itself the old culture persists. But in the levels between 4·5 and 2·5 below Vassits' datum obsidian is rare, and Milojčić sees Baden influence in the pottery. Between the last two occupation levels were found vases belonging to the Middle Bronze Age of the Lower Maros, assignable to period V of the Danubian sequence. So unless an interruption of habitation has produced an hiatus, Danubian III, IV, and V should be contemporary with later phases of the Vinča culture!

It seems as if, having established a workable adjustment to the local environment, the self-sufficing Balkan villagers made no effort – or at least failed – to obtain regular supplies of metal. The widespread bronze types that define periods IV and V in the

Danubian province are missing in the Balkans; a formally neolithic culture persisted.

The Veselinovo Culture of Southern Thrace

According to the latest reports of Mikov and Detev, the Starčevo culture at Karanovo,[36] Banyata,[37] and Ginova mogila near Celopec[38] in the Maritza valley was immediately succeeded by one of very different aspect that may be named after another tell, Veselinovo.[39]

The permanent villages were composed of spacious houses comprising several rooms. The frame was constructed of up-

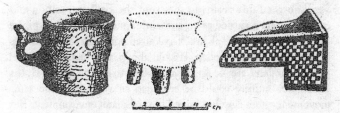

Fig. 49. Mug, tripod bowl, and 'altar' decorated by excision, Banyata II.

right wooden posts, but the walls consisted of clay mixed with straw. Their inhabitants were settled farmers who now cultivated emmer in addition to one-corn wheat. Perhaps, too, they bred, or at least hunted, horses whose bones are reported from Veselinovo.[40] Huntsmen still relied mainly on slings, but stone battle-axes may have been made for war. The pottery, even more than the architecture, reveals a thorough mastery of wood-work. For this adzes were still preferred, but axe-heads were made and perforated for mounting. The pottery marks a complete break with the Starčevo traditions. The normal ware is self-coloured, usually black and sometimes burnished. Ornament, employed so profusely before, has been abandoned save for applied strips that may terminate in spirals. During building some pots were stood on rush mats, the impressions of which are common on bases. Pithoi, over 50 cm high, were manufactured, but the most distinctive form is a straight-sided or pear-shaped mug (Fig. 49) provided with a stout handle prolonged upwards to a little pillar. The form is obviously inspired by a wooden model. So are bowls or lamps on four stout round legs and triangular ones on short flat legs. The latter are often decorated with excised chequer patterns, inspired by chip-carving (Fig. 49), and recur, similarly decorated, in the homotaxial Boian culture farther north and in the Chalcolithic of Alişar in Central Anatolia. Lop-sided bottles for carrying on the back were made in the Veselinovo level at Banyata as at Vinča (pp. 131–2).

A few very conventional figurines come from Karanovo II, but in general the Veselinovo levels are conspicuously poor in those ritual objects of clay that illustrate the ideology of the Sesklo culture in Greece and of later Balkan cultures. Indeed, the Veselinovo culture seems to interrupt the Balkan tradition and can hardly be regarded as an autochthonous development of the Starčevo complex. Its plain self-coloured pots with thrust handles in particular look Anatolian. If Mikhalic (p. 105) really be parallel to Macedonian Late Neolithic and belong to Balkan period II, the Veselinovo culture could be regarded as a result of the same movement, more closely adapted to the Balkan environment. But none of the distinctive Troadic forms, so conspicuous at Mikhalic, has yet been found *in situ* in a Veselinovo layer. There are indeed analogies to Veselinovo handles and to the 'chip-carved' lamps in Anatolia, but these are confined to Alaca Höyük, Büyük Güllücek,[41] and Alişar,[42] all on the plateau. Moreover, these are imitations of wooden models such as are common all along the southern slopes of the Balkans and the Alps, even to Italy and South France.

Now, at the eponymous site Mikov traced the development of the Veselinovo culture into one of Bronze Age type characterized by a copper shaft-hole axe, stone battle-axes, bowls with short trumpet lugs growing from the inturned rims, side-spouted bowls and jugs, and even something like a Minoan teapot. Similar material comes from Razkopanitsa,[43] Ezero, and Yunatsite,[44] where it certainly overlies Gumelniţa deposits and so belongs to Balkan IV. Of course, the stratification at Banyata and Karanovo may have been misinterpreted, and Veselinovo there may have followed Gumelniţa, as Mikov reported in 1939. Alternatively it could be assumed that the Veselinovo culture, like the Macednic Bronze Age cultures, developed at some sites parallel to, but unaffected by, the intrusive Gumelniţa settlements, and that then in Balkan IV the Veselinovo tradition triumphed over the intrusions from the north. In either case some ceramic forms of the developed Veselinovo culture from Ezero – trumpet lugs and cord-ornament, though belonging to Balkan IV – are more reminiscent of Mikhalic than anything yet observed in Karanovo II!

The Boian Culture

North of the main Balkan range, on both sides of the Lower Danube and in Transylvania on the Upper Olt, Balkan period II is occupied by an assemblage termed, after an island in the Danube, the Boian culture.[45] Comsa[46] has recently claimed to distinguish two preparatory phases during which settlements were not yet quite stable villages, when only one-corn wheat and millet were cultivated, when arrows were armed with trapezes and lunates, and when pottery was tempered with chaff and decorated only with channelled or incised lines that might form spirals and maeanders. His stages, if reliable, would give hints at the acculturation of mesolithic survivors, already postulated (p. 129), or at their absorption by immigrant farmers.

But, as found at the base of the tells of Vidra[47] and Tangaru,[48] and at the eponymous site, Boian denotes a regular village culture based on the cultivation of one-corn and emmer wheats and millet combined with stock-breeding, hunting, and fishing. The villages were made up of substantial rectangular houses, walled with split tree-trunks and wattle and daub and equipped with central fire-places and a very shallow porch, thus approximating to the megaron plan.[49] These are said to have been preceded by less substantial huts at Tangaru. Weaving is attested by clay loom-weights and cruciform whorls, like those used on the Körös. The carpenter used adzes of shoe-last form or bevelled as in the Sesklo culture of Thessaly. But they might be mounted in perforated antler sleeves as at Maglemose.

The home-made pots are obviously influenced both in form and decoration by wooden models. Characteristic are cylindrical peg-footed boxes (Fig. 50), big biconical jars, two-storeyed urns, ladles with solid handles, and tiny vases with pointed bases that stood in pairs on cubical supports. Exceptional are pedestalled bowls of Danubian II form and others on human feet. For decorating these products the potter employed the wood-carver's technique of excision, but also incision, fluting, rustication, and, exceptionally, negative painting in graphite, and crusting with colours after the firing; spirals, maeanders, and cognate repetition patterns form the basis for a rich all-over decoration.

The Boian farmers were acquainted with copper, but used it only for small ornaments and made no attempt to organize regular

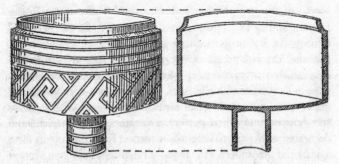

Fig. 50. Peg-footed vase, Denev ($\frac{1}{6}$).

supplies for industrial use. The only other indication of rudimentary trade is provided by bracelets of *Spondylus* shell which were as popular on the Lower Danube as in Thessaly and Central Europe. And as there, triangular and quadrangular altars were made for domestic cult, but figurines, later so common, were very rarely modelled in clay.

The Boian culture, as thus defined, eventually spread across the Balkans to the Maritsa valley, but has not been isolated sharply enough there to be attributed to Balkan II rather than Balkan III. Northward, characteristic pottery is found as far as the mouth of the Danube and the upper valley of the Oltu, while unmistakable sherds are included in the collection from Tordos on the Maros. Here its position in the Balkan sequence is well established. Boian underlies Gumelniţa in the tells of Tangaru and Vidra. Near Leţi, on the Upper Oltu, early Boian pottery is stratified above Starčevo ware but below Tripolye B_1 pottery of the Ariuşd style,

while the Boian sherds from Tordos should denote a synchronism with Vinča I.

The neolithic elements, save perhaps the emmer wheat, can simply be derived from the antecedent Starčevo culture. The antler work and the carpentry might be a legacy from surviving mesolithic hunter-fishers, represented by geometric microliths collected on some Romanian sites. These too might have transmitted the overall system of decoration using the maeander as a repetition pattern; for it was so used in late pleistocene times by the mammoth-hunters of Mezin on the löss lands of South Russia.

The Gumelniţa and Salcuţa Cultures

The Boian culture seems to have developed, though not without enrichment from Anatolia, the Aegean, and the Middle Danube, into what Romanian prehistorians term the *Gumelniţa* culture.[50] This is represented at a larger number of sites in Wallachia and Bulgaria than the Boian culture owing to the foundation of new villages by an expanding population. And it endured a long time; at least three phases can be distinguished stratigraphically at Vidra and Tangaru, but the Wallachian divisions are inapplicable in Bulgaria.

The basis of life remained unchanged save that antler harpoons, like those of the Vinča and Tisza sites, were now employed for spearing fish. But from the first a tendency to industrial specialization was manifested; in several settlements hoards of flint blades and bone tools, all fresh as if designed for barter, were uncovered. Later, in phase III, metal must have been worked by craftsmen in some sites.

Trade was also organized to some extent. In phase I at Vidra the material for stone implements was brought from Bulgaria and the Dobrudja, later from Transylvania and the Banat. Commerce brought actual manufactures, new ideas and eventually new technical processes. A binocular vase of the Tripolye A style from Moldavia or farther north and a vessel ornamented with punctured ribbons, as at Tordos and Vinča, were brought to Vidra in phase I. From the same horizon and from several Bulgarian sites come clay stamps[51] imitating Asiatic seals though decorated always with spirals. By phase II, ring-pendants, as at

Troy, Dimini, and Tordos, were being manufactured in bone, and bone copies of double-spiral headed pins. Actual pins, like Fig. 27, save that the spirals are ribbons, not wiry, were found in level III at Vidra, as at many sites and Gaborevo in Bulgaria.[52] Finally, even the Macedonian-Helladic askoi were copied locally in Vidra III and other Wallachian and Thracian sites.

By this time metallurgists, attracted perhaps by the copper lodes of Eastern Bulgaria,[53] were actually working in Bulgaria and Wallachia. The double-spiral pins they made show the Anatolian models that inspired these artisans, but they seem to

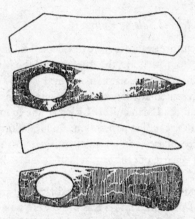

Fig. 51. Copper axe and adze from Gaborevo ($\frac{1}{3}$).

have relied on hammering, presumably through ignorance of casting,[54] and not all their products were direct copies of Asiatic forms. A shaft-hole axe and a shaft-hole adze were found together at Gaborevo (Fig. 51). Combined in a single casting, they would yield an axe-adze, and an actual specimen was found at Vidra. It may mark the starting-point of the Hungarian series of period III.

Nevertheless, the Gumelniţa economy was never transformed so that metal could take the place of stone. Throughout the period tools were normally made of stone or bone. But in addition to adzes of Boian style, flint adzes were now used; the later specimens have splayed blades or polished faces in imitation of the rare copper adzes. Hammer-axes and even simple battle-axes, all

hollow-bored as on the Middle Danube, came into fashion, and antler-axes with square-cut shaft-holes. Arrows were tipped with double-ended bone points, more rarely with triangular flint heads. Even a bowman's wrist-guard was found at Vidra III.

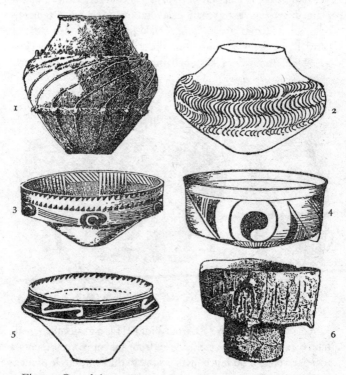

Fig. 52. Gumelniţa pottery: 1, Czernavoda ($\frac{1}{8}$); 2, Tel Metchkur ($\frac{1}{4}$); 3–4, Tel Ratchev ($\frac{1}{5}$); 5–6, Kodja Derman ($\frac{1}{6}$, $\frac{1}{4}$).

Spheroid mace-heads occur sporadically, but the culture never assumes a bellicose aspect.

The pottery carries on the old traditions. The peg-footed box went out of fashion and was replaced by the foot-base type (Fig. 52, 6), in which the foot is open to the body but closed below, and a socketed ladle of Danubian II type was introduced by phase I at Vinča. Excised decoration became less popular, but rusticated designs remained current, and graphite painting, now positive,

became the prevalent method of decoration. It was rarely supplemented by the use of white paint applied before firing. The impression of a split reed producing the so-called bracket ornament (Fig. 52, 2) was popular south of the Danube.

The relative stagnation in industry is counterbalanced or explained by an extravagant elaboration of magico-religious equipment. From phase I on, female figurines of clay were as carefully modelled as those from the middle strata at Vinča (Fig. 53). One from Vinča has shell inlays for the eyes, like Early

Fig. 53. Painted clay head, Vinča (⅔).

Sumerian statuettes. A vase from Vidra III is a grotesque female figure 42 cm high; a smaller vase from Gaborevo represents a male personage. Both products belong to the same circle of ideas as the anthropomorphic vases from Vinča. Sitting figures, male or female (Fig. 54, 1), were also made. Flat bone figurines are distinctive in all phases (Fig. 54, 3) (especially II) in Wallachia, and also in Bulgaria, where the form was also reproduced in gold leaf.[55] A much more conventional type is a simple bone prism (Fig. 54, 2); at Balbunar in Bulgaria prism figures were found in strata deeper than those containing flat figurines, but at Vidra the order of occurrence was reversed.[56] Stone idols rather like the Cycladic, were made of local Bulgarian marbles,[57] while a torso from Gumelniṭa itself replicates the Thessalian type of Fig. 31, 4, save that the inserted head is of clay, not stone.[58] In addition to female per-

sonages, males were being modelled in clay from phase II (as in Thessaly C–D), and clay phalli, like the Anatolian and Minoan, were used as fertility symbols (Fig. 54, 4). Other ritual objects are horns of consecration (phase II), model altars and thrones, and by phase III models of houses (Fig. 55), as well as models of animals and doves.

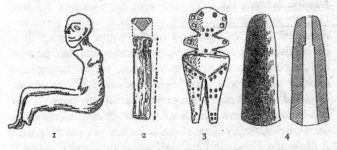

Fig. 54. Clay and bone figurines ($\frac{1}{2}$) and clay phallus ($\frac{1}{4}$), Bulgaria.

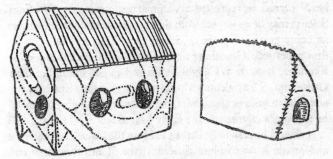

Fig. 55. Models of houses, Denev ($\frac{1}{12}$).

The dead were not objects of any elaborate cult or even ten-dence. At the base of the tell of Balbunar twenty-two contracted skeletons (accompanied in two or three cases only by flint adzes) and two trunkless skulls had been buried under the house floors; four contracted burials more richly furnished were found at Ruse. But unburied skulls and ribs hacked about have been reported from other stations as evidences of cannibalism. The skulls from Romania were dolichocranial and allegedly Medi-terranean, but two from Ruse[59] are round.

In addition to the pins already mentioned and bracelets of *Spondylus* shell, ring-pendants of bone or gold (Vidra II) and conventional bulls' heads of gold leaf adorned with punctuations (Vidra III) were worn as ornaments or charms.

The label 'Salcuţa' is applied to the version of the Gumelniţa culture found in Oltenia (i.e. on the north bank of the Lower Danube between the confluence with the Oltu and the Iron Gates)[60] and found also in the Sofia basin – above Veselinovo remains[61] – and in Bubanj II on the Upper Morava.[62] It is distinguished chiefly by ceramic peculiarities: graphite painting and bracket ornament are relatively rare, narrow flutings and crusting with colours after firing commoner. Among shapes, askoi and handled cups or mugs were particularly popular. The two-handled tankards are reminiscent of the Early Macednic, but some are ridiculously like the Silesian Jordanova type of Fig. 94.[63] A distinctive Bulgarian form is a lamp in the shape of a goat.[64] Most of the Gumelniţa ritual objects, including even prismatic bone figurines, recur in a Salcuţa context. Finally, a stone 'sceptre head' carved to represent an animal's snout (Fig. 76)[65] from Salcuţa may be an import from the steppes as another came from an ochre grave (cf. p. 203). So no very sharp frontiers can be drawn between Gumelniţa and Salcuţa. Even on the slopes of Rhodope, Banyata III might be classed as Salcuţa rather than Gumelniţa. The Salcuţa culture presumably developed on the same Boian basis as Gumelniţa, but was more strongly influenced by the Vinča culture and the Early Macednic.

It should be easy to fit Balkan III into the Danubian sequence and assign it an absolute date in virtue of the Danubian and Aegean parallels in Gumelniţa and Salcuţa assemblages. Clay stamps are proper to Danubian II, but battle-axes and axe-adzes belong there to period III. The double-spiral pins, the askoi, and the Salcuţa mugs are Early Aegean types, but of course none are actual imports. If taken as denoting synchronisms, they should date the third phase of Gumelniţa and Salcuţa not later than 2000 B.C.

In that case we should have painfully little archaeological material to fill the next thousand years. The Lower Danube and Eastern Thrace were incorporated, no more than the Western Balkans, in either the Danubian or the Aegean commercial system.

The bronze types defining Danubian IV and V are, if possible, even worse represented here than on the Morava and the Bosna. Half a dozen local copies of Late Minoan I horned rapiers have turned up in Bulgaria, but all are strays. Apart from urnfields of period VI along the Lower Danube, Bronze Age graves are lacking in Bulgaria. The funerary record begins, richly, with the Early Iron Age. Material from domestic sites is scarce and poor, compared with the rich deposits of Gumelniţa and earlier cultures from so many sites, and it still looks 'neolithic'.

Above the Gumelniţa levels at Vidra is a thin deposit of the Glina culture, the product of a less sedentary, more pastoral and warlike society. Though copper or bronze was worked, metal did not replace stone in industry or armament. Painted pottery and female figurines have alike disappeared. Homotaxial assemblages are rather more substantial in Bulgaria. At Yunatsite,[66] in the middle (II) levels above a Gumelniţa layer (I), Veselinovo handled vases with pillar handles are said to be associated with askoi that would have been expected in the lower, Gumelniţa, level. Higher up in Yunatsite III, immediately below a Thracian settlement of the seventh century B.C., occur cups and tankards with pointed bases. These are found also in late houses at Razkopanitsa[67] on the Struma, in Karanovo V, Veselinovo and a few other Bulgarian sites, and in Oltenia[68] and in the Niš basin of the Morava.[69] Jugs and cups with oblique mouths, presumably descended from Anatolian beaked jugs, are found in Karanovo V, Banyata IV, the earlier houses at Razkopanitsa, the highest levels at Ruse.[70] All this pottery, self-coloured and rarely decorated, looks at least as Anatolian as the Veselinovo ware from Karanovo II. It might be derived therefrom if a long Gumelniţa occupation did not intervene (cf. p. 136).

Hence if we placed even the first two phases of Gumelniţa in the third millennium, we should get the impression that the large sedentary population, attested by the numerous Gumelniţa tells, was either decimated or relapsed into shifting cultivation. Be that as it may, one conclusion can be drawn. Neolithic societies in the Balkans quite quickly adapted the South-West Asiatic rural economy to their intermediate environment and elaborated or adopted a similar ideology appropriate to settled village life. They did not take the next step towards civilization – to adjust their

7 Danubian Civilization

Period I

Immediately north of the Serbian Danube and the Save begin löss-clad plains and slopes which extend, not without formidable interruptions, right up to the edge of the moraines in Poland, Germany, and Belgium. These Central European löss lands had been frequented in Aurignacian and Solutrean times by mammoth and reindeer-hunters, but mesolithic successors of such food-gatherers survived only on isolated patches of sandy soil and among the post-glacial forests on the northern and western fringes. To food-producers, the löss lands, naturally drained, not too heavily wooded and easy to till, offered a domain where they could practise the simplest conceivable sort of farming. With unstinted water supplies and seemingly boundless territories the peasant was free to shift his hut and break fresh ground as soon as his former fields showed signs of exhaustion. And in fact we find prevailing throughout Central Europe a system of nomadic cultivation that does look really primitive – such as the earliest food-producers, undisciplined by environmental limitations, might be expected to invent.

The cultures[1] based upon this economy exhibit considerable uniformity throughout the löss lands. Though the temporary nature of the settlements excludes tell formation and the stratigraphical chronology derived therefrom, the cultural sequence is well established. Throughout the area three main periods can be recognized before the Early Bronze Age, which coincides with period IV. In period I we can distinguish three main groups: the Körös culture, already described under Starčevo in Chapter VI, the Bükk culture in North-Eastern Hungary and Slovakia, and the Danubian I extending from Western Hungary to the northern confines of the löss.

The löss lands west and north of the Danube were first occupied by a neolithic population whose whole culture down to the finest details remains identical from the Drave to the Baltic and from the Dniester to the Meuse.[2] This is the best known culture in Central Europe and perhaps the most classically neolithic in the ancient world. Hence the term Danubian I may be legitimately applied to it in preference to the clumsy and inaccurate terms 'linear pottery' or 'spiral-maeander' culture.

The Danubian I economy was based on the cultivation of barley, one-corn, and perhaps also emmer[3] wheats, beans, peas, lentils, and flax, in small plots tilled with stone hoes. Only small herds of stock were kept; bones of sheep, Bezoar goats, oxen, and pigs turn up in settlements, but animal dung was never incorporated in hut walls, as is usual where the farmyards are well stocked. To hunting the Danubians made no resort. Danubian I settlement sites are dotted very densely all over the löss lands, but none shows evidence of prolonged occupation. That is a result of the Danubians' crude agricultural technique, one still illustrated by some hoe-cultivators in Africa today. They cultivated a plot till it would bear no more and then another, and so on until they had used up all the land round the hamlet; thereupon they shifted bag and baggage to a new site on fresh virgin soil.

Yet these shifting cultivators lived in commodious and substantial rectangular houses[4] from 10 to 40 m in length and 6 to 7·5 m wide; five rows of posts supported a gabled roof and walls of wattle and daub or split saplings (Fig. 56). Four hearths in a row were identified on the floor of a house, 33·5 m long, at Postoloprty in Bohemia,[5] but at other sites remains of fireplaces or ovens are curiously missing. Outside the long houses irregular pits, once termed pit-dwellings, had been dug to get clay and subsequently used as rubbish-pits, silos, pig-sties, or working-places. Intersections of house plans at many sites prove intermittent return to settlements that, nevertheless, did not grow into stratified tells. On the assumption that all contemporary houses were exactly parallel, Sangmeister infers[6] that Köln-Lindental,[7] the best explored Danubian village, had been occupied seven times and at its largest comprised twenty-one households. But of course the 'household' must have been more like a clan than a pairing family. In its latest phase Köln-Lindental was surrounded with a trench and palisade. Sangmeister suggests that each occupation

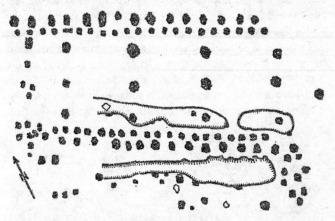

Fig. 56. Small Danubian I house from Saxony; the walls marked by a double row of posts, $\frac{1}{250}$. After Sangmeister.

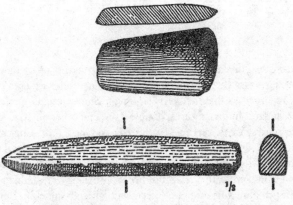

Fig. 57. 'Shoe-last celts.' After Seger ($\frac{1}{2}$).

might last ten years and postulates abandonment for regeneration of scrub for fifty years.

The rest of the Danubians' equipment was equally home-made. Shoe-last celts of stone (Fig. 57) served, if mounted on knee-shafts, as hoe-blades and adzes, or, if perforated, as axes and hammers. Knives, sickles, and scrapers were made on flint blades. No whorls nor loom-weights attest a textile industry; the flax found at Köln-Lindental may have been grown for oil. At Statenice in Bohemia,[8] a bone implement like the spatulae of the Körös was found.

Two sorts of pots (Fig. 58) were manufactured – hemispherical bowls and globular bottles (some flattened for carrying on the back) – provided with 3, 6, or 9 lugs and clearly derived from gourd models. The resemblance is often enhanced by zig-zag incised lines reproducing the slings in which gourds are carried.

Fig. 58. Danubian I pottery ($\frac{3}{20}$).

But instead of skeuomorphic patterns the peasants often incised on their vases the continuous spiral and maeander designs that are regarded as distinctively Danubian. Some designs, perhaps late, suggest human figures, double-axes, and other objects. And some coarse vases were just rusticated as on the Körös. Lugs may be modelled to resemble animals' heads as on the Vardar and the Morava, while the incised double-axe patterns may be inspired from Crete or North Syria,[9] but probably belong to Danubian II.

In principle this economy was essentially self-sufficing. But in practice materials had to be carefully selected and often transported over long distances. The green schist, used for adzes at Köln-Lindental, must have been brought 60 or 70 miles from the Hunsrück or the Taunus; Niedermendig lava from near Mayen was used for querns in Belgium.[10] Such partiality for selected materials, without destroying self-sufficiency, encouraged intercourse between distinct communities. In fact, a few vases, made from local clays in the Main valley, were transported to Köln-Lindental, 50 miles away. Moreover, in Moravia, Bohemia, Thuringia, and even the Rhine valley ornaments made from the Mediterranean *Spondylus* shell were worn as in Thessaly and on the Middle Danube; they must have been handed on by some sort of inter-tribal exchange from the Aegean or the Adriatic! So too African ivory reached Flamborn near Worms.[11] The interchange of goods, thus disclosed, developed into something like regular trade. Particularly on the borders of the Danubian province in Brandenburg, Holstein, and West Poland, hoards[12] of shoe-last adzes turn up. Like the later hoards of bronzes, these must be the stocks of specialized travelling merchants. Individuals must already have been at least supplementing their livelihood by satisfying the Danubians' prejudices in favour of selected materials and extending their activities to other still mesolithic tribes. Such were surely the forerunners of the bronze-merchants described on p. 171. And workshop debris in villages may indicate even industrial specialization within a community.

The Danubians were a peaceful folk. The only weapons found in their settlements are disc-shaped mace-heads, such as had been used by the predynastic Egyptians, and occasional flint arrow-heads. They were democratic and perhaps even communistic; there are no hints of chiefs concentrating the communities' wealth. Nor did deities fulfil that function. As expressions of ideology clay figurines or schematic representations of the human form are rare, confined to peripheral areas, and probably late enough to be attributed to the south-eastern influence that is conspicuous in Danubian II. Nothing like the ritual paraphernalia, distinctive of South-West Asian and Balkan cultures, has survived. Nor is an elaborate ancestor cult illustrated by many ceremonial burials.[13] Cemeteries are practically confined to the Rhine valley. There the dead were generally interred in the contracted position, more rarely cremated. The few skulls examined are all dolichocranial and in a general way Mediterranean. One from an Alsatian cemetery[14] had been trephined.

The culture just described had reached Germany by 4000 B.C.[15] and lasted a long time; on Sangmeister's estimate the seven settlements at Köln-Lindental occupy between them 430 years.

It can hardly have appeared simultaneously at all points within the vast area eventually colonized. But save in ceramic decoration, no development can be recognized. In the Rhineland and Belgium, styles in which the spirals and mæanders have disintegrated and simple lines are combined with punctuations, comb-imprints, and cord-impressions have been shown stratigraphically to be late. So too the 'music note' style in which lines are supplemented by pits, like breves, is often regarded as late, but Soudsky[16] has challenged this assumption. The densest concentration of sites with simple linear decoration still seems to lie on the Upper Elbe and the Upper Rhine, but these just happen to be the best explored parts of the löss lands. Only since 1950 has Danubian I pottery – of the music-note style – been identified on the Dniestr and the Sereth,[17] but that is no proof that these outposts were really planted in the last areas to be colonized!

But it is significant that the main concentrations do lie north of the Bakony and the Carpathians, i.e. north of the ecological limit beyond which gourds will not harden. If First Danubian pots be really substitutes for gourd vessels, they may have been made by preceramic farmers, spreading from the southern cradle of cereals, when they had reached the areas where their traditional receptacles were no longer available. Such immigrants, bringing the materials and technique of farming, would then have reached the Danube basin before the emergence there of the Starčevo culture. Alternatively, Danubian I might be a secondary neolithic culture, created by autochthonous hunter-fishers who would have learned farming and pot-making from the Starčevo immigrants. As there is at present no evidence for a mesolithic population on the Danubian löss lands and mesolithic survivals appear only late in Danubian industry,[18] the former hypothesis is the more plausible. The Danubian penchant for *Spondylus* shells is a positive argument for a southern origin, but the bone spatula from Statenice is strong evidence for some sort of connection with Starčevo.

The Bükk Culture

In Eastern Slovakia and North-East Hungary the Bükk culture[19] may be regarded as a parallel to Danubian I in the latter part of period I, though it is more nearly contemporary with Vinča I than with Starčevo. In the Bükk economy, in contrast to the First Danubian, hunting and fishing (with hook-and-line as well as with nets) were as important as farming. No houses have been identified, but caves were used for habitations – according to Hillebrandt[20] mainly as winter shelters. Hollow-bored stone axes and perforated antler mattocks were used as well as the usual Danubian adzes. The Bükkians controlled the obsidian deposits of the Hegyalya near Tokaj and made from the volcanic glass knives and scrapers, but no bifacially worked arrow-heads.

The pottery which defines the culture is of high quality, usually grey. The commonest form is a hemispherical bowl, like the First Danubian, and decorated, like the latter, with spirals and maeanders in an all-over style but enriched with fine embroideries. Besides such Danubian forms, bowls with tubular spouts and fruitstands were made. Besides grey ware, a kiln-fired buff fabric was manufactured and decorated with thin lines of warm black paint forming patterns in the Bükk style. In both fabrics the designs include human figures,[21] and some fruitstands have human legs as at Thermi. Otherwise figurines are missing as in Danubian I.

The inclusion of the Bükk culture in period I may be justified by a grave at Nagytétény (Pest) furnished with early Bükk and late Danubian I vases and by observations at sites where Bükk pottery lay in the same stratum as Danubian I or below that yielding Tisza sherds of period II.[22] But elsewhere Bükk and Tisza remains are contemporary[23] and the culture must largely belong to period II. The ritual anthropomorphic vases and clay copies of cylinder seals[24] attributed to the Bükkian may be due to Vinča I-Tisza influence. The technique of painting could, however, be derived from Starčevo, though fruitstands are normally Danubian II.

Period II

The Tisza Culture

On the löss lands east of the Tisza, occupied in period I by the Körös and Vinča or Bükk cultures, the Tisza culture of period II had developed a rural economy better suited to regular agriculture and directed particularly to exploiting the fish abounding in the rivers and the game haunting their banks. The settlements do not form tells, but the houses were superior to those of the Körös folk. At the village of Kökénydomb,[25] the dwellings – rectangular houses measuring up to 7·2 m by 3·4 m, entered through the long side and decorated with painted clay models of bulls' heads – were strung out in a single row along the river bank. The fisherman now èmployed harpoons of antler (Fig. 47) (as at Vinča) and double or triple rings of bone in addition to nets.[26] Stock-breeding and agriculture still provided the basis of life. Grain was stored in large clay jars or rectangular vessels, 70 cm by 50 cm by 65 cm in volume and exactly like the wooden bins used locally today.[27]

The general economy remained neolithic. The materials for axes were drawn from the Banat, Transylvania, and Northern Hungary, but obsidian was no longer imported. Shells were still imported from southern seas and typical vases were exported to Vinča and Silesia (p. 132), but clay 'stamp seals' were no longer used.

Pots, including cylindrical jars and large oval bowls, suitable for cooking fish in, may be provided with indented lugs like the Early Macednic, or short, tubular spouts, sometimes fitted with strainers. They are decorated with coarse incisions in a thick slip, sometimes supplemented by crusting with red or yellow colours after firing. The designs are grouped in vertical panels in contrast to the Danubian all-over style and are often derived from basketry.[28] The motives include concentric circles and maeanders, conventionalized faces and hut roofs.

Clay figurines were no longer manufactured, but a cognate ideology may be implied by large vases in human form,[29] as at Vinča, Vidra, and Tsani. Clay rattles in animal form may have been used in ritual. The dead were ceremonially buried flexed in small cemeteries. Shell or marble buttons with shanks were worn as brow-ornaments.

154

In the Tisza culture elements from Bükk and Vinča have perhaps been blended. The rural economy could be derived from that of Vinča, although less sedentary. The ideology expressed in anthropomorphic vases and metopic composition, could likewise be derived from the south-east. Now Schachermeyr[30] has enumerated thirty-five motives, some of them significantly improbable, common to Tisza and Dimini ceramic decoration, and a Late Neolithic vase from Olynthus[31] might pass for an actual Tisza product. If the Dimini culture must be brought from north of the Balkans into Greece, the Tisza culture has the best claim to its parentage. But then the relative ages of the Tisza and Vinča cultures in terms of the Aegean sequence would need revision.

The Lengyel Cultures

On the löss lands, colonized in period I by First Danubian peasants, the remarkable cultural uniformity thus created dissolved in period II to give place to a multiplicity of distinct regional cultures as a result of extraneous influences as well as mere divergent development. From the Drave to the Upper Danube, in Austria, the Upper Elbe in Bohemia, and the Upper Vistula,[32] the period witnessed the spread of the South-West Asian-Balkan ideology reflected in female figurines, model houses, clay stamps, and a taste for coloured vases, and of a rural economy in which cultivation was better balanced by stock-breeding though it did not yet allow settlement in one spot long enough for tell formation. The result was not a single culture even in this limited region, but several related cultural facies. As none exhibits a well-defined spatial distribution, all may still be grouped together and designated by the name given to the first one recognized, the Lengyel culture.[33]

Some settlements at least were fortified. At Hluboké Mašovky in Southern Moravia an area of some 15 acres (60,000 sq m) was enclosed by a flat-bottomed fosse supplemented by a stockade, the gate being flanked by stout projecting walls as at Troy.[34] So near Zlota on the Vistula[35] two adjacent settlements, possibly of a later stage, were surrounded by entrenchments. Small rectangular houses, probably divided into two rooms that are best known outside the Lengyel province at Ariușd in Transylvania and in Rössen and Michelsberg settlements round the Alps, replaced the earlier long communal houses. From within our area we have only clay models.

Commerce, as in Danubian I, is most clearly attested by the importation from the south of *Spondylus* and *Tridacna* shells. North Hungarian obsidian was distributed all over the Middle

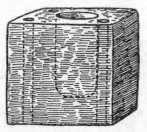

Fig. 59. Clay block vase, Streliče I, Moravia ($\frac{2}{3}$).

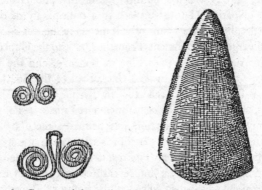

Fig. 60. Copper trinkets ($\frac{1}{2}$), and triangular axe ($\frac{2}{3}$), Jordanova. After Seger.

Danube basin and northward to Moravia, Western Galicia, Silesia, and Bohemia, but in the northern districts it is found only in the earliest settlements, as if stocks had been brought by the colonists but not subsequently replenished by trade. Cubical blocks of clay, perforated at the corners, in which one, or exceptionally two, cups have been hollowed out[36] (Fig. 59) have been claimed as copies of Early Minoan block vases of stone. Clay imitations of stamp seals are attributed to the later phase of the period in Moravia, and by that time copper trinkets began to be distributed in Moravia and Silesia (Fig. 60).

Besides shoe-last adzes, triangular greenstone axes (Fig. 60), hollow-bored axe-hammers and antler axes were employed. A few spheroid mace-heads and flint arrow-heads and, in Bohemia, stone arrow-straighteners,[37] may point to warlike behaviour. Whorls and loom-weights attest a textile industry.

Characteristic pot forms are hollow-pedestalled bowls (Fig. 61, 1), ladles with socketed handles (Fig. 61, 2), biconical jars

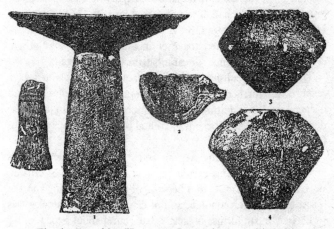

Fig. 61. Danubian II pottery, Lengyel. 1, 3, 4 (⅙); 2 (½).

(Fig. 61, 3), and variants on the older bottles. Bowls are flat-bottomed and often carinated, but inturned rims do not occur till the end of the period. Handles remain unknown. The most characteristic and nearly universal ware is black-polished, as in the Vinča and Larisa cultures. It may be decorated with crusted patterns in red, white, and yellow colours applied after firing, that may be supplemented by incised lines or low round bosses (Fig. 61, 3, 4). Buff and red wares also occur, and in Moravia[38] characterize a second phase of the culture. There the red ware may be burnished and ornamented with designs in white paint or covered with a white slip on which the design is painted in red, as in Middle Neolithic Thessalian or Tripolye B wares. In the latest Moravian phase, coloured decoration was abandoned altogether. While crusted spirals were everywhere employed and in Hungary composed in the old Danubian style (Fig. 61, 1), basketry patterns, breaking up the surface into panels as in the Tisza stymole, were even more popular.

A South-West Asian ideology found expression in female figurines, models of animals and doves, and zoomorphic vases. But in Hungary regular cemeteries of well-furnished graves containing flexed skeletons attest already ancestor tendence; at Zengovárkony near Pécs, seventy-eight graves (including six double burials of male and female – ? satî) divided between eleven groups (? lineages) had been uncovered by 1939.[39] Farther north Danubian II burials are rare; at one Moravian site twelve skeletons were found buried together in a shaft grave,[40] at others cremations, or evidence for cannibalism,[41] are reported.

The Lengyel culture could most readily be explained as a result of the further extension of the south-eastern influence that induced the Vinča culture on the Danube. But if such influence be denied, Lengyel might claim a parental relation to Vinča and so to Larisa!

Comparisons with the Aegean and Anatolia offer ambiguous possibilities for dating period II. The resemblances of crusted ware to that of phase C in Thessaly, of the indented lugs on the Tisza to Early Macedonian, and of clay stamps and block vases to Early Minoan forms, suggest a date round about 2500 B.C. for the period's beginning. On the other hand, pedestalled bowls, very much of Danubian II form, may go back to the fourth millennium in the chalcolithic of Ališar, at Kum Tepe and in 'neolithic' Crete; the red on white painted sherds from Moravia recall equally ancient Thessalian fabrics. On this evidence 3000–2600 would seem just as plausible as 2500–2200 as the historical dates of period II.

Danubian I Survivals in the North

The expansion of Danubian II farmers, like that of their precursors in Danubian I, was a slow process. Indeed, it had begun while Danubian I folk were still spreading down the Oder, the Elbe, and the Rhine valleys. Since period II begins with the emergence of the Danubian II and Tisza cultures in the Middle

Danube basin, we may say that Danubian I cultures survived in the north into period II. In fact they outlasted even that period in remote places. Moreover, the Danubian I expansion did not take place *in vacuo*. In the hill countries between the Danube and the Rhine and in Thuringia, along the rivers of the North European plain and on the sand-dunes of Silesia and Poland, still lived

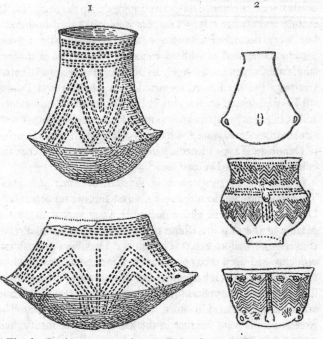

Fig. 62. Stroke-ornamented vases, Bohemia ($\frac{1}{5}$, $\frac{1}{4}$); Rössen vases, Central Germany ($\frac{1}{10}$).

scattered groups of Tardenoisian, Maglemosian, and Swiderian food-gathers. Some of these were absorbed into Danubian communities or copied the Danubians' way of life. Thus arose various cultural groups,[42] essentially Danubian in economy and equipment, but diverging from the norm in details, particularly in ceramic art. Hence the groups are defined by their pottery. And most flourished in period III too.

(1) *Stroke-ornamented ware* (*Stichbandkeramik*) (Fig. 62, 1)

distinguishes a group which arose probably in Bohemia and spread thence back into Moravia, and into Bavaria, Central Germany, and Western Poland in the wake of the Danubian I groups, and under pressure from the same economic forces. Economically it differs from Danubian I only in a tendency to supplement farming by hunting, for which transverse arrow-heads[43] of Tardenoisian ancestry were employed. The arrow-shafts were straightened on grooved stones, as in the Danubian II culture and farther east.[44] The pots were still round-bottomed, but were decorated exclusively with skeuomorphic zig-zag patterns composed of ribbons executed by a series of distinct jabs instead of continuous lines. In Bohemia, Bavaria, and Central Germany the dead were cremated.[45] In Moravia and Poland stroke-ornamented ware occurs in late Danubian II settlements, and at Gleinitz in Silesia an imported Tisza vase was found with stroke-ornamented ware,[46] while at Vochov near Plzen a figurine of Danubian II type turned up in a similar context.[47] Hence the culture thus defined at least lasts into period II.

(2) The *Rössen group* arose in Western Bohemia and Saxo-Thuringia through the adoption by Forest-folk of a fundamentally Danubian equipment and economy.[48] They spread down the Main and then up the Rhine to Switzerland, and into France through the Belfort gap.[49] Though the Danubian agricultural economy had been taken over entire, hunting retained much of the importance that it had enjoyed in the ancestral Forest culture. The increased competition for land, due to the rise of this and other new groups of cultivators, may by now have led to war. The Rössen people were the first in the Rhine valley to fortify their settlements, while weapons – transverse and hollow-based arrow-heads, disc-shaped mace-heads and the old perforated antler-axes of the Forest-folk – were relatively common. The Rössen folk lived in rectangular houses with vertical walls and gabled roofs supported by three rows of earth-fast posts,[50] and they also erected rectangular granaries. But their settlements were no more permanent than those of the preceding groups. Their pots are hemispherical or globular in profile, but are often provided with stand-rings and are decorated with rectilinear patterns imitating basketry and executed in stab-and-drag technique (Fig. 62, 2). Exceptional forms are quadrilobate dishes with analogues in the

Balkans and North Italy and a small clay barrel with closed ends and an opening in the side, a form well-represented in Troy I.[51]

As ornaments the Rössen folk wore marble bracelets, disc-beads of shell, bored tusks and deers' teeth and marble buttons identical with those from Lengyel. The dead were buried contracted in cemeteries. One skull from Alsace had been trepanned.[52]

The buttons of Danubian II type from the graves at Rössen in Central Germany prove that the group even there belongs to period II, while on the Isar, in Alsace, and in the Wetterau, Rössen house-foundations have disturbed the ruins of those left by later Danubian I peasants. On the other hand, on the Goldberg, in Württemburg, the Rössen village was succeeded by a settlement of the Western Michelsberg culture that generally belongs to period III. Hence Rössen flourished in period II.[53]

The Danubian I peasants themselves persisted, wandering about during period II and in the Rhine basin even into period III, perserving their culture intact, but not unaffected by the example of their neighbours and rivals. Plastic suggestions of a human face from Köln-Lindental, in the manner of Trojan face-urns, may belong to this phase.[54] Even in Central Germany the later Danubian I pottery is associated with the stroke-ornamented ware of period II. Such late Danubian I people fortified Köln-Lindental. Pressure on the land was becoming serious. In addition to the natural increase of the population and the competitive groups resulting from the conversion of food-gatherers into cultivators, new groups were spreading from the south-east and from the west.

Period III

By period III the natural growth of peasant populations, the conversion to food-production of food-gathering communities, and immigrations of fresh tribes from beyond the löss lands had produced a pressure upon the soil that entailed adjustments in everyday life. Inferior lands above the löss were exploited; hunting and pastoralism became more important economically, and in fact in the temperate zone they would be more productive than hoe-agriculture. Settlements were often planted on hilltops as well as in the valleys, and were frequently fortified.[55] Competition for land assumed a bellicose character, and weapons such as battle-axes became specialized for warfare. The consequent preponderance of the male members in the communities may account for the general disappearance of female figurines. Part of the new surplus population may have sought an outlet in industry and trade; imported substances such as Baltic amber, Galician flint and copper begin to be distributed more regularly than heretofore. Warriors would appreciate more readily than cultivators the superiority of metal, and chiefs may already have been concentrating surplus wealth to make the demand for metal effective. Its satisfaction was none the less dependent on the diffusion of the requisite technical knowledge, whether by immigrant prospectors or captives, from the south-east.

A general picture of the period in the löss lands would present a bewildering variety of small conflicting groups. Some of these are admittedly intruders and can be better described elsewhere. From the West, Michelsberg folk (p. 342) spread as far as Upper Austria, Bohemia, and Central Germany, while Beaker-folk (pp. 270–71) reached the Danube near Buda-Pest and spread across Germany and Czechoslovakia as far as the Vistula. From the Pontic–North European plain warriors using battle-axes and cord-ornamented pottery spread as far as Bavaria, Bohemia, and Moravia, and even into the Middle Danube basin. In other groups there is an injection of types (collared flasks, globular amphorae, and so on) which we shall find in Chapter 10 to be genuinely Northern. But these hardly suffice to demonstrate a large-scale 'Nordic' invasion of the Danubian province. We shall describe here only certain cultures which remain fundamentally Danubian even though they be found on fortified hilltops or in caves.

Bodrogkeresztur designates the culture into which the Lengyel culture developed through a Tiszapolgár stage in North-East Hungary and beyond the Tisza, whence it spread north to Silesia.[56] It is known almost exclusively from cemeteries larger than those of previous periods. That at the patent station comprised at least fifty graves, at Jaszladány forty, at Pusztaistvánháza thirty-two,[57] while at Tiszapolgár-Basatanya 158 graves have been

excavated out of an estimated total of 225.[58] The size of the
cemeteries may be due as much to prolonged occupation of the
same village as to density of population. At Basatanya, Kutzian
could distinguish two consecutive phases, both transitional,
between Lengyel and mature Bodrogkeresztur. Double graves, in
which one body had been buried with rich furniture, the other
with none, suggest a division of society into classes.

Trade now brought to the Hungarian plain flint from Galicia,

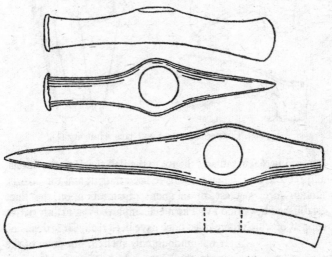

Fig. 63. Copper battle-axes, Hungary ($\frac{1}{2}$).

gold and copper from Transylvania. In the cemeteries copper is
represented by several quadrangular awls, three or four rhomboid
knife-daggers without midribs or rivet holes, a flat adze, five
axe-adzes, and at least one battle-axe.[59] Several similar battle-
axes (Fig. 63) have been found stray and disclose the translation
into metal of antler axes that in turn became the model for stone
weapons (pp. 204–5). Adzes and axe-adzes are very common stray
and sometimes occur in hoards.[60] Evidently copper was being
systematically extracted in the Carpathian basin. Roska[61] long
ago argued that axe-adzes served as miners' tools. Driehaus[62]
has now shown that the simplest types, like Fig. 64, 1 and 5, are
virtually confined to metalliferous Transylvania while the classic

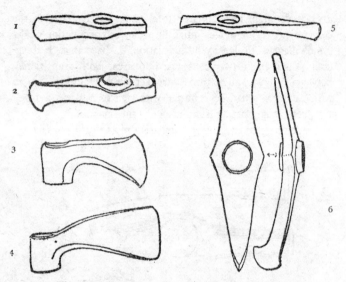

Fig. 64. Copper axe-adzes and axes, Hungary (¼).

type of Fig. 64, 6, radiates thence to the Balkans, Bavaria, Silesia, and the Ukraine. They must have been traded; and the hoards, though rare, suggest an incipient organization on the lines established by period IV. The metal employed was mainly native copper, of which there must once have been really large deposits.

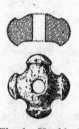

Fig. 65. Knobbed mace-head from Maros Decse (¼).

It was undoubtedly melted, but none of the products shows unambiguous evidence of having been shaped by casting in a mould,[63] but all traces would be removed by the necessary hammering.

Copper did not oust stone tools. Graves contain long knives on flint blades, polished stone adzes, hollow-bored celts and, in a late phase, triangular flint or obsidian arrowheads and a mace embellished with four projecting knobs (Fig. 65).

Technically Bodrogkeresztur pottery carries on the late Lengyel tradition and in the Tiszapolgár phase at least vessels on high hollow pedestals – though more often bowls as in Tripolye than fruitstands – were still popular.

But bowls' rims are now inverted, never expanding. Distinctive of mature Bodrogkeresztur are the so-called milk-jugs (Fig. 66, 2.)[64] Handled tankards and pyxides, very like Early Aegean ones, occur sporadically. Apart from warts and dimples, ornament is not common. Some vases, however, are decorated with cross-hatched ribbons forming maeander patterns even more like those of Dimini than the cognate Tisza designs. Late vases decorated with plastic ribs foreshadow the Bronze Age usage.

Fig. 66. Bodrogkeresztur pyxis and milk-jug. After Tompa ($\frac{1}{4}$).

Girdles of disc-beads of shell together with stray copper or gold trinkets were worn as ornaments.

Obviously the Bodrogkeresztur population was descended from the Lengyel group. But had mining and metallurgy been initiated by prospectors from the Aegean or the Caucasus? No doubt axe-adzes of different shapes were used by Early Aegean peoples and were actually manufactured – by casting in clay moulds – at Tepe Hissar in Northern Iran. Prospectors should have introduced the techniques of casting and smelting, but the Transylvanian products seem made of native copper. The forms could be regarded as translations into this 'superior stone' of Danubian II adzes, hammer-axes, and battle-axes of ordinary stone or antler. Native copper-working could perfectly well have originated in such a metalliferous region. Indeed, the Aegean axe-adzes could theoretically be derived from Transylvania while Heine-Geldern[65] has invoked axe-adzes like Fig. 80, to mark the Aryans' route to India. In other words the Aegean and Asiatic parallels to Bodrogkeresztur metal types might just as well give *termini ante*, as *termini post*, *quos*. Still, independent invention of casting is hard to admit.

The Jordanova culture of Bohemia[66] and Silesia[67] can be regarded as a parallel local development of the Lengyel tradition. It too is best known from graves – fifty-seven from the eponymous site (once called Jordansmühl) in Silesia and thirty-eight at Brześć Kujawski on the middle Vistula.[68] Metal was here used solely for ornaments – spectacle spirals (Fig. 60, 1), cylindrical ribbon armlets, and small discs bearing embossed patterns. Antler axes, deposited in men's graves at Brześć Kujawski, illustrate the weapons, copper translations of which were current south of the Carpathians. The distinctive pot-forms are mugs with one or two band handles (Fig. 94) and bowls, again with inverted rims. Bracelets were made of *Spondylus* shell or of engraved bone, while disc beads of shell were strung together as girdles or necklaces. As in the Bodrogkeresztur culture, female figurines are no more in evidence. The old ideology has been changed. That may reflect a change from a matrilineal to a patrilineal organization of society.

The copper spectacle spirals might have been inspired by Early Aegean gold ones like those of Fig. 22. If so, they would constitute a substantial argument for Oriental participation in the foundation of the Danubian III copper industry. Otherwise there are no more indications of influence from that quarter in Jordanova than in Bodrogkeresztur. Such can, however, be detected in the largely contemporary Baden culture.

The Transitional Baden-Pécel Culture

West and north of the Danube between Buda-Pest and Vienna emerged a culture complex variously designated Baden,[69] Ossarn,[70] or Pécel[71] after Austrian and Hungarian sites or 'channel'[72] or 'radially[73] ornamented' after ceramic features. Its domain extends northward through Moravia to the Upper

Elbe and the Upper Vistula and eastward across the Tisza and the Maros. Its regional manifestations in architecture and burial rites as well as pottery differ so widely as to raise doubts whether the discrepancies be due to the partial assimilation of distinct traditions or local divergences of a single tradition. Much of the data comes from isolated burials or rubbish pits; only Ossarn in Austria, Vučedol on the Drave, some sites near the Maros, and two large cemeteries near Buda-Pest have been systematically explored on an adequate scale.

While one-corn and emmer wheats [74] were regularly cultivated (very likely with the plough), stock-breeding combined with hunting made major contributions to the food-supply. Ritual burials of cattle and deer underline the importance of these activities. Experts conclude that the cattle were bred for milk, not just for flesh.[75] The bones from Ossarn [76] disclose for the first time on the Middle Danube large flocks of sheep. The first remains of horses in the province, too, have been reported from this and other sites. Perhaps they were already domesticated.[77] At least there were vehicles for horses to draw.

A model waggon, carried on four solid disc wheels,[78] from the cemetery of Buda-Kalasz affords the oldest evidence for such vehicles north of the Alps, if not in Europe as a whole. But these vehicles were not drawn by horses. At least paired oxen, buried in two rich graves at Alsónémedi,[79] must surely have drawn the hearses in which their masters were conveyed to the grave.

On the fertile plains and in mountain valleys the farmers lived on fortified hilltops or in caves. The best-attested house type is a one-roomed rectangular hut with rounded corners,[80] but at Vučedol, Schmidt [81] reports apsidal houses. Circular pits (?bothroi) are common in all settlements; at Vučedol they led into subterranean cellars excavated in the löss. At least in Hungary the size of the cemeteries – 305 graves at Buda-Kalasz, forty-one at Alsónémedi – point to large and stable villages. But these did not grow into tells, and the huts seem more appropriate to semi-nomad pastoralists. Their location, like the weapons from graves, emphasizes the martial aspect of pastoral societies.

Stone was still the normal material for knives, axes and adzes, arrow-heads, and battle-axes. But the last-named exhibit an imitation seam as if copied from a cast metal model, and Pittioni [82] assigns copper weapons, like Fig. 63, from Austria to the Baden culture. Copper ornaments alone have so far been found in graves; two in Lower Austria [83] were furnished with neck-rings of twisted wire with recoiled ends, immediate precursors of the cast ingot-torques (Fig. 69, 11–12) of period IV. Long-distance trade is positively documented by *Spondylus* and *Tridacna* shells, imported from the Mediterranean.

Spools, like the Early Troadic, and whorls attest an active textile industry. Pottery was self-coloured and generally dark-faced, occasionally mottled. A universal peculiarity is presented by large ribbon handles rising above the rims of mugs and jugs; at the top they are often deeply flanged, as in Fig. 96, or fanned out. Subcutaneous string-holes are not uncommon, and occasionally trumpet lugs (like Fig. 17, column 1) grow from the bowls. Bowls have inverted rims and, in Hungary and Slovakia, are divided into two unequal compartments and provided with conspicuous button handles. Channelled decoration is universal, but is often combined with other techniques – punctured ribbons, incised lattices, exceptional crusting combined with incision as in the Tisza culture, or even cord impressions.

Female figurines have not been recorded, but clay animal figures and models of waggons and boats may represent a survival of the old ideological tradition. It was quite overshadowed by funerary ritual. A few burials of men and women together may be taken as evidences of satî and of a patriarchal family. At Alsónémedi two centrally situated graves containing oxen and hearses must belong to chiefs interred in accordance with the tradition of royal burials that can be traced back to the Early Dynastic tombs of Kish and Ur and here marking the oldest royal funerals in Europe. The normal burial rite was interment in a contracted or flexed position, but in Hungary a small group of cremation graves has been recently reported. In a couple of Austrian tombs five or eight corpses had been buried together. Round Buda-Pest graves were grouped in distinct cemeteries; at some other sites they are said to have been dug within the inhabited area. Collective tombs containing up to twenty corpses were reported from Slovakia. [84] But in western Hungary cemeteries of cremation burials in urns constitute regular urnfields. [85] At Vučedol men were laid on the right, women on the left side.

In the Danubian sequence Baden is undoubtedly later than Lengyel. At Kiskörös[86] on the Hungarian plain a Bodrog-keresztur grave had been dug into an abandoned Baden settlement, but east of the Tisza the relation between the two cultures was reversed. At Fonyód Baden graves had been disturbed by later Early Bronze Age graves of the Kisapostag culture, while the copper neck-rings from Austria are typologically older than the torques of period IV. So the Baden culture is well fixed within period III; the extent of its overlap with the Bell-beaker culture remains to be determined. Racially the Pécel population shows a mixture of round and long heads.[87]

To Menghin, R. R. Schmidt, and Pittioni Baden is just a 'Nordic' culture, the result of an invasion from the wooded plain of Northern Europe. No doubt a few specifically Northern types, like collared flasks, occur sporadically on Baden sites as at Jevišovice in Moravia. On the other hand, peculiarities in Northern ceramic decoration have been ascribed to Baden influence,[88] and there is far more evidence for southern than for northern influences in the fundamentally Danubian Baden pottery. The distinctive channelled ornament is prominent in the Vinča culture; the incised and punctured patterns can be paralleled there and, still more precisely, in the Macedonian Late Neolithic; trumpet lugs are Troadic; flanged handles have been met in Troy while the Chalcolithic of Mersin[89] provides an exact parallel to the Baden variant. Similarly, subcutaneous string-holes recur in the Rinaldone culture of Central Italy. The wire torques from the Austrian graves can be exactly matched in 'Copper Age' burials at Ahlatlibel in Anatolia[90] and so could be claimed as concrete evidence of the south-eastern inspiration for the metallurgy at least of the Baden culture. Finally, wheeled vehicles were invented in Mesopotamia about 3000 B.C. and employed as hearses in royal funerals there by 2500. They were surely diffused thence, though the nearest analogues – spatially and chronologically – to the Baden model – from South Russia – are two-wheeled carts.

The southern connections just summarized, save the last, do not necessarily mean influences from the south. The 'torque-bearers' who introduced better metallurgical techniques into Syria[91] might conceivably have come from Central Europe, and, if so, the earlier torque from Ahlatlibel might after all be Danubian. Italian prehistorians would prefer to derive the Baden features in the Rinaldone culture from the north. If the Baden analogies in the Balkans, Macedonia, and Anatolia too could be thus interpreted, the Baden culture does exhibit all the archaeological characters – horses, wheeled vehicles, cattle and sheep, a dairy economy, patriarchal families, bows and arrows – deduced by linguistic palaeontology for the ancestral Indo-Europeans; their expansion could be beautifully documented by the connections just mentioned! Of course, such an interpretation would demand a literal inversion of current chronologies both relative and absolute. Still, these are based – mainly but not entirely – on undemonstrated postulates. With that reservation on purely archaeological evidence the Baden culture cannot begin more than a couple of centuries before 2000 B.C. and so could only be influenced by Late Neolithic and Early Bronze Age cultures of the Aegean.

The Early Bronze Age

During period III the growth of population was calling for a new economy and making labour available for industry and commerce. War was stimulating a demand for metal, and chiefs were accumulating capital; the prejudices of immigrant warriors had to be satisfied with trade-goods from the Baltic and Galicia. The Bell-beaker folk (pp. 270–76) established regular communications with the West and North and opened up new connections with the Mediterranean across the Brenner Pass. The rise of rich cities on the Levant coasts by 2000 B.C., in Crete by 1800, and in peninsular Greece by 1600 had created markets for metals and other raw materials not too far from Central European sources of supply and provided capital for their exploitation. Perhaps prospectors trained in Asiatic traditions had begun working the copper of Transylvania, Slovakia, and the Eastern Alps, and even the tin lodes of Bohemia and Saxony. At least as soon as the lords of Mycenae and Knossos began to demand amber, it became worthwhile to organize the transport of the magic resin from Denmark and at the same time the distribution of metal among the peasant societies of the Danube basin. The appearance of the metal wares thus distributed defines for archaeologists period IV.

No actual mines can be dated by direct evidence to period IV, but there are indications that the copper lodes of the eastern Alps, demonstrably mined during period VI, may have been exploited by surface workings as early as period IV (p. 352). Equally early exploitation of copper lodes near Saalfeld and of Vögtland tin has been deduced from recent analyses.[92] Moulds have been found in several settlements, but do not necessarily belong to resident smiths.

The distribution of the industry's products was effected by a regular class of itinerant merchant-artificers. Their routes are defined by hoards of finished and half-finished articles – the merchant's stock-in-trade – that had been buried when danger threatened and never recovered. They show that the merchants were following ancient Danubian traditions (p. 351) and that they dealt also in amber, gold, and presumably substances such as salt that leave no trace in the archaeological record. The amber routes are particularly well defined: the fossil resin was brought from Jutland and Sammland to the Saale valley and thence passed on through Bohemia and across the Brenner to Upper Italy and the Aegean, while a little was diverted across Moravia to the Hungarian plain and the Maros.[93] A counterpart to this export trade is certainly to be seen in segmented and cruciform beads of Egyptian or Aegean fayence common in cemeteries round Szeged[94] and in Slovakia,[95] and found sporadically in Western Hungary,[96] Lower Austria,[97] Moravia,[98] and Poland.

The activities of these merchants linked up the Central European region round the Brenner amber route into a single commercial system with branches to the tin-lodes of Cornwall and the gold-fields of Transylvania, but completely by-passing the Balkans. The types of metal ware thus diffused from the beginning of the Bronze Age produce a superficial appearance of uniformity throughout the Danubian province which no longer includes the Save or Drave, the Danube below Buda-Pest, or the Tisza south of the Maros mouth. At the same time Asiatic parallels to the arbitrary metal ornaments suggest the source of the fresh chemical knowledge, the alloy of copper with tin, on which the new economy was based.

Cast neck-rings with recoiled ends (Fig. 69, 11) were not only worn as ornaments but served also as ingots and therefore are termed 'ingot-torques'. Such torques were the insignia of members of a metal-working clan or guild in North Syria about 2000 B.C.[99] and were deposited as symbols of abstract wealth in contemporary shrines at Byblos.[100] Lock-rings with flattened ends and racket pins have explicitly Sumerian prototypes;[101] knot-

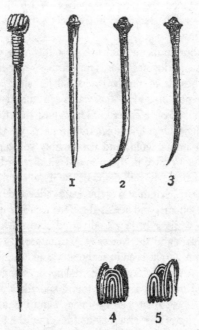

Fig. 67. Pins and earrings from Unětician graves. After Schránil ($\frac{1}{2}$).

headed pins (Fig. 67, 1, 2, 3), appearing in predynastic Egypt[102] recur later at Troy and in Cyprus: the basket-shaped earrings of gold wire (Fig. 67, 4, 5) are detached members of the Trojan ornaments shown in Fig. 22, 1. The first bronze-smiths producing for a Central European market seem to have been trained in Asiatic schools and to have introduced, together with the secret of bronze, Oriental fashions in personal adornment.[103] If so, the absence of these types on the European coasts of the

Aegean and in the Balkans requires the admission that they were introduced up the Adriatic and across the Brenner, unless they had been introduced through Troy by metallurgists working for export only till the fall of the 'second city' destroyed their market.

The novel metal tools and weapons appearing at the same time were neither so uniform in the Danubian province nor so clearly related to Oriental models. The flat axe which at Thermi had been provided with flanges by hammering (p. 74) was translated into a flanged axe, cast in a two-piece mould (Fig. 69, 1). Hence it can be inferred that Central European bronze axes, like Danubian adzes, were mounted in knee shafts. Chisels were even provided with cast tubular sockets in Moravia and Austria.[104] Only in Hungary was a shaft-tube axe of Sumerian ancestry preferred (Fig. 64, 5–6).[105] Shaft-hole axes were, however, used as weapons elsewhere in the province, while a remarkable weapon from a Saxon hoard[106] of the end of period IV seems a barbaric version of the crescentic axe represented in the Royal Tombs of Ur and rather later in North Syria.[107]

The universal weapon was the round-heeled knife-dagger (Fig. 68). Its bone or wooden hilt was hollowed at the base like the bronze hilt of the rather later dagger shown in Fig. 70, an old Egyptian trick never popular in Asia nor Greece, but traceable in Central, as in Western, Europe, on the flat-tanged daggers of the Bell-beaker folk during period III. Halberds[108] were used in Germany and Lower Austria and occasionally even in Hungary, but not in Bohemia. The type is supposedly West European, and reached the Danubian province from Ireland or from the Iberian Peninsula.

The unity created by the metallurgical industry and commerce had no political counterpart. It was imposed on a number of distinct cultures called after the sites of Perjámos[109] on the Maros, Tószeg, or Nagyrév on the Tisza,[110] Kisapostag west of the Danube,[111] Unĕtice in Bohemia, and Straubing in Bavaria, and asserting their independence not only in peculiarities of pottery and personal ornaments but even by divergences in burial rites and economic status. Most are presumably descended from local groups; for everywhere the pottery is technically in the Lengyel-Baden tradition, but everywhere, save on the Tisza, influence from Bell-beaker folk is patent even in the pottery. But the universally used strap-handled jugs and tankards with the body and neck modelled separately have nothing to do with the Bell-beakers.

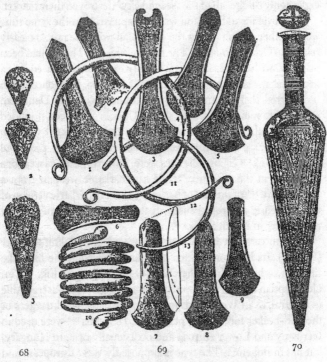

Fig. 68. Daggers from Unětician graves (¼).
Fig. 69. Hoard of Sobochleby (¼).
Fig. 70. Bronze-hilted dagger (¼).
All after Schránil.

In the Middle Danube basin settlements were founded in period IV on sites chosen primarily with a view to commerce where natural routes intersect at a ford or pass mouth.[112] And these settlements were permanent townships occupied so long that their ruins form tells. Cemeteries of contracted skeletons no less clearly attest a sedentary life; that at Szöreg near Szeged comprised 200 graves, 103 attributed to period IV and fifty-four to period V. But even these communities were more nearly self-sufficing villages than industrial cities. Bone and stone were still used for implements and even battle-axes; metal toilet-articles such as girdle-clasps were imitated in bone. The pots were hand-made, but the slipped and polished vases, red, black, or mottled, recall Anatolian and Iberic fabrics. In the basal or Nagyrév levels at Tószeg and in the older Szöreg graves the jugs have only one loop or strap handle. Later these give place to hour-glass tankards which develop in period V into metallic-looking cantharoi with quatrefoil mouths like the Middle Minoan and Hittite vases (p. 69). While the local smiths made most of the types characteristic of the period, they did not develop the flanged axe nor the same variety of pins as was popular farther north. Segmented fayence beads were, however, imported and Oriental lunula-pendants[113] were imitated, as were Aegean 'sacred ivy-leaves'.[114]

North of the Bakony and Carpathians no tells have been recognized, but cemeteries in Austria comprising over a hundred graves[115] must belong to permanent villages, occupied even into period V (sixteen rectilinear houses have in fact been recognized at Postoloprty).[116] All the foregoing graves contained contracted skeletons. Only in the Kisapostag group and the earliest graves near Szeged was cremation the normal practice. Their cemeteries are indeed urnfields like that of Troy VI. Of course, cremation had been practised locally by some Baden communities and also by Bell-beaker folk in Hungary. In South Bohemia, Poland, and Thuringia Unětician burials have been found under barrows (p. 274).

The Unětician culture proper extends from the Austrian Danube to Silesia and Saxony, but is most typically developed on the Upper Elbe in Bohemia and along the Saale and Oder. Here, owing to the proximity of the Ore Mountains and the amber trade across the Brenner, the metal industry developed most luxuriantly. By casting in valve-moulds, the celts were equipped with high flanges and the knot-headed pin was translated into the distinctive 'Bohemian eyelet-pin' (Fig. 67, 2). Towards the end of period IV core casting allowed the manufacture of socketed spear-heads and socketed chisels. Moreover, Unětician smiths could produce not only ornaments of sheet bronze but also bell helmets if, as Hencken[117] has shown grounds for believing, the specimen found a century ago at Beitsch in Saxony was really associated with Unětician ingot-torques and a triangular dagger. Amber, gold, and Mediterranean shells were freely imported, but fayence beads are rare and the segmented variety (like Fig. 157) is not found north of Brno.

The hand-made pots agree in fabric with those from Perjámos, but the most distinctive shapes were at first pouched jugs and

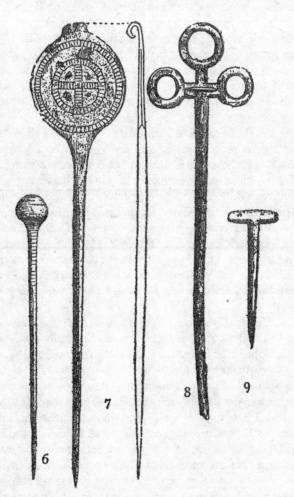

Fig. 71. Bulb, disc, trilobate, and crutch-headed pins from later Unětician graves. After Schránil (½).

mugs sometimes decorated with cord-impressions or incised lines (Fig. 72).[118] Then in the classical phase of Unětice (IVb) these are transformed by flattening out the belly into keeled mugs and jugs. Neumann[119] has analysed the constituents of Unětician pottery into elements derived from the Bell-beaker and Corded ware groups and a southern component. His analysis summarizes the constitution of the whole culture. Bell-beaker folk established the requisite commercial connection, battle-axe warriors made the demand for metal effective, metallurgists from the south may

Fig. 72. Marschwitz and early Unětician pottery, Silesia and Bohemia. After Stocký.

have provided the technical basis, but the foundation was still Baden and so Danubian.

The development of the Central European bronze industry was undoubtedly correlated with that of the amber trade across the province; the guaranteed market that alone could make regular trade among barbarians worth while was in Mycenaean Greece and Crete. It is undoubtedly assumed that the initiation of the industry was equally due to prospectors, ultimately relying for a livelihood on the purchasing power of East Mediterranean cities. On this assumption the Oriental types reproduced by Danubian smiths should provide limiting dates for period IV. The limits thus given prove to be unexpectedly wide. Most of the ornaments mentioned on p. 172 had been current in Egypt or Mesopotamia long before 2000 B.C. Even the ingot-torques, introduced into Syria about that date, had earlier wiry precursors at Ahlatlibel, as in Austria (p. 168). So period IV might begin before 2000 B.C. But regular trade with the Aegean is attested first about 1600 B.C.

The initial assumption, however intrinsically probable, has not yet been demonstrated by actual dateable imports; for segmented fayence beads were current in Hither Asia for a millennium before 1400 B.C. Now the metal-working clan, who introduced ingot-torques with core casting and other advances into Syria, are thought to have been immigrants. As no other cradle has been found for them, they might have come from Central Europe. In that case their advent a century before or after 2000 B.C. would be a *terminus ante quem* for the beginning of Danubian IV. So too the amber beads from the Shaft Graves of Mycenae at least prove that the commerce that enriched the Unětician culture was fully established before 1550 B.C. Crescentic necklaces with pattern-bored spacers, like the Mycenaean, in Bavaria and Alsace are found in graves of period V. So 1550 should be near the end of period IV. If so, the strikingly close Middle Minoan and contemporary Hittite analogies to the quatrefoil cantharoi that developed from the Perjámos tankards in period V (p. 175) become chronologically significant. Moreover, by 1200 B.C. fibulae and other Central European or North Italian types were appearing in Greece, and the types in question are more proper to period VI than to period V.[120] If, then, period V – the Middle Bronze Age – ended about 1250 B.C., and began in 1550, period IV, the initial phase of the Continental Bronze Age, might very well have occupied five centuries and begun before 2000 B.C. On the available Central European evidence, 2100 is as likely a date as 1700 for the start of the Early Bronze Age.

But whether Perjámos and Unětice are to be compared to Sargonid cities in Mesopotamia or early Mycenaean townships in Greece, they must rank several stages lower in the cultural scale. Economically they have not reached the level of the Early Aegean townships of the Peloponnese or the Troad. Most of the population must remain peasants. But one industry at least did absorb a few of the farmers' younger sons; trade did indirectly secure a share in the Oriental surplus to supplement home-grown supplies. The smiths, the only specialist craftsmen recognizable in the archaeological record of period IV, displayed far more originality and inventiveness than their fellows in Asia or Egypt. And their products were more democratic. Even in period IV they were making sickles while Egyptian peasants were still reaping with flints. By period VI their successors would have invented an axe of bronze that was as efficient and as cheap as an iron one, and an armament with which European barbarians could challenge the well-equipped armies of Oriental monarchies.

8 The Peasants of the Black Earth

On the löss-clad flanks of the Carpathians, in the valleys of the upper Oltu and the Seret, and on the parkland plateau extending north-eastward across the Prut, the Dniestr, and the Southern Bug to the Dniepr, there developed, on a Starčevo foundation enriched by Danubian elements, a remarkable farming culture named after Tripolye, a site near Kiev.[1] Though its authors were throughout farmers and lived in large villages of substantial houses, they seem, like their kinsmen farther west, to have practised a sort of shifting cultivation.[2] Hence the village sites are very numerous – twenty-six have been identified in 110 sq miles just south of Kiev – but none formed tells. A few sites – Nezviska[3] on the Dniestr, Cucuteni[4] and Izvoare[5] on the Prut, Traian[6] on the Seret – were occupied more than once. The stratigraphy there observed justifies a division of the culture into four main stages: A, B1, B2, and C.[7] It is based primarily on a stylistic analysis of the ceramic decoration in which local divergences may have sometimes been mistaken for discrepancies in age. Phase A is confined to a few sites on the upper reaches of the Prut, the Dniestr, and the Bug. The valleys of the Oltu and Dniepr would then have been colonized in phase B1 (AB). Only in phase C does Tripolye pottery occur in settlements of quite different cultures on the steppes and in the forests north of the Teterev.

The basis of life was throughout the cultivation of wheats – *Triticum monococcum*, *dicoccum*, and *vulgare* – barley, and millet, and the breeding of cattle, goats, sheep, and pigs.[8] Cows were always the most important stock; horses'[9] bones occur in all stages, but perhaps represent game animals save in the latest stage. Hunting was at all times important, but the percentage of game bones in the food refuse declines from 52 in stage A to 20 in stage C. Fishing must also have made a substantial contribution; hooks of copper or bone are found even on phase A sites, while along the Dniestr remains of fish over 1·5 m long have been reported. Net-fishing may be inferred from clay sinkers. Finally, the collection of shell-fish and berries added substantially to the food-supply.

The settlements are normally located on spurs of löss, protected on three sides by ravines. At the time of their occupation the plateaux were moister than today, liable to swamping, covered with damp woods and inhabited by tortoises, otters, and water-rats.[10] Most sites were probably defended by ditch and rampart. Those at Ariuşd [11] on the Oltu (phase B1) enclosed 1¼ acres that would accommodate at most twenty-one houses arranged in three rows. Hăbăşeşti on the Seret [12] comprised perhaps forty-four dwellings, while as many as 150, mostly B2, are reported from Vladimirovka. Normal villages of phases B2 and C consisted of thirty to forty-two houses usually arranged radially on the circumferences of one or more concentric circles 200 m to 500 m in diameter.

Only alleged pit-dwellings of phase A have been described; the houses of later phases are represented by the celebrated *ploščadki*, areas of baked clay resulting from the burning and collapse of walls and floors. The walls of wattle and daub heavily plastered with clay and straw were supported by earth-fast posts at Ariuşd in phase B1; their sockets define houses measuring 8·25 by 5·4 m and divided into two rooms by a partition. Ovens were found in both rooms, a hearth in the outer one. In plan and internal arrangements these houses are identical with those of Rössen and contemporary settlements round the Alps (Fig. 137), and assumed for period II along the Middle Danube. In phases B2 and C, posts planted in sleeper beams seem to have served to support only a skeleton frame and the roof-tree, the walls being built of compacted earth – kerpitsh. In most villages a few houses were small and one-roomed, 7 by 4 m in area and containing only a single oven. The average house measured about 14 by 5·5 m and contained two to four ovens. The largest house recorded measured 27 by 6·5 m and was divided into five rooms, four furnished with one oven each, the fifth with two. The most puzzling features in many houses are the hard-baked and well-smoothed clay floors on which ovens, querns, and vases stood and on the undersides of which imprints of close-set timbers are preserved.[13]

The large ovens, 2 m or more square, were made of clay on a framework of saplings. In addition, some rooms were furnished with raised benches of baked clay, and – at least in phase B2 on the Bug – also with cruciform pediments ornamented on their surfaces with engraved lines or with paint. Russian archaeologists agree that these last were offering-places. Six or seven fragmentary models illustrate the interior of a Tripolye house, showing the porch, the oven, the cruciform pediment, the jars of grain, and the quern just as excavators have found them (Fig. 73). All these models stand on legs and so suggest that Tripolye houses were really raised on piles. That would be quite reasonable as the sites were liable to swamping; it would at once explain the burning of the clay floors and of the wooden beams under them. But there is no excavational evidence for this very plausible hypothesis. Russian excavators frequently refer also to half-subterranean dwellings or *zemlianki*, but the plans look almost as dubious as those of Danubian 'pit-dwellings'.

Kričevskii believed that the large houses with three or more rooms resulted from the enlargement of one-roomed houses to accommodate married children of the latters' builders. The enlarged family would keep together, as in the recent Slav *zadruga*. If so, the sites in question must have been occupied for at least two generations.

Tripolye farmers were generally content to use local materials for their equipment which consequently looks purely neolithic. Adzes were made of local stone, often rather soft, but axe-hammers or even simple battle-axes were perforated with a hollow borer, and mattocks or adzes were made from bored antlers (Fig. 75, 15). Weapons are not common. Triangular flint arrow-heads occur sporadically from phase B1 at least. A knob bed mace like one from Danubian III is reported from a B2 site near Kiev,[14] while model battle-axes – surely warriors' weapons – were made at Ariuşd and Hăbăşeşti in phase B1.

Trade secured farmers even at Petreny on the middle Dniestr obsidian from west of the Carpathians by phase B2. Copper too was similarly obtained from the very first, but in phase A[15] was

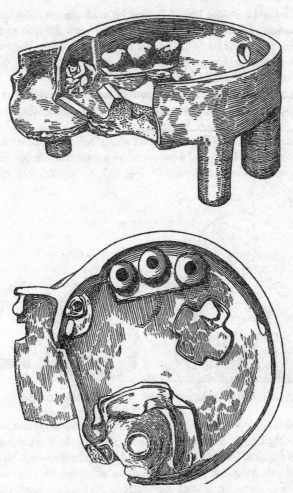

Fig. 73. Model hut from Popudnia.

employed only for fish-hooks, rings, bangles, and beads; one fragment analysed contained 30 per cent of zinc, so native copper at least is excluded. In phase B1 copper was used occasionally for making flat adzes, while a B2 site yielded a copper pick-axe, allied to the Transylvanian axe-adzes of Danubian III. Phase C is certainly contemporary with the frankly Bronze Age Usatova culture (p. 191), but even in B1 a knot-headed pin is reported from

Sabatinovka on the Bug.[16] It may be evidence for Asiatic inspiration of the school of metallurgy that grew up west of the Black Sea, but it could just as well be derived from the Perjámos and Unětician cultures in the Danube valley. In that case phase B1 of Tripolye would fall already into Danubian IV.

The products of Tripolye potters have been celebrated in archaeological literature for nearly a century. In every village local potters made vases of sophisticated forms and substantial dimensions and fired them in kilns to a hard red or orange ware. A model vertical kiln and remains of an actual one stacked with vases were found at Ariușd[17] (Fig. 74), perforated clay grills

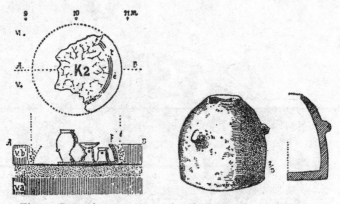

Fig. 74. Potters' oven and model, Ariușd (Erösd). After Laszló.

from Hăbășești[18] may have served to separate the firing chamber from the hearth. Yet housewives most probably made at home the pots required for domestic use instead of purchasing them from a full-time specialist potter; for stocks of prepared clay were discovered in some houses and instruments for decorating vases in many. Actually two wares are found on most Tripolye sites – a coarse ware tempered with shell and a finer fabric with chaff or sand temper. The former, not reported from phase A sites, is ornamented with a comb, impressed into, or drawn over, the wet clay; its affinities lie with the products of surviving hunter-fisher societies in the boreal forest zone of North-Eastern Europe.

The finer wares, red or orange in hue, were richly decorated. In all phases the patterns might be outlined with deep channelled grooves supplemented with dots and, in phases A and B1, filled with rouletted lines; the curved stamps of antler, bone, or shell used to produce such lines have been found on several sites[19] (Fig. 75, B1, 12). Broad flutings were sometimes employed with, or instead of, grooves in phase A and especially in B1.[20] Exceptionally these devices were enriched by incrustations in ochre or with lines of white paint applied before firing to the red ground in phase A. The most familiar decoration in phases B and C was, however, painted – in white or red (mainly in B1), outlined with black on red, or red outlined in black on a white slip. Warm black, sometimes supplemented by thin lines in red, on buff or orange was the favourite style in phases B2 and C. In phase A running spirals, used as a repetition pattern, formed the basis of the decoration, but they gave place to closed S spirals in phase B1. In the sequel these dissolved into circles and the old all-over composition gave place to a tectonic arrangement emphasizing the vase's articulation.

From the first the vase forms are highly sophisticated and too varied even for enumeration. Tubular stands (Fig. 75, B1, 2) are confined to phases A and B1. Fruitstands (Fig. 75, B1, 1) were most popular in phase B1 and in that phase alone are accompanied by jars on profiled and perforated pedestals. 'Binocular vases' (Fig. 75, B11, 7) were characteristic at all periods. Vases in the form of animals, usually bulls, or anthropomorphic, may rank as ritual vessels, but a 'bird vase' of phase A[21] could just as well be regarded as an askos.

In the light of the total excavation of Kolomiščina Tripolye society would seem to have been as democratic and equalitarian as the Danubian of Köln-Lindental, since the size of the houses was determined by the number of families inhabiting them jointly. But at Fedeleşeni, a Moldavian village of stage B1, Nestor[22] mentions that one house was more richly furnished than the rest and contained a stone animal sceptre-head (Fig. 76) as if it had belonged to a chief. Moreover, the mace-head from Veremye might be interpreted as a symbol of authority.

The ideology of the Tripolye farmers was as 'Asiatic' as that of their Balkan and Danubian II contemporaries. In addition to the cruciform 'altars', many houses were littered with clay figurines and models. The former, predominantly female, in phases A and

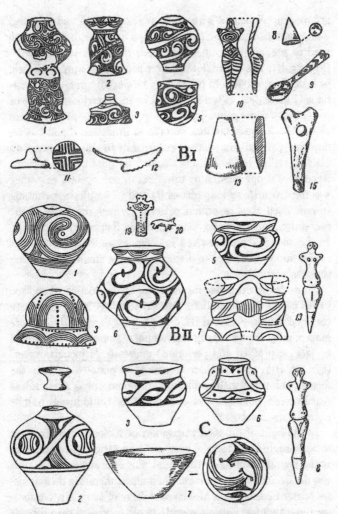

Fig. 75. Tripolye types (after Passek).
B I: Polychrome pottery ($\frac{1}{12}$) and ladle, figurine, clay cone, and
stamp ($\frac{1}{4}$), comb for decorating pottery, stone adze, antler pick.
B II: 1 ($\frac{1}{20}$), 3, 7 ($\frac{1}{10}$) grooved, 5–6 painted ware ($\frac{1}{16}$), Pyaniš-
kovo; Vladimirovka.
C I: 1–3 Popodnia; 6–8 ($\frac{1}{10}$), Staraya Buda.

B1 were steatopygous, and in phase B1 richly ornamented with incised spirals (Fig. 75, B1, 10), though fiddle-shaped types like Fig. 8, 2 were also common at Hăbăşeşti.[23] In phase B2 the figurines are flat, often perforated for suspension and painted (Fig. 75, B11, 13; C, 8). Males are represented sporadically even in phase A, phalli[24] too in phase B1. Clay stamps occur only in phase B1 and are confined to sites between the Oltu and the Prut – Ariuşd, Cucuteni, Hăbăşeşti, and Ruginoasa; one bears a filled cross design, the rest spirals (Fig. 76).

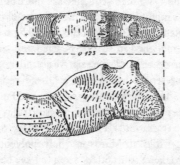

Fig. 76. Stone sceptre-head, Fedeleşeni and clay stamp, Ariuşd.

As ornaments, besides copper and very rare gold trinkets, clay beads, some star-shaped, were worn at all periods. Copper beads and bored deers' teeth seem confined to phases A and B1, to which belong also laminae from boars' tusks perforated at the four corners. Clay cones, common in phase B1 (Fig. 75, 8) may have been gamesmen, though one is surmounted by a rough human head.

The position of the Tripolye phases in the Balkan sequence is fairly clear. On the Seret, phase A is preceded by Boian, while a broken binocular vase was found as an import in the earliest Gumelniţa level at Vidra (pp. 139–40). At Verbicoara in Wallachia, polychrome sherds, attributed to phase B1, were found in the Salcuța layer, while the sceptre-head from Fedeleșeni is paralleled at Salcuța itself. On the Upper Oltu, remains of the Ariușd, B1, version of Tripolye are superimposed on early Boian strata. On the Dniestr at Nezviska, the settlement with early B1 pottery overlies the late Danubian I village (p. 152), but at Traian, Danubian I sherds are reported from a Tripolye A layer.[25] Hence, while phase A may overlap with Boian in Balkan II, most of phases A and B must be parallel with Gumelnița and Salcuța in Balkan III.

Links with the Danubian sequence are more ambiguous. The clay stamp-seals might be used as a basis for synchronizing phase B1 with Danubian II, and so might the Ariușd figurines that, as in Moravia, were modelled in two parts separately and then stuck together. On the other hand, the relative abundance of metal, the battle-axes, represented by models, a bossed copper disc from Hăbășești[26] would all be more appropriate to Danubian III. So the jars on high profiled pedestals of phase B1 have their closest analogies in the transitional Tiszapolgár pottery that is likewise Danubian III, while at Marosvasarhely polychrome B1 and decorated Bodrogkeresztur pottery seem to have been associated. An even lower limit in terms of the Danubian sequence would be given by the one possible import found in a Tripolye settlement: the knot-headed pin from Sabatinovka, if imported from Bohemia or Hungary, would mean that Tripolye B1 did not end before Danubian IV began. But of course the pin might have come from Asia. That Tripolye C lasts into and perhaps beyond Danubian IV is nearly certain.[27] Here Tripolye has been assigned to periods II, III, and IV, but perhaps its several phases should each be set a period later.

In its economy, as in its art, the Tripolye culture is so fundamentally Danubian that one might speak of a Dniestro-Danubian cycle of cultures. The Danubian element can be most economically derived from the colonists established at Nezviska and elsewhere in pre-Tripolian times. But they had been preceded by earlier Starčevo settlers, if not by the hypothetical hunter-fishers who might have remained in occupation of the region since the Ice Age (p. 128). Indeed, the latter now become almost tangible in the coarse ware found on all Tripolye sites and related to that of the more boreal hunter-fisher tribes of the Eurasiatic taiga. It is now no longer necessary to look to Central Asia to account for the painted Tripolye vases, since the Starčevo pioneers painted their vases and must have possessed the vertical kilns requisite for producing light-faced wares.

The Tripolye ideology and the elaborate ritual paraphernalia that expressed it were of course shared by the Tripolye farmers with their cultural antecedents in South-West Asia, but equally with neighbouring Gumelniţa, Vinča, and Danubian II societies; it could have reached the Tripolye province thence, if not earlier with the Starčevo colonists.

The Beginnings of Metallurgy on the West Pontic Coasts

By Tripolye phase C, and probably earlier, there had arisen on the steppes bordering the Black Sea a local metal industry serving stratified societies, best represented in the Usatova culture,[28] so named after a village and cemeteries near Odessa. Warlike chiefs, leaders of a pastoral aristocracy, were enabled to exercise an effective demand for metal armaments by concentrating the surplus wealth produced by their pastoral followers and by their Tripolye subjects.

The new pastoral aspect of the economy is disclosed by the very numerous animal bones from the village and the prominence among them of sheep and horses, now surely domesticated; the percentages are: 37·8 sheep, 31 cows, 15·5 horses, only 2·2 pigs. Game accounts for only 28·4 per cent of the total.[29]

The rulers were buried under barrows which form two cemeteries near the village. A chief[30] was interred contracted on one side or on his back in a central shaft grave encircled by a ring of slabs on edge. Under one barrow a slab in the kerb had been engraved with very rough representations of a man, a stag, and perhaps a horse.[31] Before the barrow was heaped, one or two slaves or dependents would be slain and interred in accessory graves. Bones of animals and statuettes, too, were buried in separate pits.

Contrasted with these almost royal tombs are the flat graves belonging presumably to the cultivators. These are shallow pits, each covered by a flat slab and containing a single contracted skeleton. That these cultivators were an off-shoot from Tripolye

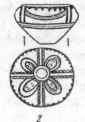

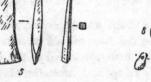
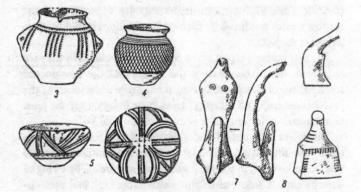

Fig. 77. Usatova types.

(*Top*) Usatova Barrows: 1–2, cord-ornamented and painted vases
($\frac{1}{8}$); 3–5, copper objects ($\frac{1}{2}$) barrow I; 6–10, figurine ($\frac{1}{4}$), painted
pot ($\frac{1}{8}$), copper spirals, bored wolf's teeth ($\frac{1}{4}$) barrow II.
(*Below*) 3–7, cord-ornamented and painted pots ($\frac{1}{8}$), clay figurine
($\frac{1}{4}$) from other barrows; 8, figurine from Usatova settlement
(after Passek).

communities may be inferred from survivals of the Tripolye ideology and ceramic art. Figurines were still made in clay though stylized almost beyond recognition (Fig. 77, 6–8).

In the village and both under the barrows and in flat graves well-fired vases, painted and fashioned in the Tripolye technique, occur side by side with coarser vessels ornamented with cord impressions. The designs on the painted pots can be regarded as degenerations of the good spiral ornament of Tripolye A and B1, and some old Tripolye forms are reproduced. The cord-ornamented pottery must represent the new pastoral element; some of the jars could be regarded as degenerations of Thuringian amphorae (Fig. 77, *top*, 1, 3), but the impressed cord designs are more elaborate than any from North or Central Europe and include the imprints of crocheted necklaces, maggot patterns, and horseshoe loops.[32]

Trade brought amber, presumably from the Baltic, antimonite allegedly from Turkey, and substantial supplies of copper. The metal was cast into characteristic local types. The most distinctive is a kite-shaped riveted dagger with a midrib on one face only (Fig. 77, *top*, 4), but flat axes and quadrangular awls were also made. The shaft-hole axe from Cucuteni may also be a product of Usatova industry, since a typical dagger comes from the site. Small spiral rings of copper or silver were worn as well as necklaces of bored deers' teeth. The stone industry is comparatively poor. A perforated antler axe had been buried with one of the chiefs and so must rank as a battle-axe, as in the Danubian III graves of Brześć-Kujawski.

Ustatova ceramic and metal types occur in a number of barrow graves on the steppes between the Tripolye province and the Black Sea and in a few marginal Tripolye villages.[33] The first two villages at the fortified site of Mikhaĭlovka[34] on a tributary of the Lower Dniepr may well have been occupied by a kindred society, again predominantly pastoral. Metal was certainly worked here too, but no distinctively Usatova types have been published in 1956.

Kričevskiĭ[35] and Passek treated the Usatova culture as the final result of the conversion of the Tripolye economy to pastoralism, Briusov,[36] however, could easily show that Usatova represented a distinct culture not later than Tripolye B2 or at least C. A Tripolye component is indeed obvious enough. The origin of the pastoral element will be considered in Chapter 9. What of the metal industry?

The distribution of the distinctive metal types leaves little doubt that the raw material reached the Black Sea coasts by sea. If that means that the knowledge of metal-working was introduced by prospectors from the Aegean or Asia Minor, it cannot be claimed that their local products reproduced any specific southern models. The technique of casting midrib daggers in a one-piece mould is a barbarism quite foreign to any of the advanced schools of metallurgy and paralleled only in the Iberian peninsula and South France. Usatova metal types give no clue as to the origin of their makers nor as to the absolute date of the Usatova culture. Relatively it might be assigned to period IV or a late phase of period III in the Balkan sequence. In the Danubian sequence it should occupy a similar position. Usatova must surely be earlier than period V, since Hungarian bronzes of that phase are quite common in the province.[37] A little support for an equation with Danubian IV might be derived from the kite-shaped daggers of the East Polish and Slovakian Tomaszów culture,[38] at least in plan they recall the Usatova type and they are associated with segmented fayence beads. Still the latter might be correlated with the amber beads from Troy II and Usatova as indicative of a trade in metals and Sammland amber in the IIIrd millennium.

9 Culture Transmission over the Eurasian Plain?

Last century anthropologists regarded the Eurasiatic plain as a corridor through which Asiatic hordes, precursors of the Huns and the Tartars, swept neolithic culture to Western Europe. Their guess is hardly confirmed by the evidence of the spade. But of course confirmatory evidence would be hard to obtain; predominantly pastoral and *ex hypothesi* mobile communities need leave no durable equipment that archaeologists could recognize, and certainly would leave no stratified tells in their wake. Stock-breeding is indeed not attested earlier near the eastern than near the western extremities of the plain, but only in the sense that no geological nor pollen dates are available in the former area while the culture sequence as distinguished in 1956 seems less varied, and therefore shorter, than farther west. No doubt in the wide chilly forest zone a 'palaeolithic' economy based on collecting, hunting, and fishing along the shores of meres and rivers persisted long, albeit made increasingly sedentary by the emphasis on fishing. Farther south, in the wide belt of parkland and the steppe zone bordering the Black Sea, collections of flint tools may indicate a continuity of settlement from late pleistocene times. Chopping tools, sharpened by a tranchet blow (p. 43), are reported from the parklands of Volhynia, Podolia, and the Ukraine.[1] Only in a few stratified caves in Crimea[2] can even the relative antiquity of the archaic flints be determined, and even there, though microliths are associated with pots with pointed bases[3] no very high antiquity need be assigned to them since geometric microliths may survive quite late.

Still less can such collections be cited as documenting precocious animal husbandry, since no bones survive on sandhill sites.

The flints collected from dunes between Lake Aral and the Oder may have been left by ancestors of the herdsmen who reached Denmark in Atlantic times, but there is not a scrap of evidence that they were.

On the fringe of the vast löss lands, colonized by primary neolithic Danubian, Starčevo and Tripolye peasants, there did indeed emerge communities of herdsmen, known almost exclusively from graves. Do these represent pastoral tribes separated out from the more agricultural Dniestro-Danubian societies? Or are they local mesolithic communities converted by their neighbours' example to food-production? Or, finally, are they immigrants from the steppes farther south and east? There, too, are barrow graves of a peculiar kind, the so-called ochre graves.

The Ochre Grave Cultures of the Pontic Steppes

The true steppe zone extends from the Dobrudja and the wooded outposts of the Carpathians round the Black Sea coasts to the Caucasus and beyond the Volga to the Altai. The steppes are covered with barrows of all periods down to the late Middle Ages. The prehistoric ones, generally small, cluster in little cemeteries, presumably marking some sort of tribal territory, and most cover many successive interments. On the strength of his excavations between the Donets and the Don, Gorodtsov defined three main stages on periods distinguished primarily by tomb types – first shaft graves (*yamy*), next pit-caves ('catacombs') and finally wooden cists (*sruby*). Hence the archaeological record in South Russia has been divided into yamno, catacomb, and srubno periods, and this terminology is retained even though it is now established that catacomb graves are confined to the Black Sea coasts and the valleys of the Donetz, the Don, and the Manyč, and define a culture rather than a period of time. On the slopes of the metalliferous Caucasus, however, some barrows are so rich that a finer typological division into five periods has been established by Yessen.[4] His phases I and II correspond roughly to the old Early Kuban[5] and more roughly to Gorodtsov's *yamno* stage,[6] while his group III may equal Middle Kuban and catacomb. But these burials under round barrows are not the earliest. Just as the funerary record in Britain begins with collective burial under long barrows, so in South Russia it begins with multiple burials in long trenches or under long mounds.

In all these graves the skeletons lie extended, usually covered with red ochre and arranged in groups. At Vovnigi,[7] near Dniepropetrovsk, 130 skeletons in three layers were lying side by side under a sandhill. At Mariupol on the Sea of Azov[8] 120 adults and six children had been buried in groups across one long trench filled with red earth. At Nalčik[9] a low irregular mound covered 130 contracted skeletons, again buried in groups and covered with red pigment. Such numbers exceed those recorded from any mesolithic cemetery of food-gatherers so that the denial of neolithic status may be unjustified. Actually flint celts with polished blades were found at Mariupol together with stone beads and bracelets and a variety of ornaments carved out of wild beasts' teeth and boars' tusks. Two skeletons were accompanied by knobbed mace-heads (cf. Fig. 65), interpreted as emblems of chieftainship. A female figurine of stone lay in one grave at Nalčik, and pottery in others. However these communities got their food, they were not economically isolated. A pendant of porphyry imported from the Urals occurred at Mariupol; a copper lock-ring and beads of 'vitreous paste' and carnelian at Nalčik. The last-named ornaments are explicitly results of connection with Oriental civilization, and even the knobbed maces from Mariupol may be thus interpreted, since the type was common in Mesopotamia from Early Dynastic times.

The burials just described recall most strikingly those of mesolithic Natufians in the Wad cave on Mount Carmel, but agree in several points also with those of neolithic hunter-fishers on Gotland and on Olenii Island in Lake Onega. They are not for these reasons necessarily earlier than the single burials, sometimes accompanied by metal objects, under the commoner round barrows. Indeed, knobbed mace-heads father west are Danubian III or Balkan III (p. 164). On the other hand, microliths are found in Early Kuban barrows.

The earliest food-producers detectable on the steppes in South Russia are those buried under round barrows in the *yamno* graves. In these, remains of domestic animals – only sheep have been recorded – are exceptional, while bones of game, flint arrow-heads, and bone harpoons do attest hunting and fishing.

Finds from domestic sites,[10] however, prove that cows, sheep, goats, and probably horses and pigs were bred and millet cultivated. The stock-breeders were interred, thickly sprinkled with red ochre, lying on a bier or bed of rushes on the back with the legs drawn up or more rarely extended, sometimes in a tent-shaped mortuary house,[11] at the bottom of the shaft, which was roofed with birch poles resting on ledges in the sides (as in the Shaft Graves of Mycenae).[12] In the Ukraine, rudely anthropomorphic stelae covered some graves.[13]

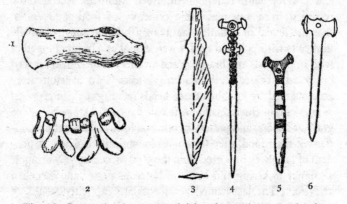

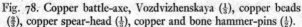

Fig. 78. Copper battle-axe, Vozdvizhenskaya ($\frac{1}{5}$), copper beads ($\frac{2}{3}$), copper spear-head ($\frac{1}{3}$), copper and bone hammer-pins ($\frac{1}{2}$).

In no grave does much furniture survive – at best a pot, some hunting or fishing tackle, necklaces of bored teeth and – only in the latest graves – a hammer-headed pin of bone (Fig. 78, 5–6).[14] The pot, if present, is an ovoid beaker, often plain, sometimes decorated with pits below the inturned rim or even with cord impressions[15] (Fig. 79, 4).

A lucky chance has revealed dramatically how unreliable negative conclusions, based on the inevitable deficiencies of the archaeological record, may be. Under a large barrow of the period, 'Storozhevaya', near Dniepropetrovsk[16] an exceptional conjuncture has preserved remains of a wooden cart with two solid wheels, 48 cm in diameter, that served as a hearse. It demonstrates at once that wheeled vehicles were used by the steppe folk, that these had not only domesticated but also harnessed oxen – or conceivably horses – and that they recognized chiefs who enjoyed the privileges of Sumerian kings.

On the slopes of the Caucasus such chiefs secured more substantial emblems and instruments of authority. A celebrated barrow near Maikop[17] is representative of the eleven rich 'royal burials' that constitute Yessen's group I. The tomb was a tri-

Fig. 79. Vases: 1, from Catacomb grave, Donetz ($\frac{1}{3}$); 2–3, from pit-graves, Yatskovice, near Kiev ($\frac{1}{6}$); 4, from *yamno* grave Donetz basin ($\frac{1}{4}$); 5, B funnel-beaker from Denmark ($\frac{1}{4}$).

partite wooden chamber in a deep shaft encircled by a ring of boulders. A prince had been buried in the main chamber under a canopy adorned with gold and silver lions and bulls. A male and a female corpse occupied the remaining compartments, less richly furnished, but all the bodies were covered with red ochre. The royal weapons (Fig. 80) include a transverse axe, certainly, and a straight axe together with an axe-adze[18] that looks like a combination of the other two, but also rhomboid arrow-heads of flint and microlithic lunates of mesolithic ancestry. A gold flask with a silver ring round the neck, jars of silver and of stone, and imitations in reduced grey pottery are certainly Asiatic.

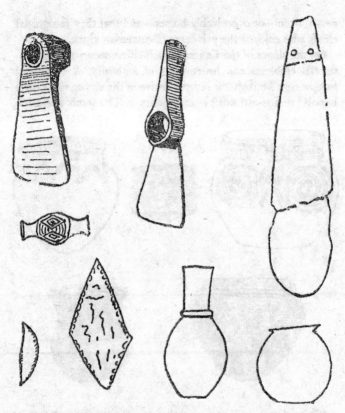

Fig. 80. Transverse axe, axe-adze, knife, and gold and silver vases ($\frac{1}{4}$), carnelian bead and flint arrow-heads (1), from Maikop barrow.

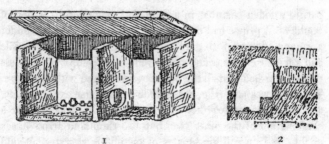

1

2

Fig. 81. 1, Megalithic cist, Novosvobodnaya; 2, Catacomb grave, Donetz basin.

Beads of turquoise and lapis lazuli had been imported from Iran, meerschaum[19] from Anatolia. Two silver vases are engraved with local mountain scenes and a procession of animals – two kinds of ox, a mouflon, a tame boar, Przewalski's horse, and a panther.

Yessen's second and rather less homogenous chronological division within the Early Kuban period is represented by the furniture of the tombs in two huge cairns at Novosvobodnaya (generally but incorrectly termed Tsarevskaya).[20] Both were megalithic cists divided into two compartments by porthole slabs (Fig. 81, 1). Cist II measured internally 1·80 m+1·15 m by 1·60 m by 1·20 m, and was surrounded by a ring of orthostats over a metre high. The princely dead, one wearing a linen garment, dyed red and purple, a cloak of camel's wool covered with a black hide and profusely sprinkled with red ochre, were provided with shaft-hole axes, bidents, spear-heads, cauldrons, ladles, wands, and drill bits of copper, together with flint arrowheads and globular clay vases (Fig. 82). The spear-head is directly derived from an Early Sumerian type and the bident and gouge have an equally Early Sumerian pedigree, but exact parallels to them and to the ladles, perhaps also to the wand, can be cited from Hissar III[21] in Northern Iran. The pottery, on the contrary, undoubtedly resembles the Central Russian Fatyanovo ware and the Globular Amphorae of Central Europe (pp. 215, 240).

A dozen other burials are assigned to this second phase of the Early Kuban period and enlarge the repertory of types attributable to it. They include battle-axes[22] both in copper (Fig. 78, 1) and stone and probably a clay model of a covered cart[23]; the latter, if really Early Kuban, demonstrates the use of wheeled vehicles and ox traction on the slopes of the Caucasus as on the steppes.

Yessen[24] insists that none of the metal ware from any Early Kuban tomb is a local North Caucasian product; all are imports or loot from more advanced regions south of the range. By the Middle Kuban period resident or itinerant smiths were producing local types of tools, weapons, and ornaments, and Oriental imports have disappeared.

The North Caucasian smiths manufactured flat axes, chisels[25] with an incomplete socket, made by folding the butt end round a mandril, flat daggers the tang of which expands for the

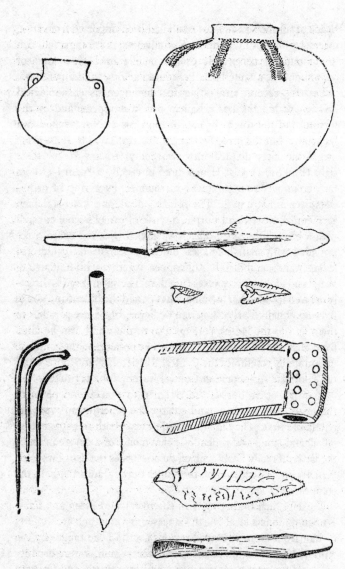

Fig. 82. Pottery ($\frac{1}{6}$), weapons and tools ($\frac{1}{2}$), and pins ($\frac{1}{3}$) from tomb at Novosvobodnaya.

pommel,[26] shaft-hole axes with a drooping shaft-hole and long narrow body, and ornaments – including elaborate versions of the hammer-pin (Fig. 78, 4) – on which filigree work has been ingeniously imitated by *cire perdue* casting. Most of these types recur farther north in the catacomb and contemporary shaft graves. Their extension suggests that the rich copper resources of the Urals were now being exploited. Querns, pestles, flint sickle-teeth,[27] and animal bones attest a regular farming economy to support the metal-workers and the chiefs.

On the Caucasian foothills, south of the Kuban and the Terek, the Middle Kuban graves are more varied and more numerous than the Early Kuban. None are so obviously 'royal' as those described above, but many must belong to small chiefs. The catacomb graves that define a contemporary local culture extending from near Odessa to the valleys of the Donets, Don, Manyč, and Upper Kuban-Terek and just into Daghestan (Fig. 81, 2) are really pit-caves under barrows. Most contain only a single corpse, but some served as family tombs housing as many as seven persons. There is explicit evidence of one or even two females having been slain to accompany their lords.[28] Round-headed persons now appear and these perhaps practised annular deformation of the skull.[29]

Additions to armaments peculiar to the catacomb graves are heeled battle-axes,[30] like Fig. 35, arrow-shaft straighteners, and sling bullets. The pottery, distinctive of the period, is represented by flat-bottomed vases profusely decorated with the imprints of cords, whipped or braided cords, and shells sometimes forming spiral patterns (Fig. 79, 1).[31] Peculiar to the Manyč and Kuban-Terek group of catacomb graves are cruciform-footed lamps – shallow saucers, divided into two unequal compartments and standing on four solid and united feet. They are richly decorated in the style of the period.

Other characteristic pots and catacomb types recur in shaft graves in several regions. On the Lower Volga, one grave probably of this period under a very large barrow contained no less than three carts with tripartite disc wheels, while a clay model of a covered cart lay in an 'offering place' above the shaft mouth.[32]

The catacomb type of tomb and its distribution suggest Aegean inspiration. Cranial deformation had been practised in

Cyprus from neolithic times.[33] A few beads of 'paste', presumably fayence, reported from catacomb tombs and copper imitations of winged beads (Fig. 78, 2) might be derived from the same quarter. A hoard of metal objects from Četkovo near the mouth of the Dniepr,[34] probably assignable to this period, comprises double-axes, presumably of Minoan or Helladic manufacture. Conversely, the unfinished battle-axe from the Early Macednic site of H. Mamas (p. 106) belongs to a distinctively South Russian family first appearing in the catacomb phase. On the other hand, the cross-footed lamps are absurdly like Starčevo forms from Moldavia and Hungary (Fig. 46) and still more the later Vučedol type. Moreover, the 'pit-caves' of the Vučedo culture at Vučedol are rather like catacomb graves.

But if the chiefs of the pastoral clans were imitating the fashions of Aegean colonists of the Black Sea coasts, nothing of precise dating value has come from their tombs. The battle-axe from H. Mamas alone could be invoked to justify a partial synchronism between the Middle Kuban-Catacomb period and the Early Aegean.

The actual Oriental imports in the Early Kuban tombs are not incompatible with such a dating, but are all too long-lived to confirm it. The transverse axe from Maikop is a type of undoubtedly Mesopotamian origin, but was current from 3000 B.C. for nearly two millennia.[35] The type was being cast in clay moulds at Shah Tepe in Transcaspia,[36] while axe-adzes of the Maikop variant were being similarly manufactured in the contemporary settlement of Hissar III.[37] The grey ware from Maikop likewise recalls Iranian fabrics of the Hissar III phase. There too the ladles, bidents, and drill-bit from Novosvobodnaya can be paralleled,[38] but just as well in the Early Sumerian metalwork of Ur. Only the hammer-pins are more illuminating, for the type is comparatively rare. In Anatolia, gold specimens occur in the Royal Tombs of Alaca,[39] at Ahlatlibel, in Troy IIf., and in the Middle Helladic Greece. Moreover, bone hammer-pins have been found in a Danish passage grave of Northern IIIc and in Central European graves of Danubian III or IV. In time the Pontic pins should come at least between the Anatolian and the Central European examples.

Now the rare gold pins from the treasures of Anatolian princes may well be luxury versions of a Pontic type. If so, their absolute date – certainly about 2000 B.C. – is a *terminus ante quem* for the creation of the type in South Russia. Hammer-pins are not attested before the Middle Kuban phase in Cis-Caucasia and mark the end of the *yamno* period of the steppes. Thus the beginnings of the Ochre Grave culture should go back well into the third millennium. So too *yamno* graves in Eastern Poland had been dug before the dry Sub-Boreal climate had promoted the formation of black earth.

Only in the light of these chronological considerations can possible contributions from the Steppe societies to the development of European culture farther west be evaluated. That they did really transmit ideas westward is proved by the hammer-pins just mentioned and by the animal sceptre-heads from Romania (p. 144); one of these came from an ochre grave in the Dobrudja[40] and there is another from Cis-Caucasia.[41] Yet early Central European metallurgy cannot be proved to owe anything to the Caucasian school. To derive the great family of Transylvanian axe-adzes from the single Maikop specimen seems far-fetched. Nor are the later Hungarian shaft-tube axes obviously related to the Maikop-Novosvobodnaya type and its Middle Kuban derivatives. Even at Usatova no types are distinctively Caucasian, and at Mikhaïlovka metal had been worked in the first settlement perhaps before makers of *yamno* pots arrived there in the third.

Wheeled vehicles, horses, and even sheep are in a different category. Genuine ochre graves under round barrows in Romania, Eastern Slovakia,[42] and Eastern Poland[43] do attest infiltrations of herdsmen from the steppes into the zone of temperate forest. But the position of these graves in the Danubian sequence is still undetermined. Farther west cord-ornamented pots from barrow-burials[44] and globular amphorae from porthole cists have been claimed at once as indications of a wider expansion and as proofs that the steppe folk themselves came from Germany!

For the moment it will suffice to insist that there is no evidence for an origin in Central Asia. Relations can indeed be traced right to the Yenesei. There the earliest steppe culture, termed

Afanasievo,[45] is characterized by ovoid vases resembling those from European *yamno* graves; but they seem later, being accompanied by *catacomb* types; and they accompany skeletons of Europeoid type. At the same time the ovoid *yamno* pots are strikingly like those made by the hunter-fisher folk of the Eurasian taiga from the Baltic to Lake Baikal. But these hunter-fishers were mostly Lapponoid, the Steppe herdsmen Europeoid.

Battle-Axe Cultures

All the cultures that emerge round the fringe of the territories colonized by Dniestro-Danubian peasants on the wooded North European plain from the Middle Dniepr to the Lower Rhine exhibit so many common features that they may be designated by a single name, Battle-axe cultures. That does not imply that all are branches of a single culture. By divergences in burial rites, armament, and pottery we may distinguish a number of cultures, of which the most important are: (1) the Single Grave culture of Jutland with relatives in North-West Germany and Holland; (2) the Swedish Boat-axe culture with extensions east of the Baltic; (3) the Saxo-Thuringian or 'Classical' Corded Ware culture; (4) the Oder culture; (5) the Middle Dniepr culture; and (6) the Fatyanovo groups in Central Russia.

All these cultures were based primarily on stock-breeding and hunting, but always combined with cereal cultivation. In all groups at least the earliest graves contain a single skeleton[46] buried in the contracted position. Timber linings to the grave pit have been observed in groups 1, 2, 3, and 6. Save in groups 2, 4, and 6, the grave was normally surmounted by a barrow. Grave goods common to all groups include stone battle-axes, necklaces of bored teeth, and a pottery drinking-vessel that may be termed a beaker and that may everywhere be ornamented with cord-impressions. All the battle-axes in this series are characterized by drooping blades – that is the blade expands only downwards in contrast to the symmetrical splay of Baden and polygonal battle-axes. Though each group is distinguished by peculiar local types, in nearly every area are to be found specimens of a simple type, like a stone version of Fig. 63, 1, and at least in Jutland these are stratigraphically, as well as typologically, the oldest.[47] Finally, on all early drooping-bladed battle-axes a longitudinal ridge imitates the seam of a casting and reinforces the metallic impression given by the splayed blade though the original model were antler.[48]

North Sea–Baltic Battle-Axe Cultures

Towards the western extension of the plain between the Vistula and the Rhine the pastoral societies represented by barrow cemeteries were juxtaposed to and contrasted with more sedentary farmers. After such farmers had already reached Denmark, a herding group who sometimes decorated their funnel-beakers (Fig. 79, 5) with cord imprints had cleared tracts of Denmark and Southern Sweden for pasture in Late Atlantic times. They do not seem to have settled permanently, since forests soon returned and smothered the pastures they had cleared.[49] A second and more drastic clearance by fire was made in Jutland, and this time no regeneration of forest followed.[50] A new wave of herdsmen had colonized Jutland, and their free-grazing stock ate up the young tree seedlings. Archaeologically these graziers are known only by little cemeteries of barrows, and so they are termed the Single Grave folk.

In Jutland the Single Grave folk[51] replaced all remnants of the Gudenaa hunter-fishers and came to occupy the interior of the peninsula to the exclusion of the Megalith-builders, but never engaged in that commerce the results of which allow the several phases of Megalithic culture to be arranged in the general scheme of prehistoric chronology. Contact between the two groups was, however, sufficiently frequent to allow the chronology for the Northern Stone Age, set forth on p. 222, to be applied also to the Battle-axe cultures. A reliable chronology of these cultures' own development can in turn be based upon successive interments under the same barrow, as on the Pontic steppes.

The oldest graves (Bottom Graves or Undergrave), timber-lined pits[52] dug in virgin soil and designed to hold a single contracted corpse, contain the finest battle-axes (often very metallic looking) and beakers with an S profile decorated with cord imprints round the neck (Fig. 83). Next, in graves on the ground surface (Ground Graves or Bundgrave), large enough to hold an extended skeleton, the axes deteriorate and the beakers are decorated with incised herring-bones. Finally, the Upper Graves (Overgrave) in the body of the mound contain flower-pot vases decorated with rouletted zig-zags, degenerate axes, and even flint daggers such as are found in the latest megalithic tombs. They denote the fusion of the two cultures, with that of the Battle-axe folk triumphant.

The furniture of the Upper Graves shows that the latest phase of the Battle-axe culture in Denmark falls into Northern period IV. The prior development represented by only two or three interments in the same barrow cannot cover a vast number of years – indeed perhaps only three generations. But it begins already during Northern IIIb or IIIc.[53]

In Sweden[54] separate graves containing contracted skeletons, but not surmounted by barrows, are contrasted to the collective tombs of the agricultural megalith-builders and to the extended burials of a native food-gathering population. They are furnished at first with battle-axes, gouges of flint or greenstone, facetted polishing stones, and shallow beakers decorated round the neck with cord imprints. The battle-axes (Fig. 83), termed boat-axes, are always provided with a shaft-tube which gives them a very metallic look. Indeed, a copper boat-axe was found in East Russia, but the tube might be suggested by the tine stump through which the shaft-hole of some antler axes has been bored. Pottery of this type has been found associated with that in vogue about the middle of the Passage Grave phase (Northern IIIc), while later graves containing rouletted vases like the bottom row in Fig. 83 admittedly belong to Northern IV. Very similar graves with just the same kind of battle-axes are found in Norway[55] and on the opposite coasts of the Baltic in Esthonia and Finland. The distribution of these graves, confined to South-Western Finland with a sharp frontier between them and the encampments of the native hunter-fishers, leaves no doubt that the Boat-axe folk were intruders.[56]

On the heathlands of North-West Germany and Holland[57] many barrows (two dated by radiocarbon to 2480 and 2240 B.C.) covering Single Graves reveal an extension of the Battle-axe cultures to the English Channel. Many barrows are demarcated by a ring of upright posts; some, that may belong to period IV, cover small mortuary houses[58] and so may rank as chieftains' tombs. The earlier graves are furnished with battle-axes akin to Jutland types, but less finely worked, and S beakers, bearing cord or herring-bone ornament, and exceptionally also with

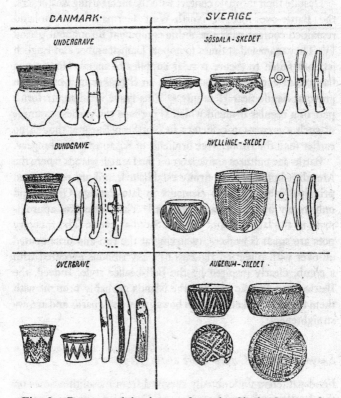

Fig. 83. Pottery and battle-axes from the Single Graves of Jutland (left) and Sweden (right). After *Fv*, 1922 ($\frac{1}{10}$).

amphorae of Saxo-Thuringian form. But the Battle-axe folk here came into contact with local Megalith-builders (p. 239) and Bell-beaker folk from the west and developed hybrid cultures. S beakers are not seldom found with the later burials in megalithic tombs; from the Bell-beaker group the Battle-axe folk took over their bow and the wrist-guards appropriate thereto and even adopted the roulette technique for ornamenting their beakers and spread the designs in zones over the whole vase-surface in the style regularly applied on Bell-beakers. Nevertheless, the Battle-axe component remained dominant in the resultant fusion.

Despite their intimate contact with the metal-using westerners, the Battle-axe folk in North-West Germany and Holland remained content with a neolithic equipment throughout period IV. They managed at times to import Danish amber and English jet, but failed to secure regular supplies of metal. However, a flat axe of copper was found with an S beaker in a cremation grave at Sande near Hamburg.[59] This grave incidentally forms part of a regular urnfield which is perhaps the earliest example of such a cremation cemetery in Northern Europe, though no earlier than the Bronze Age urnfields of Kisapostag in Hungary.

Battle-axe cultures arrive later on the Danish islands where the Megalith-builders were firmly established, and are represented principally by intrusive elements in late Passage Graves and only rarely by true separate graves.[60] The battle-axes approximate to the later Jutland or even Swedish types. The funerary pots are squat S beakers, recurving at the rim and ornamented all over with rouletted zig-zags or wavy ribbons executed with a comb, clearly inspired by the Bell-beaker style. Indeed, the Battle-axe folk who reached the islands probably brought with them the Bell-beaker culture's bows and wrist-guards and arrow-straighteners.

Saxo-Thuringian Corded Ware and its Congeners

Food-gatherers undoubtedly survived from mesolithic times on the heaths and boulder clays of Central Germany and on the sandy lands farther east fringing and interrupting the löss. But here Battle-axe cutlures represent neither the first food-producers – those were the Danubians (pp. 147, 161) – nor yet the sole result of the acculturation of residual food-gatherers or of the internal development of Danubian society itself. The most important – the *Saxo-Thuringian* to whose pottery alone the term Corded Ware was originally applied – emerges in Central

Germany and Bohemia as only one among several groups, all more pastoral and more warlike than any Danubians.

Its distinctive cemeteries of barrows or flat graves are concentrated in the Saale basin, but extend south-east into Central Bohemia and westward to the Rhineland and even Central Switzerland. While common enough on the löss, Saxo-Thuringian barrows are still more prominent on heaths and uplands, as if hunting and stock-breeding had been the foundations of the economy. Yet the cemeteries are too extensive to belong to

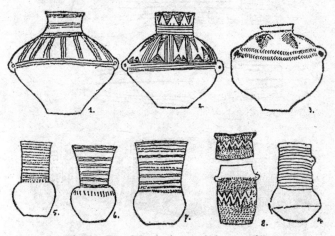

Fig. 84. Saxo-Thuringian corded ware ($\frac{1}{10}$).

nomads, and grain imprints on vases[61] prove some sort of cultivation.

Characteristic of Saxo-Thuringian corded ware is the conjunction of amphorae (Fig. 84, 1–3) with the usual beakers which here have an ovoid body contrasted with a long straight neck (Fig. 84, 4–7). Ornament is effected, as usual, on the earlier vases by cord impressions which then later give place to stamped herring-bone patterns (Fig. 84, 3). Equally distinctive is the faceted battle-axe (Fig. 85, 1), though this is not often found in graves and then not with the earliest pottery.[62] Its peculiar form may show some influence from spiked club-heads[63] of mesolithic ancestry (the Vögtland type), but stray copper battle-axes

209

exhibit much the same form[64] and the influence of antler weapons is admitted. Actual antler axes, asymmetrical stone axes like Danubian 'ploughshares', almond-shaped celts of flint or greenstone mounted as adzes (one was found thus mounted in an antler haft) and occasional spheroid mace-heads or rough flint daggers also served as weapons.

Small rings of copper and even spirals of poor bronze sometimes served as ornaments. But though these were allegedly

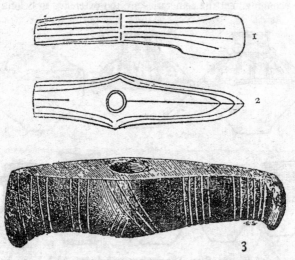

Fig. 85. 1 and 2, Thuringian faceted battle-axe ($\frac{1}{3}$); 3, Silesian battle-axe ($\frac{1}{2}$).

made from local ores,[65] the Saxo-Thuringians remained content with a neolithic equipment and armoury. The best evidences for trade of any kind are a carving in Sammland style and a few other amber beads. Discs made from local shells but ornamented with a cross[66] constitute the most distinctive additions to the usual bored-teeth necklaces. One man, buried with a herring-bone beaker and a tanged copper spear-head or dagger, had worn a hammer pin of Pontic type as a head ornament.[67]

Normally the Saxo-Thuringians were interred in simple pit graves, rarely in wood-lined shafts, by no means always covered by barrows. North of the Unstrut, modest megalithic cists, measuring up to 3·5 m. by 2·25 m., were often used as collective sepulchres.[68] The practice was presumably borrowed from adjacent Northern or Horgen megalith-builders (p. 235), but might have been inspired from the Kuban[69] since some are divided by a porthole slab as in Fig. 81, 1. Trephined skulls occur in both Central German and Bohemian graves. In some tombs, mostly late and more often in Western than in Central Germany, the bodies have been burned. Exceptionally the cremated remains lay in wooden mortuary houses.[70] The latter prove that some Saxo-Thuringian groups were led by chiefs and that the herdsmen lived in substantial houses with at least a porch in addition to a living-room.

The later phases of the Saxo-Thuringian culture admittedly last into period IV, and grave-groups[71] establish synchronisms with Globular Amphorae and Walternienburg 2 in period III. A beginning in period II might be deduced from corded ware sherds in Danubian village-sites and faceted battle-axes associated in hoards with shoe-last celts, but the associations are not very reliable.

Westward, burials under barrows accompanied by corded beakers and amphorae and faceted battle-axes document an extension of Saxo-Thuringian culture to the Rhine. Beyond it in Switzerland, in the latest occupation levels of the neolithic Alpine lake-dwellings, sherds of corded ware mark the replacement of the Middle Neolithic Horgen population or the superposition thereon of a pastoral aristocracy such as we met at Usatova. Eastward, too, barrow-burials if accompanied by cord-ornamented vases that could be derived from amphorae like Fig. 84, 1–3, are likewise attributed to colonists from Saxo-Thuringia. So in Sammland[72] are graves furnished with amphorae and beakers, and in a couple of cases with bone hammer-pins, while at least three faceted battle-axes are reported from the province. Here corded ware is found also in the substantial houses of farmers who combined cultivation and the breeding of cattle, sheep, and pigs with hunting, fowling, and fishing with bone harpoons.[73] But with the supposedly Saxo-Thuringian pots go other vases that may represent an East Baltic version of the Ertebølle or First Northern culture.

On the Polish löss lands within the great elbow of the Vistula, already intensively colonized by Danubians by period II, corded beakers and amphorae are associated with Oder flower-pots, handled cups, funnel-necked beakers, and globular amphorae that elsewhere denote distinct groups, in the *Złota culture* (Fig. 86).[74] Extensive cemeteries of contracted skeletons, generally in flat graves, sometimes in pit-caves, mark the population as sedentary. Ritual burials of cattle, pigs, and horses demonstrate

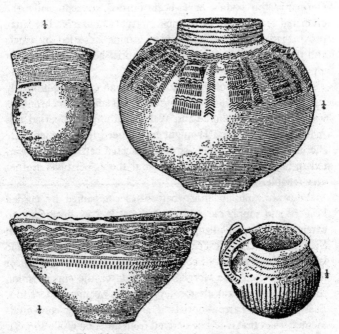

Fig. 86. Złota pottery. After Kozłowski.

the economic importance of these domestic animals. Battle-axes are not very often included among the grave goods, but such as occur are typologically early.

In Eastern Moravia [75] one barrow at Němetice covered a shaft grave containing an amphora and a beaker, and another barrow one furnished with a faceted battle-axe. But other graves here, as also at Drevohostice and Prusinovice, contained battle-axes of Silesian type (Fig. 85, 3) and keeled mugs with cylindrical necks and strap handles derived from the Jordanova group; others again Bell-beakers.

Then in East Galicia[76] some barrows, girt with a circular trench and heaped after the black earth's formation – and therefore later than those mentioned on p. 213 above – cover graves containing corded amphorae and beakers and copper trinkets. So do the flat graves of the Tomaszów culture[77] forming large cemeteries and representing a sedentary population extending across the Carpathians into the Nitra valley of Slovakia.[78] These burials are furnished with segmented fayence beads like those from the Tisza-Maros region (p. 171) and occasional round-heeled triangular daggers. The Tomaszów cemeteries therefore extend over period IV.

Still farther east the corded ware from Usatova (p. 191) has been claimed as evidence that the pastoral aristocracy there superimposed on Tripolye peasants was of Saxo-Thuringian extraction! Even the Middle Dniepr culture[79] has been regarded as an offshoot of the Saxo-Thuringian. 'Amphorae' do no doubt occur in the urnfield of Sofiivka[80]; among the grave goods associated with 141 cremations are also stone battle-axes, flat axes and daggers of copper, flint celts and sickles, and vases painted in late Tripolye style (as at Usatova). Barrows of this culture, however, do not seem to have contained amphorae; the beakers are sometimes ovoid as in *yamno* graves (Fig. 79, 3), more often basket-shaped (Fig. 79, 2).

The Oder and Marschwitz Cultures

On the other hand, between these alleged outposts of Saxo-Thuringian culture and its centre on the Saale-Elbe intervene other groups distinguished by corded ware and battle-axes of quite different forms. The *Oder* culture in Brandenburg shares with the Saxo-Thuringian the usual beaker, but is distinguished by the absence of amphorae and the presence of cylindrical 'flower-pot' vases, sometimes with ledge-handles.[81] Such are found in pit graves, occasionally under barrows and at least once containing red ochre, but also in slab cists of Central German type. Other grave goods include small battle-axes, flint adzes with a pointed-oval cross-section, and Danubian 'ploughshares' as in Saxo-Thuringia. While occasionally associated with Globular Amphorae or Walternienburg 3–5 pottery (p.

239), a few bronze ornaments and Scandinavian flint daggers [82] show that the Oder culture lasted well into period IV.

In the *Marschwitz culture* of Silesia and Moravia this persistence is more amply demonstrated. The graves contain flower-pots of Oder form, but these are accompanied by pouched jugs, decorated with cord-impressions, but of early Unětice shapes (Fig. 72, 1). With them go battle-axes made of Sobotka serpentine [83] (Fig. 85, 3), rather like the Fatyanovo form but also wrist-guards, derived from the Beaker folk, and even bronze ornaments. The whole group occupies economically as well as geographically an intermediate position between the Bronze Age Unětician culture of Bohemia and the still neolithic culture of the middle and lower Oder.

The Fatyanovo Culture [84]

In the forest zone of Central Russia the first reliable indications of the neolithic economy are afforded by bones of domestic cattle, swine, sheep, goats, and horses, and grain-rubbers from graves of the Fatyanovo cycle of cultures. These have been divided into three local groups which differ in age as well as in spatial distribution, by Kritsova-Grakova. [85] The earliest is the Moscow group on the Oka and Kliazma, next the Yaroslav group on the Upper Volga to which the eponymous cemetery belongs. The Čuvaš group on the lower Kama near the confluence of that river and the Oka with the Volga should begin latest.

The graves, never surmounted by barrows and normally containing one contracted skeleton, rarely a male and female together, occasionally cremations, [86] form cemeteries of half a dozen to a score, and occur both in the low-lying basins, long occupied by the hunter-fishers, and also on the uplands right to the Volga-Oka watershed, where the gatherers had never settled. This extension is itself a symbol of the new economy since the uplands are better suited to tillage and grazing than the chilly vales, [87] but it was possible only with aid of the polished flint celts that occur alike in men's and women's graves, [88] since the new territory was densely wooded. At the same time bones of pike and teeth of bear, wolf, fox, lynx, and reindeer, as well as shells, used for ornaments, attest a persistence of the old economy of the Forest.

But now cattle-raising provided a prize for more serious warfare than the hunter-fishers had indulged in, and so the graves are furnished with an armoury of weapons strange to the older forest dwelling-places. Stone battle-axes accompany every male interment. The finest, the classical Fatyanovo axes (Fig. 87, 1)

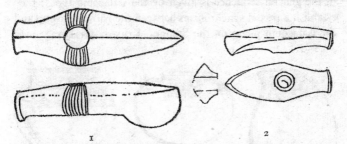

Fig. 87. Fatyanovo battle-axe and Finnish boat-axe ($\frac{1}{3}$).

are confined to the Yaroslav group; some of the rest can be treated as degenerations of these,[89] but at least one, from the Trusovo cemetery in the Moscow[90] group, belongs to the heeled type proper to the Catacomb culture of the steppes. Another grave contained a pair of arrow-shaft straighteners,[91] yet another a Pontic hammer-pin. In chieftains' graves in the Yaroslav and Čuvaš groups copper shaft-hole axes accompany or replace the stone weapons, but miniature clay battle-axes were buried with children in the Yaroslav group.[92]

Flint strike-a-lights with tinder too were sometimes[93] buried with the dead. Perforated clay discs, some 5·5 cm. in diameter,[94] are doubtless model wheels and attest familiarity with wheeled vehicles.

The numerous pots tend to be globular, provided with flat bases, sometimes ornamented, and distinct necks, but never with handles; so none could be called an amphora! In the Moscow group early vases are ornamented with cord impressions (Fig. 88, 1); elsewhere combs or other stamps were used.

Peaceful if irregular commerce brought the Fatyanovo warriors occasional amber beads,[95] silver earrings, disc-pendants, lock-rings, cuff armlets, and neck-rings of copper.

In the Vaulovo cemetery two rich graves, each containing male and female skeletons buried together and furnished with copper shaft-hole axes, surely belong to chieftains. Graves in the same cemetery, containing respectively the skeleton of a boar and that of a kid, suggest to Kraĭnov [96] the totems of two clans.

A clue to the relative position of the Central Russian cultures in the general sequence is given by the Catacomb types; they establish a partial synchronism between the Moscow group and the Catacomb phase on the Steppes. Kritsova-Grakova [97] uses

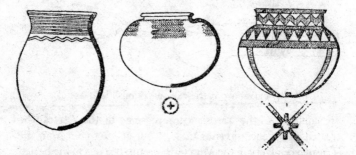

Fig. 88. Fatyanovo pottery of the Moscow, Yaroslav, and Čuvaš groups.

the cuff-armlets from Mytiščensk to establish a synchronism between the Yaroslav group and Unětice; though the agreement is not exact, Danubian IV should be an upper limit for the Yaroslav group.

The copper axes from the Yaroslav cemeteries approximate closely to those included in the hoards found at Seima and Galič [98] (Fig. 89). These presumably represent southern imports intercepted by the Fatyanovo population that must have controlled the fur trade so important in the first millennium B.C. But both hoards contain types that would be more appropriate to the *srubno* phase in the Pontic sequence. But by that time the Čuvaš version of the Fatyanovo culture was developing into the fully metal-using Abaševo culture.

Bader and other Russian prehistorians [99] in the thirties regarded the Fatyanovo culture as a development of the native culture of local hunter-fishers to exploit the new sources of food made available by the introduction of cereals and domestic stock. These were admittedly introduced from outside into the woodland zone of Central Russia. Anthropometric studies of the Fatyanovo populations by Trofimova[100] have subsequently shown that the cultivators and stock-breeders themselves must be immigrants; for the skulls, Europeoid or Mediterranean, are in sharp contrast to those of the autochthonous hunter-fishers,

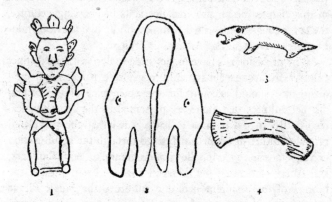

Fig. 89. The Galič hoard, 1–4 ($\frac{1}{3}$).

which are Lapponoid. Briusov[101] proposes to derive the Moscow group at least from the Middle Dniepr culture. But, after all, the origin of the latter is not at all clear, and Briusov himself admits the possibility of a more western origin for the Yaroslav group. German and many other Western prehistorians, emphasizing – and perhaps exaggerating – the similarities of the classic Fatyanovo pots to Saxo-Thuringian and Globular Amphorae, have thence deduced an invasion of Central Russia by warriors from Central Germany, Scandinavia, or Sammland.[102] But of course the Fatyanovo cultures are not mere transplantations of any one of the known western or southern Battle-axe cultures and 'amphorae' are not necessarily derived from Saxo-Thuringia. The Fatyanovo battle-axes derive from East Poland.[103]

The cultures of several peoples that in historical times spoke Indo-European languages could plausibly be derived from those described in the preceding pages. The list could be further enlarged if cord-ornamented sherds from Greece, Macedonia, and Thrace (pp. 110, 137), and battle-axes from Troy and the Caucasus were accepted as evidence for kindred cultures in the Balkans and Anatolia. Hence, if the several cultures considered in this chapter be all provincial variants of one single culture, the latter could be identified with that of the hypothetical Indo-European parent stock, 'Aryans' or 'Wiros'.

Many prehistorians have in fact tried to derive all the distinct cultures from one primary culture whose expansion and local divergence should account for the emergence of the several distinct cultures that alone are presented in the archaeological record. By 1910 Kossinna[104] had argued that the postulated primary culture developed in Jutland through the acculturation of Maglemosians by Ertebølle immigrants and megalith-builders, and Åberg elaborated his thesis in 1918.[105] From Jutland the bearers of the resultant neolithic culture – the Single Grave culture – would have spread across Central Europe to the Aegean and the Caucasus.

Danish prehistorians, however, are unanimous in regarding the Single Grave culture as intrusive in Jutland. Even German prehistorians, since the 'Versailles Diktat' detached South Jutland from the Reich, have preferred to transfer the cradle of the Single Grave and other Battle-axe cultures, and so of the Indo-Europeans, to the more thoroughly Germanic soil of Saxo-Thuringia![106] There should be the focus from which the warriors radiated not only to the Balkans and the Ukraine but also to Sweden, Denmark, and Switzerland!

On the contrary, near fifty years ago J. L. Myres suggested reversing Kossinna's migrations and deriving the Single Grave, Saxo-Thuringian, and other Battle-axe cultures from the Pontic steppes. Borkovskij[107] pointed out how well the ovoid beakers from *yamno* graves could serve as prototypes for the Central and North European vases. Forssander[108] inclined to think that the makers of Globular Amphorae (below, pp. 241–2), coming from the Caucasus and bringing with them the idea of the porthole cist, affected the development of the Central and North European cultures, which would still have been rooted in the Saxo-Thuringian. The discovery of Pontic hammer-pins in a Danish passage grave of Northern IIIc and in more or less contemporary Corded Ware graves in Central Europe and Sammland, has provided some concrete, if by no means conclusive, evidence in favour of a Pontic origin. Still the Ochre Grave culture, the oldest concretely recognizable on the steppes, on the one hand does not exhibit even in germ all the distinctive traits common to the Battle-axe cultures, and on the other hand contains elements not replicated in any of them. In a word, the Pontic steppes can offer a concrete ancestor for all no more than Jutland or Saxo-Thuringia.

A satisfactory explanation of the distribution of our battle-axes, of cord-ornamented vases, and of amphorae decorated like Figs, 42 and 84 in Central Europe, Central Russia, Greece, and the Troad, would be provided by Sulimirski's postulate of an early herding culture in the woodlands between the Vistula and the Upper Dniepr. The hypothetical cattle-breeders would, Sulimirski[109] suggests, have used wood-and-leather vessels that, translated into clay, assumed the form and decoration of the amphorae. They expanded first to Central Russia, the East Baltic, and the Eastern Balkans, but to Jutland and Saxo-Thuringia only after adopting the practice of barrow-burial from Ochre Grave pastoralists who had advanced as far west as the headwaters of the Vistula, if not farther (p. 203). The main defect of Sulimirski's account is that the assumed East Polish–Byelo-russian culture is still not directly documented archaeologically. But, after all, such documentation will be hard to find (p. 193), and the presumptive cradle-land is virtually unexplored.

Marxist prehistorians in the U.S.S.R. have rejected any explanation of the agreements between the several Battle-axe cultures in terms of migration or conquest. They would result from parallel or convergent developments of local societies in accordance with general laws of social-economic progress. In temperate Europe, with a neolithic equipment, pastoralism combined with hunting was the most productive rural economy, and with pastoralism are associated a patriarchal social organization, differentiation of status, and warfare. The Battle-axe cultures would represent 'pastoral tribes separated out from the mass of agricultural barbarians'. In a remarkable article Kričevskii[110] showed how many of the features of the Battle-axe cultures of Danubian III – even cord ornament on vases and ochre in graves – were explicitly foreshadowed in Danubian cemeteries and settlements of the preceding period. Some such account has the incomparable advantage of economy; it makes minimal draughts on undemonstrable assumptions and undocumented entities. It is not incompatible with the belief that 'the battle-axe' – i.e. the copper translation of an antler axe (Fig. 87, 2–3) and 'wheeled vehicles' – concretely the idea of making wooden discs and mounting local sledges upon them – were diffused. Only dogmatists need assume that the battle-axes were brandished by conquering hordes or that the waggons carried migrating tribes. Yet human agents were inevitably involved. In neither case do 'traders' fit the bill. We might postulate behind the known Battle-axe and Steppe cultures, a loose continuum of scattered groups of herdsmen or indeed of hunter-fishers; for our tangible pastoral groups might have arisen from the one-sided acculturation of savages, as well as from specialization among barbarians. Seasonal shifts of pasture or hunting expeditions would guarantee sufficient intercourse between the several groups for the transmission of ideas. Such transmission is established for the period of the fully differentiated Battle-axe and Steppe cultures. Perhaps it should be postulated earlier to explain the association of wheeled vehicles with chieftains' funerals and the spread of plough cultivation in Central Europe.

The coveted amber of Jutland, whose magic virtue was appreciated as far away as Greece by the sixteenth century, attracted a commerce which brought fresh ideas and foreign manufactures to Denmark. Thus stimulated, the local farmers developed an exceptionally rich culture on the fertile morainic soils left by the recent retreat of the ice-sheets. At the same time extensive peat bogs provide unusually favourable conditions for the preservation of relics and for the reconstruction of the environment in which they were made and used. Finally, since the beginning of the nineteenth century Swedish, and still more Danish, antiquities have been systematically studied by successive generations of gifted investigators. By 1812 Thomsen had established the system of the Three Ages, still used by all prehistorians, and had divided the prehistoric period of the North into Stone, Bronze, and Iron Ages. By 1870 Worsaae had distinguished an Earlier and a Later Stone Age that subsequently became Mesolithic and Neolithic respectively. Finally, Montelius divided the Northern Neolithic Age into four periods – Neolithic I, II, III, and IV – based on the typology of flint axes (Fig. 90) and megalithic tombs.

During the 1920s the existence of Montelius' Neolithic I as an independent period was seriously questioned; for it was then represented solely by flint axes with pointed butts, found without context. The remaining periods were designated by the names of the megalithic tombs by which Montelius had characterized them – Dolmen (*dyss, dös*), Passage Grave (*ganggrift, jaettestuer*), and Stone Cist (*hällkist*) periods. But since 1945 Danish and Swedish prehistorians[1] have adopted a triple division into Early,

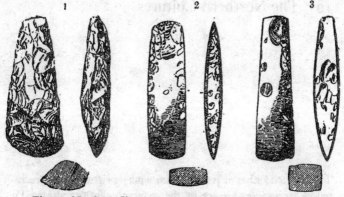

Fig. 90. Northern flint axes arranged according to Montelius'
typology. By permission of Trustees of British Museum.

Middle, and Late Neolithic (EN, MN, and LN), each subdivided. The subdivision of Early Neolithic was originally based on the typology of the funnel-beaker – the most distinctive vase in the dominant culture which is usually called after it, not at all euphoniously, the Funnel-Beaker culture (*Trichterbecher* or *Tragtbaegre kultur* – abbreviated TRB culture). But the subdivision of Early Neolithic had in practice the effect of re-establishing in somewhat different form a pre-Dolmen phase equivalent to Montelius' Neolithic I. Hence in the sequel his numeration will be retained albeit for the sake of brevity alone. Its correlation with other nomenclatures can be effected with the aid of the following table:

Montelius	*TRB*	*Tombs*	*Flint Axes, etc.*
Northern Neolithic I A B	Early Neolithic A B		Pointed-butted
II	C	Dolmens	Thin-butted
III *a* *b* *c* *d*	Middle Neolithic I II III IV	Passage Graves	Thick-butted
IV	Late Neolithic	Stone Cists	Daggers

Montelius' typological system had been worked out on the basis of closed finds from the West Baltic coasts and is still substantially valid there, though no one now supposes that Dolmen, Passage Grave, and Long Cist mark stages in a self-contained evolution. But his disciples and imitators have clumsily extended his system beyond the regions for which it was devised and have used it as a frame of reference into which cultural phenomena in Central Europe, South Russia, and even Turkestan must be fitted! From a fog of misconceptions and distortions they have evoked a 'Nordic myth'. The 'Nordic' cultures, crystallized in Montelius' II, would have expanded in periods III and IV till they reached the Balkans, Anatolia, and the Caucasus.[2] These fantasies were never accepted in Denmark and have recently been emphatically rejected in Sweden and even Germany. An explicit refutation here is accordingly superfluous. None the less, it will be convenient to base our survey on the Danish and Swedish record which is incomparably more complete, though not necessarily longer or originally richer, than that from the Continent.

The Early Neolithic Period of the West Baltic

The first farmers to reach Denmark are represented by the bones of cows and sheep or goats and by sherds bearing impressions of one-corn, emmer, club, and dwarf wheats and of barley[3] found in several votive deposits, in certain 'Ertebølle kitchen middens', and in one or two pure domestic sites, all of the Atlantic phase. In all cases the farmers' archaeological personality is expressed in flat-bottomed funnel-beakers and amphorae of Becker's A group. Troels-Smith[4] insists that these pots are made by the same technique of ring-building as the standard Ertebølle jars and lamps, though their walls are thinner, and are associated with the latter in many kitchen-middens. Hence he concludes that the Ertebølle culture of Late Atlantic times was in fact the culture of the A group of First Northern Neolithic farmers.

Becker,[5] on the contrary, in 1954 described a pure assemblage of A types – including flat clay discs or baking plates – from a site that was not a normal kitchen-midden (Fig. 91), So he maintains the contrast between intrusive neolithic farmers and sur-vivors of the older mesolithic population of hunter-fishers. In 1956, therefore, it would be premature for an English author to try and define too precisely the economy and the stone indus-tries of the earliest or A group of neolithic farmers recognized on Danish soil. So much at least is certain.

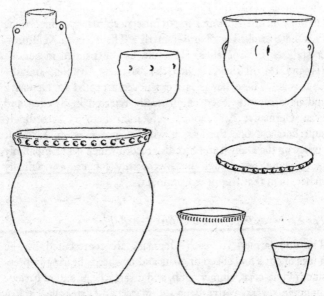

Fig. 91. A-type funnel-beakers (*bottom*), amphora, 'baking plate,' etc. (⅛). After Becker.

About 2600 B.C. (according to a radiocarbon estimation) A farmers were cultivating cereals (including *Triticum monococcum* and the hexaploid club wheat *Triticum compactum*) and breeding domestic stock. The latter were not allowed to graze freely but were tethered by day and stalled at night, being fed during winter on leaves – a small decline in elm pollen, coinciding with the farmers' appearance, has been attributed to the provision of winter fodder.[6] In the kitchen-middens, bones of game and fish still predominate. A few polished flint celts with pointed butts (Fig. 90, 1) are the only notable additions to the mesolithic stone industry.

No graves attributable to phase A have been identified, but votive deposits in bogs give some indication of the current ideology. They include beside human and animal bones – presumably from sacrifices – amber beads, the magic value of the resin having been recognized even in Boreal times.

Amphorae and funnel-beakers like the Danish A type have been found in North-Eastern Germany and Poland.[7] They may mean that the First Northern culture in its A form extended over a wide area of the wooded plain south of the Baltic.

In Denmark these cultivators with their tethered stock were followed by other farmers with larger herds who burnt wide tracts of forest for pasture and plots and cultivated thereon emmer wheat and barley. A layer of ashes in the bogs, followed by a sharp decline in all tree pollen, marks the arrival of these B-group farmers.[8] Doubtless their flocks and herds grazed freely in the clearings, but their masters cannot have remained very long at any one place since in time the forest regenerated. Nor did they drive out their precursors. At Havnelev[9] in Zealand a settlement of B farmers is marked by numerous rubbish pits. In them the bones of cows, sheep or goats, and pigs preponderate over those of game animals. Polished thin-butted axes were used side by side with the mesolithic flake axes. The blade tools were inferior to the Ertebølle types, but polygonal battle-axes of polished stone (Fig. 92) were already in use. The funnel-beakers were sometimes decorated with cord impressions below the rim (Fig. 79, 5), but were round-bottomed, as were the contemporary amphorae and collared flasks. But not far away on the shore at Strandegaard Ertebølle folk were still living almost exclusively by hunting, fishing, and collecting with a mesolithic equipment.

Similarly at Siretorp in Scania[10] herding folk, using funnel-beakers adorned with cord impressions and sometimes exhibiting corn imprints, twice encamped on the same strip of sandy shore. Between the two periods of herder settlement, Ertebølle hunter-fishers had occupied the site. To the B farmers may be attributed a grave at Virring in Jutland,[11] large enough to contain only a single contracted adult skeleton, but no bones survived.

Pottery appropriate to the B group of First Northern farmer-herders has been found all over Denmark and right across Southern Sweden to the east coast.[12] On the Continent, B vases are not readily distinguishable from those just attributed to the A group.

In Northern Neolithic II – Early Neolithic C the First Northern culture even in Denmark dissolves into several local sub-cultures. All are characterized by the same type-fossils – funnel-beakers, collared flasks, amphorae, thin-butted flint axes, polygonal battle-axes, etc., but are mutually distinguished by divergences in pot forms and decoration and by burial rites.

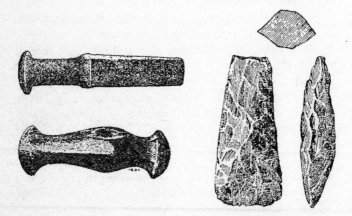

Fig. 92. Tongued club-head, Denmark, polygonal battle-axe, Jordanova ($\frac{1}{3}$), and flint axe of Eastern type ($\frac{1}{2}$).

By this time, too, Denmark and Southern Sweden themselves form only quarters of a larger province eventually extending from the Vistula to the lower Rhine.

Everywhere farming provided the basis of life, but some Danish groups followed the practice of their A ancestors in animal husbandry while others may have grazed stock freely, as in the B phase. By judicious burning of scrub, using the ashes as fertilizers, substantial communities could live together for a generation or more. The village of Barkaer in Jutland[13] consisted of fifty-four one-roomed houses arranged on either side of an open space in two continuous rows, each 85 m long.

The farmers still used thin-butted axes of flint with rectangular cross-section and mounted directly on wooden handles, but now also others of fine-grained rock, sometimes splayed at the blade.[14] Numerous weapons survive – arrows, their shafts polished on stone straighteners like Fig. 113 and tipped with transverse flint heads, polygonal battle-axes, and tongued club-heads like Fig. 92. The stone celts and battle-axes with splayed blades evidently copy metal models. In fact, many minute scraps of copper were observed at Barkaer while a contemporary earth-grave at Salten in Jutland [15] contained a bossed copper disc that can be exactly matched in the graves of Brześć Kujawski (p. 166). This import not only established an exact synchronism between Northern II (EN.C.) and early Danubian III, but also

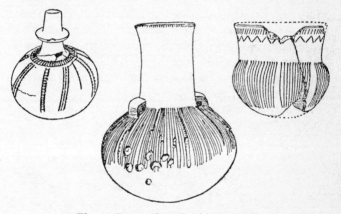

Fig. 93. Pottery from Danish dysser ($\frac{1}{4}$).

indicates the source of the metal, already known in Northern Neolithic II, albeit only as a luxury material.

The pottery of Neolithic II (Fig. 93) is a development of that made in Neolithic I, but is now more often decorated with pits, ribs, or impressions of whipped cords so as to produce vertical patterns. Variations in techniques and pattern serve to distinguish three or four local groups.[16] As charms and ornaments amber beads, sometimes decorated in the drill-technique inherited from Maglemose times and strung together in necklaces of several strands kept apart by spacers, were worn.

One classical method of disposal of the dead, or perhaps only of deceased chiefs, which gives its name to the whole period in Denmark, was ceremonial burial in a megalithic dolmen or dyss. In its oldest form a dyss is a small chamber formed by four uprights supporting a single large capstone, and less than 6 ft long by 2 ft wide.[17] Such small chambers sound as if they were designed to contain a single corpse only; though as many as six skeletons[18] have been found in one, they cannot rank as collective tombs. Later, one end-stone is generally lower than the remaining uprights, leaving an aperture through which subsequent burials might be introduced after the completion of the tomb. A rare and archaic-looking variant of the dolmen is an enclosure of inward-tilted slabs not supporting a capstone, but converging,[19] just as in Portugal. Small polygonal chambers with a rudimentary passage and rectangular chambers with more than two side-stones have also yielded relics of the kind described above and are accordingly classed as dysser by Danish authorities. Dolmens of all types were normally partially buried by mounds, sometimes round but often long and rectangular and demarcated by a peristalith of large boulders.

The distribution of dolmens along the Danish coasts indicates

Fig. 94. Grave 28 at Jordanova. After Seger.

a population of accomplished seafarers. Indeed, both the basis of the new economy and the metal tools that were imitated in stone might have reached Denmark by sea. But no regular supplies of metal were obtained by this or any other route. The economy of the dolmen-builders is typically neolithic though they lived when societies in Central Europe or Britain were already in a Copper Age.

But even in Denmark and Schleswig-Holstein people, perhaps descendants of the B group herders, might be buried in non-megalithic earth graves accompanied by a typical 'dolmen' equipment of thin-butted axes, collared flasks, etc.[20] In such burials one or rarely two corpses were laid extended on the ground surrounded by a setting of boulders, as in Fig. 94, and sometimes covered with an elongated mound (in contrast to 'Battle-axe' burials, contracted in a pit under a round barrow).

The Danish Passage Graves

In Northern III about the time of the last marine transgression new influences affected both the architecture of the megalithic tombs and their furniture. The spacious passage graves that partly replaced the dolmens were used as collective sepulchres by clans for several generations; for they may contain as many as a hundred skeletons[21] and pottery of several styles the succession of which serves as a basis for the subdivision of the period. But owing presumably to the need for fresh land as old plots became exhausted, the settlements were shifted more often and yield as a rule pottery of only one stylistic phase.[22] A settlement of the first phase at Trøldebjerg on Langeland[23] consisted of several apsidal huts, 13 to 18 ft long, and a continuous row of rectangular buildings with a total length of 71 m. Two of these were certainly houses, each about 28 m long and apparently subdivided so that one end was occupied by humans, the other by cattle. The gabled roof, about 11 ft high, sloped down to the ground on one side and on the other rested on a wall only 6 ft high. (Obviously these houses have nothing to do with the Aegean and Balkan megaron type but derive directly from the Barkaer form.) They could accommodate a household larger than the 'natural family' – i.e. a clan – whose deceased members might rest in the spacious passage grave.

Hunting was now relatively unimportant. Hexaploid wheat in addition to one-corn, emmer, and flax were certainly cultivated, but, as in England, wheat was far more popular than barley.

Specialization in industry is attested by the existence of communities of flint-miners and by specialized tools such as gouges for the carpenters. Trade was sufficiently developed to secure for the Passage Grave builders a certain number of metal tools and ornaments. A hoard found in Bygholm in Jutland[24] and dating from the very beginning of the period, comprised four flat axes, a dagger with an imitation midrib on one face, like Fig. 132, 5, and two arm-cylinders. A distribution map of copper axes in Denmark and Schleswig-Holstein suggests that they were imported by sea, though most of them must have come from Hungary.[25] Halberds have a similar distribution to axes and certainly were brought by sea from Ireland.[26] Amber was presumably the principal export bartered for metal and was very likely worked locally to form necklaces. Beads reached Brittany, Central France, and the Iberian Peninsula, and, as we saw, were common throughout Central Europe in Unětician times. In exchange the Danes obtained hammer-headed pins of Pontic type[27] by phase III. But the supplies obtained by such barter were quite insufficient to allow metal even to compete with stone and bone. Even the ornaments imported are mostly inferred from bone imitations made locally.

The emergence of Battle-axe folk during the period (p. 206), combined with the increased competition for land as the population grew, intensified militarism. The outstanding weapons are stone double-axes, imitating Aegean metal models transmitted up the Danube thoroughfare (Fig. 95, 4), flint daggers, disc-shaped mace-heads of Danubian origin and transverse flint arrow-heads.

The earlier pots, including funnel-necked beakers, are decorated with patterns executed with whipped or braided cords and arranged vertically or in panels, thus carrying on the Early Neolithic traditions. [28] Still in the settlement of Trøldebjerg the distinctive innovations of deeply cut or stamped incisions in what Sophus Müller called 'the grand style' and even cardial decoration (p. 407) already appear and with them new Danubian forms – the pedestalled bowl and the socketed ladle.[29] In a later settlement, like Blandebjerg,[30] phase IIIb, the technique of deep incision is completely dominant and is used to form basketry patterns on angular vases, inspired by basket models (Fig. 95, 1) and derived from North-West Germany or the early Walternienburg group of Central Germany. Next in IIIc the profiles are rounded off (Fig. 95, 2) and rouletted lines, presumably derived from the Bell-beakers (pp. 274–5), replace the cardial technique in shading. Finally, in phase IIId the shapes are further simplified while simple incision or stab-and-drag lines were preferred to rouletted ones for the sparing decoration. This, however, includes oculi motives (Fig. 95, 3), recalling the Copper Age of Almeria.

Of the domestic pots, 50 per cent were decorated in IIIa at Trøldebjerg, but the percentage had fallen to 4 per cent at Lindø in IIId. Still, at all times some vessels were ornamented with

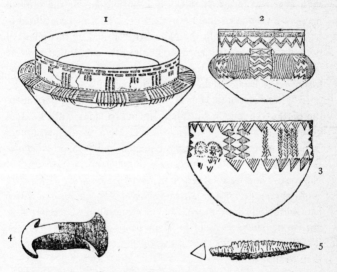

Fig. 95. Pottery ($\frac{1}{7}$, $\frac{1}{6}$), double-axe ($\frac{1}{4}$), and arrow-head ($\frac{1}{3}$) from Danish Passage Graves.

pits in the native Ertebølle tradition, indicating how large a proportion of the old population was absorbed in the new farming societies.[31] Yet of course unabsorbed groups of food-gatherers survived.

As in Early Neolithic times, a non-megalithic branch of the First Northern[32] culture survived in the succeeding period. But among the better-known Megalith-builders, soon after the beginning of Northern III,[33] came in the practice of collective burial in a megalithic passage grave. The latter cannot be regarded as an independent development from the dyss – such tombs were still used – as Montelius' disciples have contended, but reflects fresh influence from the West, explicitly imitating the corbelled tholos of the Atlantic coasts (p. 262). The earliest passage graves, standing closest to the models, are polygonal chambers sometimes with a cell attached, entered through a long passage and covered with a circular mound. In later versions the chamber is elongated at right angles to the passage. Passage graves served of course as family vaults. Some contain as many as a hundred skeletons. But in others the earlier interments with their gear had been removed and reburied outside the vault to make room for subsequent burials. Votive offerings continued to be deposited in bogs during Northern III, and by this phase, if not before, there is evidence for a cult of the axe. But at no time did the manufacture of female figurines in any durable material form part of First Northern ideological activity.

In Middle Neolithic II or III a new group of warlike herdsmen, the Battle-Axe folk, had invaded Jutland (p. 205), while kindred groups occupied the Danish islands. Then bands of hunter-fishers[34] from the Scandinavian peninsula began crossing the Belts to win raw flint which they traded far into Sweden and Norway. They were armed with heavy bows from which they could shoot the curious arrow-heads of Fig. 95, 5. The latter may ultimately be derived from the mesolithic Garnes point, but immediately seem to be translations of bone models; for they have a triangular cross-section more appropriate to bone than to flint work.

Imported objects or copies thereof found, sometimes in stratified horizons, in passage graves establish the chronological relations of Northern Neolithic III with cultural sequences in other provinces. A Bell-beaker, probably of Bohemian manufacture,[35] thus provides a synchronism between Northern IIIc and a late phase of Danubian III; the metal ware from Bygholm, if of Danubian origin, should not be very much earlier in the same period. The contemporary fruitstands and socketed ladles, made locally in the North, cannot then be contemporary with their Danubian II analogues, and are in fact associated with handled cups and tankards derivable from Baden and Bodrog-keresztur types. At the same time the hammer-pin establishes a quasi-synchronism with the Middle Kuban and Catacomb phases in South Russia.

The First Northern Culture on the Continent and Its Origin

The West Baltic cultures whose development during the local Early and Middle Neolithic stages has just been surveyed were just regional variants of a wider culture the unity of which has been typified for prehistorians by the ubiquity in one form or another of the Funnel Beaker. As this vase does not yield a euphonious culture name in English and still less in French, and as almost any open-mouth bowl – even the 'Arpachiya milk bowl' of Mesopotamia in the fourth millennium[36] – could be called a funnel-beaker (!) – I have substituted the term 'First Northern'.

This First Northern culture is far less homogeneous than the Starčevo, First Danubian, or Tripolye culture. In addition to the Northern province whose diversity has just been disclosed in the last two sections, Eastern, Southern, and Western provinces have been recognized since 1912 but are even less unitary and less fully explored than the Northern. Yet certain distinctive peculiarities other than ceramic are common to all four. Everywhere the subsistence economy was mixed farming combined with hunting and gathering, though there may have been the variations in animal husbandry that pollen-analysis alone has revealed in Denmark and more hunting in the Continental than in the Peninsular provinces. In the South province, positive evidence for cultivation with the aid of an ox-drawn plough is provided by a clay model of a pair of yoked oxen from Kreznica Jara near Lublin.[37] But it cannot be proved that plough cultivation was an original trait and not a secondary borrowing from, for instance, Baden neighbours. Horse bones have been reported from many settlements but may have belonged to game animals[38] since wild horses had roamed the North European plain since Pre-Boreal times (p. 43). Centrally perforated clay discs,[39] about 4 cm in diameter, may represent model wheels rather than spindle whorls, but no vehicles survive.

Hunters used arrows, armed normally with transverse heads but occasionally also with lozenge-shaped points, and doubtless clubs. Flint was preferred for axes, but in the East and South provinces these do not have the rectangular cross-section favoured in the North and West, but resemble Fig. 92, 3. The material was extensively traded from Rügen, and in Galicia banded flint was won by regular mining,[40] while the village on Gawroniec Hill can properly be described as an axe-factory.[41]

Though a trade in flint had been thus early organized, the organization did not extend to the distribution of metal, which, though known, was very little used. So, too, amber ornaments

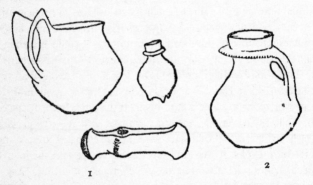

Fig. 96. Furniture of a grave at Zastow ($\frac{1}{7}$), and collared flask from grave at Nalenczow ($\frac{1}{2}$).

were occasionally worn, but only in quantities that could have been obtained from local moraines supplemented by irregular barter. Warlike behaviour is abundantly attested by stone battle-axes, usually of the polygonal type and always with symmetrically splayed blades in contrast to the drooping blades of Battle-Axe cultures.[42]

In pottery, divergent modifications in the form and decoration of the ubiquitous funnel-beakers, collared flasks, and amphorae illustrate divergence of taste between local groups and influences from other societies. So in the South group the attachment of strap handles or nipple feet to flasks and beakers, and still more the flanged character of the handles (Fig. 96, 1),[43] might have been suggested by Baden. Basketry ornament, popular in the West group, might be inspired by Rössen or by the basketry vessels of an hypothetical pre-existing hunter-fisher population.

But, as in Denmark, fruitstands and socketed ladles must be derived ultimately from Danubian II.

In the ideological domain, votive deposits in bogs are reported at least from the East group. Female figurines were nowhere manufactured, but figures of animals were sometimes modelled in clay in the South group, as in the Baden cultural province. The characteristic burial rite everywhere was to inter a single corpse extended in an earth grave – i.e. on the ground surface surrounded by a kerb of boulders.[44] But, save in the South group, some persons – perhaps only 'chiefs' – were interred in stone or perhaps wooden chambers under long or round barrows. In the East group the Kuyavish graves of Western Poland[45] must have been wedge-shaped mounds, up to 80 m in length, bordered with stone kerbs and containing the burial near the broader east end (Fig. 97). West of the Oder,[46] trapeze-shaped mounds of more modest dimensions enclose a cists of slabs without entrance passage (such are termed long dolmens). In the West group[47] long oval or rectangular mounds bordered with large boulders covered at first closed chambers and later chambers as long as the barrow generally, provided with a short entrance passage in the middle of one long side, and popularly termed Huns' Beds. These North-West German and Dutch passage graves were collective tombs, presumably inspired by the same ideology as their Danish-Swedish counterparts under round barrows. They contain, like the latter, fruitstands and socketed ladles, decorated with basketry patterns, but also collared flasks similarly decorated.

Thus in the West group contradictory chronological conclusions could be drawn from the tomb types and their furniture. On the typology established for the North group, the collective tombs, the basketry ornament on the pottery, and the fruitstands and socketed ladles would be MN., the collared flasks EN.[48] Did the innovations reach North-West Germany and Holland from the Atlantic coasts and the Danubian province before they reached Denmark and Sweden? That would be *a priori* likely. But still farther south in Westfalia and Hesse collared flasks appear in long cists with porthole entries identical with those of the Paris basin (p. 363) and of Sweden in LN. times.[49] Now the slabs of the cist at Züschen, Hesse, are carved and the carvings

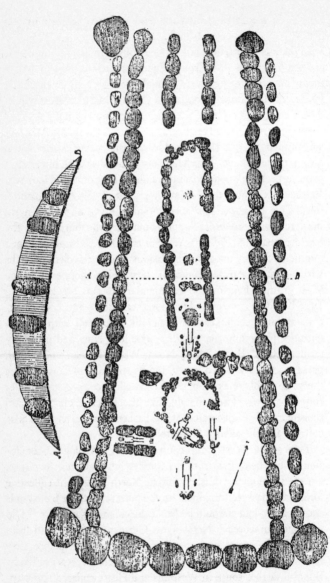

Fig. 97. Kuyavish grave, Swierczyn. After Kozłowski.

seem to include representations of ox-carts.[50] On the other hand, among the sparse ceramic finds, two tombs are said to have yielded minute sherds of Rössen pottery.[51] These sherds, if really part of the tomb furniture, would accord with the collared flasks in making these West German long cists EN. in terms of the Northern sequence. But then they would be a whole period earlier than the LN. Swedish tombs of identical plan!

Now, since in 1910 Kossinna purported to explain the distribution of funnel-beakers, collared flasks, and amphorae on the Continent as the result of an expansion of Ur-Indogermanen from Denmark, it has been tacitly assumed that the Continental cultures characterized by these vases are later than their nearest Danish analogues of Northern II (EN.C). Such a relation may still hold good for the West group. But the imported disc from a Neolithic II grave at Salten (p. 227) now proves that the South group was by then already established between the Warta and the Oder. So there is no longer any reason to doubt that the long barrows covering dolmen-like chambers and earth graves furnished with funnel-beakers, collared flasks, and amphorae in Poland and North-Eastern Germany were in fact substantially contemporary with the Danish dolmens and earth graves of EN.C. In this case the analogues to Early Neolithic A-B vases, found – twice under long barrows – between the Vistula and the Elbe, may be as old as the Danish specimens. Thus, though best known from the West Baltic coasts, the First Northern culture in its earliest manifestations may already have occupied the whole area from the North Sea to the Upper Oder, from the Vistula to the Elbe. 'The origin of the First Northern culture' thus means the origin of this widespread complex.

Outside this region no single culture is known that exhibits all the distinctive traits – ceramic forms, battle-axes, arrow-heads, burial rites, bog offerings – enumerated above. On the other hand, survivals of mesolithic Forest culture traditions (transverse arrow-heads, tranchet axes, antler axes, extended burials, etc.) are conspicuous in the First Northern neolithic culture. Since even in Boreal times the Forest culture must have spread more widely on the Continent than the surviving bone tools can show, and a local invention of pottery cannot be excluded, the archaeological content of the First Northern culture could be explained as an autochthonous development of that vigorous and adaptable culture save for the cereals and domestic stock. The question of its origin would then be reduced to this: Whence did the Forest-folk acquire these and learn the arts of cultivating and breeding them?

Of course, pottery might provide some clue. Hinsch[52] has convincingly stated the case for deriving First Northern pottery from the Western neolithic. Becker,[53] too, would admit Western – or more precisely Michelsberg – inspiration in his B-group vases. Troels-Smith,[54] however, insists that the rural economy as well as the pottery of the A group agrees with that of the Michelsberg and Cortaillod cultures. Vogt,[55] on the contrary, has contended that Michelsberg itself is not a Western culture but an offshoot of the First Northern. His thesis has been substantially strengthened by the subsequent publication[56] of baking plates, distinctive of the Michelsberg culture, as an integral element in the First Northern from its earliest, A, phase. Indeed, the striking similarity of British and Breton long barrows (pp. 376–7), for which no satisfying explanation has yet been found in South-Western Europe, to Kuyavish graves and long dolmens[57] might provide an argument for admitting at least a First Northern element even in the Windmill Hill and Armorican Early Neolithic cultures. Still, the First Northern is not an offshoot of any known Western culture.

That is not to say it could not spring from some earlier and less-specialized assemblage from which such Western cultures as Windmill Hill and Michelsberg might also have arisen. Or it could be argued that on the now submerged coasts of the North Sea representatives of the Forest culture's coastal variant learned farming from pioneer Western immigrants. That too, however, makes excessive draughts on the unknown, since neither the Mesolithic coastal culture nor that of the Western pioneers is tangibly represented in the existing archaeological record.

On the other hand, First Danubian farmers had demonstrably spread right to the Baltic coasts between the Oder and the Vistula and, west of the Elbe, had advanced into territories later occupied by First Northern farmers.[58] In Denmark itself, while no Danubian settlements occur, stone implements of Danubian type have been found, some on Ertebølle sites.[59] The First Northern long barrows could well be regarded as durable imitations of the external appearance of a Danubian I long house.[60] Finally, the *Triticum monococcum*, demonstrably cultivated in Northern IA could hardly have reached Northern Europe save through the Danubian province. East of the Oder – admittedly rather hypothetical – Forest hunter-fishers could have learned from the pioneer Danubian outposts to breed stock and till the soil.

Still, it remains possible that predominantly pastoral tribes without pottery, with no specialized kit of stone tools nor ideology expressed in funerary monuments or figurines of clay, pushed in through Volhynia from the south-east. But for such an invasion there is of course no positive evidence.

Middle Neolithic Northern Cultures on the Continent

During what corresponds to Northern Middle Neolithic, the West, South, and East groups of First Northern cultures in contact with surviving mesolithic groups and remnants of the Rössen, Jordanova, and Michelsberg cultures dissolved into a multiplicity of local groups, known mainly from grave-finds and distinguished primarily by ceramic peculiarities.

In the West group the Elbe-Weser culture carried on the traditions of burial in Huns' Beds and earth graves and of basketry vases. But Bell and S beakers found even in Huns' Beds illustrate the increasing dominance of Beaker and Battle-axe folk over the First Northern elements, and also the late survival of the culture in Danubian III. A gold armlet with expanded terminals from an earth grave at Himmelspforten near Stade[61] should in fact belong to Danubian IV.

The *Walternienburg-Bernburg culture*[62] developed on the Lower Saale and in Havelland out of the local branch of First Northern, termed the Baalburg culture,[63] through the so-called Salzmunder culture of MN.1.[64] The angular vases, distinctive of Walternienburg 1, obviously copy basketry models (Fig. 98), but in subsequent phases the basketry origin seems to have been forgotten. Pottery of this sort is found in simple pit-graves, grouped in small cemeteries, in megalithic cists or galleries, in Huns' Beds with lateral passage and in cists of thin slabs. Axe-heads were made by preference of Wida shale from the South Hartz; the rest of the Walternienburg equipment seems to be derived indiscriminately from various Northern and foreign cultures. It includes double-axes of Passage Grave type, amber beads, crutch-headed pins, perhaps derived from the Pontic hammer-pins, and metal ornaments of Unětician type or bone copies of such. The culture, while beginning in Northern period III, lasts therefore well into Danubian IV.

In part of the areas formerly occupied by the East and South

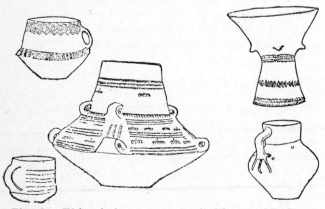

Fig. 98. 1, Walternienburg vases, 2, Latdorf drum, and Baalburg jug.

groups emerged the culture typified by and named after the *Globular Amphorae*.[65] The type-vase, like the other vessels habitually associated with it, is clearly a copy of leather models and is always decorated in a very distinctive manner round the neck, with fillets hanging over the shoulder (Fig. 99). The characteristic vases are accompanied by small trapeze-shaped axes and chisels of flint, frequently of the banded variety mined in Galicia, transverse and tanged arrow-heads, bored teeth and boars' tusks, amber beads and, east of the Oder, ornate bone girdle-clasps. Antler axes, double-axes of stone, flint knives and other articles were occasionally borrowed from contemporary groups. Ring-pendants of bone and other ornaments characteristic of the Scandinavian long cists, and bronze rings and spirals demonstrate the survival of the culture during period IV.

The makers of these vases might be interred, extended, in simple trench graves forming cemeteries of not more than twelve graves, cremated, or buried, generally squatting, in collective tombs, containing as a rule not more than seven corpses and generally less. The collective tombs are sometimes megalithic cists or large cists made of thin slabs. The latter are often divided into two compartments, sometimes by a porthole slab.

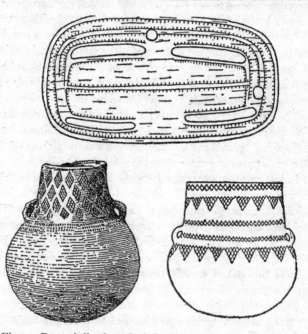

Fig. 99. Bone girdle-clasp. Podolia (⅔), and globular amphorae, Saxo-Thuringia and Podolia (¼).

The principal concentration of Globular Amphorae is in the Saale-Elbe region and Havelland, but they extend northward to Rügen, southward into Bohemia, and eastward through Galicia into Volhynia and Podolia. In Bohemia[66] Globular Amphorae are sometimes found on hilltops in fortified settlements, but even in Volhynia and Podolia they are normally found alone in characteristic slab-cists, subdivided and containing up to six skeletons.[67] Even the pottery from the cists, divided by porthole slabs, at Novosvobodnaya in the Kuban valley (p. 198), is reminiscent of the Globular Amphorae.

Evidently these vases were made by swine-breeders who roamed about in small groups far and wide, presumably mainly as hunters and swineherds, but doubtless engaging in casual robbery and trade. They were thus agents in the distribution of amber, Galician flint, and even metal trinkets, but developed no specialized industries of their own that we can recognize.

In Holstein a Globular Amphora was associated with pottery of Northern Neolithic IIId or even IVa,[68] while in Kuyavish graves Globular Amphorae represent the latest intrusions. An oft-quoted report of the association of a Globular Amphora with Danubian Ib pottery at Klein Rietz is quite unreliable and intrinsically improbable.[69] In the Danubian sequence they cannot be earlier than period III; the Bohemian sites that have yielded specimens belong at earliest to the Baden culture.

Kossinna derived the Globular Amphorae from those of the Danish dolmens and made them the symbols of his second wave of Indo-Germanic expansion from the West Baltic coasts. The culture they typify is still considered by all German writers 'Nordic' and is now supposed to have developed between Elbe and Oder and thence spread eastward. But, if so, why did it not spread westward too? Forssander,[70] on the contrary, suggested that the culture arose somewhere in the Pontic zone and that its authors introduced into Northern Europe not only Galician banded flint but also porthole cists, such as we have in fact met in Novosvobodnaya; presumably the idea then spread from Central Germany both to Sweden and to the Paris basin. In fact, it is not easy to derive the culture simply from the First Northern, but it remains essentially a culture of the woodland zone and its outposts in Volhynia are separated by a huge tract of steppe, bare of comparable finds, from the Caucasian group of porthole cists.

Sometimes associated with Globular Amphorae are curious tubular pots like Fig. 98, 2 (top), often embellished with crosses and other symbolic figures and generally interpreted on the strength of good ethnographic parallels as drums. Most come from the Elbe valley in Saxo-Thuringia and Bohemia, but they are not peculiar to any one culture; the jug from Latdorf is a

Baalburg type and some Moravian drums[71] were found in a Baden context.

We must accordingly imagine numbers of small groups, each distinguished by peculiarities in pottery and sometimes also in burial rites or equipment, wandering about the North European plain simultaneously. Especially in Central Germany, groups adhering respectively to Walternienburg, Globular Amphorae and Battle-axe traditions must have been not only contemporary but also in close spatial contact. And they must have encountered also Danubian peasants making stroke-ornamented ware and others making Jordanova pots to say nothing of makers of collared flasks and miscellaneous megalith-builders. It is not surprising that such groups frequently interchanged ideas – perhaps they intermarried; the wonder is that they retained the individuality of their ceramic traditions so long. The number of distinct types of pottery tends to give a quite exaggerated idea of the density of population and the duration of Northern Neolithic III. Actually the several kinds of vases must have been made by relatively small and nomadic groups, several of which must have been living side by side. It is only by trying to arrange all groups in a sequence, which may really be valid at one particular site, that period III becomes inordinately inflated. But that it overlaps with Danubian IV may be once more demonstrated by the metal trinkets associated with Globular Amphorae and Walternienburg vases.[72]

The Northern Late Neolithic Period

During the fourth period of the Northern Stone Age the sharp contrast between Megalith-builders and Battle-axe folk began to break down in Denmark and Southern Sweden. Though each party still retained its traditional burial practices, there is little difference between the furniture of the Long Stone Cists, collective tombs that carry on the megalithic tradition, and that of the Upper (Separate) Graves of the Battle-axe population. But it is the culture of the latter that is dominant.

The area of settlement remains unaltered, but the population has perhaps increased: in Västergötland there are 4,266 relics belonging to period IV, as against 3,106 from the preceding period.[73] These figures further indicate that the Stone Cist period can hardly have been shorter than that of the Passage Graves. But the general economy remained unaltered. The importance of agriculture may be inferred from the number of flint sickles, curved in imitation of metal models. But weapons

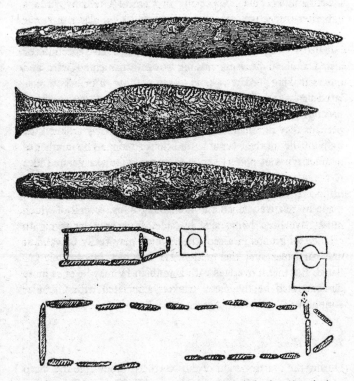

Fig. 100. Flint daggers (Denmark, ⅓) and porthole cists (Sweden) – types of Montelius' IV.

are still the most prominent relics. The flint axes now regularly imitate metal axes with a splayed blade; but the faces are seldom polished; indeed, polished flint axes made in period III were sometimes flaked all over for use in period IV. Battle-axes were still used, but are less shapely and less metallic. The classical weapon was the dagger, at first lanceolate in form but culminating before the end of the period in the famous fish-tailed form

(Fig. 100).[74] The arrow-heads are hollow-based rather as in the Copper Age of Iberia.

The fish-tailed flint daggers certainly copy the bronze-hilted daggers of Central Europe. The models for these and other weapons were indeed imported from time to time. A certain number of bronzes from Italy, Central Europe, and Britain have survived from this period, stray or in hoards. And before the period ended smiths may have been producing for a local market in Schleswig-Holstein and even Southern Sweden.[75] To obtain metal for rearmament the northerners had to rely chiefly on the export of amber. Every scrap of the precious gum was reserved for foreign trade, so it could no longer be used locally for charms. In the tombs the place of amber beads is taken by long pendants of slate, ring-pendants of stone or bone, and a few metal trinkets of Unětician type.[76] But for all their sacrifices the Northerners' equipment and economy remained essentially neolithic throughout period IV.

The practice of collective burial persisted, alongside burial in separate graves in the mass of the barrow. But the passage grave gave place to the long stone cist or gallery grave generally sunk in the ground. These are not, as Montelius thought, the result of a degeneration of the passage grave.[77] One group might be treated as an evolution of the dolmen, but even so that evolution must have been inspired by new ideas from outside the Northern province. A group of Swedish cists, built of thin slabs and often subdivided by a porthole slab, must be derived from the Paris basin, presumably through the Westfalian group mentioned on p. 235. Even the splay-footed pot, characteristic of the French Horgen culture (p. 364), was reproduced in a variant in Sweden and Denmark.[78] These new ideas must have been introduced by immigrant families joining the established communities. But the normal pottery of the period is represented by flower-pot forms imitating wooden models and decorated with rouletted zig-zag ribbons (Fig. 83, bottom left) perhaps derived from the Oder Battle-axe culture.

Imitations of Unětician pins and Unětician gold ornaments associated with even the early flint daggers show that the fourth period of the Northern Stone Age did not even begin till the Early Bronze Age was well established in Central Europe and in

Britain. Though metalworkers and traders were spreading northward, the Northern Stone Age outlasted Danubian IV. In Denmark and Scandinavia the Bronze Age proper begins first in the Middle Bronze Age of Hungary and Britain.[79] Till that date metal was too scarce for bronze weapons to be buried with even the richest chief. And one of the earlier graves furnished with products of the local Northern bronze industry (at Liesbüttel in Schleswig-Holstein) contained an imported spearhead of a type characteristic of Middle Bronze Age 2 in Britain,[80] while British palstaves of the same typological age are included in contemporary Danish hoards.[81] If the preceding phase of the British Bronze Age be correctly dated to the fifteenth century by the fayence beads then imported (p. 392), Northern Neolithic IV must have lasted till 1400 B.C. in the sense that till then metal weapons were not normally deposited in native graves in Denmark, Southern Sweden, and the adjacent parts of North Germany. A segmented fayence bead was, however, found in a grave of Bronze Age form in North Jutland.[82]

The Saale-Warta Bronze Age

Round the salt deposits and ore lodes of the Saale and Elbe, and along the trade-route leading thence to the East Baltic amber coast, a peculiar version of the Unětician culture had arisen by the beginning of Northern period IV. Metal had been brought thither in the time of the Jordanova culture and weapons already by the Beaker-folk in Danubian III. These or some other unidentified prospectors may have begun the exploitation of the ores of Vogtland and exported their winnings as ingots in the form of the sacred double-axe.[83] For double-axes with a shaft-hole too small to take a real shaft are concentrated in that region and strung out thence across Switzerland to Central France. At the same time, connections with the Pontic zone to the east are attested by the hammer-pins mentioned on p. 210. In the sequel Unětician farmers had spread down the Elbe and the Oder to the Saale and Warta.[84] Their poor graves contain a few Unětician ornaments – but not the oldest forms such as knot-headed pins – but their pots with provincial conservatism preserved the pouched form that had gone out of fashion in Czechoslovakia after the earliest phase of Danubian IV.

The local bronze industry was based on the same Unĕtician tradition, but it was fertilized by the importation of Britannico-Hibernian manufactures[85] and very likely by the immigration of Irish craftsmen. Its products were exported to the still neolithic North and raw amber obtained in exchange. Some of this was re-exported in the raw state to England, there to be worked up into amber cups and crescentic necklaces. Local chieftains succeeded in concentrating the profits derived from this commerce and thus accumulated capital for the industry's further development. Their rich burials under imposing barrows present a striking contrast to the flat graves of Unĕtician farmers and confer a distinctive character upon the Bronze Age of the province quite reminiscent of the Kuban.

At Leubingen,[86] for instance, an old man and a young girl had been interred in a lean-to chamber of stone slabs and oak beams (Fig. 101) enclosed by a circular fosse 20 m in diameter,

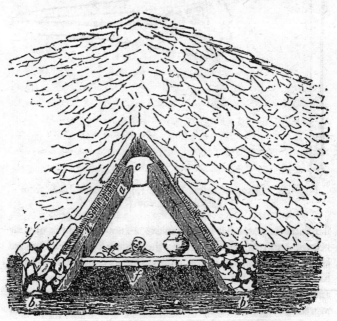

Fig. 101. Section of Leubingen barrow.

and furnished with bronze rounded-heeled daggers, gold pins and lock-rings of Unětician types, a halberd derived from the Irish series, a massive gold bracelet, and a perforated stone axe (or ploughshare).

Even richer burials were discovered in a barrow cemetery at Łeki Małe in Poznania during 1953.[87] A wooden chamber built in a shaft grave at the centre of a barrow, 30 m in diameter, had contained the remains of a man and a woman. The former was accompanied by a bronze-shafted halberd like Fig. 102, 1, a

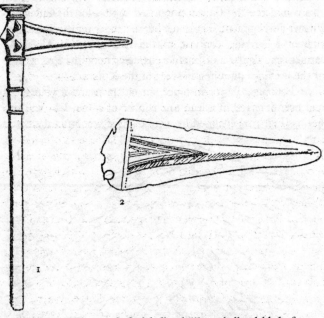

Fig. 102. 1, Bronze-shafted halberd ($\frac{1}{6}$), 2, halberd-blade from Leubingen barrow ($\frac{1}{3}$).

flat knife-dagger, a flat Unětician axe, a knot-headed pin of poor bronze, and two gold lock-rings, the woman by only two bronze bracelets. A secondary grave on the periphery contained a bronze-hilted dagger of Elbe-Oder type, an axe, a Bohemian eyelet pin and three gold lock-rings. Horses, oxen, pigs, and sheep were represented, in that order of frequency, among the remains of funerary feasts under the barrow.

Such richly furnished barrow burials must belong to chieftains who had won economic power as well as authority by taking toll on the trade that traversed their territories. They established no kingdoms guaranteeing order and security beyond the narrow limits of tribal domains. A large number of merchants' hoards of bronzes and amber beads vividly illustrate the dangers to which traders and perambulating metal-workers were exposed between these local realms.

These hoards, together with the grave goods just mentioned, show how by blending varied foreign traditions in producing for their warlike patrons local craftsmen had created a variety of original types[88] – halberds, modelled on late Irish types, but decorated with grooves and triangles and ultimately mounted on bronze shafts (Fig. 102, 1), curious narrow 'double-axes', daggers with bronze hilts, cast in one piece with the blades either oval in imitation of daggers like Fig. 70, or flat like the gold-studded Anglo-Armorican weapons,[89] and what may be clumsy imitations of the elegant crescentic axes of the Kings of Ur.[90] Their products were exported to North Germany and across Poland to Sammland.[91] Thence and from Denmark came in exchange amber beads to be used in turn for barter with England, Bohemia, Hungary, and Italy.

Though definitely Early Bronze Age, the graves and hoards containing these products need not be early within Danubian IV. As compared with Britain, the actual imports establish synchronisms only with phase II of our Early Bronze Age. In Central European terminology graves and hoards containing true Middle Bronze Age – Reinecke B-C – types are practically non-existent in just those parts of Central Germany and Poland where the chieftains' graves occur;[92] there the archaeological record seems to recommence with the Lusacian culture generally attributed to Danubian VI! That might suggest that the Saale-Warta culture occupies part of Danubian V too.[93] On the other hand, in Southern England and in Brittany we shall witness the abrupt emergence of richly furnished barrow graves whose furniture, though still Early Bronze age, exhibits specially close affinities with, if not derivation from, that of the Saale-Warta chieftains' tombs,[94] and the English graves at least seem fairly well dated by Aegean connections between 1600 and 1400 B.C.

11 Survivals of the Forest Culture

The circumpolar zone of Eurasia, extending from the Norwegian coasts across the Baltic and the North European plain far into Siberia, offered no propitious soil to neolithic cultivators, but was rich in game, wild fowl, fish, nuts and berries such as mesolithic Forest-folk had pursued or collected round the North Sea and the western Baltic in Boreal times. By then the Forest-folk had perfected an efficient equipment for the exploitation of these natural resources. They continued to use a similar equipment long after farmers had colonized Denmark and Southern Sweden; for the coniferous forests or taiga to the north constituted a botanical environment very similar to that of Britain and Denmark in the Boreal phase. In it much of the Maglemose culture survived. Now, the survival of equipment implies also continuity of tradition prescribing its manufacture and uses. And continuity of tradition means in turn some continuity of population too. However much immigration or invasion have modified its genetic constitution, cultural traditions have been preserved locally for eight or nine thousand years (cf. p. 49).

But continuity of culture is not equivalent to immutability. In fact, the environment was neither static nor uniform. Cultures were modified to take advantage of new opportunities, were differentiated to exploit local resources, and were enriched by inventions and borrowings. Nor was the population of the European taiga zone homogeneous; by Sub-Boreal times Mongoloid, Lapponoid, Europeoid and hybrid types are represented in the graves.

Throughout the period here considered the Forest-folk remained food-gatherers. All indeed possessed domestic dogs which were sometimes fed on fish,[1] but nowhere were animals bred for food save in Eastern Sweden, where the hunter-fishers, perhaps inspired by the example of the B group herders (p. 225), kept pigs of native stock. On the Norwegian coasts, round the Baltic and along the shores of the White Sea the pursuit of aquatic mammals provided an important element in the food supply and evoked a specialized equipment of harpoons, ice-picks, and blubber-axes, while fishing was universally a major economic activity. Hence the most permanent settlements were close to the coast or along the shores of lakes and rivers. Even these – the so-called Dwelling-

Fig. 103. 1, F.II pit-comb vase from Karelia ($\frac{1}{6}$); 2, vase of East Swedish style from Åland Islands ($\frac{1}{6}$); 3, flint figures from Volosovo ($\frac{3}{10}$).

places (Bopladser) – seem mere encampments where not more than ten households congregated temporarily. Large cemeteries of forty-nine graves on Gotland[2] and of 150 on Deer Island in Lake Onega[3] do not necessarily imply large and permanent villages.

But despite their comparatively nomadic mode of life, all the hunter-fishers save those in Northern Norway made pots from Sub-Boreal times on, and these help to define local and chronological groups. From Sweden to Siberia indeed all pots were manufactured by the same technique of ring-building,[4] all taper downward to a rounded base and all may be decorated with horizontal rows of pits, frequently combined with zones of comb-impressions.[5] The whole ceramic family is therefore termed 'pit-comb ware'. But west of the Baltic most vases have a concave neck separated from the conical body by a shoulder, while farther east neckless ovoid vessels predominate. Within these branches variations in the technique and arrangement of the decoration demarcate stylistic groups and phases. In Sweden[6] and Finland[7] four consecutive styles can be arranged in chronological order by the relations of the coastal dwelling-places on which typical sherds occur to the receding shore of the Litorina Sea; for the land here was still rising, so that the higher a camp is above the present strand the older it should be. The Swedish scheme can be correlated with the subdivisions of the Northern Neolithic indicated in the last chapter and less precisely with the Finnish. An extension of the latter to North and Central Russia has been attempted by Finnish prehistorians, while Gurina[8] has outlined a roughly parallel sequence based on observations round Lake Onega and the White Sea. But other Russian authorities[9] reject such generalizations and deny the extension of pit-comb ware to the Urals altogether.[10] Nevertheless, we shall apply the Finnish scheme to the whole region, using the expressions F.I, F.II, F.III, and F.IV to denote similar styles and to indicate relative positions in local sequences rather than contemporaneity throughout the zone, and assigning to F.O assemblages not associated with pottery that are probably pre-ceramic.

F.O then denotes the Suomusjärvi culture, characterized by rough stone adzes (Fig. 104, 2) and slate points[11] that in Finland appear in Atlantic contexts and do recur in the Urals, and assemblages of Maglemosian types in North-West Russia similarly dated by Russian pollen-analysts.[12] F.I pots, decorated with broad zones, sometimes of whipped-cord impressions, are reported from the Baltic coasts to Lake Onega and the White Sea and from one site in the Upper Dniepr basin.[13] F.II would be well represented also in Central Russia and up to the Urals if it include stylized representations of aquatic birds.[14] (Fig. 103, 1.) Subsequently local divergences are too great to allow of correlations presumably owing to the rise of Battle-axe cultures on the Baltic coasts and in Central Russia. But pit-comb ware of F.IV styles was still being made by hunter-fishers when a few socketed celts of Late Bronze Age types and even iron were reaching Finland and Northern Russia.

For fishing, leisters with bone prongs (Fig. 105, 6) more or less like the Maglemosian, were in use throughout our period from Norway to Siberia. Fish-hooks of the Boreal Pernau type (Fig.

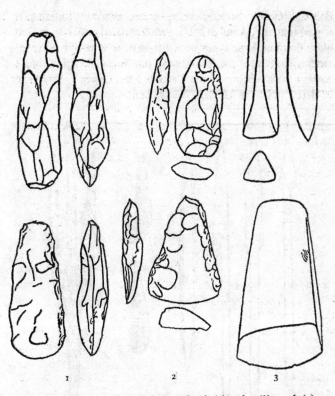

Fig. 104. Nøstvet (1) and Suomusjärvi (2) celts ($\frac{3}{8}$), and (3)
polished chisel and adze ($\frac{1}{2}$).

105, 5) survived too in North Russia and even on the Desna, but
by the Sub-Boreal were supplemented throughout the zone by
composite implements with a notched shank of stone or bone and
a separate barb.[15] But net-fishing was at least equally important.[16]

Of the Maglemosian hunting-equipment, slotted bone points
survived everywhere, conical bone arrow-heads[17] and the type of
Fig. 105, 3 as far as the Urals and from F.O to F.IV. Flint tips for
arrows and darts with little invasive retouch on the bulbar surface,
occurring in F.O and F.I sites may be derived from the Swiderian
and were copied in slate. Rare transverse arrow-heads,[18] found
with the oldest F.I pottery in Finland and on early sites along the
Oka, could be derived from the Ukraine as well as from the West

253

Baltic. Bifacially trimmed arrow-heads, generally leaf-shaped, appear first in F.II and in F.III were translated into slate, as were older flint and bone types with a triangular or rhomboid cross-section (Fig. 106, 3). Rhomboid club-heads like Fig. 106, 4, current from Norway to the Urals and the Lower Volga,[19] may be descended from Maglemosian spiked weapons.

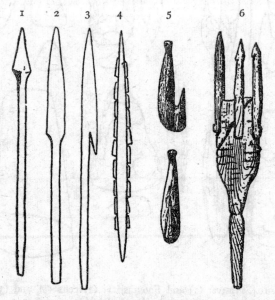

Fig. 105. Eastern Maglemosian types (⅓), 1–4, Esthonia, after Clark; 5, Ukraine; 6, leister from Ural peat bogs (⅙).

For woodworking, antler wedges[20] and socketed bone chisels remained in use in Norway as in North Central Russia, but in the north were supplemented by more efficient adzes, gouges, and chisels of polished stone (Fig. 104, 3); in Central Russia such tools of polished stone are not apparently found before the rise of the Fatyanovo culture. So too the Maglemosian boars' tusk knife survived in Norway, Sweden, and Central Russia,[21] but was translated into slate in the north, giving rise to forms like Fig. 106, 1.

For land transport the man-pulled sleighs of Boreal age were supplemented by dog sleighs, represented by runners found from Sweden to the Urals and dated in Finland as early as F.II.[22]

A still heavier sledge, suited for reindeer traction, is attributed to 'the transition from the Stone to the Bronze Age' in Finland. Skis too are attested in Finland and Sweden.[23] For use on water, the skin boats, inferred for the Maglemosian, are actually depicted in a Norwegian rock engraving,[24] while paddles of the Maglemosian type have been dug up from Ural peat.

Each little group of hunter-fishers could be self-sufficing, but

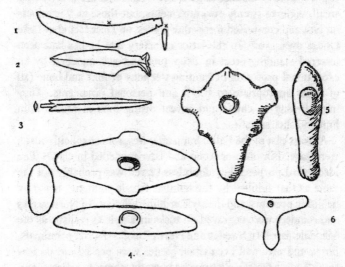

Fig. 106. 1–3, Slate knives and dart-head, Sweden (¼), 4–5, stone mace-heads, Finland (¼), and 6, slate pendant (½).

this economic independence did not exclude interchanges of goods and materials. Indeed, the seasonal hunting trips, imposed by their predatory mode of subsistance, might well be combined with inter-communal barter and easily grow into trading expeditions. So Russian flint was largely imported into Finland during F.II, but was ousted by Scandinavian flint in F.III.[25] Chisels like Fig. 104, 3, were manufactured east of the Baltic, but were imported into Sweden.[26] Forest folk had discovered the amber deposits of Sammland and carved it in their own naturalistic style, but exported it to Norway, Central Germany, Finland, and Central Russia.[27] Becker[28] has convincingly attributed to Forest hunter-fishers the surprisingly wide distribution of South Swedish or Danish flint attested by regular hoards of celts from Northern Scandinavia while Clark[29] has envisaged an export of dried cod from Norway in return.

The ideology, as far as it is expressed in the archaeological record, was as uniform as the economy on which it reposed. So the dead were always buried extended, often accompanied by lumps of red ochre or sprinkled with that colouring matter, either on camp sites or in distinct cemeteries.[30] The latter are usually very small, eight to twenty-two interments, but those at Västerbjers on Gotland comprised forty-nine graves, on Deer Island in Lake Onega over 150.[31] In the latter cemetery five bodies had been interred standing erect in deep pits and accompanied by an exceptional profusion of hunting weapons of flint and bone (all of types appropriate to F.O!) and personal ornaments. They must belong to chiefs and reveal distinctions in rank within hunter-fisher societies.

At least east of the Baltic human figures, some explicitly male, were carved in bone or wood and later modelled in clay.[32] The ideological purpose they doubtless served was probably not the same as that fulfilled by the familiar female statuettes made by neolithic peasants, and the style is quite different. In Norway elks and reindeer were engraved on rocks in a style as realistic as the Magdalenian.[33] In Sweden and North Russia[34] figures of animals, birds, and men and even ritual scenes were pecked out on ice-smoothed surfaces in a far more conventional manner. Beasts and birds were carved realistically in bone, stone, and wood by all the Forest hunter-fisher tribes, but curious little flint sculptures[35] are concentrated rather in Eastern Russia from the Oka to the White Sea.

The authors of these relatively uniform cultures did not constitute a racially homogeneous population. Most of the skulls from sites in North and Central Russia are described as Lapponoid, some as Europeoid, Mongoloid or hybrid,[36] and even on Gotland one skull has been diagnosed as Mongoloid.

The most economical account of the hunter-fisher cultures just surveyed would be to treat them all as derived by divergent adaptation from the North Sea – West Baltic Maglemosian of the Boreal phase. The anthropological data would suffice to exclude such an oversimplification. Becker,[37] without of course denying its Maglemosian constituents, regards the culture symbolized by the pit-comb ware of Scandinavia as introduced there immediately from beyond the Baltic. Russian prehistorians deny vehemently all dependence of the Central Russian, Uralian, and Siberian aspects on the Baltic cultures. According to Briusov,[38] the Urals would have been colonized in early post-glacial times from the Aral-Caspian basin, Central Russia and the East Baltic from the Pontic region; the classical cultures distinguished by pit-comb ware would have crystallized in the Oka-Upper Volga and Upper Dniepr basins. His account involves rather heavy draughts on ignorance. The early cultures of the North Pontic zone and Transcaspia are still very ill-defined. The chronological relations of assemblages from the Ural peat bogs, from sand-dune sites in the Oka-Volga basin, and even from the White Sea-Onega-Ladoga belt to those collected round the Baltic are quite ambiguous. Few pollen-diagrams[39] have been published, and their interpretation in terms of the West Baltic zonation remains disputable.

Types proper to the Boreal phase round the Baltic do indeed occur in the Ural bogs, but their context is unknown. They might theoretically have spread westward rather than eastward, but without independent evidence of date no final decision is justified. So, too, ovoid pots, similar in technique to the Swedish and Finnish, are found both in Siberia[40] and across the Pontic steppes to the Caucasus.[41] The coarse ware, associated with Tripolye pottery at all stages, is technically akin to pit-comb ware. Whipped cord patterns that might have inspired Finnish styles I and II[42] were at some time very popular in the Ukraine and Dniepr basin. But the relative antiquity of all these phenomena is uncertain. The apparent brevity of culture sequences round the Urals, in Central Russia, and in the Ukraine gives the West Baltic a semblance of priority. But that brevity is partly due to deficiencies of exploration and of publication and, in so far as archaeological events are occasioned by climatic changes or land movements, to the greater stability of the continental environment.

The archaeological data here summarized do prove that the hunter-fisher populations of the taiga zone, however sparse, constituted a continuum for cultural transmissions all through the circumpolar zone of Eurasia and between it and the parklands and steppes to the south. They prove too that this was not a one-way traffic, but they give no measure of the relative importance of contributions from the east, the south, and the west respectively. The technique of bifacial retouch on flint flakes and blades is more likely to have reached the north from the south-east than from the south-west; the contemporary appreciation of amber must have been diffused in the opposite direction. The heavier bow introduced into Denmark by the pit-comb traders may have been of the composite type attested in Siberia by the Serovo stage[43] and ancestral to the Turko-Mongolian type, but even the Maglemosian bows had been re-inforced with sinews. The transmission through the food-gathering cultures of the taiga of Asiatic contributions to European civilization is in fact better attested in Sub-Boreal than in Boreal times, but still eludes precise evaluation.

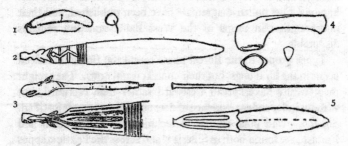

Fig. 107. Knives and axe from Seima hoard: 1, ($\frac{1}{2}$); 2, ($\frac{1}{6}$); 3, (detail of 2), ($\frac{1}{3}$); 4–5, ($\frac{1}{6}$).

The cultural continuum thus constituted was disrupted by the arrival of warlike farmers and herdsmen of the Boat Axe and Fatyanovo cultures. The former occupied the East Baltic coastlands, but beyond a frontier, sharply defined in Finland,[44] left undisturbed the old hunter-fishers. These preserved intact the old ceramic tradition of pit-comb ware, though they sometimes used asbestos as temper for the pots, and continued to rely on stone implements and weapons with the addition of local imitations of boat axes even when a few imported socketed axes of Swedish Mälar and East Russian Ananino types[45] proclaim that the Final Bronze Age had already been reached in Denmark and Southern Sweden. So too in Central Russia the Fatyanovo warriors did not replace the older population of the Volga valley. Camp sites, yielding pottery made in conformity with the old prescriptions, though now sometimes decorated with textile impressions, illustrate the survival of a predominantly neolithic hunter-fisher population when socketed celts and other metal types represented in the hoard from Seima (on the Oka west of Gorki)[46] were filtering in from the Late Bronze Age cultures of the srubno phase to the south and east. The realistic elk's head of the Seima knife-handle (Fig. 107, 2–3) has indeed analogues in Siberian and Chinese bronze-work,[47] but springs from the naturalistic art of the Eurasiatic hunter-fishers and can be closely matched not only on stone battle-axes that have turned up from Norway to the Urals[48] but also on the bone dagger from the Deer Island cemetery on Lake Onega. But such belated survivals of the Stone Age lie outside the scope of this book.

Megalithic Tombs

The diffusion of Oriental culture in Western Europe must have been effected in part by maritime intercourse. And evidence of such intercourse is supposedly afforded by the architecture of groups of tombs spread significantly along the coasts of the Mediterranean and the Atlantic and along terrestrial routes joining these coasts. Judged by their contents, the tombs in question do not belong to a single culture and were not therefore erected and used by a single people. But architectural details recur with such regularity at so many distinct places that a general survey of the main types at this stage will save repetition.

The most intriguing tombs of the series, which consequently received the first attention from archaeologists, are built of extravagantly large stones. They are therefore termed 'megalithic'. But as the same plans are followed in tombs built in dry masonry with small stones and in others excavated in the ground (*rock-cut tombs*) the application of the term to the whole series is misleading. In Portugal,[1] for instance, beehive chambers entered through a low, narrow passage were excavated in hillsides where the soft limestone facilitated digging. Where the subsoil was shallow and the rock hard, the same plan was reproduced above ground in dry-stone masonry roofed by corbelling if the local sandstone or schists broke naturally into convenient slabs. Where the rock is more refractory, like granite, large blocks set on end, *orthostats*, supporting large capstones or lintels form the framework for chamber and passage. And tombs constructed by all three methods often contain the same furniture.

Many authorities[2] therefore contend that in such regions the method of construction is conditioned by local geology alone. That thesis will be adopted in the sequel with the reservation that it is not universally applicable. 'Rock-cut' tombs could easily have been excavated in the chalk of the English Downs, but in fact the burial chambers here were always built above ground. At Antequera and other cemeteries in Southern Spain (p. 324), orthostatic and corbelled tombs – of different plans – stand side by side. In such instances the method of construction must have been dictated exclusively by the traditional prejudices of the tombs' builders. In a preliminary survey, however, it is community of plan that is most significant.

Among a bewildering variety of local deviations it is convenient to distinguish two main types – *Passage Graves* consisting of a chamber entered by a distinct passage, lower and narrower than the chamber proper; and *Long Cists* (*Gallery Graves*) in which the chamber itself is long and narrow and entered directly through a portal without any preceding passage. But if this conventional distinction be rigidly maintained, it leads to quite arbitrary classifications. A tomb like Fig. 153 is on plan as much a Gallery Grave as Fig. 109, but by its furniture and method of construction it belongs to the same group as Fig. 152. Long Cists may be covered by long or round barrows and so may Passage Graves. No complex of relics is peculiar to one type rather than the other save that the SOM culture (pp. 263–4) is regularly associated with Long Cists of the Paris type. Hence even in Western Europe the facts do not authorize us to postulate the diffusion of two distinct versions of the 'megalithic idea'.[3]

The Passage Grave is the most widely distributed type, being common throughout the East Mediterranean area, in Sicily, Sardinia, Southern Spain, Portugal, Brittany, Central Ireland, Northern Scotland, Denmark, South Sweden, and Holland. Cellular annexes open off the main chamber in the rock-hewn tombs of the East Mediterranean, Sardinia, and the Balearic Islands and in some corbelled tombs in Southern Spain, Portugal, Ireland, and Scotland, in a few orthostatic tombs in Brittany and Denmark. Roughly circular chambers characterize the corbelled tombs of Crete and the Cyclades, the earlier rock-hewn tombs of Sicily, and many South Spanish, Portuguese, Breton, Irish, and

261

Scottish sepultures and the oldest Danish ones. A corbelled passage grave of circular plan is often called a *tholos* (Figs. 44 and 108).

In rock-cut tombs the passage is often a descending ramp. Where the ground surface is nearly level it may be reduced to a stepped shaft, producing the pit-cave (Fig. 25, 2) already encountered in Greece and South Russia and to meet us again in Sicily. If the chamber is cut in the face of a cliff, the passage may be abbreviated to a mere doorway as often in Sicily (Fig. 108). A

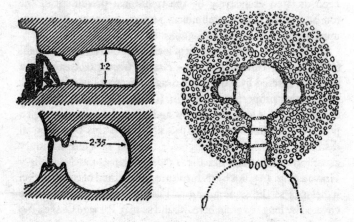

Fig. 108. Rock-cut tomb, Castelluccio, and corbelled tomb, Los Millares.

well-marked variety of passage grave, built with large orthostats, has been termed an undifferentiated passage grave because the passage gradually expands towards the chamber which is generally bottle-shaped. Near Arles and in the Balearic Isles the rock-hewn chambers are themselves long and narrow and not preceded by any length of passage though cellular annexes sometimes open off the chamber (Fig. 109). In Menorca the same type is reproduced above ground in dry-stone masonry in so-called navetas.

The long stone cist or *gallery* reproduces this Balearic plan in orthostatic masonry. In Sardinia the orthostats support dry-stone walling corbelled in to a barrel vault. But in the classic form represented in the Paris basin, Brittany and Jersey, Belgium,

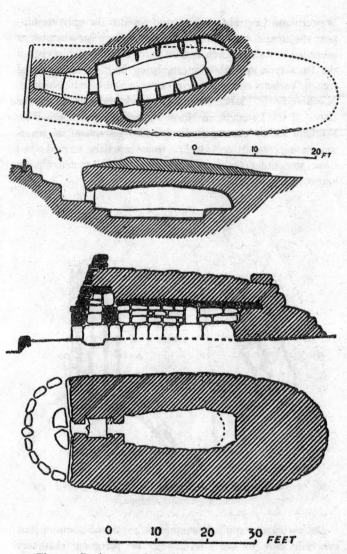

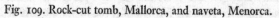

Fig. 109. Rock-cut tomb, Mallorca, and naveta, Menorca.

Western and Central Germany, and Sweden the uprights support the lintels, and the long narrow rectangular chamber is preceded by a short porch as wide as the chamber. Most cists of the Paris type are subterranean, being built in an excavated trench. Variants on the long cist occur in South Italy, Sardinia, Northern Spain, France, Britain, Denmark, and Holland. On the slopes of the Pyrenees, in Northern Ireland, and South-West Scotland gallery graves are divided into a series of intercommunicating compartments by low, transverse slabs, termed *septal stones*, sometimes combined with upright portals; such tombs are known as *segmented cists* (Fig. 110).

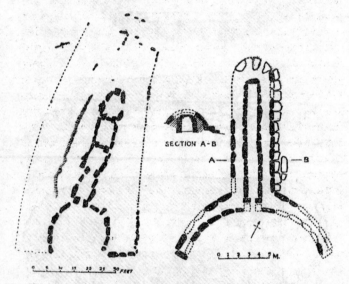

Fig. 110 Segmented cist in horned cairn, North Ireland, and Giants' Tomb, Sardinia.

Dolmen is a term applied sometimes to any megalithic tomb, but generally only to small rectangular or polygonal chambers without entrance passage, formed of three to six megalithic uprights. Even when thus restricted, the name obscures the genetic and functional variety of the monuments to which it is applied. Some 'dolmens', for instance in Sardinia[4] and in the Cotswolds,[5] appear to be just the most stubborn remains of more complex monuments destroyed by cultivators or road-builders. Some are closed chambers, not collective tombs. Others are obviously just abbreviated gallery graves.[6] To avoid confusion we have used the Danish name *dyss* (plural *dysser*) for dolmens which are marked by furniture as well as structure as a distinct type. But even the classical *dyss*, as defined on p. 228, might be regarded as a segmented cist abbreviated to one compartment only.

The portal of the tomb was treated with special care, and one form – termed the porthole slab – must be mentioned here. A round or sub-rectangular aperture, 45 to 80 cm (1 ft 6 in to 2 ft 8 in) across is cut out in a slab – or in the proximal edges of two juxtaposed slabs – which closes the entrance to chamber or passage (Figs. 81 and 100). Porthole slabs were a regular feature in Caucasian 'dolmens' and occur even in the Indian ones. They form the portals to megalithic cists and rock-cut tombs in Sicily, to the gallery graves of Sardinia, to corbelled and other passage graves in Southern Spain,[7] to long cists of the Paris type not only in the Seine valley, but also in Brittany, Jersey, Central Germany, and Sweden; they were even incorporated in the megalithic temples of Malta.[8] A porthole stone often enhances the resemblance of a built tomb's doorway to the entry into a natural or artificial cave. The desire to emphasize the similarity has in fact been suggested as an explanation for the porthole stone's origin.[9] But a porthole slab was employed to form the portal of a tomb cut in friable rock at Monte Salia,[10] and the device does not always simulate a cave mouth at all realistically.

Built chamber tombs, when not erected in an artificial excavation, were probably always put underground artificially by burial in a mound or cairn. The latter was always carefully constructed and was often, if not always, supported by a built masonry revetment wall, or by a peristalith of large uprights. Masonry revetments are well illustrated in the Balearic *navetas*, in some Almerian round cairns, and in the long cairns of the Cotswolds and Northern Scotland. But it is doubtful whether these finely built walls were intended to be seen in Britain, since the faces were masked deliberately by an 'extra revetment'[11] of slabs piled obliquely.

The passage or portal of a chamber tomb often gives on to a forecourt so carefully planned that it must have played an essential part in funerary ritual. Semicircular forecourts cut in the rock precede some Siculan tombs, and are delimited by built walls in front of Sardinian gallery graves and North Scottish passage graves and by orthostats in front of tholoi at Los Millares in Almeria and Barro in Portugal and of North Irish and South-West Scottish segmented cists[12] (Figs. 108 and 110). In England the forecourts are more often cuspidal in plan, as are those connected with one or two Mycenaean, Danish, Swedish, and Armorican passage graves.[13] More careful examinations of the environs of chamber tombs or of the barrows covering them will certainly reveal the presence of forecourts in other regions. Despite their careful construction, the forecourts in Great Britain are generally found filled up with earth and rubble. This filling may be deliberate. In any case the entrances to tombs have usually been intentionally blocked up and hidden. That need not mean, as Hemp[14] has inferred, that the numerous skeletons found in such tombs had all been laid to rest simultaneously, after which the vault was finally sealed up. The intiated could always rediscover the entrance and remove the blocking, as happened at Mycenae (pp. 121–2). Irrefutable evidence of the use of tombs for successive interments is forthcoming from one or two graves in Scotland, Brittany, and Denmark,[15] as at Mycenae.

The distribution of chamber tombs is presumably due to the spread of some religious idea expressed in funerary ritual. Save in Egypt, they seem everywhere to have served as collective sepulchres or family vaults. A family likeness between the skeletons buried in the same tomb has been reported in England and Denmark[16] as at Mycenae, and the features noted in Crete (p. 59: fires kindled in the chamber, confusion of bones) are repeated almost universally. Collective burial alone can hardly represent the unifying idea, since collective burial in natural caves was practised even in mesolithic Palestine (p. 58). It has indeed been suggested that the tombs were just copies of cave ossuaries,[17] and Wheeler[18] describes the erection of megalithic tombs as 'the mass production of artificial caves' by populations accustomed to collective burial in natural ones. But in Scotland and elsewhere perfectly good natural caves were neglected; collective burial comes in simultaneously with megalithic sepulchral architecture. But megalithic tombs were not always used as communal ossuaries. The finest *tholoi*, the Mycenaean, were designed for a single chieftain and perhaps his spouse. The most elaborate rock-cut tombs of the Marne contain only a few skeletons, the rest a hundred or so. Moreover, burial practices were far from uniform. While inhumation, generally in the contracted attitude, was everywhere the normal practice, cases of cremation have been reported from many South Spanish, South French, Armorican, and British tombs and are conclusively attested in Northern Ireland.

It is in fact only detailed agreements in seemingly arbitrary peculiarities of plan and in accessories, such as porthole slabs and forecourts, that justify the interpretation of megalithic tombs as evidences of the diffusion of ideas. The grave goods afford little support for this interpretation. They are characterized at first by purely local idiosyncrasies and would suggest to the typologist differences in date. In Egypt, Cyprus, and the Aegean even the earliest tombs contain a relative abundance of metal objects, and such are not uncommon even in the first Siculan and Sardinian vaults. Moreover, in all these regions chamber tombs continued to be built and used even in the Iron Age. In Portugal, as in Malta, some megalithic tombs seem to be genuinely pre-metallic, but in most tombs in the Iberian Peninsula and South France, too, despite numerous stone tools, the grave goods are explicitly Copper Age, while during the Bronze Age collective burial in chamber tombs went out of fashion. In Brittany metal is exceptional in chamber tombs. In Great Britain and the rest of North-Western Europe such tombs contain an exclusively neolithic furniture and in general went out of use as bronze became available.

This disparity has been used to support the thesis that megalithic tombs, invented in the extreme north or in Portugal in a fabulously ancient Stone Age, were carried thence to reach South Spain in the Copper Age and the Aegean in a still later Bronze Age. In reality the quantity of metal from the tombs is no criterion of their absolute age. In North Europe we have proved conclusively that at least the later 'Stone Age' passage graves and long cists were in use during the full Bronze Age or Danubian period IV in Central Europe and that none of the dysser even need be appreciably older than period III. On the short chronology outlined on p. 392 megalith building in Denmark should begin about 2500 B.C., or several centuries later than the Early Minoan and Cycladic tombs, to say nothing of the Egyptian.

The extreme rarity of metal and indeed of other imported objects in the megalithic tombs of Northern and North-Western Europe seems an almost fatal objection to the theory that the idea of building such tombs was diffused by 'prospectors' or 'Children of the Sun'[19] setting out from Egypt or some other East Mediterranean centre to settle in regions where ores or precious stones, valued for magical qualities as givers of life, were to be found. There is a general, but far from exact, correlation between the distribution of such substances (for instance, copper in the Iberian Peninsula, the Pyrenees, Sardinia, Ireland, Galloway, and the Crinan district, tin in Galicia and Cornwall, gold in Brittany, Ireland, and the Strath of Kildonan, pearls in Orkney, amber in Jutland, etc.) and foci of megalithic architecture. The tomb furnitures afford surprisingly little evidence for the exploitation of these resources (no Scottish copper, gold, or pearls have been found in a local megalith) and none whatever of Egyptian or Aegean imports obtained in exchange for their exportation. Yet such products would be expected in the graves of merchant princes enjoying such prestige that they could persuade local savages laboriously, if rather barbarously, to copy for them the sepultures appropriate to their rank at home, and inspired also with the desire for securing their own immortality by necklaces of pearls and gold beads.

The rarity or complete absence of imports from megalithic tombs is furthermore a serious obstacle to their correlation with any independent sequence of cultures by which their relative or absolute age might be determined. Once in Sicily, very frequently in Sardinia, the Iberian Peninsula, South France, and Brittany, occasionally in Scotland and even Denmark, Bell-beakers or their derivatives are found in megalithic tombs of almost every form. From individual tombs in Brittany, Spain, Scotland, and Denmark[20] it has been proved conclusively that the Beakers were associated only with the later interments in the tombs concerned. The Beaker-folk cannot therefore have been the vehicles in the original diffusion of the 'megalithic idea', nor can their expansion, which reached the Danube basin late in period III, fix the relative age of the earlier chamber tombs.

Gallery graves in Central France, Brittany, and Jersey and even in the Balearic Islands and Southern Sweden regularly contain relics of the Horgen culture (p. 245). Indeed, it may be said that Horgen folk diffused the Paris type of long cist to Brittany and across Germany to Sweden. In Central Europe the Horgen culture too seems to belong to a late phase of period III, and lasts into IV. But megalithic tombs are not attached to the best-dated Horgen settlements, and the long cist may be a secondary accretion in their culture.

In default of better founded chronologies, a resort to typology is tempting. In Scandinavia the sequence, dyss (dolmen), passage grave, long stone cist really seems to hold good, though it is no longer regarded, as it was by Montelius, as a self-contained process of evolution and degeneration. Similar sequences have been applied by Leeds, Obermaier, and Bosch-Gimpera[21] to the Iberian Peninsula, and by Mackenzie to Sardinia.[22] Bosch-Gimpera, by labelling some ruinous tombs in Northern Portugal 'dolmens', traces their development into orthostatic passage graves, rock-cut tombs, and lastly tholoi. But of the Iberian Peninsula Forde could write[23] quite justly, 'small passage dolmens have a poorer, but not earlier furniture and represent a provincial degradation typical of peripheral areas'. In the sequel, however, it has been established that some orthostatic passage graves are really earlier than any tholoi in Portugal, while the still unpublished furniture is said to confirm the yet higher antiquity of 'small dolmens', containing it would seem only a single burial. Mackenzie's 'dolmens' in Sardinia prove on closer examination to be just badly ruined Giants' Graves.[24] Only in Denmark is the priority in time of the simplest types proved by grave goods. But even in Denmark out of hundreds of dysser only fifty-seven are dated by their contents to Northern II; a very large proportion must have been built, like the passage graves, during period III.[25]

No new typology need be attempted here. The architectural agreements cited reveal the megalithic province as a cultural continuum. Within that continuum culture grows in every aspect poorer as we pass westward and northward from the East Mediterranean to Scotland and Denmark. We see the same sort of cultural zoning that has been disclosed in the Danubian corridor and on the Eurasiatic plain.

Beaker Traders

The Beaker-folk was a principal agency in opening up communications, establishing commercial relations, and diffusing the practice of metallurgy. We have already mentioned their activities in Central Europe, and they will meet us so frequently in the West that a brief characterization becomes convenient at this point.

Beaker-folk can be recognized not only by their economic activities but also by the distinctive armament, ornaments, and above all pottery, associated together everywhere in their graves. Indeed, the inevitable drinking-cup, which gives a name to its users, may be more than a readily recognized diagnostic symptom; it symbolizes beer as one source of their influence, as a vodka flask or a gin bottle would disclose an instrument of European domination in Siberia and Africa respectively. Millet grains[26] were in fact found in a beaker in Portugal.

The Beaker-folk are known principally from graves which never form large cemeteries. When their pottery and other relics are found in settlements, they are normally mixed, save perhaps in Central Spain, with remains distinctive of other groups. Thus Beaker-folk appear as bands of armed merchants who engaged in trading copper, gold, amber, callaïs, and similar scarce substances which are frequently found in their graves. The bands included smiths – the mould for casting a West European dagger was found in a Moravian Beaker grave[27] – and women who everywhere fashioned the distinctive vases with scrupulous attention to traditional details of form and ornament. They roved from the Moroccan coasts[28] and Sicily to the North Sea coasts, and from Portugal and Brittany to the Tisza and the Vistula.[29] Sometimes they settled down, by preference in regions of natural wealth or at the junctions of important routes. At times they obtained economic and political authority over established communities of different cultures, formed hybrid groups with these, and even led them on farther wanderings; the Beaker groups that invaded Britain give indications of composite origin.

A detailed study of Beaker pottery does not disclose a single and irreversible expansion. It suggests an early uniformity so remarkable as to be hardly explicable merely by the rapidity of a migration and the conservatism of the migrants followed by the

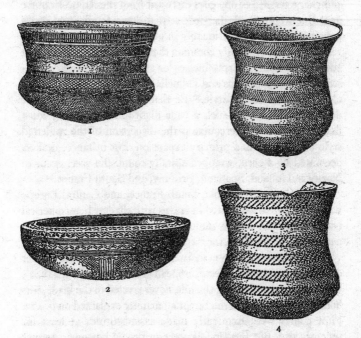

Fig. 111. Beaker pottery: 1, ($\frac{1}{3}$) and 2, ($\frac{1}{5}$), Palmella, Portugal; 3, La Halliade, South France ($\frac{1}{3}$); 4, Villafrati, Sicily ($\frac{1}{2}$).

emergence of distinct local groups, but the maintenance of intercourse between some of these at least. The 'classical' or 'Pan-European' beaker (Fig. 111, 3–4),[30] made of relatively fine grit-tempered ware coated with a burnished slip that is liable to peel off and brick red to black in colour, is decorated with zones of 'rouletted' hatchings, alternating with plain zones. The 'rouletted' decoration is executed with a comb with very short teeth, separated by extremely narrow interstices and probably with a curved edge. It yields a practically continuous 'hyphenated line' of round or, more often, rectangular dots, separated by low septa. The horizontal zones may be combined with a radial decoration on the base.

This classic Pan-European style is represented in nearly every region[31] reached by the Beaker-folk, though it grows less common and characteristic as one goes eastward from the Rhine-Brenner line. But wherever Beaker-folk settled down at all, local styles grew up. These are presumably in general later and specialized variants on the originally common theme. On the other hand, an Iberic style using sharply incised or stamped lines (well represented at Ciempozuelos and Palmella) (Fig. 111, 1–2) is possibly older than the classic style.[32] Be that as it may, some local or derivative styles have such a wide distribution that they must denote secondary intercourse if the dispersion of the rouletted style be ascribed to a primary expansion. For instance, beakers decorated by a cord, wrapped spirally round the vase, occur in Northern Holland, Scotland, Brittany, and South France.[33]

In the Iberian Peninsula, South France, and Central Europe beakers are often associated in graves with shallow hemispherical bowls decorated in the same technique but more often with patterns radiating from the base (Fig. 111, 2).

A distinctive weapon associated everywhere with the Beaker complex is the tanged West European knife-dagger (Fig. 113, 2). The tang may be flanged; the hilt, never riveted to the blade, was hollowed at the base in the Egyptian manner explained on p. 173. Flint copies were frequently made as substitutes at least for funerary use. But Beaker-folk were primarily bowmen. Arrows were normally tipped with tanged-and-barbed flint heads in Western Europe, with hollow-based heads in Holland, Central Europe, and Upper Italy. In Central Europe (including Italy and Poland), Holland, and Great Britain, rarely also in Brittany, but only once certainly in Spain,[34] the Beaker archer wore a concave plaque of stone perforated at the four corners as a *wrist-guard* for protection against the recoil of the bow-string (Fig. 112). In South France, Brittany, and Bohemia[35] thin strips of gold-leaf (Fig. 113, 4), similarly perforated for the same purpose. Thick clay plaques of the same plan, but flat and also perforated at the corners, are found on Beaker sites in Portugal and Spain and may

Fig. 112. Beaker, wrist-guard, and associated vases, Silesia.
After Seger (¼).

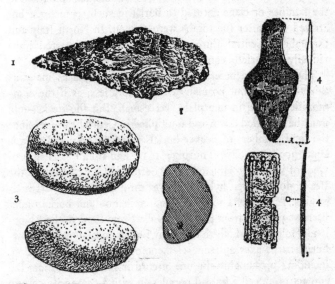

Fig. 113. West European dagger (Bohemia) and flint copy
(Silesia); arrow-straightener (Wiltshire); gold-leaf from wrist-
guard and copper awl, Bohemia (½).

also have been used as wrist-guards. Stone arrow-straighteners,[36] used by Beaker-folk in Bohemia and Poland and also in Sardinia, do not seem to be an original part of their equipment since in Central Europe they appear in pre-Beaker times, in Britain only in the early Middle Bronze Age, well after the Beaker invasions were over.

A distinctive element of the Beaker-folk's costume was a button of stone, bone, amber, or jet with V perforations.

In Northern Sicily, Sardinia, the Iberian Peninsula, South France and Brittany, and the Channel Islands, Beakers and their normal associated armaments are found, generally accompanied by relics distinctive of other cultures, in collective sepulchres – natural caves,[37] rock-cut tombs,[38] tholoi,[39] orthostatic passage graves,[40] gallery graves,[41] and segmented cists.[42] In no case, however, do they demonstrably accompany the primary interments, while in isolated instances they were proved to be secondary (p. 378). Beaker-folk had sometimes obtained admission to the families or clans entitled to burial in such sepulchres, but arrived only after the tombs were erected. In North Italy and throughout Central Europe, Beaker-folk were interred individually and strictly contracted, in simple trench graves.

These form cemeteries comprising in Moravia as many as thirty graves,[43] but normally considerably less, as if the communities settled in one place were small. But the Beaker-folk must have settled down and multiplied in Central Europe, since the total numbers of Beaker burials recorded from Bohemia is about 300, from Saxo-Thuringia 103,[44] and from the small province of Veluwe in Holland 150.[45] Settled in Central Europe, the Beaker-folk formed hybrid cultures through contact with other groups. In Moravia some adopted cremation and burial under barrows perhaps from Battle-axe folk. From these in the Rhineland, Holland, and North Germany Beaker-folk adopted barrow-burial, battle-axes, and some elements even in ceramic decoration, including presumably the use of cord impressions. In fact the contact produced a hybrid population with a composite culture and art. At least the B2 and C groups of Beaker invaders in Britain are offshoots of such a hybrid.

The people buried with Bell-beakers at Ciempozuelos, near Madrid[46] and almost invariably in Central Europe and Britain, are round-headed, and brachycranial skulls are found in nearly every collective tomb that yields Bell-beakers, even in regions so dominantly Mediterranean as Sardinia and Sicily. In Germany,[47] though not representing a strictly homogeneous population, skulls from Beaker cemeteries regularly comprise a novel racial type, better known in the Iberian Peninsula and ultimately of East Mediterranean stock. In this instance, therefore, it looks as if culture and race coincided and one might legitimately speak of a Beaker race. Even in Central Europe Beaker skulls had been trephined.

Both in form and decoration Bell-beakers of the classic style and the associated bowls look like copies of esparto-grass vessels such as are made in the Sudan today.[48] Beaker-like vases decorated with zones of incision which might be clay translations of such basketry vessels occur in Egypt in the early 'Tasian' phase of culture.[49] Potsherds found in a still undatable settlement on the western edge of the Nile valley at Armant and in a 'neolithic' context in the Sudan and Africa Minor[50] show roulette decoration, though rather coarser than that on classical beakers, while typical beakers have been found in a cave on the Moroccan coast.[51] A hollow-based hilt like that regularly attached to West European daggers was attached to flint and copper blades on the Nile in Predynastic times.[52] Hollow-based arrow-heads were characteristic of the 'neolithic' Fayum and of Early Predynastic Egypt. There is accordingly some evidence for an African element in the Beaker culture. Still most authorities hold that the culture as we know it took form in Andalusia or on the lower Tagus,[53] though plausible typological arguments favour a North-West German origin.

The Beaker-folk's expansion, from whatever cradle it started, was presumably rapid. It thus constitutes a convenient chronological horizon in several otherwise separated areas. But the number of beakers and the variety of their decorations in each area imply that such vases must have been in fashion for several generations. It is therefore a grave error to treat all beakers as contemporary.[54] Such vases mark rather a substantial period of time, not everywhere of equal duration. In Central Europe beakers go back to period III. On the other hand, in Moravia, Bohemia, and even on the Rhine, beakers[55] are associated in graves with round-heeled riveted daggers typical of period IV and in Austria[56] with mature Unětician forms. A beaker, with exact parallels in Bohemia and in Sardinia too, reached Denmark, in Neolithic IIIc. And the bronzes of period IV are often decorated with patterns that recur on beakers. In other words, beakers remained in fashion into period IV in Central Europe and the Beaker and Unětician cultures overlap. Beakers do not denote a point in time. But the Beaker cultures are everywhere on the same economic plane. Judged by form and decoration, most British and Central European Beakers seem to be later than the 'classic type', those from the edge of the Beaker territory – Scotland and Poland – looking particularly late.

Spreading westward by sea, the neolithic economy would be expected to reach the Apennine Peninsula next after Greece. This expectation is justified by quite early settlements in Apulia, in Sicily and on the adjacent Aeolian Islands, and along the coast of the Tyrrhenian Sea. But ecologically Italy is less uniform than Greece. In the south and on the Tyrrhenian coasts a rural economy that had worked in the Levant would still serve. It would need drastic adjustments to meet the more continental conditions that reign on the northern slopes of the Apennine chain. In fact, the two sides of the Peninsula enjoyed very different fortunes in the neolithic phase, but during the Bronze Age a remarkable degree of uniformity was attained.

The general outlines of Italian prehistory were sketched last century by Pigorini and Orsi and summarized for English readers by Peet.[1] After fifty years of stagnation they have been corrected and filled in largely as a result of stratigraphical excavations by Bernabo Brea in Liguria, on the Aeolian Islands, and in Sicily. His division[2] of the Italian Neolithic into Lower, Middle, and Upper will be followed in the sequel.

The Neolithic Colonization of South Italy and Sicily

In the south and in Liguria the record begins with settlements characterized best by rough-looking but well-fired vases of quite sophisticated shapes that agree very closely both in technique, form, and ornament with the 'barbottine' ware of Starčevo, that we have encountered all over the Balkan peninsula. That their makers came by sea is clear from the coastwise distribution of the sites and the occupation of small islands in the Tremiti and Aeolian archipelagoes. It must have been the rich deposits of obsidian that attracted early neolithic voyagers to the Aeolian Islands: for fertile though they be, water supplies are totally lacking. In fact, the volcanic glass was extensively exported and used in neolithic villages all over the mainland and Sicily. These first settlers might have come direct from the Balkans, but the occurrence, together with simple rustication, of patterns executed with the edge of a shell (generally *Cardium*) and in particular the so-called rocker motive might suggest a parallel but independent movement from the Levant where this motive was popular on neolithic pottery. Still, 'rocker patterns', executed with a notched stamp if not a shell edge, occur on 'neolithic' pottery in the Urals, in the Sudan, and widely in North Africa, and cannot all be plausibly traced to a single origin! This distinctive pottery is found only exceptionally[3] unmixed with other styles. Hence the Lower Neolithic culture, introduced by these maritime colonists, cannot be further defined. In Sicily it developed directly into the Stentinello culture. This takes its name from a village on the shore just north of Syracuse, but is represented at similar sites at Matrensa and Megara Hyblaea. All three villages lie near the coast on level ground, but were girt with rock-cut ditches and internal ramparts of some kind. At Matrensa the ditch was interrupted by frequent causeways as in English and Rhenish neolithic camps. On these sites, as elsewhere in Sicily and at Castellaro on Lipari, the rough-looking rusticated pottery is associated with a very fine local ware characterized by the use of a greater variety of stamps, more diversified motives, their composition to form well-ordered patterns (in contrast to the casually scattered finger-tip or cardial impressions of the 'rough ware'), and an equal diversity of shapes; the latter include simple round-bottomed types such as are attributed to the 'Western Neolithic' in Chapter 15, and also sophisticated vessels with, for instance, ring handles rising above the rims.

The economy evidently was based on cultivation, stock-breeding, hunting, fishing, and collecting, but no weapons survive save sling-bullets. Blade tools of local flint or of obsidian from Lipari include neither bifacially worked nor geometric types. Ground stone celts were rare.

The only burial attributable to the Stentinello culture is that of a skeleton in a round pit lined with slabs on edge. Nor do female figurines survive to attest a fertility cult of the Asiatic–Balkan type. A few clay animal heads may be ritual or merely ornamental.

While the Stentinello culture was still flourishing in Sicily, the Middle Neolithic phase in Apulia had already been initiated with the advent or development of a distinct culture which will here be called the Molfetta culture, characterized by painted pottery. It is known from numerous ditched enclosures, revealed by air photographs,[4] of which only a few have been excavated.[5] The enclosures can, from the plans alone, be classified as villages and homesteads. The former cover very large areas often subdivided into an inner enclosure, containing within its ditch smaller round enclosures and representing the inhabited area, and a larger outer space, presumably fields or pastures. The inner enclosures, of which there may be 100 in one village, measure sixty to fifty feet across and must be farmyards, like Irish raths, each corresponding to one household. Homesteads too may be divided up into an infield or yard of about an acre in area and a larger demesne outside it. Bradford from air-photographs alone has identified over 200 villages and homesteads in an area of less than 1,500 square miles. So the neolithic population must have been quite dense even if not all sites were Middle Neolithic.

The population was engaged in breeding cows, pigs, sheep, and allegedly buffaloes,[6] while sickle-teeth and saddle querns[7] demonstrated the cultivation of cereals which were stored in the numerous pits that are found within the farmyards. Again the sling is the sole weapon attested. Obsidian was imported from the Aeolian Islands. Ground stone celts were supplemented by roughly flaked chopping-tools. The pottery[8] comprises on the one hand hard-fired burnished ware, generally red and often decorated with rectilinear patterns scratched after firing, and on the other light-coloured fabrics painted with designs in red, or red and black. Some vases show a nose and two eyes, just below the rim, as in the Trapeza ware of Crete.[9] Similar painted vases may illustrate the spread of the Molfetta culture to the Aeolian Islands, Ischia, and Capri,[10] but on Sicily it is represented only by stray painted vases (Fig. 114, 3) found on Stentinello sites. On Lipari[11] some of these vases are provided with vertical subcutaneous handles, foreshadowing a device already encountered in Central Europe in the Baden complex, and to meet us shortly in the Rinaldone culture of Central Italy. And the painted ware is associated with black burnished vases, some provided with broad ribbon handles as in Early Neolithic Greece. These black vessels are sometimes crusted after firing with red or black colours or incised with maeanders or less often spirals in a manner that really recalls Dimini and Balkan-Danubian styles.

The Molfetta culture is usually supposed to have been introduced into Apulia from the Balkan peninsula. But except for the maeander and spiral patterns on Lipari no decisive parallels can at present be found on that side of the Adriatic.

The Later Neolithic Phases

A second division of the Middle Neolithic (M.N.II) is conveniently defined on the mainland and on the Aeolian Islands by the 'fine painted ware' classically represented at Serra d'Alto near Matera. The walls and ditches of the enclosures had been allowed to collapse or fill up,[12] but the sites were still inhabited or used as burying-grounds. Much of the old culture persisted, but ceramic forms and decorations are quite novel. The vases, including on Lipari[13] rare square-mouthed vessels, are painted, but only in warm black, and with stumpy spirals or maeanders and step, ladder, or windmill motives (Fig. 114, 1–2). One vase from Apulia stood on model human feet. Long horizontal tubular handles, perforated axially, are quite distinctive; they might be surmounted by conventionalized heads of bulls or rams.

The dead were buried flexed in pits lined with stones and provided with a special niche for the feet.[14] Rare clay stamps or *pintadere*,[15] long and narrow in plan in contrast to the Aegean-Balkan forms, may belong to the ideological equipment, but clay figurines are missing save on Lipari.

The Serra d'Alto culture, like its predecessor, is generally considered to be instrusive in Apulia and of Balkan origin. Similar painted pottery has in fact been found in the cave of Khirospilia on Levkas, and the *pintadere* could be derived from Balkan clay stamps. But no exact counterpart to the culture has been identified outside Italy. Now Puglisi[16] has recently reported Mycenaean sherds associated with typical 'fine painted ware' in the Caverna de Erba in the heel of Italy. If his observations be confirmed, the whole culture sequence in South Italy, Sicily, and Malta will have to be drastically curtailed. But on the acropolis of Lipari Serra d'Alto pottery is stratified well below the layer containing abundant L.M.I imported vases, while Diana and other groups, distinguished mainly by typology, should be intercalated before this horizon.

In the Late Neolithic phase, more sharply distinguished in the

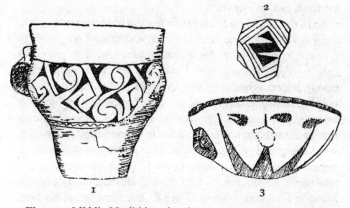

Fig. 114. Middle Neolithic painted pottery: 1–2, black on buff, Serra d'Alto ware, M.N.II; 3, red and black on buff, Megara Hyblaea ($\frac{1}{4}$).

village of Diana on Lipari than on the mainland, painted wares went out of fashion to give place to highly burnished red vases. These still retained the horizontal tubular handles of Serra d'Alto which, at first of exaggerated length and expanding towards the ends like trumpet-lugs, subsequently degenerated into unpierced ridges. But by this time fresh impulses were reaching the province. At Diana on Lipari occur a few bifacially trimmed hollow-based arrow-heads and even metal slag.[17] On the mainland at Bellavista near Taranto[18] polished vases with Diana handles but also spouts were found in a small cemetery of rock-cut collective tombs.

The phenomena just mentioned herald the transition to a new division of the archaeological record traditionally termed Chalcolithic, most clearly documented in Sicily. There the Serra d'Alto culture had been represented only by a few typical vases found as far west as Palermo.[19] Vases of Diana style are more widespread and occur even on Stentinello sites, though perhaps in intrusive graves. But in the chalcolithic cultures of Sicily the Stentinello tradition seems to be blended with, or transformed by, fresh foreign impulses.

So in the San Cono culture[20] we find both single interments in stone-lined pit graves, as at Molfetta, and at least one rock-cut pit-cave, used however for a single interment. The pottery is dark-faced, sometimes incised and incrusted with red or white colour, but occasionally painted in bright red before firing. Small polished celts, hitherto rare, are now common, and bifacially trimmed arrow-heads appear, as at Diana. Metal is practically unrepresented, but obsidian was freely imported and rough celts, some sharpened with a tranchet blow, were manufactured in regular factories on the slopes of the Iblean Mountains and systematically distributed.[21] From this culture developed in North-Western Sicily that termed Conco d'Oro,[22] known mainly from small groups of pit-cave tombs each containing one, or exceptionally two corpses; sometimes two chambers open off a single shaft. Hollow-based arrow-heads, stone beads, and an axe-amulet are among the grave goods, and a variety of pots. Besides self-coloured wares decorated by incision or rarely with white paint, clear buff ware was manufactured and covered all over with a dark slip that might be used as a ground for designs in white paint. Cups and mugs are provided with good handles, some nosed; 'salt-cellars' – paired bowls linked by a high loop handle – were conspicuous. The tomb type, the pot forms, and the dark-slipped pale ware vaguely suggest East Mediterranean influence. On the other hand, a Bell-beaker, imported from Sardinia or Spain, was found in a sepulchral cave at Villafrati, and another Beaker, perhaps a local imitation, came from a Conco d'Oro tomb at Carini.[23] The Conco d'Oro culture lasted until the Casteluccio culture was established in South-Eastern Sicily, and Late Minoan

I pottery was reaching the Aeolian Islands in the fifteenth century.[24]

By then the Serraferlicchio[25] pottery style of Southern Sicily had developed and disappeared. The vases, red surfaced and painted in black, include handled mugs, amphorae, and spouted jugs that look vaguely Aegean though the patterns can be best matched in the 'Neolithic' of Acarnania. On the Aeolian Islands[26] the period is represented by the village of Piana Conte, where imported vases of Serraferlicchio style were found together with local vases provided with vertical subcutaneous string-holes or horizontal tunnel-handles.

The Sicilian Bronze Age

The foreign influences foreshadowed in these rather nebulous transitional cultures culminate in the rise of the Castelluccio

Fig. 115. Bossed bone plaque, Castelluccio. After Evans ($\frac{1}{2}$).

culture, Orsi's Siculan I, in South-Eastern Sicily. Now actual Aegean imports supplement ceramic and architectural analogies and provide an historically dated horizon not only for the environs of Syracuse but for Malta and the Aeolian Islands too.

In Eastern Sicily, as on the Aeolian Islands, the lowland coastal villages had been replaced by little townships planted on naturally defensible hilltops or promontories and well fortified. The walled areas were still small; in two cases the estimate given is one hectare or $2\frac{1}{2}$ acres. But large cemeteries of collective tombs imply a substantial population settled in one place for several generations; thirty-two tombs have been actually examined at Castelluccio, twenty at Syracuse, eleven at Monte Salia, and each tomb contained from fifty to 200 corpses.[27] The population, of course, still depended primarily on farming – the bones of horses are now reported in addition to those of food animals – but produced a surplus to support craftsmen and traders.

Flint was still systematically mined at Monte Tabuto by expert miners who were presumably specialists. Metal was imported and apparently worked locally into simple flat axes (known only by a couple of miniatures made for funerary purposes), triangular riveted daggers and ornaments such as spectacle-spirals, and tubes of coiled wire. However, metal was so rare

Fig. 116. Early Apennine Copper and Early Bronze Age pottery: 1–2, pit-cave, Otranto; 3, 'dolmen' of Bisceglie; 4–5, Castelluccio ware ($\frac{1}{4}$).

that polished stone axes and roughly flaked picks were still made and used even for carving the tombs. Stone beads were manufactured for the first time.

Foreign trade is explicitly disclosed by bossed bone plaques (Fig. 115) found in several tombs,[28] in the ruins of Troy II, in a Middle Helladic layer at Lerna (p. 115), and in the 'neolithic' temple of Hal Tarxien in Malta. Its effects may also be recognized in a bone pommel[29] of the same type as the Trojan pommel shown in Fig. 21, 3, in a Middle Helladic matt-painted cup from tomb V at Monte Salia, and in numerous axe-amulets, but some alleged 'amber' beads may be made of a local resin.

Pottery remained a domestic industry, but the forms of the handmade vases – hour-glass tankards, high-handled mugs (Fig. 116, 4–5) and pedestalled bowls with handles joining bowl and stem – are quite alien to the Stentinello tradition. They may

Fig. 117. View into chamber tomb, Castelluccio.

be plain or painted in black on a reddish ground with geometric designs. On some vases from Vallelunga the black is outlined in white, giving somewhat the effect of Dimini ware.

The dead were now buried in rock-cut tombs of East Mediterranean style (Fig. 108). The chambers are generally more or less circular in plan and may be preceded by a smaller ante-chamber. When cut in a vertical cliff face, the entrance is normally a small window-like aperture, rebated to receive the blocking stone. The blocking stone in one tomb at Castelluccio was carved with spirals in low relief; the entrance to the inner chamber of another tomb in the same cemetery was closed by two carved slabs, which, combined (Fig. 117), produce the effect of the funerary goddess carved on many megalithic tombs in France and on the stele from Troy I mentioned on p. 76. The tombs often open on to a semi-circular porch or forecourt cut in the rock, the walls of which were in at least one case carved with pilasters.[30] In some late tombs at Monteracello the vault had been reproduced above ground in a rectangular cist (2·05 m by 1·2 m square) framed with four large slabs on edge in one of which a square window had been cut out, converting it into a sort of porthole slab.[31] The disused galleries of flint-mines were also used as burial-places. All these tombs served as family vaults in which numerous skeletons were deposited, sometimes seated as if at a feast. Ritual objects from domestic sites include clay horns,[32] used perhaps against the evil eye. Such horns had, however, been used already at Serraferlicchio and in contemporary sites on the Aeolian Islands.

In a general way the Castelluccio culture, economy, and funerary ritual might be attributed to a further extension of the causes that occasioned the rise and westward expansion of Early Helladic culture in Greece. But the sepulchral architecture has more analogies to the West than to the East. The pottery, despite Early Helladic parallels (e.g. to the tankards of Fig. 116, 2), has been more aptly compared by Bernabo Brea[33] to Anatolian wares – particularly the Cappadocian current at the time of the Assyrian colony at Kül-tepe between 1950 and 1850 B.C. The bossed bone plaques may be just versions of the gold ornaments from the earlier Royal Tombs of Alaca, but find their closest analogues in Troy and Middle Helladic Lerna (pp. 80–81). The matt-painted cup from Monte Salia unambiguously attests contact with Middle Helladic Greece, probably after rather than before 1600 B.C. More precise limits can be deduced from Aegean imports on the Aeolian Islands.

The islands had now become points of trans-shipment for coastwise trade between the Aegean and the West or lairs for pirates who preyed thereon. In contrast to the earlier open villages, settlements of the Early Bronze Age Capo Graziano culture (so-called after a site on that promontory of Filicudi) are located on naturally defensible sites or fortified.[34] That on the acropolis of Lipari comprises over ten oval huts with stone wall bases and internal diameters between 3·2 m by 3·0 m and 4·5 m by 3·1 m which are grouped round a much larger oval building in an inner enclosure that seems a sanctuary rather than a chieftain's palace. Though the culture is termed Bronze Age, no metal survives – collective tombs that might have contained some had been pillaged long ago – and obsidian was still quarried and worked. But a relative abundance of Minoan and Mycenaean vases attest frequent contacts with the Aegean. Most sherds are L.H.I–II, only a tiny handful might be L.H.IIIa. Hence the Capo Graziano villages flourished mainly between 1500 and 1400 B.C. Only a couple of sherds of Castelluccio ware have been recognized on the Aeolian Island sites. On the other hand, the earliest Bronze Age pottery of Malta is related to native Capo Graziano ware, while imported specimens of the latter have been reported from Conco d'Oro tombs at Villafrati.[35]

Hence in North-Western Sicily the Conco d'Oro culture must have lasted till 1500 B.C. Only thereafter was it replaced by the Castelluccio culture. By 1400 B.C. in South-Eastern Sicily the latter culture had been replaced by that now named after a cemetery at Thapsos – Orsi's Siculan II.

By then Sicilian economy had been transformed into one of full Middle Bronze Age type by the incorporation of the island into the Aegean commercial system. Late Helladic III pottery,[36] gold rings, bronze vessels, mirrors, rapiers,[37] and fayence beads were imported from Greece. Aegean influence was so strong that Evans[38] suspected a Cretan colonization of the island under a Minoan prince.

But basically the Thapsos culture was rooted in the native traditions of the island. Pottery was not industrialized. The handmade grey vases, though unpainted and decorated in a novel style, preserve many Castelluccio forms. Large cemeteries of rock-cut tombs carry on equally old traditions. But though the cemeteries comprise far more tombs, each chamber contained far fewer corpses, serving as the burying-place of a single family, as at Mycenae.

Ischia,[39] the Aeolian Islands, and the adjacent promontory of Milazzo in Sicily were also now incorporated in the orbit of Mycenaean trade, but not in the Thapsos culture. They seem rather to be frontier posts between the Aegean and the Continental–West European commercial systems. The cemetery of Milazzo[40] consists not of chamber tombs but of pithos burials;

these reproduce the practice of Argaric Spain, of Anatolia, and of Middle Helladic – but not Mycenaean – Greece. The grave goods include amber, imported from the Baltic, and fayence from the Aegean. On the acropolis of Lipari and in the natural fortress of Milazzesi on Panarea [41] imported Mycenaean vases and Thapsos pottery turn up in villages of oval, or exceptionally rectilinear, houses, built on stone foundations – twenty-three survive at Milazzesi. Native vases, inscribed with characters derived from the first Minoan linear (A) script, show how deeply Aegean influence had penetrated the islands' culture. Associated are ritual objects of clay, almost identical in form and size with the anchor

Fig. 118. Knife and razor, Pantalica ($\frac{1}{2}$).

ornaments so popular in Greece and Thrace in the Early Aegean period – nearly a millennium earlier. A hoard of imported beads found on Salina contains more segmented fayence beads than have been found in the whole of Britain! But side by side with these Aegean and Sicilian elements are sherds of early Apennine ware. They indicate strong influence, if not some actual colonization, from the Italian mainland as early as 1350 B.C. Thereafter the Aeolian Islands were annexed to the mainland province of the Apennine culture, doubtless as a consequence of the invasion by Ausonians, of which Diodorus has preserved a tradition.

An extension of this current to Sicily may be inferred from an urnfield at Milazzo; [42] the cremation rite is that proper to the mature Bronze Age of peninsular Italy; the funerary vases are of Apennine type. But one at least is decorated in the old Thapsos style. Thus the cremationists should have arrived at latest about 1150, which would agree strikingly with the traditional dates given for the arrival of the Sicels by Hellanikos and Thucydides! But in South-Eastern Sicily the old tradition of inhumation in chamber tombs was maintained in the cultures of Pantalica and Cassabili [43] (both were included by Orsi and Peet in Siculan II).

But here too ceramic styles have changed, Mycenaean imports have ceased, the settlements and cemeteries have been transferred from the coastal plains to more defensible fastnesses farther inland. Some of the metal-work is still based on Mycenaean traditions (shaft-hole axes, knives like Fig. 118, 1). Razors and fibulae conform to Continental types. By the Late Bronze Age even Sicily was dominated by the traditions of Temperate Europe.

The Early Metal Ages in South Italy

In tells[44] and caves[45] strata containing plain burnished leather-coloured pots of Apennine types seem to be immediately superimposed on those yielding Serra d'Alto ware, and the local Apennine culture they typify lasted, through a period when Mycenaean pottery was imported, into the Iron Age. The Mycenaean levels should correspond to the Thapsos phase in Sicily and the Middle Bronze Age of Upper Italy. Earlier phases may be represented in some sepulchral caves,[46] chamber tombs,[47] and 'dolmens'.[48]

The latter are either passage graves with a chamber, no wider than the passage, or long cists, one actually a segmented cist.[49] One was provided with a porthole slab, placed however in one side instead of at the end.[50] Of the furniture, a few amber beads and a cup with an axe-handle (Fig. 116, 3) survive. Identical cups will meet us in Liguria, South France, and Catalonia associated in the latter regions with a late phase of the local megalithic culture. So it looks as if the South Italian dolmens were an offshoot of the South French megalithic culture. Puglisi[51] suggested that it was brought through Corsica and Sardinia by pastoral groups, who, landing in Tuscany, would have helped to develop the Apennine culture which they brought with them by land routes to the southern extremity of the peninsula.

But some interments in chamber tombs and natural caves may be earlier, for some of these contain Diana ware (pp. 281–2) or vases with striking parallels in Thessaly III.[52] The chamber tombs themselves might denote Aegean influence as in Sicily and equally early.

If so, similar funerary practices should reveal the same influence in Central Italy too. After all, in historical times the first

Greek colony in the West was planted at Cumae near Naples, not in Sicily nor the heel of Italy. A cemetery of pit-cave tombs at Paestum (Gaudo) near Salerno[53] might represent a precursor a millennium earlier. Most chambers contain only one, or at most two, flexed skeletons, but some were genuine collective tombs with seventeen or even twenty-six corpses, while occasionally two chambers open off a single pit. The funerary pottery, monochrome, generally black, rarely ornamented with incised designs, includes some very Aegean-looking forms, notably askoi and pyxides with string-hole lids, while 'salt-cellars', globular vases with strap handles, and some other types could be paralleled in the Conco d'Oro (p. 282) as well as in Apulia. Transverse arrowheads were found in one tomb, but bifacially trimmed tanged arrow-heads and lance-heads and a single copper dagger with prominent mid-rib are types proper to the Rinaldone culture farther north. Of thirteen skulls examined, five were brachycranial, three longheaded.

Trade from such a 'colony' might have promoted the rise in Central Italy of the *Rinaldone* culture, first distinguished from the North Italian Remedello culture by Laviosa-Zambotti in 1939.[54] It is represented by burials in pit-caves or natural grottoes in Latium[55] and Tuscany.[56] There are tin lodes in Tuscany and there a sepulchral cave in Monte Bradoni contained two V-bored buttons of metallic tin, a dagger like Fig. 121, *a*, of Early Minoan affinities and brachycranial skeletons. Kite-shaped or triangular daggers and flat, or exceptionally hammer-flanged, axes recur in other Rinaldone tombs. But while the tomb form and the metal gear may be of Aegean inspiration, other items in Rinaldone equipment are not. Bifacially trimmed daggers and tanged arrow-heads of flint are common to all the 'chalcolithic' cultures of the peninsula. Stone battle-axes with symmetrically splayed blades must be connected with the 'polygonal' weapons of Northern Neolithic II or their copper prototypes of Danubian III. In the pottery, which is dark-faced, burnished but undecorated, the most distinctive form is a bottle provided with no handles but vertical subcutaneous string-holes like those of the Danubian III Baden culture or of M.N.I on Lipari. But at Punta degli Stretti (Grosseto)[57] good Rinaldone types seem associated with an axe-handle cup like Fig. 116, 3.

Thus if southern and western influences travelled northward along the Tiber-Arno corridor, it provided a channel also for cultures, adapted to the Temperate zone, to spread south, and in the Apennine peninsula these proved the more viable.

The Apennine culture that succeeds Rinaldone in Central Italy and that had reached the Tyrrhenian coasts and South Italy by Mycenaean times is still known almost exclusively by its highly characteristic pottery. This has indeed been found in some semi-megalithic tombs under round cairns in Tuscany which, resembling the late passage graves of the Causses d'Aude, might provide the required link between South France and the South Italian 'dolmens'.[58] But these tombs had been re-used in Etruscan times and robbed of any non-ceramic grave goods. Most of the pottery comes from hilltop settlements, much eroded, and from caves used for collective inhumations over a long period.[59] The distinctive monochrome burnished pottery is characterized by an exuberant development of bizarre handles (cf. Figs. 116, 1–3, and 119), all inspired by wooden models. Some vases are decorated with incised punctured ribbons forming spirals and maeanders, as at Butmir and Vinča, or with excised ornament imitating the chip-carving of wood, as in the West Alpine Vučedol culture. Such metal-work as is associated is all based on North Italian and Central European traditions, but is more appropriate to the Middle and Late Bronze Age.

No doubt the amber trade across the Brenner went on to Greece, either along the Adriatic or across Italy by the Arno and the Tiber. But the inhospitable Italian coasts of the Adriatic offered no convenient halting-places to merchantmen, while the rough herdsmen and farmers of Central Italy do not seem to have benefited by any transit trade. Many Apennine sites yield so many stone tools as to look quite neolithic.[60] Metal types, proper to Danubian IV, are very rare in Italy south of the Po basin. A single hoard from Montemerano near Grosseto comprising halberds and a dagger with triple midrib [61] is the sole link with an equally isolated cist grave furnished with a flat axe, a bronze-hilted dagger and perhaps a halberd at Parco di Monaci near Matera. The funerary caves of Central Italy do indeed contain amber beads, but associated with daggers, swords, winged axes, fibulae and other types not known before Danubian V.

ducted by L. Bernabo Brea since 1939.[63] It is not applicable to the whole of Upper Italy; for Liguria belongs still to the Mediterranean zone and was in historical times a backward and provincial area. And so in this cave stone axes were plentiful right up to the last occupation layer, where the pottery is appropriate to the fourth or fifth century B.C. Still the succession provides the only available standard. Twenty-eight separate layers containing pottery could be distinguished above a deep deposit of palaeolithic and mesolithic occupations. The nineteen lowest have been grouped together to represent three main periods – termed respectively Lower, Middle, and Upper Neolithic by the excavator, while the topmost eight contain Chalcolithic, Bronze Age, Iron Age, and Roman remains.

The first neolithic occupants of this cave, and of many others in the coastal zone of Italy and France, were a branch of those maritime colonists who landed also on Sicily and in South Italy. Continued contact with that area is illustrated at Arene Candide by obsidian from Lipari. But some fusion with the local mesolithic population probably took place in Liguria.

In the Middle Neolithic layers (24–17) this old tradition is blended with Danubian II and Western elements. The former are exemplified by socketed ladles, clay stamps or *pintadere*, female figurines, moulded in two parts and then stuck together, and the selection of *Spondylus* shells for bracelets. Microliths, plain potsherds,[64] arc-pendants (like Fig. 147),[65] and others made from hares' phalanges[66] may rank as Western elements since they occur in the 'Cortaillod culture' of South France. Finally, obsidian and sherds painted in M.N.I style from Lipari[67] prove continued relations with the south and synchronize the Ligurian with the South Italian sequence. Middle Neolithic pottery in Liguria was generally smooth, dark-faced, and decorated, if at all, with scratched lines. The most distinctive form is the square-mouthed vase (Fig. 120, 2) which was equally popular in the Po basin and was sometimes reproduced on Lipari in a M.N.I context. Among the scratched patterns are 'Danubian' spirals.

The dead were buried individually and contracted in little stone cists within the cave. These closely resemble the Chamblandes cists of the Upper Rhône valley and might be linked therewith by similar graves in the Aosta valley.[68] They would then disclose movements of persons, perhaps herdsmen with their flocks, across the Alps in Middle Neolithic times and help to confirm a synchronism between Swiss Lower Neolithic and Ligurian Middle Neolithic.

In the Upper Neolithic of Arene Candide (layers 13–9) figurines, *pintadere*, and decorated pots have disappeared. The layers are characterized by plain Western pottery more akin to the Chassean of South France than to the Lagozzian of Lombardy; for pan-pipe handles are common as in France. In the immediately succeeding layers appear cups with axe-handles that

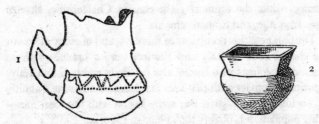

Fig. 120. 1, Vase from lake-dwelling at Polada ($\frac{1}{4}$); 2, Square-mouthed neolithic pot from Arene Candide ($\frac{1}{6}$).

we have classed as Early Metal Age in South Italy. Even the Upper Neolithic in Liguria is perhaps equivalent to the Chalcolithic of Central Italy and the Po valley.

In the more continental environment of the Po valley and the Alpine foothills neolithic culture is less well defined and certainly less homogeneous than on the Tyrrhenian coasts. The *Lagozzian* of the Lombard lake-dwellings is, judged by its pottery, certainly 'Western', but not identical with the Cortaillod culture of the Swiss lake-dwellings nor yet with the Upper Neolithic of Arene Candide,[69] while microlithic flints indicate a survival of mesolithic traditions. In Emilia, south of the Po, the late F. Malvolti[70] established a succession of three cultures – Fiorano, Chiozza, and Pescale. But these are little more than ceramic styles, though in the second obsidian and square-mouthed vases[71] suggest relations with Liguria and a quasi-synchronism with the Middle Neolithic there.

The archaeological record becomes coherent only in the 'Aeneolithic Period' of Italian terminology and discloses the Remedello culture fully formed in the Po valley. Extensive cemeteries [72] of contracted or flexed skeletons – 117 at Remedello (Brescia), forty-one at Cumarola, thirty-six at Fontanella – sometimes arranged in regular rows, reveal substantial communities occupying the same site for several generations. Metallurgical industry and rudimentary trade were now combined with farming, hunting, and fishing. The coppersmiths produced flat axes, some with notched butts or low-hammered flanges (as at Thermi), daggers of two types (Fig. 121), and occasional halberds. The one type

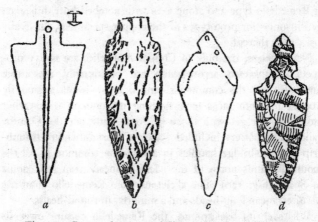

Fig. 121. Copper daggers and flint copies, Remedello ($\frac{1}{3}$).

of dagger with a tang to which the hilt was attached by rivets with a conical head is clearly a derivative of the Early Minoan group. The other form, kite-shaped, was hafted in the Egyptian manner with a hollow-based hilt held in place by several small rivets (cf. p. 173).

Despite the contemporary exploitation of Tuscan tin suggested by the tanged dagger from Monte Bradoni (p. 290), trade was not regular enough to supply the Remedello smiths with material for bronze, and even copper was relatively scarce. So polished stone axes were still used, and tanged, riveted kite-shaped and unriveted West European daggers were each copied locally in flint (Fig. 121). Axes were hafted with the aid of antler sleeves perforated with square-cut holes for the shaft. Still even silver was obtained, perhaps from Sardinia. But the forms produced by the silver-smith suggest more far-flung intercourse. A hammer pin from Remedello itself resembles, but rather remotely, Pontic *yamno* types. A gorget from a tomb at Villafranca near Verona [73] recalls the Irish lunulae, but also may be compared to a copper gorget from a tomb dated to period III–IV at Velvar in Bohemia. Finally, stone battle-axes, sometimes with knobbed butts,[74] could be treated as a reflex of intercourse with the copper-miners of Upper Austria. And there, in the lake-dwellings of the Mondsee and Attersee, have been found rhomboid daggers of Remedello type and stone axes with notched butt, mistaken by Pittioni [75] for prototypes of the copper specimens, but really just copies thereof.

Nevertheless, the bulk of Copper Age relics are native products. Transverse arrow-heads are presumably mesolithic survivals, but the commoner tanged arrow-heads splendidly worked on both faces have nothing in common with earlier industries nor yet with those of South Italy nor the Danube valley. The pottery included vessels with rudimentary thumb-grip or nose-bridge handles in a tradition common to all the mountain lands north of the Mediterranean from Macedonia to Spain (Fig. 120). The skeletons from Remedello comprise Mediterranean long-heads and a minority of round-heads.

Whatever its background, the Remedello culture owes its character partly to a northward extension of intercourse with the Aegean, motivated by the tin lodes of Tuscany and attested there, as in the Po valley, by daggers of Early Minoan type. At the same time contributions by the Bell-beaker folk must be admitted. Bell-beakers were found in three graves in the Province of Brescia, one with a characteristic West European dagger; and stray sherds of the same ware are reported from Remedello itself.[76] The Bell-beaker folk may have introduced from the west the halberd and perhaps the gorget and assisted in opening up intercourse with the Danube valley. The battle-axes may well be contributions from Central Europe, perhaps even from farther east, but hardly suffice to prove an intrusion of Battle-axe folk. The daggers of Early Minoan type provide a vague upper limit, somewhere about 2300 B.C., for the beginning of the Remedello culture. Since amber and fayence beads are missing from the graves, the cemeteries had presumably gone out of use before the regular trade between Mycenae and Bohemia was established about 1600 B.C. So, too, Danubian IV bronze types are missing from the Remedello cemeteries. The Beaker graves do indeed establish a connection with period III in the Danubian sequence, but no one knows whether they belong to the beginning or the end of the long period represented by the Remedello cemeteries.

The Bronze Age begins with the extension to Upper Italy of the Danubian commercial system. Types of period IV – flanged axes like Fig. 69, 3, round-heeled and bronze-hilted daggers, ingot torques and even a few Unětician eyelet pins are not uncommon. Some, like the pins, must have been imported from beyond the Alps. Many were made locally by itinerant or resident smiths who worked in populous settlements – lake-dwellings on the shores of the eastern lakes, marsh villages like Lagazzi south of the Po, the celebrated terremare on the southern margin of the marshy plain and caves on the Apennine foothills.

The eastern lake-dwellings, among which Polada [77] is taken as the type site, though Ledro [78] and Barche de Solferino [79] have been better explored, may like Lagazzi [80] have been founded before the terremare. They have yielded pottery carrying on the older Remedello tradition, hollow-based flint arrow-heads, arrow-shaft straighteners, a few wrist-guards and buttons with V perforation going back before period IV, but only a few later bronzes appropriate to period V. The terremare, on the contrary, are genuine tells – sites of villages occupied for many generations – from which come Middle and Late Bronze Age relics and only a few distinctive of period IV. All alike were farming villages. Their fields were certainly tilled with the plough; the oldest dated European plough, made entirely of wood, comes from Ledro, while ploughs drawn by two or four oxen are depicted in rock-engravings high up in the Alps round Monte Bigo. [81] The cereals [82] were reaped with angled sickles of wood armed with flint teeth; the type is illustrated by a complete specimen from

Solferino and was literally translated into metal in the Middle Bronze Age (Fig. 119, 5). In addition to cows, pigs, sheep, and goats the *terremaricoli* – but probably not the earlier lake-villagers – kept horses and controlled them with bits furnished with antler cheek-pieces. Carts with solid disc wheels may well have been drawn by oxen, but a model six-spoked wheel from Solferino and a complete wheel from Mercurago could have belonged to a horse-drawn chariot. The latter specimen, which may belong to period VI, illustrates the peculiar type later distinctive of Classical Greek country carts.[83]

The lake-village of Ledro covered only 5,000 square metres; Lagazzi was a cluster of ten huts, probably round, but the *terremare*[84] may cover from four to eighteen acres. The regular plans, popularized by Pigorini, have been shown to be products of his imagination. We do not know the plans of the houses, nor even whether the villages were from the outset defended by a moat and casemate rampart; Säflund considers these defences additions made in the Late Bronze Age.

The pottery throughout imitates wooden models such as have actually been preserved in all stages of manufacture at Ledro. In the Polada group, that carries on the Remedello tradition, relatively simple nose-bridge and elbow handles (Fig. 120, 1) predominate and plainly give expression to a fashion detected all along the mountain zone from Northern Anatolia through Thrace and Macedonia to the Pyrenees. In the Lagazzian wares, derivable perhaps from the Lagozzian,[85] begins a fantastic elaboration of handles towards cornute types (Fig. 119, 1) that culminates in the *terremare* and eventually spread south to the heel of the peninsula.

Moulds for casting Early Bronze Age types occur in many settlements, but may have been used by perambulating merchant-artificers who distributed metal-ware as a sideline of the amber trade across the Brenner; one such left in the cave of Farneto near Bologna the only surviving example of a mould for a flanged axe. Many hoards containing ingot torques, daggers, and other Early Bronze Age types illustrate the travels of these merchants and the danger attendant thereon. Middle Bronze Age types are not thus represented in hoards as if some degree of security had been established throughout the Po-Adige basin by period V.

Moulds and other metallurgical appliances are relatively common in the *terremare* and may well denote the workshops of resident smiths. The earlier metal types are mostly derivable from the Unětician, as if the local bronze-smiths had been trained in the Danubian school. But halberds are more likely Iberian, and if so, imply the incorporation of Western traditions in the nascent North Italian school. To these must be added the development of the local Remedello tradition, inspired, as suggested above, by Early Aegean models. Fresh links with the Levant are not discernible.

North Italian metallurgists had evolved original forms of axe and dagger even in the Early Bronze Age and developed these into original types in the succeeding phase. They are generally credited with several more pregnant inventions, in particular that of the safety-pin[86] (Fig. 122) that was introduced into Greece in the

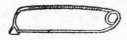

Fig. 122. Peschiera safety-pin (fibula) ($\frac{1}{2}$).

thirteenth century and diffused in Central Europe chiefly in period VI, but this claim has been challenged on behalf of the Unětician culture! It was indisputably a North Italian craftsman who at this time found a patron at Mycenae itself (p. 122) for whom he cast medial winged axes. Other North Italian innovations are flanged sickles, double-edged razors, 'Peschiera daggers' (double-edged knives with flanged handles) (Fig. 119, 3, 4, and 5) and cut-and-thrust swords.[87]

No graves attributable to the Early Bronze Age lake-dwellers nor to the *terremaricoli* are known. A Middle Bronze Age cemetery of extended skeletons accompanied by Central European rapiers at Povigliano near Verona[88] may be attributed to a group of invaders from beyond the Alps. The urnfields connected with some *terremare* are attributed by Säflund[89] to a fresh wave of conquerors who would have occupied – and fortified – the village sites only in the Late Bronze Age. Finally, the Apennine herdsmen continued to practise collective burial in natural caves.

The ideology of some Bronze Age societies found expression in the celebrated rock-carvings round Monte Bigo near the 7,000-ft

14 Island Civilizations in the Western Mediterranean

It is possible to sail coastwise from the Aegean to Italy and Sicily without ever losing sight of land. Progress thence westward meant embarking on the pathless ocean without any guiding point in the heavens like the Pole Star by which a mariner might set his course.[1] Sicily must have set a bound to regular intercourse between the Aegean and the western world in so far as such intercourse depended on following the northern shores of the Mediterranean. Land routes across North Africa and even coastal routes along the inhospitable southern shores of the Mediterranean were of course available, however difficult they may have been. But they traversed territories so little explored archaeologically that the effect of communications along them can hardly be even inferred. We can therefore scarcely expect to find the West Mediterranean islands clearly revealed in the archaeological record as stepping-stones in the transmission of culture wholes from East to West, nor to be able adequately to assess the part they may have played in transmission from Africa northward.

The Megalithic Civilization of Malta

The barren little islands of Malta and Gozo are last remnants of a land-bridge from Africa to Europe and offer natural havens to mariners blown by mischance or groping their way deliberately westward from the East Mediterranean. They were unsuited to Old Stone Age hunters, and, save for a questionable Neandertaler, were uninhabited thereby. In the Holocene they supported a surprisingly dense population of farmers who developed a vigorous insular culture,[2] through two main periods.[3]

The most enduring and distinctive monuments of period I are megalithic 'temples', built of really gigantic stones, and labyrinthine burial-vaults ingeniously carved out of the limestone with stone tools. And so today the most truly native monument of Maltese culture in the twentieth century A.D. is the village church of Musta, near Valetta, roofed with a dome larger than that of St Paul's Cathedral. Like it, the neolithic temples and tombs are eloquent of a devotion to immaterial ends which inspired the island farmers to produce a surplus above immediate needs. And they suggest how 'circulation' of this surplus wealth was effected through unproductive works, that, just because they were unproductive, could be repeated again and again.

Stratigraphical observations justify the division of period I into three phases, A, B, and C, distinguishable by pottery styles and temple plans. The first colonists who have left distinct traces in the archaeological record and who presumably initiated this unproductive activity seem to have come from Sicily since they introduced a version of the Stentinello type of impressed pottery. The temples of period IA, built of undressed stones, possess a simple trefoil plan. This was elaborated in phase B by the addition of an extra apse and further complicated in the culminating phase C. By this phase the slabs had been beautifully dressed with stone mauls and sometimes pitted all over decoratively. Some are carved in low relief with spirals or even processions of animals and men.[4]

Community of tradition between this temple architecture and the sepulchral architecture of West European collective tombs[5] is revealed in many details of plan and construction – semicircular forecourts in front of shrines (Fig. 123); the deliberate use of enormous blocks; porthole slabs as doorways; roofing of apses by corbelling[6]; walls in which uprights set with their broad faces in line with the wall alternate with slabs projecting at right angles thereto;[7] cup-marks on many stones.

In fact, in the islands themselves chamber tombs were hewn in the rock to accommodate collective burials throughout period I, and even in phase A some replicate the trefoil plan of the temples. Most early tombs, however, were little more than rock-cut pits containing skeletons sprinkled with ochre.[8] But at Hal Salflieni near Valetta a vast and complicated hypogaeum had been carved in the living rock. Starting simply in phase A (to judge by the potter), it was gradually enlarged till by phase B it already comprised many underground rooms with several chambers opening off a central hall. In phase C it was further elaborated and decorated with spiraliform paintings and skeuomorphic carvings.

Cult objects from the temples of phase C include limestone statuettes[9] a foot or more in height representing an obese female personage standing, seated, or reclining on a couch and sometimes wearing a skirt recalling Minoan or Sumerian fashions, as well as betyls, bells, altars, and other models in stone. Most belong to

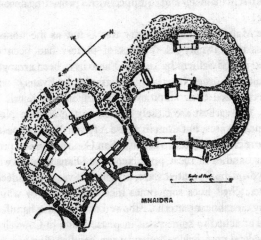

MNAIDRA

Fig. 123. Plan of 'temples' at Mnaidra, Malta, Period IC.

phase C, but from a tomb of phase A2 near Zebbug[10] came a fragmentary statue menhir, comparable to those of South France and to the stele from Troy I.

All these works were executed without the aid of metal tools; the culture of period I was in this sense neolithic. But flint was imported – probably from Sicily – by phase A and obsidian from Lipari in phase C at least. The flaked stone implements are of the simplest kind without bifacial working, and ground stone celts are extremely rare. Querns were made from Sicilian lava while pebbles of fine grained rock were imported for the manufacture of charms and ornaments. Among these, axe-amulets are very common, pendants in the form of doves and other shapes rare.

Finally, a bossed bone plaque, identical with those from Castelluccio tombs and resembling those from Troy and Lerna, from the Tarxien temple is generally assigned to period IC. As ornaments may be regarded hemispherical buttons with V perforation, found already in phase A,[11] beads of *Spondylus* shell and bone, and in phase C winged beads.

Vases, too, were carved in stone, probably already in phase A but with exquisite skill by phase C. Then quite complicated shapes, familiar in pottery, were reproduced in stone and even fitted with tunnel or nose-bridge handles. A giant cup from Hagar Qim is 6 ft in diameter and equipped with a projecting nose-bridge handle!

The Maltese ceramic industry was as fine as the stone-work. No less than twenty-six varieties of pottery had been distinguished at Hal Saflieni by 1910.[12] These have been arranged in a chronological order, based on stratigraphy, by Evans,[13] who has also recognized their affinities with Sicilian and South Italian wares. The earliest are closely related to the Middle Neolithic Stentinello wares, but even in phase A (Evans's A2) appear vases still more closely related to the later San Cono group and probably tubular handles of the Upper Neolithic Diana type, as well as a little red-on-buff painted ware. In phase B vases were decorated with scratched lines sometimes incrusted in red or white and forming curvilinear patterns. Elbowed or triangular handles were already attached to some vases in phase B and in C develop into fully fledged nose-bridge and even axe-handles (like Fig. 116, 3), while tubular lugs had been converted by a local evolution into the so-called tunnel handle;[14] that is a clay tube attached horizontally to the inner wall of the vase the contours of which are interrupted only by two apertures corresponding to the tube's ends. Such handles appear in the Piano Conte phase of the Chalcolithic on the Aeolian Islands and will meet us again in Sardinia. Axe-handles too are appropriate to the Early Bronze Age of Italy.

Judged by ceramic analogies, therefore, the age of temple-building and tomb-cutting on Malta should have begun late in the Middle Neolithic of the Italian scheme, used in the last chapter, and continued well into the succeeding Chalcolithic. The bossed bone plaque from Tarxien, if correctly attributed to period I, should mean that period IC overlaps with the Castelluccio culture of Sicily. It should, however, end therein since the earliest pottery of period II can best be paralleled in the Capo Graziano culture of the Aeolian Islands that can be synchronized both with Castelluccio and with L.M.I. Sepulchral architecture would suggest rather different correlations with Italy. Chamber tombs there are at earliest Upper Neolithic, most explicitly Chalcolithic. In the West, too, V-perforated buttons are most commonly associated with Bell-beakers that are late Chalcolithic.

If the first settlers on Malta and Gozo were Sicilian in ceramic tastes, their ideology was rather East Mediterranean. But the architecture that expressed it is more West Mediterranean; the best analogies for the trefoil temples may be found in the corbelled tombs of Los Millares (pp. 320–23). Ideological megalithicism seems again a West European disease. The statue menhir could indeed as well be a symbol on its way from Troy to South France as a contribution from that direction, but V-perforated buttons are explicitly Western. Allowance must certainly be made for West European stimuli at the birth of the islands' remarkable culture. Fresh inspiration from the East may be suspected in promoting the brilliant efflorescence of phase C, but despite analogies to the spiral carvings and painting on Middle Minoan Kamares cups[15] and on the Shaft Grave stelae from Mycenae, concrete evidence for this is lacking.

Whatever its origins, the megalithic culture of period I was brought to a violent end by an armed invasion or a religious revolution. As a result the temple complex of Hal Tarxien was diverted from its primary use and made a cemetery for cremation burials. With these were deposited[16] little triangular daggers and flat or hammer-flanged axes of copper or bronze, pottery in an absolutely new tradition, and clay figurines curiously stylized to a disc with projections.[17] The novel pottery includes vases with oculi ornaments, handled mugs, askoi, and two-storeyed urns. Beads of silver, fayence, and shell were worn as ornaments.

On the typological systems, valid for the East Mediterranean and for peninsular Italy, the metal gear would be Early Aegean and Chalcolithic respectively, though in Sardinia almost equally archaic bronzes survive in hoards attributable to the first millennium. The pot forms, too, are definitely Early Aegean and find vague analogies in the Chalcolithic Paestum cemetery. But in

Sicily and Sardinia askoi and similar Aegeanizing forms reappear after 1200 B.C.[18] The new burial-rite might be connected with the urnfield invasion that had reached Northern Sicily about that date. Indeed, a few sherds of Apennine ware have turned up in the cemetery and on other period IIa sites. However, cremation had been practised at Boğaz Köy and Troy much earlier in the second millennium and might have reached Malta direct from that direction. Still, the closest parallels to the pottery of period IIa are found in the village of Capo Graziano on Filicudi, the occupation of which was roughly contemporary with Castelluccio and L.M.I–II but lasted nearly to 1400 B.C.[19] That is not to say that the cremationist invaders came from the Aeolian Islands, but does suggest that the Maltese Bronze Age began a little before 1400 B.C.

It failed to develop. Bronze merchants would not accept the spiritual commodities that had satisfied pedlars in flint and obsidian, and the Maltese had nothing else to offer. Nor could they, like the Aeolian Islanders, become intermediaries in Mycenaean trade with the West; for even voyagers to Spain preferred the coastwise route up the Tyrrhenian Sea to a direct crossing exposed to the western gales in the fifteenth century A.D., a fortiori in the fifteenth century B.C.[20] No later bronzes survive in the islands. Still new settlers arrived and converted some old temple sites, like Borg in-Nadur[21] into fortified villages. They introduced new pottery types, quite unlike those of the Tarxien cemetery, and made pottery anchor ornaments. A single Mycenaean (L.H.IIIb) kylix is the sole import or piece of loot that survives from period IIb. It serves to date the phase to the thirteenth century and so confirms the dating of phase IIa. Moreover, some vases from the Thapsos cemeteries round Syracuse are thought by Bernabo Brea[22] to be imported products of the Borg in-Nadur culture. But anchor ornaments, just like Fig. 38, appearing about the same time also at Milazzesi in the Aeolian Islands, had been Early Helladic in Greece and so took a thousand years to reach Malta!

In the sequel Malta made no further contribution to European culture. In fact it was only during period I that the island culture was original and creative. Even then its contributions to the

European heritage can only have been immaterial and may well have been illusory.

Sardinia

Sardinia, though apparently uninhabited in the Old Stone Age, is large enough despite its mountainous character to support numerous, if mutually isolated, farming communities in its valleys and plains. Moreover, it possesses natural resources – obsidian, copper, and silver – to attract industrial colonists. When the archaeological record opens clearly, all these opportunities

Fig. 124. Tripod bowl, San Bartolomeo (⅙), and vase-handle of nose-bridge type, Anghelu Ruju (½).

were already being exploited. The evidence is derived in the main from natural caves and rock-cut tombs used as collective sepulchres for many generations. Relics of different periods accordingly occur generally mixed together.

Only in the cave of San Bartolomeo[23] near Cagliari in the south of the island is a stratigraphical separation possible. In an upper layer here the grave goods comprised Beakers, tripod bowls decorated in Beaker style (Fig. 124, 1), West European daggers and a flat axe of copper, and a prismatic V-perforated bone plaque – in fact a typical 'Copper Age' assemblage. Below and separated by a layer of stones from the 'Copper Age' burials was an earlier funerary deposit comprising, as well as skeletons, simple obsidian implements and hemispherical and carinated bowls, one adorned with a stellate pattern of finely incised hatched ribbons. Technically the last-named vase recalls some vessels from Villafrati in Sicily, from Hal Saflieni in Malta, and from pre-

Beaker horizons in South France. The pottery from the sepulchral cave of San Michele (Ozieri)[24] includes vessels of the same type, but others with tunnel-handles quite like the Maltese but decorated with semicircles executed in cardial and stab-and-drag technique that is represented at San Bartolomeo only in the upper level.

Sardinian culture of Beaker and post-Beaker age is better represented by the rock-cut tombs, locally termed *domus di gianas*. Some of these family vaults may have been dug even in pre-Beaker times, since sherds of the incised fabrics represented in the lower level at San Bartolomeo occur in them, but others were excavated, or in any case still used, in the first millennium B.C. Generally the tombs are isolated or grouped in twos or threes, but at Anghelu Ruju,[25] a cemetery of no less than thirty-one chamber tombs has been systematically explored. The burial chambers here tend to a rectangular plan, are often preceded by an antechamber, and entered either by a stepped pit or a passage. Subsidiary chambers may open off the principal compartment. The inner portals may be carved to suggest a lintelled wooden doorway like the façades of Early Cypriot tombs.[26] In two cases rock pillars were left standing in the chamber. On such pillars and on the walls bulls' heads or high-prowed ships have been carved in low relief (Fig. 125). Traces of red ochre were found on the floors of two tombs. Normally the bodies were buried in the contracted attitude, but in two tombs (XV and XXbis) cremated remains were found in small niches and in tomb XX a baby's skeleton in a jar.

A series of intermediate forms leads from the subterranean *domus di gianas* (Witches' Houses) to the megalithic tombs built above ground and termed locally *tombe di giganti* (Giants' Tombs) – rock-cut tombs roofed by corbelling in megalithic style,[27] megalithic extensions built on in front of rock-cut tombs,[28] *domus di gianas* with the rock face above and around the entrance carved to reproduce the portal and forecourt of a Giants' Tomb.[29] Similarly Mackenzie[30] has constructed a typological series leading from simple 'dolmens' to the classical Giants' Tomb – a long narrow gallery walled with megalithic slabs, roofed by corbelling, covered by a cairn enclosed by masonry walls and entered through a low arch cut in a tall upright slab or stele from a semicircular space flanked by masonry walls (Fig. 110). Of course, such a series can be reversed as it is a pure *a priori* construction and unsupported by a reliable series of closed grave finds. The so-called 'dolmens' have yielded no datable furniture. Some are just remnants of Giants' Tombs.[31] The distribution of the latter does not agree so exactly with that of the *nuraghe* as to prove contemporaneity.[32] Nuragic and even Roman [33] relics have been found in Giants' Tombs. But of course such finds do not establish erection in the Iron or Late Bronze Age.

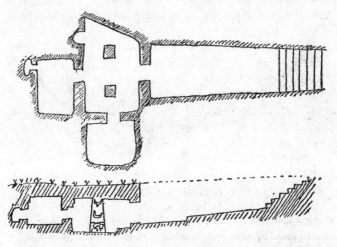

Fig. 125. Plan and elevation of tomb XXbis at Anghelu Ruju.

The grave goods recovered at Anghelu Ruju give the best available picture of Sardinian culture before the Nuragic age, though tomb-robbing in antiquity has stripped that picture of any pretence at being complete. Metal was used, but apparently only sparingly; only two or three West European daggers, one flat axe, one arrow-head, several quadrangular awls, some beads, bracelets and atypical pins of copper and olive-shaped beads, and a ring of silver have escaped the ancient plunderers. Martial activities are indicated by numerous weapons—the copper daggers, spheroid mace-heads of stone, arrow-heads (triangular, tanged, tanged-and-barbed, and even serrated) of flint together with wrist-guards (these, however, having for the most part only two perforations, may have been used as whet-stones as in Crete) and an arrow-straightener of pumice. In the pottery we might distinguish: (i) carinated vases, and cylindrical pyxides, vaguely Aegean in form; (ii) vessels decorated with semicircles and other patterns formed either of (*a*) finely incised hatched ribbons or of (*b*) stab-and-drag lines; (iii) Bell-beakers and tripod bowls like Fig. 124, 1; (iv) carinated cups and other vessels with nose-bridge handles (Fig. 124, 2), which persist into the Nuragic age.

As ornaments and charms, stone bracelets and rings, axe-amulets, disc-beads of shell, and tortoise beads (Fig. 126, a, c, f) and conical buttons with V perforations were worn. Finally, three

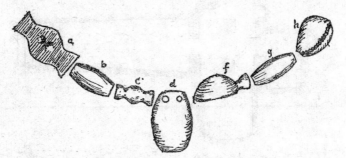

Fig. 126. Necklace from Anghelu Ruju (⅔).

tombs contained marble idols, which, although made of local stone, look like deliberate imitations of Early Cycladic models.

Plainly many streams have converged in the Copper Age culture of Anghelu Ruju. Its debt to Crete was admirably summarized by Patroni:[34] 'Not only the form of the tombs but also the shape and decoration of some of the vases in them recur in Crete. The symbols sculptured on the walls and the statuettes of marble show relations of a nature superior to any external relations of commerce; for they denote a profound affinity of thought and culture.' Giuffridi-Ruggieri adds anthropological arguments. Noting that fifty-three skulls from Anghelu Ruju were long-headed and ten round, and that a similar mixture is detectable in Crete, he concludes that Sardinia was invaded at the end of the third millennium by a mixed race of Cretans. (It would be safer now to say 'East Mediterraneans, including the round-headed type that reappears among the Beaker-folk' (pp. 274–5).) The invaders, combined with some small pre-existing population also of Mediterranean stock, created the Copper and Bronze Age civilizations of Sardinia.

If Giuffridi-Ruggieri be right, the finely incised wares of our group (ii) might be taken as representative of the 'pre-existing population'. These fabrics are certainly related to those of Malta, Apulia, and Sicily on the one hand, of South France on the other. Their origin is not thereby determined. The Beaker-folk's effective contribution is demonstrated by their pottery, armament, and ornaments. Some beakers from Anghelu Ruju resemble especially those from Almeria, but one is almost identical with specimens from Bohemia and Denmark.[35] The arrow-straightener, too, though locally made, is a Central European trait in the West Mediterranean. But a beaker from a rock-cut tomb at Cuguttu[36] has a rudimentary thumb-grip handle.

This and related nose-bridge handles and many other traits, especially the V-perforated tortoise beads and prism-shaped buttons, betoken particularly intimate relations with Catalonia and South France. In South France such handles belong to a horizon explicitly later than wares like our group (ii) and on the whole post-Beaker (p. 361). In Sardinia they persist into the Nuragic age.

Despite the industrial development and wide cultural relations attested at Anghelu Ruju, no urban civilization arose and Sardinia held aloof from any comprehensive system of foreign commerce that might bring datable foreign manufactures into the archaeological record. Judging by sepulchral architecture, island culture developed insensibly into the extremely insular Nuragic phase. This development did not take place without renewed contact with the East Mediterranean. A Cypro-Mycenaean copper ingot stamped with Mycenaean letters was found on the island. About 1200 B.C. maritime raiders, termed Sh'rd'n', appear in the Egyptian records. They are depicted protected by horned helmets and round shields and armed with swords precisely like those of bronze statuettes from the Sardinian *nuraghi*. Whether the Shardana originated in Asia Minor, like the Etruscans, and only settled in the Western Mediterranean after raiding Egypt,[37] or were actual descendants of the Copper Age Sardinians,[38] their connection with the island in its Nuragic age is indisputable, as is the stimulus given to West Mediterranean development by their experiences in the East.

But the result was not the establishment of a city-state organization such as the Etruscans created. In the island the highest social unit was a cluster of round huts sheltering beneath the dry-stone tower – *nuraghe* – of the clan chief. Architecturally as well as sociologically these complexes are significantly like a modern Nigerian village.[39] Mines and smelting furnaces, as well as many hoards belonging mostly to founders, disclose indeed an active and efficient metallurgical industry.

On the whole, indeed, the Late Bronze Age industry of Sardinia, like those of peninsular Italy and Sicily, was based on Central European traditions. Yet the variety of types comprised in the hoards would suggest trade with, or raids on, both the Aegean (double-axes, axe-adzes) and Atlantic coasts (double-eared palstaves, carp's-tongue swords). But the island industry was extraordinarily conservative. Hoards of Nuragic age may contain every sort of axe[40] from flat or flanged types assignable by typologists to the Copper or Early Bronze Age, up to socketed forms of the Late Bronze Age and of stabbing weapons from archaic round-heeled daggers[41] to carp's-tongue swords. Luckily a few imported manufactures prove that these archaic types were still current in the eighth or even seventh century B.C., when the Etruscan Iron Age was in full bloom in Italy.[42]

Yet the nuragic bronzes appear in the archaeological record as the immediate successors of the Copper Age types just as nuragic pottery occurs already in the rock-cut tombs of Anghelu Ruju itself. We have unconsciously overstepped the chronological boundaries of this book. The excursus demonstrates how dangerous it would be to apply to the West Mediterranean typological systems that may work well within the Danubian and British commercial spheres and how difficult it is to fill with developments in tools and vessels, weapons and tombs any vast interval between the prehistoric Copper Age or Beaker period and the proto-historic Bronze Age of the eighth century B.C. Archaeologically a millennium is not very plausible, two quite incredible.

In the Balearic Islands the archaeological record begins with the megalithic culture. In Mallorca the normal family vault was a rock-cut tomb.[43] The chamber (Fig. 109) takes the form of a long narrow gallery round which runs a shallow bench divided into several stalls by low ridges of rock. One or more cells may open off the chamber, and it may be preceded by an antechamber. The entrance is a low arch or window cut in the rock and may give on to an uncovered forecourt excavated in the hillside. In Menorca the form of the underground gallery is reproduced above ground in megalithic chambers enclosed in boat-shaped constructions walled with cyclopean masonry and termed navetas. The end at which the chamber opens is flattened and sometimes even concave in plan.[44]

Evidence of early contact between the islands and the Aegean is afforded only by a matt-painted beaked jug of Middle Cycladic type like Fig. 41, 3, certainly an import but found without definite context on Menorca. Otherwise the earliest contacts with the outer world are provided by a single sherd of Beaker ware[45] from the rock-cut tomb of Felanitx, and a conical button with V perforation from the tomb of Son Mulet. Both are indicative of the activities of Beaker-folk on Mallorca. On the other hand, splay-footed vases typical of the Horgen culture from a rock-cut tomb at Sa Val[46] prove connections northward, as do the similarities of the Balearic tomb plans to those of the Rhône and Seine valleys.

The bulk of the sepulchral pottery from the rock-cut tombs, however, consists of plain vases sometimes provided with upstanding lugs but never with true handles. Technically this fabric resembles the Argaric ware of the East Spanish Bronze Age, and several forms can be matched in the same context. But simple round-bottomed and carinated vessels preserve the traditions of the oldest West European neolithic ceramics.

Little metal survives among the grave goods. Round-heeled daggers of 'Early Bronze Age' type were recovered from Sa Val and several other tombs,[47] but one tomb yielded an identically shaped dagger of iron!

Indeed, the cultural history of the Baleares is parallel to that of Sardinia. There is no obvious break between the 'Copper Age' culture represented in the rock-cut tombs and that represented in the 'talayots'. The latter are fortified hamlets, counterparts of the Sardinian nuargic settlements, and like these, the talayots[48] continued to be inhabited into the Iron Age. As in Sardinia, the archaeological material from the Balearic Isles does not show sufficient typological development to justify a very high dating for the local megalithic culture. If, like Hemp,[49] we treat the Mallorcan rock-cut tombs as the starting-point for the French series of gallery graves, we must still insist that a reversal of the relations would accord far better with the tombs' furniture and any chronology based thereon.

15 The Iberian Peninsula

The Iberian Peninsula [1] offers the natural channel through which Oriental influences, whether transmitted by land ways across North Africa or by sea along the Mediterranean, might penetrate to Atlantic Europe. In the Peninsula a substantial Old Stone Age population had probably been augmented at the end of the pleistocene by makers of microliths in the Capsian tradition (p. 41). Some of these may indeed have brought with them at least domestic sheep and goats if not some rudiments of agriculture. Their traditions of flint-working and of parietal art at least can be recognized in cultures that are admittedly neolithic.

Now Spanish prehistorians today recognize two 'Neolithic' phases, I and II, followed by a 'Bronze Age I', equivalent to the old 'Copper Age', that is divided into phases A and B; the old 'Early Bronze Age' (El Argar) thus becomes Bronze Age II. And within the Neolithic they have long recognized two parallel cycles – the Almeria culture and the Cave culture.

Maritime Neolithic Settlements

The Cave culture used to denote a very heterogeneous assemblage; for at all times hunters, herdsmen, pirates, and outcasts have taken shelter in caves for shorter or longer periods. But in some caves both in the Peninsula and in South France, as in Liguria, it is now possible to distinguish at the base of deep deposits a recurrent assemblage of pots and implements. This is just that culture, characterized by Cardial ware, already encountered in South Italy and Liguria. It is found all round the West Mediterranean coasts in North Africa,[2] the Iberian Peninsula,[3] and South France[4] too. But at least in its earlier manifestations it is strictly confined to the coastal regions where the Mediterranean environment is preserved in its most distinctive form.

It was carried by groups of hunters and stock-breeders, known almost exclusively from their occupation of caves. This circumstance has unduly exaggerated the rôle attributed to animal husbandry in the economy; for herdsmen periodically shelter in caves even though they have homes in permanent farming villages. Actually the Cardial herdsmen did cultivate cereals; in their deposits have been found not only grains of barley,[5] sickle-teeth, and querns, but also – both in Spain[6] and Provence[7] – bone spatulae of the specialized type used by Starčevo folk in the Balkans for collecting flour (p. 124). Perhaps they followed that system of cultivation, still observable in Corsica and Liguria, by which the scrub is burnt off and the grains planted between the trees still left standing.[8] But for hunting they employed bows and arrows armed with microliths and clubs, weighted with percussion-perforated stone heads[9] – both items that could have been borrowed from local 'Tardenoisians'.

The flint-work is generally very simple. Axes, in preference to adzes, were made from fine-grained rock. The pottery shows leathery forms, generally round based and sometimes provided with small strap handles. The vases have been profusely decorated by impressing the edge of a shell or other stamp in the wet clay. The impressions are normally arranged to form skeuomorphic patterns recalling wicker cases in which pre-ceramic vessels might have been carried.

Bracelets of shell or stone were worn as ornaments together with necklaces of bored teeth. The dead seem to have been buried in caves, used as collective ossuaries.[10]

The coastal distribution of this culture leaves no doubt that it was diffused by seafarers. Though very similar pottery is distributed very widely in North Africa down to Tibesti and Khartoum,[11] there are no convincing grounds for supposing that the maritime distribution of our culture began from Little Africa rather than the Balkan or Levant coasts. Cardial decoration is found on some of the earliest neolithic pottery of North Syria. On the other hand, Starčevo ware is related to Cardial and associated with the bone spatulae that occur in no other context. It certainly seems that the earliest neolithic cultures, adapted respectively to Balkan and West Mediterranean environments, at least sprang from a common root.[12] In the latter area Cardial herdsmen may well have mingled with surviving mesolithic hunters and with neolithic farmers of Capsian tradition. And so a certain continuity of tradition may be observed in the cave deposits. But the varied styles of pottery and kinds of stone tool grouped together in earlier books to constitute a 'Cultura de las Cuevas' are no more homogeneous culturally or chronologically than the relics from the several strata of Arene Candide. But in Spain they can seldom be distinguished stratigraphically. At least at El Pany near Barcelona, however, collective burials with Cardial ware were stratified below Bell-beakers of Bronze I.[13]

The Almeria Culture

A second and possibly earlier stream of neolithic colonists, come this time from Africa, introduced a different culture that is first recognizable in Almeria and therefore thus designated.

The neolithic colonists settled generally on hilltops like the type site, El Garcel,[14] overlooking the fertile valleys; they arrived at a time when pines still grew on the now treeless hill. In addition to breeding stock and cultivating cereals they may have introduced the culture of olive-trees since olive-stones were found, but grape-seeds are said to be derived from wild vines.[15] The grains were reaped with sickles armed with serrated flint teeth, like those from the pre-dynastic Fayum, stored in subterranean silos and ground on saddle-querns. Tied to the soil by their fruit trees, the villagers lived in round or oval huts, partly excavated in the soil but roofed with a superstructure of wattle-and-daub. Huntsmen still used microlithic arrow-heads – micro-gravers found at El Garcel may be by-products in the manufacture of these.

Carpenters employed ground stone axes, adzes, and gouges. A textile industry is implied by biconical whorls. Pottery was undecorated and vases were never provided with true handles though singly or even doubly perforated lugs were applied. Forms include jars with pointed bases (Fig. 127, 3) like the early Egyptian (Gerzean) and North African,[16] curious bottles, oval in plan, that also recur in North Africa, and sack-like leathery vessels related to the neolithic pottery of the Fayum and Merimde[17] in Egypt. The leathery sack-like forms continued to be popular in all later phases of Almerian culture. In Siret's second neolithic phase as represented at Tres Cabezos[18] they are provided with upstanding perforated lugs (Fig. 130, 1), while bowls may be carinated, and even double-vases were made as at Merimde in Egypt. Vessels were also woven of esparto grass.

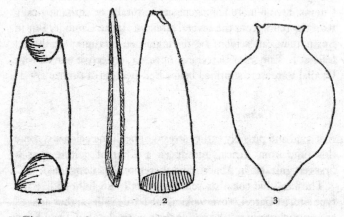

Fig. 127. 1, Gouge, El Garcel (½); 2, schist adze, Portugal (½); 3, jar, El Garcel (⅛).

Disc-beads of shell, made also by African Capsians, and bracelets of *Pectunculus*[19] shell and stone, beads of callaïs and later of steatite were worn as ornaments. The dead were buried collectively in natural cave ossuaries or in stone-walled but closed cists, usually circular in plan and covered by low tumuli.[20] Even at El Garcel a very crude fiddle-shaped stone, rather like Fig. 8, 14, may represent a 'Mother Goddess'. She is slightly more recognizable in stone figures from the tombs that may, however, be Neolithic II.

Vaufrey[21] reports 'the whole assemblage from El Garcel' – flints, celts, and even pots – 'is an almost exact replica of the neolithic of Capsian tradition' as found throughout the Maghreb. The African origin of the Almeria culture is thus established. But bifacially trimmed arrow-heads and richly decorated pottery are missing from its neolithic I phase. Hence the Straits may have been crossed before the main expansion that Vaufrey has traced took place in Africa. And the radio-carbon date of 3050 B.C. for the Capsian neolithic in the Maghreb[22] need not be accepted as an upper limit for its arrival in Europe.

A parallel colonization of the west coast may perhaps be inferred from plain baggy pots and microliths, similar to those from El Garcel, found in megalithic passage graves that are at best Neolithic II (p. 326 below). Perhaps the first phase of this western colonization will be documented if the furniture of the Portuguese 'dolmens' be published. These are reported[23] to be megalithic cists, each containing a single corpse accompanied by archaic microliths.

On the east coast Spanish prehistorians have traced the spread of the Almeria culture northward to Catalonia by a series of burials of contracted skeletons in simple pit graves. Their furniture includes tanged and transverse arrow-heads, *Pectunculus* bracelets, callaïs beads, and plain 'Western' pottery – once indeed a 'square-mouthed vase'.[24] Though formally neolithic, these Almerian cemeteries in the north may be relatively late, but at least once the distinctive plain pottery has been found stratified below Beakers.[25]

On their way north these Almerians must have come into contact not only with Cardial herdsmen but also with descendants of older, mesolithic, tribes. Interactions with the latter must be responsible for the curiously African character of some of the East Spanish rock-shelter art. Pericot indeed now believes that the practice of decorating shelter walls with lively but impressionistic scenes of animals and the chase began in the Solutrian phase of the old Stone Age. But some still quite lively paintings depict side by side with gathering activities sheep, equids, and even a rider.[26] If these neolithic elements be derived from the Almerian of Capsian – i.e. North African – tradition, the stylistic similarity of some East Spanish paintings to those of Libya[27] or even Rhodesia would be more comprehensible. But the paintings in question are demonstrably older than more conventionalized paintings the figures of which can be matched on Copper Age I vases (Fig. 128) and tomb walls. Rock-shelter art of this later conventionalized type is not confined to the eastern coasts, but occurs widely in the Peninsula[28] and along the Mediterranean coasts even east of the Rhône.[29] It must be the work of roving hunting and herding groups whose palaeolithic traditions had been enriched by interaction with Almerian and other neolithic farmers.

Fig. 128. Stages in conventionalization of parietal art in Spain. After Obermaier. A, Maimon; B, Figuras; C. La Pileta.

The Rise of a Metal Industry

The Peninsula was rich in gold, silver, copper, lead, and even tin. The discovery of these natural resources permitted the development of a new economy in which industry and trade could absorb some of the rural population, as in the Eastern Mediterranean. It was presumably initiated by actual prospectors, probably by veritable colonies, from that direction. It is in fact first and most brilliantly attested in Almeria at sites adjacent to the Mediterranean coasts whence colonists come by sea from farther east could conveniently exploit and work neighbouring lodes of argentiferous copper and lead ores. The type station, Los Millares,[30] a few miles up the Andorax from the modern port of Almeria, has indeed all the aspects of an Aegean township, covering 5 hectares ($12\frac{1}{2}$ acres) and protected by a wall and fosse. Outside the wall lay a cemetery of a hundred-odd collective tombs said to have held up to a hundred interments. A similar settlement was established at Almizaraque about a mile up from the mouth of the Almanzora. Others may be inferred from corbelled tombs at Belmonte, Purchena, and Tabernas.[31]

Most of the townsmen were of course farmers who cultivated emmer and hexaploid wheat, barley, beans, and flax.[32] But the population included also metallurgists, presumably initiated in the East Mediterranean and interested especially in silver and gold. Slags from Almizaraque attest the extraction of silver, copper, and lead. Siret[33] believed that clay arcs, perforated at both ends and up to 22 cm long, formed parts of a reverberatory furnace. But the exact Anatolian parallels to such arcs, that are characteristic of most sites of Bronze I, suggest that they really served as loom weights. The copper-smiths were masters of only the simplest techniques of forging and open-hearth casting. So they manufactured only daggers with a midrib on one face (like Fig. 132, bottom), as at Usatova, or quite flat and tanged (of West European type) together with long narrow flat adzes, cutters, as in the Cyclades, quadrangular awls, and even saws.

Trade brought to Los Millares hippopotamus ivory and ostrich egg-shells from Africa, turquoise, callaïs, amber, and jet from undetermined sources. But stone was still normally used instead of metal for axe-heads, and flint was now superbly worked by pressure flaking for arrow-heads, dagger or halberd blades (Fig. 129, 4), as well as knives and sickle-teeth. Apart from transverse arrow-heads which were still used, 68 per cent of the specimens from Los Millares are hollow-based, 17 per cent tanged-and-barbed, 7 per cent leaf-shaped (Fig. 129, 5). Thick plaques of clay, perforated at the four corners, may have been used as wrist-guards or loom-weights.[34] A stone plaque perforated at each end from Belmonte was used as a whetstone.

The pottery on the whole carries on the native Almerian tradition, but some vases are decorated with incised patterns that include oculi motives (like Fig. 130, 2) and conventionalized stags (Fig. 130, 3), with small knobs or even painted in warm black on a light ground. New forms include squat birds' nest pyxides, sometimes with plaster necks, cylindrical tumblers and little globular vases with short necks as well as a few multiple vessels. Beakers were found, apparently as an intrusive element in only four tholoi at Los Millares, in one each at Belmonte, Purchena, and Almizaraque, and in five cists. Vases were also made out of plaster to imitate ostrich eggs, and unguent flasks were carved out of ivory or white limestone.

As toilet articles and ornaments, bone or ivory combs were worn at Los Millares, the clothing fastened with shanked stone buttons, and simple disc or barrel beads of stone, shell, talc, and

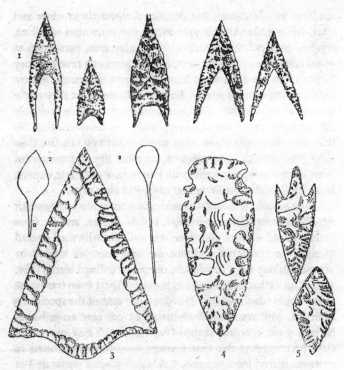

Fig. 129. Flint arrow-heads: 1, Alcalá ($\frac{1}{1}$); 5, Los Millares ($\frac{1}{2}$).
Halberd blades; 3, Casa da Moura; 4, Los Millares ($\frac{1}{2}$); 2,
Palmella points ($\frac{1}{2}$).

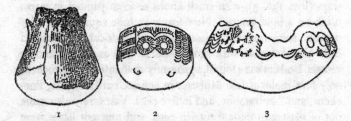

Fig. 130. 1, 'Late Neolithic' vase from Tres Cabezos; 2-3,
symbol vases from Los Millares.

imported materials were hung on strings round the neck. At Almizaraque, conical and prismatic buttons with V perforation and a grooved bone toggle of a type found at Troy and Ališar were used as dress-fasteners, and in the tholos at Tabernas and probably also in that at Llano de Media Legua on the Almanzora, bone pins with grooved cylindrical heads (like Fig. 132) were found.

The Almerians were, however, deeply preoccupied with immaterial ends. The collective tombs were constructed with great care; sixty-five of those at Los Millares, as at Almizaraque, Belmonte, Tabernas, are corbelled tholoi (Fig. 108), often with cells opening off the chamber or passage, and with porthole slabs for entries,[35] covered with circular cairns supported by a built retaining-wall on to which straight or curved walls may be built to frame a forecourt. Wooden pillars are said to have supported the roofs. A few of the earlier tombs at Los Millares are rectangular or trapezoid megalithic cists from 2 to 5 m long, preceded by a short entrance passage. Ritual objects include owl-eyed female figurines made by painting bovine phalanges (Fig. 131, 1), or stone and ivory cylinders, plain plaques of schist (Los Millares), and flat stone figures without faces like Fig. 8, 13, and, at Almizaraque, bone models of sandals. Axe-amulets were worn as charms at Los Millares and elsewhere.

The urbanization of Almerian economy seen at Los Millares and Almizaraque is presumably a reflection, however indirect, of Oriental cities' demands for metal. But the townships thus created, themselves constituted local secondary centres of demand and radiated their influence right across the Peninsula. Westward, parallel or colonial settlements sprang up all across Andalusia to the coasts of Portugal along the natural route, followed by the modern railways from Almeria to Algarve, and principally at focal-points (now junctions) thereon or in metalliferous districts.

On the plateau of Granada[36] are several large cemeteries of collective tombs round Guadix, Gor, and Gorafe, composed partly of tholoi, more often of cists of the Almerian form and frequently entered through porthole slabs. The tombs contain typical Almerian products – oculi vases, flat stone idols, phalange idols, ribbed cylinder-headed pins – as well as a few Beakers. Yet other tombs of the same form in these cemeteries contain pottery

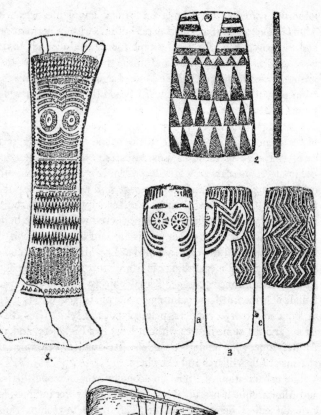

Fig. 131. Ritual objects: 1, Almeria; 2 and 4, Portugal; 3, Granada (¼).

and bronzes characteristic of the succeeding Argaric Bronze Age. Farther west at Antequera[37] and in the ancient Betica,[38] the route is marked by superbly built tholos tombs. But near the princely tholos of Romeral at Antequera is a small cemetery of rock-cut tombs[39] that reproduce in miniature the plan of the tholos but contained mainly Argaric bronzes. On the other hand, stroke-burnished ware from villages near Jerez and Carmona[40] points to fresh impulses direct from the East Mediterranean. But at Campo Reale near Carmona, Bonsor[41] found burials in 'silos' – really chamber tombs – accompanied by polished stone axes, plain pottery, and a little painted ware akin to the Almerian and the characteristic clay arcs.

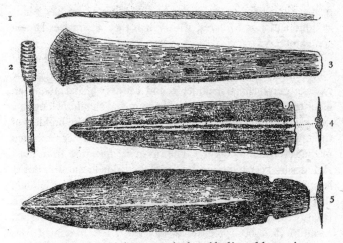

Fig. 132. Copper daggers and adze, Alcalá, and bone pin, Cabeço da Ministra ($\frac{1}{2}$).

Then, in Algarve, a metalliferous region where the rocks are suited to dry-stone masonry, a cemetery of seven tholoi at Alcalá[42] marks the site of a smaller Los Millares. The tombs contained flat adzes, notched daggers with midribs on one or both faces (Fig. 132), awls and saws of copper, superbly worked hollow-based arrow-heads of flint (Fig. 129, 1), undecorated vases of Almerian type, a marble paint-pot, a clay arc, hammer beads, and beads of amber, callaïs, and jet, but not Beaker ware nor West European daggers. Corbelled tombs extend along the Portuguese coasts as far north as Torres Vedras (Peña and Barro with semicircular forecourt).[43] Tombs at Monge and San Martiñho, Cintra,[44] excavated in the rock but roofed by corbelling, illustrate the transition from the built tholos to the rock-cut tomb.

Tombs of the latter class, agreeing in plan with the tholoi and, like them, sometimes preceded by an antechamber, a curved forecourt or a long entrance passage divided by rock-cut versions of the porthole slab form regular cemeteries at Palmella,[45] Alapraia,[46] Estoril, and other sites round the Tagus estuary.[47] From their situation at the river mouth and from the tomb furniture these cemeteries of the Palmella culture might belong to maritime colonists from the East Mediterranean like Almizaraque and Los Millares, with which they are in fact largely contemporary.

But in the hinterland, including the stanniferous plateaux of Northern Portugal, are cemeteries of four or five megalithic passage graves (antas) under round cairns which embody an older tradition of sepulchral architecture and should belong to a native population of neolithic ancestry (p. 319) – the builders of the unpublished 'dolmens'. Nearly all antas had been pillaged in the seventeenth century. The surviving furniture from most includes beakers and typical relics of the Palmella culture. But at least two[48] were demonstrably earlier than 'Almerian' tholoi that had been built up against them under the same cairns. And from a couple of very simple passage graves (Fig. 133) the original furniture has been recovered intact.[49] Each interment was accompanied by an axe and an adze, a set of geometric microliths and a couple of plain round-bottomed 'Western' pots and a plate of red-slipped ware. So the first megalithic passage graves in Portugal were built by a neolithic population akin to the Almerian and at a time at least culturally equivalent to Neolithic II in Spain. Yet larger, and presumably later, tombs reproduce in orthostatic masonry all the features of the tholoi and rock-cut tombs[50] with their divided passage and even porthole slabs.[51]

The only settlement yet explored in Portugal is Vila Nova de S. Pedro,[52] not on the coast, but well in the hinterland of Lisbon. It was founded before Beaker ware became fashionable locally,[53] but was occupied throughout the 'Copper Age' (Bronze I) and until Argaric types were locally produced in Bronze II. The villagers cultivated hexaploid wheat,[54] barley, and beans and

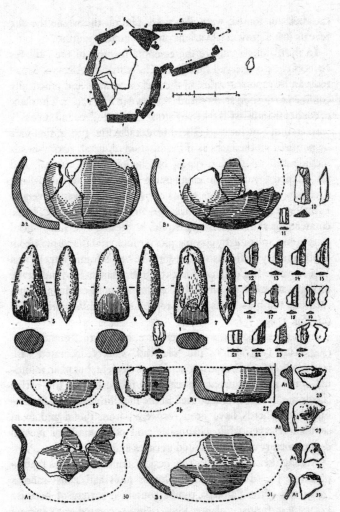

Fig. 133. Plan of 'neolithic' passage grave (*anta*) and part of furniture; Alemtejo. After Leisner. Pottery and celts ($\frac{1}{6}$), flints ($\frac{2}{6}$).

engaged in stock-breeding and hunting. Local copper ores were smelted at the site and the metal worked into flat axes, saws, and other types,[55] though perhaps not before Bronze II. The domestic pottery is characterized by reinforced rims, surprisingly like those of neolithic Britain.[56] But beakers and other vases, found in the rock-cut tombs, were also used, and on the whole the site reveals just a provincial variant on the Palmella culture.

In the Palmella culture the essential features of the Millares economy are conserved though less fully than in Algarve. Metal tools and weapons are rare in the rock-cut tombs and practically confined to the odd arrow-heads[57] shown in Fig. 129, 2. The place of copper in industry is taken by stone axes and adzes and superbly worked flints, including halberd blades like Fig. 129, 4, that may be polished on the faces as if in imitation of metal. Arrow-heads include still microlithic types, but hollow-based, tanged, and leaf-shaped forms, none comparable in delicacy to those from Alcalá, occur in the proportions of 72, 19, and 9 respectively at Palmella. Trade brought gold, callaïs, amber, and ivory, while the connections with Almeria are explicitly attested by cylinder-head pins from tombs and by clay plaques perforated at the corners from contemporary settlements. But tortoise beads from Palmella and Vila Nova de S. Pedro conform to the Sardinian-Provençal type of Fig. 126, while a pair of basket-shaped gold earrings from a rock-cut tomb at Ermageira[58] reproduce a familiar Irish type (cf. Fig. 154).

In the Palmella pottery Beaker ware, both of the 'grand style' (Fig. 111, 1–2) and of the 'classical' variety decorated with rouletted zones, is the most conspicuous element, but plain round-bottomed and carinated vessels may just carry on the native 'neolithic' tradition, illustrated in the megalithic tombs. Stroke-burnished sherds have been recovered from tholoi and from sepulchral caves while channelled and other kinds of incised decoration are also represented in caves and settlements.

Among the ritual objects too, besides familiar Millares types – phalange (S. Martiñho) and cylinder idols and schist sandals (Alapraia) – the Palmella tombs contain a variety of peculiar Portuguese forms – plaque idols richly decorated with incised patterns (Fig. 131, 2), schist croziers, similarly decorated, marble copies of shafted hoe-blades, large crescentic 'collars' of lime-stone,[59] and pendants in the form of a rabbit.[60] The owl-face of a funerary goddess and even representations of a copper dagger were carved or painted on the uprights of some tombs.[61]

Similarly on the east coasts from Almeria northward to Cata-lonia rural communities continued to bury the dead in natural cave ossuaries. While they relied mainly on stone for axes, they obtained objects of copper, and beads of callaïs, learned to work metals and copied locally such Almerian types as cylinder-head pins and painted phalange idols.[62] Flint daggers and hollow-based arrow-heads of Portuguese form are not, however, found north of Almeria. The local pottery preserves the rounded Almerian shapes but is generally mixed up with decorated 'Cave wares' and beakers. A round-headed minority is represented in most of these caves.

From many Copper Age tombs and settlements, especially in Portugal, but also in Almeria, bones of horses – or just possibly asses – have been reported.

We might thus recognize in the Copper Age Almerian (Los Millares) Andalusian, Algarvian, Portuguese, and East Spanish cultures though the first four might be grouped together as local facies of one Early Hispanic culture. Should we distinguish a sixth entity – a 'pure' Beaker culture in the Peninsula. Beakers of the Pan-European type, like Fig. 111, 3–4, with their usual accompaniment of West European daggers and arrow-heads but no wrist-guards, have been found in every type of Copper Age tomb – tholos, rock-cut, megalithic, natural cave – but far more frequently in Portugal than in Almeria. But there are local variants on this standard model. Fig. 111, 1–2, illustrates a Portuguese variant that may be found in the same tomb as the Pan-European form.[63] Beakers, decorated in this style, are associated with chalices of Argaric shape at Acebuchal near Carmona in Betica.[64] In two tombs at Gandul in Betica beakers were associated only with the latest (Copper Age I) and presumably intrusive, interments and must thus be later than the erection of the tombs. Similarly, at Vila Nova de San Pedro Beaker ware was missing from the oldest habitation deposit. On the other hand, at Los Millares, Leisner assigns beakers to the earliest phase. So it is impossible in the south of the Iberian Peninsula to isolate an assemblage of relics and rites that should distinguish archaeologically a Beaker people from the rest of the interrelated societies responsible for the Early Hispanic culture. Physically Beaker-folk were undoubtedly represented among those societies, and, assuming they were of East Mediterranean origin, should have been among the first colonists thence who founded those societies.

Yet they did not arrive as Beaker-folk since Beakers are not known in the East Mediterranean nor yet at Paestum, where the physical type is represented.

Presumably they separated out from them in the Peninsula. Margaret Smith has shown that the beaker cannot be derived from the native Cave culture pottery of Betica [65] and that the Tagus estuary is the most likely focus for the wide dispersion described in Chapter 12. But unless the fine bifacially worked arrow-heads they carried with them evolved in the Peninsula from microlithic forms as Siret suggested, we might suspect that they had been joined by a contingent of bowmen from the Sahara, where such arrow-heads were made in profusion, whether as a local continuation of the Aterian tradition or under inspiration from the Fayum neolithic.

The foundation of the Copper Age cultures in the Peninsula, as in Italy and Sardinia, is generally attributed to an actual coloniz-ation by East Mediterranean prospectors. But these colonists did not, like the Phoenicians and the Greeks, bring shiploads of manufactured articles; not a single East Mediterranean export has been recognized on any Peninsular site before the Argaric period. The metal gear, locally made by the immigrant smiths, was technically inferior to that current in the East Mediterranean even during the third millennium – but after all the 'prospectors' would have been looking for silver and gold, not copper. Some Millares pot forms have general parallels in the Early Minoan ossuaries of Crete,[66] the stone figurines are obviously like Cycladic and Anatolian ones, the owl-face engraved on plaques and vases or painted on phalanges and caves belongs to the same 'goddess' whom the Sumerians depicted on the handles of funerary jars and the Trojans on a stele and on face-urns. The plaque-idols like Fig. 131, 2, are very like Egyptian block figures (p. 54) or Early Cypriote clay 'idols'.[67] The clay arcs have exact parallels in Anatolia, as has the toggle [68] from Almizaraque; a segmented stone bead from Palmella is quite like Fig. 12, 2, while the stroke-burnished ware from Betica (p. 324) is identical with the East Mediterranean fabric. The idea of the artificial collective tomb is East Mediterranean and was translated into corbelled vaults in Crete and the Cyclades in the third millennium. The tholoi of Los Millares are actually rather similar to Krazi in Crete (p. 59), while the contemporary cists resemble those of H. Kosmas in Attica (p. 110).

Still these analogies are distinctly vague. Collective burial had apparently been practised in the Peninsula already in the neolithic period. In Portugal even built collective tombs may be equally neolithic. There, too, megalithic tombs are demonstrably older than tholoi. Even for the Almerian tholoi Leisner has expounded a plausible evolution from the neolithic round cists. The similarity between tholoi, like those at Antequera and Alcalá and the Mycenaean looks indeed particularly striking. It is accentuated by the cemetery of rock-cut tombs near Antequera that seem to bear the same relation to the tholos as chamber tombs do to Mycenaean tholoi. But perhaps the similarity in plan is deceptive; in Greece the passage was unroofed, where in Iberia it was always covered. In any case it is no longer plausible to derive from the Mycenaean the Iberian tholoi any more than to make the latter the models for the Portuguese passage graves. Indeed, it is now just as plausible to derive the Mycenaean tholoi from the Peninsula (p. 119). Hence its East Mediterranean relations provide no indisputable limiting dates for the Early Hispanic Copper Age.

Whether as a consequence of East Mediterranean colonization or no, during the Copper Age the several societies inhabiting the Peninsula, while asserting their autonomy in divergent ceramic styles, fashions in amulets, and preferences for arrow-heads, had achieved a considerable degree of uniformity in stone and metal tools and weapons, in costume and personal ornaments and from one coast to the other. To this cultural uniformity no political union need have corresponded. Only in Andalusia and perhaps Algarve do a few monumental tombs look like princely sepulchres rather than communal ossuaries or family vaults.

The exotic materials – turquoise, amber, jet, callaïs – and foreign types, like tortoise beads, from Copper Age tombs illustrate wide commercial relations, particularly with the Northwest. The counter-balancing exports – at least before the Beaker expansions – seem to have been of a less substantial character – elements of a cult. The passage graves of Brittany are so closely related to the Portuguese in architecture and furniture as to suggest direct maritime intercourse foreshadowing that of the

Tartessians in the eight century.[69] The Northern passage graves should result from a further extension of such relations that might account for the amber at Los Millares. The symbolism and the technique of ceramic decoration in Brittany and Scotland point in the same direction, while the magic patterns on Irish bronzes[70] are inspired by the hieratic art of Palmella. In the sequel, of course, the Beaker-folk, presuming they did set out from Spain, played a decisive rôle in initiating a Bronze Age in Central Europe and Upper Italy. The main contribution of the Peninsula to Atlantic and North-Western Europe was, however, surely 'the Megalithic Religion'. With Hawkes[71] we might imagine the megalith-builders sailing from the Portuguese coasts, like the Conquistadores, to conquer for that faith a New World. Or perhaps the saints of the Celtic Church would provide a better analogy; some actually followed routes marked out by megalithic tombs while our megalith-builders have left no superior copper weapons to correspond to the fire-arms with which the Conquistadores vindicated the authority of the cross.

The great creative moment was transient. As in the seventeenth century, after the great expansion, Peninsular culture stagnated and – compared to Britain and Central Europe – declined. Even in Copper Age II decline is perceptible. According to Leisner the later tombs at Los Millares contain a poorer and less varied furniture than the earlier ones. In the succeeding Bronze Age (Bronze II), though tin was now obtainable and alloyed with copper and methods of casting were improved, Hispanic culture seems less progressive and its domain contracts.

The Bronze Age

In Eastern Spain the Copper Age culture of Los Millares develops into, or is succeeded by, a no less well-defined semi-urban culture of Bronze Age type, named after the type station at El Argar.[72] Its authors continued to live in hilltop townships, or citadels, more solidly fortified than before. There might even be galleries in the walls. The houses are agglomerations of rectangular rooms with stone foundations, but the total areas are small – the acropolis of El Officio covered $2\frac{1}{2}$ acres. The dead were no longer buried in collective tombs but individually in cists or jars among the houses; the 780 graves actually identified at El Argar give some indication as to how large the population must have become or how long the Argaric Bronze Age lasted. Metal was mined and worked locally on a larger scale than in the Copper Age and was effectively distributed throughout the province. Long-distance trade, on the contrary, languished; it brought only a few beads of callaïs and segmented beads of Egyptian fayence like those from Perjámos graves. Tin was scarce, and the smith had generally to be content with copper or poor bronze. But he could turn out flat axes with splayed blades or even with hammered flanges, awls, saws, round-heeled daggers that might be elongated into swords up to 70 cm long (Fig. 134) and specialized halberds which seem to be local translations of Copper Age flint forms.[73] Silver was sometimes used for rivets. Whetstones perforated at both ends were in regular use. Yet polished stone axes are quite plentiful on all Argaric settlements.

Round-bottomed and carinated pots might seem to carry on some Copper Age traditions (Fig. 134), but technically the fabric – red, black, or mottled – is surprisingly like Anatolian Bronze Age pottery and its Danubian IV analogues. The carinated shapes, too, but for the absence of handles, would fit well into the Unětician repertory; indeed, one mug from a typical cemetery near Orihuela is actually provided with a handle.[74]

Ornaments included diadems of silver (Fig. 134, top), beads, rings, and simple bracelets of gold, silver, or copper, perforated boars' tusks carrying tiny rings of copper wire, shells, fish-vertebrae, and various beads (none of amber). Rare burials with diadems (Fig. 134) must belong to chiefs or nobles, burials of males and females together should be instances of satî. A class division of society and a patriarchal organization are thus attested. Concurrently the cult of a mother goddess, in so far as it inspired the production of female figurines, was given up. Indeed, apart from an 'altar' surmounted by 'horns of consecration' at Campos, ritual objects are no longer conspicuous. In the mixed population, round-heads were mingled with a majority of Mediterraneans.[75]

The Argaric culture might be regarded as a continuation of the old Almerian stripped of foreign elements after appropriating the technical advances introduced therewith.[76] The Almerians, having emancipated themselves from the megalithic super-

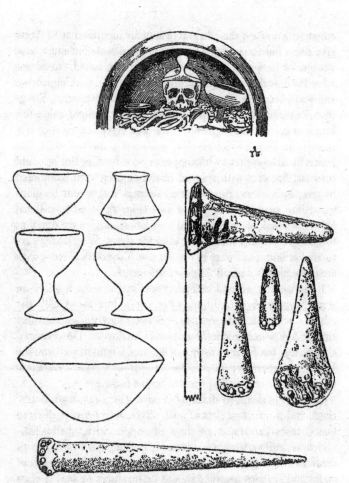

Fig. 134. Argaric burial-jar showing diadem ($\frac{1}{10}$); funerary vases ($\frac{1}{8}$); halberd and dagger-blades ($\frac{1}{8}$); sword ($\frac{1}{8}$). By permission of Trustees of British Museum.

stition, went on to develop the metallurgy introduced therewith on original native lines. Yet the novel burial practices, as strange to El Garcel as to Los Millares, but traditional in Central Anatolia and adopted in Middle Helladic Greece, suggest that this emancipation was not effected without help from the East Mediterranean. Indeed, there is better evidence for an East Mediterranean colonization of Almeria at the beginning of the Bronze Age than in the Copper Age. Agreements in burial practices are more specific. The typical Argaric chalices are just Aegean kylikes of wood or metal translated into the local pottery as they were into Minyan or painted Mycenaean ware in Greece. The fayence beads are actual Aegean imports. On the other hand, some would derive the innovations of the Argaric culture from Upper Italy. Italian prehistorians, however, prefer to regard the halberd-brandishers there as immigrants from the Peninsula.

The segmented fayence beads from Fuente Alamo in any case prove that the Argaric culture was flourishing at latest by 1400 B.C. If due to Aegean colonists, it could not have started much before 1500, since even the Minyan kylikes are Late Helladic (p. 113). How long it lasted is still more uncertain. There are no connected remains outside the Argaric citadels and graves till the Iron Age began after 1000 B.C., so that Almeria is in much the same plight as Sardinia. Outside that province the position is still worse.

Typical Argaric cemeteries, well provided with metal tools, as far north as Alicante and Valencia[77] illustrate the effective extension of the Almerian economic system. But in the province of Alicante itself in the Alcoy district on the hilltop citadels of Mola alta de Serelles[78] and Mas de Menente[79] axes of Argaris type were cast, or Argaric riveted daggers used, but the round-bottomed bowls and globular jars preserve purer traditions of the Almerian culture in contrast to the sharper profiles of Argaric pottery, while polished stone axes were still regularly employed.

Westward in Granada some megalithic tombs in the cemeteries of Gor, Gorafe, and Los Eriales contain Argaric bronzes, ornaments, and pots. So at Alcaïde, near Antequera,[80] rock-cut tombs, reproducing exactly the plan of the built tholos, contain relics of Argaric type. Otherwise there is nothing in South Spain till the Iron Age. In Portugal cemeteries of cist graves containing (? Argaric) carinated pottery are rare and mainly concentrated in Algarve.[81] Sometimes the capstones of the short cists are carved with representations of developed metal axes.[82] Apart from cist graves, only the megalithic passage graves and natural cave sepulchres are available to fill the gap in the funerary record between the Copper and Late Bronze Ages; carinated and even handled pots from such might well be 'Bronze Age'. On the other hand, bronzes of highly specialized type, especially two-eared palstaves,[83] show that there arose in North Portugal and Galicia during the Late Bronze Age an important centre of metallurgy the products of which were exported to Britain in a revival of the old trade that had been reflected in the earrings of Irish form from Ermageira and lunulae from Galicia.[84]

With this revival the Peninsula's Atlantic coast or at least its stanniferous northern part at length became again a creative centre of metallurgy and trade, of which Avienus' verses have preserved a memory.[85] Yet this Late (Atlantic) Bronze Age began only after 1000 B.C. No Middle Bronze Age is defined by typological landmarks. Into this vacuum the poor Early Bronze Age cists and even some Copper Age collective tombs might easily slide! Between 1550 and 1400 B.C. indirect commerce between Britain and Mycenaean Greece by some western route is positively attested. Were Alcalá – and Los Millares – points on that route? An affirmative answer seems quite plausible[86] and the extra-short chronology for the Hispanic Copper Age cannot be refuted just by the vague parallels in the third millennium we have cited. But then the Peninsula's claim to cradle the Beaker-folk would become precarious unless the chronology for Temperate Europe be similarly telescoped!

The diversified region north of the Pyrenees and west of the Rhine and the high Alps, which had been steppe and parkland during the Ice Age, in the subsequent forest period still supported Azilian descendants of the Magdalenian reindeer-hunters and salmon-fishers, of Tardenoisian immigrants from Africa, and of Forest-folk who spread southward. These autochthonous food-gatherers were converted gradually to a food-producing economy by the spread of an exotic neolithic culture, and, multiplying in response to the new opportunities of livelihood, accelerated its expansion. This conversion itself might indeed have taken place in Provence and round the Pyrenees, where the Cardial herdsmen, as shown in Chapter 15, had implanted their neolithic culture and economy. It is, however, generally attributed to a second wave of immigrants who would have introduced a Western Neolithic culture and spread it thence to more temperate regions, indeed to the Alps and the Channel. Even on the latter view the primary Western farmers admittedly mixed with native food-gatherers and, in adapting their rural economy to the novel environment, took advantage of their experience and equipment. Moreover, in South France the postulated Western immigrants have left only ambiguous traces of their passage, and the Western culture they should have brought with them is largely an inference from the 'Western' cultures of Lombardy, Western Switzerland, Central and North France, and Southern England.

No doubt in a number of South French caves Cardial ware is replaced in higher strata by plain leathery pots that can be more or less exactly matched on the one hand in the Lagozza, Cortaillod, Chassey, and Windmill Hill cultures,[1] on the other in the Almeria culture and its Portuguese counterpart (p. 319), while similar pots occur in the basal levels of caves outside the narrow zone colonized by Cardial herdsmen. It is less clear whether other distinctive traits occur so early in South France or, if they do, whether they be distinctive of the Western Neolithic. Leaf-shaped arrow-heads are thus found[2] and are distinctive of the earliest Neolithic in Britain, but not of Lagozza or Cortaillod. Antler sleeves for celts so distinctive of Cortaillod occur early in Aude and Ariège,[3] but are missing from the deepest levels in Gard as from Lagozza and Windmill Hill. Hares' phalange pendants again occur[4] in Gard as in South Spain and in Cortaillod and in the Lower to Middle Neolithic of Liguria. Hence the South French caves have yielded some material, stratified below Beaker layers, which could be treated as intermediate between the Almeria culture on the one hand, the Ligurian Middle Neolithic and the Alpine Cortaillod cultures on the other. In the last-named assemblage we have the fullest picture of the Western, indeed of any, neolithic culture available in Europe.

The Early Neolithic Phase on the West Alpine Lakes

The Swiss lakes have provided not only an unique picture of neolithic equipment and economy, owing to the preservation by the waters of organic materials, but also the clearest record of cultural development in Western Europe, thanks firstly to the stratigraphical excavations on Lake Neuchâtel, initiated by Paul Vouga in 1919, and to the subsequent observations of E. Vogt[5] and others which have clarified and extended Vouga's sequence. The names Cortaillod-Michelsberg, Horgen, and Corded Ware denote three culture periods that follow one another in that order on all the Alpine lakes and bogs. But the earliest neolithic colonization of the area is not represented by lacustrine habitations at all, but is known exclusively from cereal pollen blown into some peat mosses from cultivated fields adjacent to unidentified settlements on what is still dry land.[6]

So the oldest 'lake-dwellings' in Western Switzerland were erected by farmers who arrived with a complete neolithic equipment, constituting what is termed the Cortaillod culture – now divisible into an Early and a Late phase.[7] But the majority of

Swiss prehistorians by 1956[8] have become convinced that 'lake-dwellings' were not raised on piles above the waters but erected on solid, if rather moist, ground, strung out along the shore between the reed belt and the strand scrub, which had then been left dry owing to the contraction of the lakes in late Atlantic and Sub-Boreal times. Similarly the so-called 'stacked platforms' (*Packwerkbauten*) were not artificial islands floating in bogs, but houses built on firm peat the floors of which required frequent renewal owing to subsidence.

The farmers cultivated wheats (*Triticum monococcum, dicoccum*, and *compactum*) and barley, and also peas, beans, and lentils.[9] Plums and apples were at least gathered; apples were eventually cultivated by the Lake-dwellers, though not certainly in the Cortaillod phase, and a sort of cider brewed from them. Horned cattle (*Bos brachyceros*) were bred together with minor herds of pigs and small flocks of sheep and goats.[10] Cattle were tethered and fed on leaves during the winters.[11] A neolithic (? Cortaillod) yoke[12] survives, and Vouga considers some stone implements to have been used as ploughshares, but more probably the land was tilled only with antler hoes.[13]

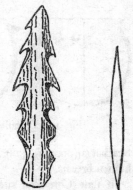

Fig. 135. Antler harpoon ($\frac{2}{5}$) and bone arrow-head ($\frac{1}{3}$). Switzerland.

Game contributed much less to the community's diet than domestic stock. But the huntsman used arrows tipped with double-ended bone points (Fig. 135), or more rarely with transverse or triangular flint heads. Fish were caught in traps, in nets weighted with grooved stones and suspended from birch-bark floats, and were also speared with antler 'harpoons' (Fig. 135).

Wood-work was done with stone axes and rare adzes made from suitably shaped pebbles or sawn-out blocks of fine-grained rock. They were mounted directly in straight shafts or in tapering antler sleeves (Fig. 139 A) which were fitted into straight wooden shafts. Antler axes and picks with square-cut shaft hole were also employed.

A local flax was cultivated for its seeds and for its fibres, which were woven into linen, but the spinner did without whorls. Skins were doubtless largely worn; bundles of bone spines, like the antler combs of Michelsberg and Windmill Hill, could have served for leather-dressing. Baskets were plaited with great skill.

Early Cortaillod pots are of simple leather forms without handles save for lugs, which may be perforated with several vertical holes (Fig. 136). In the Late phase much more sophisticated forms were produced and vases were often decorated[14] with strips of birch bark, stuck on with birch-pitch to form patterns, including the magic concentric circles popular at Conguel and

Fig. 136. Cortaillod pottery. After *Antiquity* ($\frac{1}{4}$).

Beacharra (pp. 369, 378), or just with paired nipples simulating human breasts.

In Late Cortaillod sites appear some vases of Rössen style or at least influenced by Rössen and others of Michelsberg affinities. And on all Cortaillod sites flint instruments were made exclusively of a translucent yellow flint, strange to the Neuchâtel basin but of unknown provenance. Otherwise Cortaillod sites have yielded no conclusive evidence for trade.

Combs for the hair were made of wood. As ornaments were worn beads of steatite, wood, and bored teeth, cranian amulets (p. 362), pendants made from segmented tines, from perforated phalanges of hares, boars' tusks, perforated at both ends, and wooden models of clubs.

No cemeteries attached to the lake-side villages have been found, but some human bones, broken to extract the marrow, turned up in the villages – as if the peasants had practised cannibalism – while two measurable skulls proved to be dolichocranial. On the other hand, Sauter[15] has argued that cist graves of the Chamblandes type belonged to Cortaillod people.

Cemeteries of such graves,[16] containing single contracted skeletons or a male and female together, extend from the vicinity of Basel in the Aar valley to the Upper Rhône and thence beyond the Great St Bernard along the Aosta valley into Upper Italy. The grave goods – unpolished flint axes, a triangular axe hammer, hollow-based arrow-heads, coral and Mediterranean shells, a copper disc, a cranian amulet, and a V-perforated button – are certainly very poor, but look late. The 'Chamblandes culture' has therefore generally been assigned to Swiss Middle or Late Neolithic. But its distribution agrees very closely with that of the Cortaillod culture, and the grave-type is identical with that characteristic of the Middle Neolithic levels of Arene Candide.

Chronologically the Cortaillod culture, at least in its Late phase, can be conclusively equated with the Rössen culture, again mainly with its later manifestations,[17] thus giving a partial synchronism between Swiss Lower Neolithic and Danubian II. A knobbed battle-axe, however, from the Late Cortaillod layer at Seematte,[18] must mean that Swiss Lower Neolithic lasts into Danubian III and Northern E.N.c. A radiocarbon estimate for the pre-Rössen Cortaillod of Egolzwill 3[19] put the oldest tangible phase of Lower Neolithic at 2740±90 B.C. – a figure that would be perfectly reasonable for Danubian II too, but only on a 'long' chronology.

In the Cortaillod culture such elements as mounting celts with antler sleeves, antler harpoons, microlithic arrow-heads, can economically be derived from the mesolithic heritage. Of the constituents that make it neolithic, one-corn wheat must be Danubian. But it could have been introduced by the Rössen colonists (pp. 160–61), for it is not yet attested before their influence becomes perceptible, and no distinctively Danubian artifacts, necessarily older than Rössen, have yet been found in the West Alpine area. So it still seems most likely that the primary impulse – i.e. the cereals and domestic stock together with a tradition of leathery vessels, cranian amulets, hares' phalange pendants – that engendered the pre-lake village cultivations and the pre-Rössen Cartaillod culture of Egolzwill[20] came up the Rhône despite the ambiguity of the analogies in South France.

North of the Cortaillod province, in lake-side villages on the Lake of Constance, in moor villages in northern Switzerland and Württemberg, in hilltop camps in South-West Germany, and at the flint-mines of Spiennes in Belgium, the place of Cortaillod is taken by a quite different culture – named after the hilltop camp at Michelsberg[21] in Baden.

The moor villages may comprise up to twenty-four houses

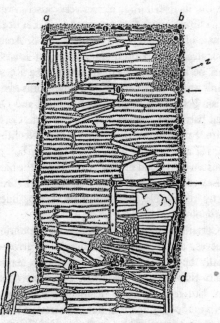

Fig. 137. Plan of a house at Aichbühl ($\frac{1}{150}$).

grouped along regular corduroyed streets.[22] In land settlements as many as seventy-five houses have been recorded, but, since a hut might be pulled down at its owner's death, they cannot all be regarded as contemporary. The houses themselves were again rectangular, varying in size from 6 by 3·6 m to 5·3 by 3·2 m or less, but normally divided into two rooms with a hearth in the inner and an oven in the outer (like Fig. 137). The dry land stations in Germany were generally defended by flat-bottomed ditches and palisades; the ditches of many camps are interrupted by frequent causeways as in England.

The rural economy seems very similar to that of the Cortaillod and First Northern A cultures. But there are some hints of more pastoral clans separating out from the mass of Michelsberg villagers and presumably allowing their stock to graze freely. The principal crop in Württemberg[23] was barley, but wheats (*T. monococcum*, *dicoccum*, *spelta*, and *compactum*) too were grown, and apples, strawberries, and other fruits collected. Flour was not, according to Guyan,[24] converted into bread, but eaten as a sort of gruel, but the ovens, so conspicuous in most villages, must surely have served for baking bread. Guyan[25] believes that the villagers practised shifting cultivation, deserting their homes at intervals but returning to the same site as soon as the scrub had grown up again on their old clearings. The villages were certainly occupied over considerable periods, during which the house floors at least had to be renewed more than once – at Ehrenstein near Ulm as many as thirteen times.[26] The evidence here suggests not reoccupation but continuous habitation on the same site for fourteen years or probably longer. Finally, hunting played a far more prominent rôle in the Michelsberg subsistence economy than it did in that of the Cortaillod farmers; bones of game animals, including horses,[27] form a relatively high proportion in the food refuse.

Secondary industry and trade played a recognizable part in the Michelsberg economy. Thus at Spiennes in Belgium[28] lived a community of specialized flint-miners skilled at sinking shafts and digging out subterranean galleries. Indeed, the Michelsberg settlers there constituted a specialized industrial community, supplementing their livelihood by exporting the products of their mines and workshops – and Spiennes was no isolated phenomenon within the Western complex. It implies also the development of hunting expeditions and transhumance into something like regular commerce. Hoards of Western axes in Southern Germany may belong to Michelsberg traders. As a result of such trade some communities, like that at Weiher near Thayngen, eventually obtained copper axes and amber beads.

But on the whole Michelsberg equipment is typically neolithic and agrees generally with that of Cortaillod; axes were preferred to adzes and often mounted in antler sleeves. The pots are generally plain and many could be called leathery in shape. But many have flat bases and jugs have genuine handles. Sup-

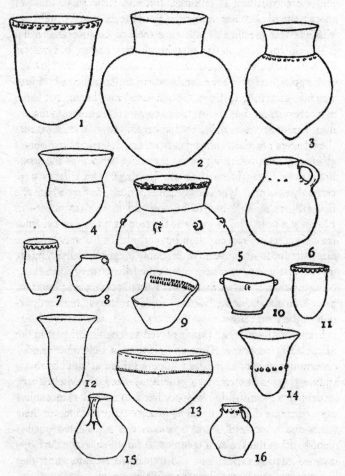

Fig. 138. Michelsberg pottery.

posedly distinctive forms are 'tulip beakers' (Fig. 138, 1, 12, 14) and flat round plates, reputedly used for baking cakes, which, however, recur in a First Northern context (Fig. 91). A few contemporary sites in Württemberg have yielded vases of more or less Michelsberg shapes but decorated with fine incised patterns reminiscent of Chassey (p. 354). These represent the 'Schussenried' style, but do not suffice to define a distinct culture.[29] For leather-dressing, bunched antler combs were employed at Spiennes as in Southern England.

The dead were normally buried, contracted or extended, within the confines of the settlements, but small cemeteries comprising up to seven graves have been recorded. On the other hand, at Ottenbourg and Boitsfort in Belgium[30] cremations have been reported under long mounds, but the latter may be the ramparts of fortified villages rather than barrows. The skulls examined proved to be dolichocranial to mesaticranial, none brachycranial.

In Switzerland, Michelsberg[31] is partly parallel to Cortaillod, and both overlap locally with Rössen. But farther east on the Goldberg in Württemberg[32] the Michelsberg settlement succeeded the fortified Rössen village. Thus in the Danubian sequence Michelsberg could not be placed before the final phase of period II. Its persistence well into period III can be deduced from polygonal battle-axes and even copper celts from Michelsberg settlements.[33] Indeed, Baden influence has been recognized in the pottery from some eastern sites.[34]

The main concentration of Michelsberg settlements lies on the Neckar and the Middle Rhine.[35] There are outposts on the Saale, in Bohemia, and near Salzburg. Settlements in Belgium and in the Aar valley likewise look peripheral. This distribution might well prompt doubts as to the Western origin traditionally attributed to our culture. Indeed, Vogt has argued that the Michelsberg culture is just a south-western extension of the First Northern culture of (Northern) Early Neolithic times (p. 237). The Michelsberg rural economy is in fact strikingly like that of the A group of First Northern as described by Troels-Smith, and the ceramic agreements are even closer than Vogt imagined. All might perhaps be explained more simply by positing an acculturation of Forest hunter-fishers in Western Germany by immigrant Danubian peasants, parallel to that assumed farther east to account for the First Northern itself. But if the latter originated farther south-east. Vogt's account would seem the most probable, at least until a primary Western Neolithic immigration be better documented.

The Middle Neolithic Horgen Culture

On Lake Neuchâtel, after a flood which overwhelmed the Early
Neolithic stations, many sites were reoccupied and new ones
founded by people of a quite different culture[36] – the Horgen
culture. It is recognizable too above a Michelsberg settlement at
Greifensee, on many lakes and probably also in land stations.[37]
Economically the Middle Neolithic witnesses a cultural regres-
sion. On Lake Neuchâtel agricultural equipment is poorer (no
more 'plough-shares'); hunting contributes more to the meat

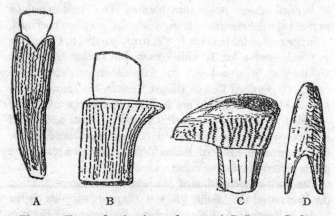

Fig. 139. Types of antler sleeves for axes: A–B, Lower; C, first
in Middle; D, first in Upper Neolithic; Lake Neuchâtel (⅔).

supply than stock-breeding, the percentage of bones of game as
against those of domestic beasts rising from 30 to 45 per cent;
local flint replaces the imported material. But triangular perforated axes now reach the Rhône valley, copper double-axes
were copied in stone and unbored Western celts were mounted
as axes in perforated or heeled antler sleeves and as adzes in
socketed ones (Fig. 139, B). Continued inter-communal specialization is illustrated by an axe-factory at Mumpf, Aargau. The
pottery is coarse, badly baked, and ornamented only with raised
cordons (what used to be regarded as early because crude), but
the vases have flat and even splayed bases (cf. Fig. 146). Spindle
whorls of stone, however, came into use.

Even architecture declines; while some Horgen houses from the Lake of Constance are long rectangles, as at Aichbühl, the occupants of other sites, like Dullenried, were content with small rectangular houses with a peaked roof, more suited to pastoral nomads than sedentary cultivators.[38]

Such a reversion to hunting and pastoralism was formerly attributed to adversities overtaking the West Alpine farmers. Really it reflects the advent of fresh settlers with stronger mesolithic traditions. Judged by its pottery, its perforated antler sleeves, its arc pendants, and other artifacts, the Horgen culture is only an aspect of that which we shall meet (pp. 363–4) in the collective tombs of the Seine-Oise-Marne basins.[39] Moreover, even gallery graves of the Paris type were built near Lake Neuchâtel and on the Upper Rhine, while five megalithic cists are known in the area.

The Altheim culture of the Upper Danube basin may be regarded as an eastern extension of the Horgen culture. On the Goldberg[40] in Württemberg the Altheim village, consisting of one-roomed huts like those of Dullenried grouped in clusters of four or five, was superimposed on the ruins of the Michelsberg settlement and thus occupies the same stratigraphical position as Horgen layers in the Swiss sites. It too belongs to period IIIa, but the Altheim culture is so closely linked with the East Alpine that it can best be considered on pages 349 ff. below.

Upper Neolithic and Chalcolithic Periods

Though separated by a 'flood layer' from the Middle, the Upper Neolithic strata on Lake Neuchâtel[41] exhibit essentially the continued evolution of the Horgen culture; there are new types of antler sleeve (Fig. 139, D) and tanged-and-barbed or hollow-based arrow-heads. But battle-axes indicate that warlike tribes were already reaching the western lakes. On Lake Zurich[42] typical corded ware from the immediate successor of a Horgen village attests already the sway of Battle-axe warriors.

In the Chalcolithic phase on Lake Neuchâtel[43] their sway was extended westwards; for cord-ornamented sherds and fine battle-axes are found in the Chalcolithic villages. The barrows of the invaders covering cremation burials were raised in the interior. But in the western lake-villages the native tradition is presumably illustrated by coarse wares decorated with finger-printed cordons. This decoration at the same time recalls that of some pottery in North Spain, South France, and Liguria. On the Lake of Geneva south-western connections are more explicitly attested by polypod bowls,[44] like the Pyrenaean vase of Fig. 144. A sur-

plus, perhaps exacted by Battle-axe chieftains, was now available to purchase foreign material; rare objects of metal including flat axes and riveted daggers, Grand Pressigny flint from Central France, and, on the Lake of Geneva, winged beads (like Fig. 143, *j*, *n*) from the Midi[45] occur in the lake-dwellings. But not till the Late Bronze Age did bronze-smiths, supplied with raw materials by regular commerce, establish themselves in the lacustrine villages. Stray axes and triangular and rhomboid daggers, appropriate to periods IV and even V, together with bone copies of Unětician pins (Fig. 140), have indeed been collected from many 'neolithic' (in Vouga's sense Chalcolithic) lake-dwellings.[46] But the economy remained formally neolithic.

Fig. 140. Bone copies of Unětician pins (½).

The West Alpine Bronze Age

But to prosperous villages on dry land must belong cemeteries of richly furnished flat graves in the Rhône and Aar valleys.[47] In them the deceased, buried contracted, were equipped with flanged axes, triangular or ogival daggers, ingot torques, and ring-head, trilobate, trefoil, racket, bulb-headed, or even knot-headed and Bohemian eyelet pins. All types can be derived from Central European models and disclose the extension westward of the Danubian traditions of metallurgy. Indeed, two currents from that quarter can be distinguished:[48] the one characterized by classical Unětician pins, ingot torques, and axes brought Bohemian traditions via the Upper Danube and the Aar to the

Rhône valley; the other, distinguished by a preference for ornaments of sheet metal (Vogt's '*Blechstil*'), brought the traditions of Kisapostag and Straubing through Upper Austria and Bavaria to the Upper Rhine and to Vallais.

Copper was won from small local lodes to exploit which metallurgists penetrated far into the high Alps. They based their operations on tiny fortified villages like Mutter-Fellers,[49] Crestaulta,[50] and Borscht in Liechtenstein.[51] The villagers were primarily farmers who cultivated wheat and barley and bred cattle, sheep, cows, pigs, and goats, and perhaps horses,[52] and who must have devised a rural economy almost as well adapted to the Alpine environment as that practised there today; for the villages seem to have been permanently occupied. They included also metallurgists who smelted the local ores and developed from Danubian models local types – spatulate axes, bronze hilted daggers of Rhône type, a variety of handsome engraved ornaments. Such were exported to Upper Italy and France. In return, amber and glass beads reached Crestaulta, while a quoit-shaped fayence pendant was acquired by a resident in the contemporary village of Bleich-Arbon in North-Eastern Switzerland. Judged by the types produced, this brilliant Swiss bronze industry flourished mainly in the latter part of period IV and in period V. But despite their enterprise and originality, the Swiss smiths seem to have remained content with supplying a local market. Cut off from the great trade-routes to the Mediterranean, the West Alpine Early Bronze Age culture did not progress so far towards urbanization as did the North Italian or Hungarian.

The Eastern Alps

Altheim[53] near Landshut, Bavaria, Mondsee[54] in Upper Austria, Vučedol[55] on the lower Drave in Slavonia, and Ljubljansko Blat (Laibach Moor)[56] in Slovenia are patent stations for a series of cultures extending along the eastern slopes of the Alps from Goldberg in Württemberg to Debelo brdo on the Bosna near Serajevo. They are lake-dwellings or fortified hilltop camps; at Altheim three concentric rings of ditches and palisades enclosed an area 40 m in diameter. Their occupants lived by cultivating cereals which they reaped with crescentic sickles made from a single flint flake and, on the Austrian lakes, also apples and beans, by breeding cattle, sheep, pigs, and horses, by hunting and by fishing – in Upper Austria using double-pronged fish-spears of bone. Stone was still used for axes which might be mounted with antler sleeves and sometimes notched at the butt[57] and for weapons – knobbed polygonal battle-axes, spheroid mace-heads, daggers, hollow-based arrow-heads, and sling bullets.

But copper was generally used, too, both for flat axes and rhomboid daggers, like Fig. 121, c, and for ornaments. On the Austrian lakes and Ljubljansko Blat and at Vučedol it was also worked locally; for moulds have been found in the settlements (one from Ljubljansko Blat would yield an axe like Fig. 64, 3) as well as grooved hammer-stones. Indeed, the Austrian lake-villagers, living at the head of navigation on the Traun,[58] were supplementing the products of farming by smelting copper ores and shipping their winnings down the Danube's tributaries. So, too, Ljubljansko Blat lies at the head of navigation on the Save and may have been the precursor of the Roman station of Nauportus for trade from the Middle Danube basin to the Adriatic. Intercommunal specialization is further illustrated by 'axe-factories' on the Enns[59] and elsewhere.

Everywhere, many of the vases are coarse and decorated only with cordons though they have flat bases and include handled cups and jugs. But on the Attersee and Mondsee and in land stations in Salzburg, vases were decorated with concentric circles incised in stab-and-drag technique and filled with white paste (Fig. 141).

In the Vučedol or Slavonian ware[60] of the Lower Drave, the Save, and the Bosna the same magical motives were combined with excised patterns that imitate the chip-carving of wooden vessels, and distinctive shapes, proper to the latter, were reproduced in pottery. Among these are bowls or lamps on a cruciform foot, like those of the Starčevo culture, but even closer to the lamps from the Pontic Catacomb Graves (pp. 127, 201). But some vases from Ljubljansko Blat are provided with tunnel-handles just as in Maltese 'Neolithic B', in Piano Conte on Lipari, and in Sardinia.

Models of animals were moulded in clay on the Austrian lakes; Slavonian ideology[61] was expressed in the production also of figures of human beings fully dressed, of vases in the shape of a bird, and of models of huts, tables, and perhaps in 'horns of consecration'. At Vučedol itself the dead were buried in löss-cut 'cellars', formally like the pit-caves of the Mediterranean and the Pontic 'catacombs'.

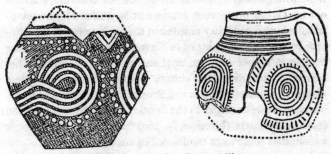

Fig. 141. Mondsee Pottery (⅓).

On the Drave, Save, and Bosna, Vučedol ware, being exclusively associated with the assemblage just summarized, may serve to define a distinct Slavonian culture. But vases, decorated in the same style and including cross-footed lamps, have been unearthed at many points – usually fortified hilltop settlements – in Hungary,[62] Austria,[63] Slovakia, Moravia, and Bohemia,[64] but always associated with relics proper to some other culture, generally

Baden. Still, in a small cemetery at Čaka in Slovakia,[65] Slavonian vases alone furnished the graves, one serving as a cinerary urn. For here the burial rite was cremation.

At the Goldberg, the Altheim settlement succeeded an occupation by Michelsberg folk, and at Vučedol Slavonian pottery was stratified above Baden wares. Hence the East Alpine neolithic cultures cannot well begin before period III. On the other hand, though ingot torques and even metal types of period V have been found in and around the Austrian lakes, the abundance of well-made polygonal battle-axes from the lake-villages suggest that their foundation should be put early in that period. Allied types occur in Slavonian contexts and in the Rinaldone culture of Italy. The latter should give a partial synchronism between East Alpine and Italian Chalcolithic.

Now, the symbolic patterns adorning Mondsee pottery are notoriously identical with motives popular on Early Cypriote Bronze Age vases, while the Mondsee daggers are at least East Mediterranean in form. If, then, Central European metallurgy were initiated by Torque-bearers from the Levant coasts (p. 177), these patterns may well be an ideological reflection of the arrival of a few Asiatic prospectors among a native Baden-Horgen population whose labour they enlisted in the exploitation of the adjacent copper lades. Analogies to Slavonian ceramic decoration at Pescale in Upper Italy (p. 295) and to Vučedol tombs in the Central Italian Rinaldone culture (p. 290) might even, if less plausibly, be interpreted as indicators of the prospectors' route, but even closer analogies in the Pontic Catacomb graves and the cross-footed lamps therefrom (p. 202)[66] might just as well mark a circuitous route from the Black Sea coasts.

In any case, if a trading-post were early established on the Mondsee during period III, it declined in importance during period IV. Trade southward was diverted to the Brenner route.[67] Carinthia, Slovenia, and Slavonia lay outside the system that distributed the metal types of period IV to Upper Italy and to the Maros valley. The Slavonian culture presumably lasted through that period, but as none of the constitutive metal types reached the province, it still looks neolithic. Even in the Eastern Alps it is not till period VI that the rich graves of the Hötting urnfield culture attest a local prosperity based on mining for copper and salt and a rural economy adapted to take full advantage of Alpine conditions. No counterpart of the West Alpine Early Bronze Age, described in the last section, is discernible in the Eastern Alps nor in the North-West Balkans.

The corridors of the Garonne and the Rhône valleys offer passage from the Mediterranean to the Atlantic West, traversed in historical times by the trade-route that carried Cornish tin to the Greek colonies round the Gulf of Lions. Along it perhaps had spread a millennium or so earlier the megalithic religion in the wake of prehistoric trade from colonies on the same shores. But still earlier the Western farmers whose arrival and spread to the north-east were postulated in Chapter 16 should have expanded also north-westward to Central France, Normandy, and Brittany. It is convenient to consider the results attributable to such an expansion before describing the impact of megalithic ideas on South France.

Chassey and Fort Harrouard

The famous but badly excavated station of the Camp de Chassey (Saône-et-Loire)[1] certainly ought to mark a stage in the assumed expansion of Western neolithic culture. It is a fortified hilltop, and from it have been gathered many objects distinctive of the West Swiss Lower Neolithic Cortaillod culture – plain leathery pots, tapering antler sleeves for axes, segmented tine pendants. But collections from the site include also types that are not older than Middle or even Upper Neolithic on Lake Neuchâtel, such as sleeves like Fig. 139, B, perforated stone axes, and tanged arrow-heads. If these denote a second phase of occupation, there are no stratigraphical observations to decide to which the decorated pottery, often called simply Chassey ware,[2] belongs. This ware bears hatched rectilinear patterns scratched on the surface after firing or on the hard-dried clay just before (Fig. 142, 2).[3] The 'vase-support' is a distinctive shape.[4] Such decoration is missing from Cortaillod sites in Switzerland, but finds analogies in Schussenried pottery farther east (p. 345). In Liguria, scratched decoration was Middle Neolithic.

After crossing the Massif Central the neolithic colonists would reach the downlands of Northern France, an area rich in flint[5] and already inhabited by mesolithic hunter-fishers, probably of

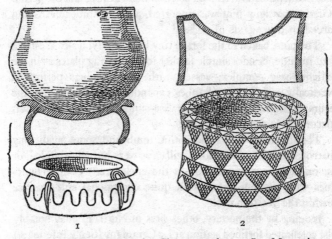

Fig. 142. Vase-supports in Chassey style: 1, Le Moustoir, Carnac; 2, Motte de la Garde, Charente.

the Forest culture. In the oldest recognizable neolithic settlements the farmers appear to have adopted much of the food-gatherers' equipment – core and flake axes, transverse arrowheads, and other items – giving the local cultures a hybrid, 'secondary neolithic' aspect. Their neolithic elements might have been contributed by Rössen farmers, spreading through the Belfort Gap as far as Yonne[6] or Danubians advancing from the Meuse to the Somme and the Marne as well as by Westerners. The best picture available of the ambiguous result is provided by Fort Harrouard[7] (Eure-et-Loire), a promontory camp about 17 acres (7 hr.) in extent, where Father Philippe could distinguish two neolithic strata.

The villagers lived by cultivating indeterminate grains and breeding mainly horned cattle; they kept also some pigs and goats and a very few sheep too, but relied very little on hunting or fishing.[8] They lived in irregular oval huts partly excavated in the ground[9] and dressed in woven fabrics, using whorls for spinning and clay loom-weights in weaving. The carpenter used polished axes of imported stone occasionally, but relied mainly on the 'mesolithic' flint tranchets and 'picks', together with rare antler axes.[10] Besides transverse arrow-heads the bowman sometimes used triangular ones. Before the end of the period Grand Pressigny flint was imported, as were amber beads and arc-shaped pendants of schist.[11]

The pots, baked in the fort in tiny kilns, are typically Western, but include, besides simple leather forms, baking plates as in the Michelsberg complex, vessels with pan-pipe lugs perforated vertically and horizontal tubes expanding at the ends like the trumpet lugs of Troy I, and vase-supports and other vessels decorated in the Chassey style.

Though there are a megalithic tomb and some small long barrows in sight of the camp, villagers were buried extended, or in one case contracted, within the enclosure.[12] Female figurines were modelled in clay, a quite exceptional cult practice within the Western cycle.

Judging by the pottery, other sites in North France, notably the celebrated fortified station at Le Campigny (Seine Inférieure) (once made the patent station for a mesolithic culture) and the Camp de Catenoy (Oise)[13] were occupied at the same time as Fort Harrouard I. At that station the second neolithic stratum illustrates a development of the older culture. While cattle-breeding predominates, a large breed of *Bos brachyceros* now coexisted with the small cattle of the older herds. Goats had died out, but game bones now amount to as much as 8 per cent of the total. And oysters and other shell-fish were imported from the coast. Finished implements, such as daggers and lance-heads of Grand Pressigny flint, were also obtained by barter. But the old types of tools, including the 'mesolithic' core and flake-axes, were still retained. The pottery shows a development of the Chassey style with much coarser incisions combined with rusticated wares.

Since the late Chassey style inspires the decoration of 'Incense Cups' at the beginning of the Middle Bronze Age in Southern England, it must follow that Fort Harrouard II falls at least into the 'Beaker' period of the West; it may indeed outlast it, since, as on the Swiss lakes, the record of settlement is continued only by the Late Bronze Age occupation of Fort Harrouard III.[14] For all we can tell, the pastoral communities of Northern France preserved their neolithic economy unaffected by the cultural impulses that crossed South-Western France.

So even Fort Harrouard I may begin relatively late; Grand Pressigny flint in Switzerland is Middle Neolithic, so are arc-pendants in both the Swiss and the Ligurian sequences. In other words, Fort Harrouard I is not demonstrably pre-megalithic or anterior to the earlier SOM tombs. Even the ceramic evidence for a pre-megalithic Western colonization is no more explicit at Fort Harrouard than at Michelsberg. An acculturation of Forest hunters by Danubians in North France, parallel to that suggested as a possible explanation of Michelsberg, cannot be ruled out. Indeed, if Michelsberg represent a south-western extension of First Northern, Fort Harrouard I could be claimed as an outpost still farther west (p. 342 ff.). Still, in 1956 the best authorities consider the neolithic elements of North French culture Western.

Brittany, too, may have been reached in pre-megalithic times by Western neolithic herdsmen-cultivators who would have joined forces with survivors of the Teviec strand-loopers. The stone-walled 'camps' of Croh Collé and Lizo have indeed yielded pottery of the channelled and later Chassey styles common in the peninsula's megalithic tombs. But leathery vases, generally plain, rarely decorated with scratched patterns and sometimes provided with trumpet lugs, found in small cist graves,[15] conform to the standard Western neolithic types. The cists recall the mesolithic sepulchres of Teviec, but contain cremated human bones. Some groups of cists, e.g. at Manio, were covered by elongated mounds of earth and stones which in plan offer the closest West European analogy to the British long barrow.[16]

If the megalithic religion were implanted round the Gulf of Lions by colonists from the East Mediterranean, a cemetery of monumental collective tombs on an island in the Rhône delta near Arles might well belong to a bridgehead station comparable to Los Millares. The tombs, cut in the rock but roofed with lintels and covered by round barrows, are in plan long galleries[17] and might have provided the models for the built gallery graves which constitute the majority of the megalithic tombs in South-West France and, south of the Pyrenees in Catalonia and the Basque Provinces.[18] Segmented cists occur in Catalonia (Puig Rodo), in the Basque Provinces and at La Halliade[19] near Tarbes; that at La Halliade was 14·2 m long, divided by septal slabs into seven compartments with a lateral compartment added at one end and covered with a cairn of stones. Others like St Eugénie near Carcassonne are subdivided by internal portals.[20]

On the other hand, passage graves in the area might be inspired from Spain. A group of corbelled passage graves in Provence[21] and Gard might be connected directly with Los Millares. A series of rectangular orthostatic chambers entered by dry-stone walled passages is strung out significantly along a line from the coast to the copper and lead deposits near Durfort,[22] Gard. Architecturally these resemble Puglisi's Tuscan 'dolmens' (p. 289), and their builders seem to have been pastoralists. Finally, many caves in the area were still used as collective ossuaries in megalithic, as in Early Neolithic, times. If burial in megalithic tombs were the prerogative of aristocratic clans, commoners may have been interred in caves.

The furniture of these various sepulchres is the principal source for any picture of the cultures of North Spain and South France during a long period, traditionally termed Chalcolithic, but certainly capable of subdivision. Two phases stand out clearly: during the first (Pericot's Bronze I) Bell-beakers were generally current; they had gone out of fashion by the second (Pericot's Bronze II and III), which might last down to the advent of Urnfield invaders with an equipment of Danubian VI types. Near Narbonne, Heléna[23] claimed to distinguish a pre-Beaker megalithic phase (Chalcolithic I), two phases with

Beakers (II and III), and two later. Other authorities,[24] however, do not accept his separation of Chalcolithic I from II. It is therefore a disputed issue whether the transformation of the neolithic cultures, described in the last chapter, into a 'Chalcolithic' one were due to the simultaneous arrival of megalith-builders and Beaker-folk or whether the latter arrived only after the former and in either alternative precisely what is to be attributed to the newcomers and what to the earlier neolithic and mesolithic groups.

In any case the subsistence economy of the Chalcolithic as thus disclosed appears more pastoral and less sedentary than the previous 'Western Neolithic'. Apart from inhabited caves, only two settlements are known – Fontbouïsse in Gard[25] – a disorderly cluster of round and rectangular huts on stone foundations – and La Couronne – a fortified site near the Rhône delta that might be comparable to Los Millares or Vila Nova de San Pedro.

But food-production was now certainly combined with some secondary industry and trade. Local ores of copper, lead, and perhaps even tin[26] were probably worked. They do not seem to have formed the basis for a metal industry capable of satisfying local demand such as arose in the Alpine valleys (pp. 348–9), and only elementary techniques of casting are illustrated by local finds. West European daggers[27] were no doubt manufactured for the Beaker-folk, and several notched daggers with a midrib on one face only (cast in an open-hearth mould) were found in a curious crematorium near Freyssinel in Lozère.[28] Otherwise metal was used mainly for ornaments. Metal daggers were replaced by bifacially flaked flint copies – some polished on one face to enhance the similarity.[29] Only in the post-Beaker phase, Heléna's Chalcolithic IV, do a few Bronze Age types appear, and these – daggers, trefoil,[30] bulb-head,[31] and racket pins[32] – are imports from Central Europe or Switzerland, not East Mediterranean (Fig. 143).

Gold was obtained in Beaker times and used to cover wrist-guards (like Fig. 113, 4), and for other purposes. Callaïs was imported at the same time, but earlier in Catalonia. Amber arrived still later, in Chalcolithic III according to Heléna, only in Bronze II on Pericot's[33] division. The sole recognizable Mediterranean import found in any context is a segmented fayence bead from the sepulchral Grotte du Ruisseau, Aude.[34] To this may be added a Middle Cycladic jug[35] (Fig. 41, 3) dredged up from Marseilles harbour and two contemporary Cypriote daggers found stray in Provence.[36] All three could, with the bead from Almeria, be accounted for by coastwise traffic with the

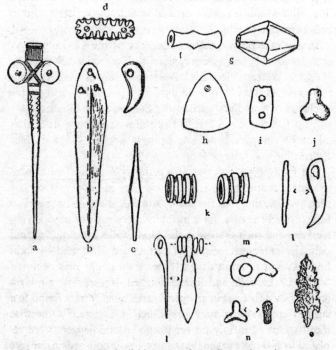

Fig. 143. Late Chalcolithic types from Cevennian cists: a–e, Liquisse; f–i, Grotte d'en Quisse, Gard; j–o, 'dolmens' of Aveyron ($\frac{2}{3}$).

West as well as by a trans-peninsular tin-trade with Cornwall. Yet in the first millennium the Greek and Sicilian manufactures that should mark archaeologically that historic route are sparse enough.[37] If the Cycladic jug be accepted as a counterpart of the Classical vases, it means that the route was open before 1600 B.C.

Most Chalcolithic pottery is based on older native traditions, but bell-beakers are of course intrusive; those of Pan-European

ornaments that were exported to or copied by other groups. For fastening their garments Beaker-folk, as elsewhere, used V-perforated buttons, but local variants[45] were devised and exported. Thus an elongated prismatic type was preferred round the Eastern Pyrenees, particularly in Bronze II, while Aude may have been the cradle of tortoise beads which were diffused thence to Sardinia and Portugal. Winged beads of East Mediterranean ancestry found a secondary centre of manufacture in South France, while some bone tubes from the cave of Treille, Aude,[46] and the dolmen of Cabut, Gironde, are vaguely like the Early Aegean type of Fig. 27, 1.

The main creative impulses of Pyrenaeic-Provençal societies were diverted to ideological ends. The overwhelming importance attached to the funerary cult is patently displayed in the innumerable megalithic tombs and cave ossuaries. But no rigid orthodoxy prevailed. Some clans adopted cremation at an uncertain date; a sort of collective cremation is reported from some caves,[47] while under a cairn near Freyssinel[48] (Lozère) fifty corpses had been burned on the spot.

South France was certainly one, and perhaps the primary, centre of the practice of ritual trepanation, though the superstition was potent also round the Tagus estuary[49] and in the SOM culture. Certainly an astonishingly large number of the skulls from the Cevennian megaliths and from the caves[50] had been trephined, some while their owners were still alive! As the cranian amulets produced by this operation were found in Cortaillod sites in Switzerland, the practice presumably goes back to premegalithic times in South France, though it persisted like so much else. In Aveyron, Gard, Hérault, and Tarn monoliths were carved with representations of a female divinity armed with an axe;[51] one such statue-menhir was used as a lintel in a corbelled megalithic tomb at Collorgues, Gard (Fig. 145a).[52] Clearly this is no 'portrait statue' but represents the same deity as the citizens of Troy I carved also on a monolithic stele. We shall meet her again in the Marne valley. Presumably these statue-menhirs mark her route northward, unless her journey should be reversed; with a change of sex the deity was carried eastward to Upper Italy (p. 299), presumably by immigrants from South France. The latter, though recognizable in pottery too, are not likely to have made contributions, such as ploughs and halberds, to the material culture of the Apennine peninsula. Sculpture and surgery in South France developed outside the frame of urban life and without relation to practical ends, as we understand them, in a society whose material culture remained fossilized for perhaps a thousand years.

Fig. 145. Statue-menhirs from Gard and sculptured tomb (b), Petit Morin (Marne).

The Seine-Oise-Marne (SOM) Culture

The adoption of the megalithic faith by a Forest population on the chalk downs of Champagne and round the Paris basin produced a remarkable culture, known almost exclusively from collective tombs and termed the Seine-Oise-Marne culture (abbreviated SOM).[53] The burial-places may be natural caves,[54] artificial caves hewn in the chalk,[55] or 'Paris cists', a specialized type of gallery grave. In the Marne[56] the rock-cut tombs form regular cemeteries; there are some fifty in the valley of Petit Morin alone. All are rectangular chambers entered by a descending ramp like the dromos of a Mycenaean tomb. A few are more carefully excavated than the rest and are provided with an antecella on the walls of which may be carved or sketched in charcoal representations of the same funerary goddess, bearing an axe,[57] as appears on the statue-menhirs of the Midi (Fig. 145). While the smaller tombs contain forty or more corpses (including some cremated bones), not more than eight bodies were deposited in the more elaborate chambers, but the funerary furniture in them is much richer. They accordingly belong to 'chiefs', while poorer common-folk were crammed into family ossuaries. The gallery graves in the valleys of the Aisne, Seine, Oise, and Eure[58] (Paris cists) are generally built of slabs erected in a long trench, a compartment at one end, divided from the rest by a porthole slab, serving as the entrance (cf. Fig. 100). The funerary goddess[59] reappears in the entrance, generally more conventionalized than on the Marne, so that only her breasts are recognizable.

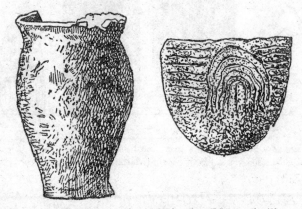

Fig. 146. Horgen pot from Paris cist (Mureaux) ($\frac{1}{6}$), and channelled vase from Conguel, Morbihan ($\frac{1}{9}$).

The grave goods disclose a warlike population living by stock-breeding and hunting, but almost certainly also tilling the soil. Its rôle in flint-mining is uncertain, but Grand Pressigny flint was obtainable, and the chieftains of the Marne secured even beads of amber, callaïs and rock-crystal and small copper trinkets. Even flanged axes of bronze have been reported from SOM gallery graves.[60] The grave gear consisted, however, of polished flint axes, normally mounted in perforated antler sleeves, antler axes with square-cut shaft-holes, very numerous transverse arrow-heads together with a very few leaf-shaped ones, daggers of Grand Pressigny flint and characteristic splay-footed vases of rather coarse ware (Fig. 146, 1).[61] The ornaments include shells, bracelets, rings, and arc-pendants (Fig. 147) of stone, a leg amulet of antler,[62] axe-amulets, and cranian amulets. Nearly a third of the population was round-headed, less than a quarter really dolichocranial. Quite a large number of individuals had undergone ritual trepanation as in South France.

The tomb plans and sculptures and the trepanned skulls suggest that the megalithic religion had reached the Seine-Marne basins from the lower Rhône. Paris cists, as slab-lined trenches, reproduce most faithfully the plan of the rock-cut tombs near Arles, and the chalk-hewn tombs of the Marne are the most Mediterranean chamber tombs north of the Pyrenees and the Alps. The missionaries who introduced the faith must have

Fig. 147. Arc-pendant of stone (⅕).

travelled fast and kept it fresh. But the SOM culture preserves so many mesolithic traits that the bulk of their converts must have been descendants of native Forest-folk. The transformation of these 'savages' into farmers may be attributed not so much to the 'missionaries' as to Danubian peasants who had established colonial outposts on the Somme, the Marne, and the Seine,[63] or to less well-documented Westerners (p. 355).

The composite warlike population thus unified by the megalithic faith soon embarked on a crusade of conquest and colonization, in the course of which some items of the faith, or at least their durable expressions, were lost or distorted. Westward the whole complex with its specialized gallery graves, porthole slabs, and splay-footed vases reached Brittany,[64] Normandy, and Jersey – but not Guernsey – while Beakers were still current there. Even the funerary goddess, albeit degraded to a mere pair of breasts, was thus carried to the Atlantic coasts. To the north-east the culture is classically represented in Belgian caves,[65] while Paris cists were built in Belgium, Westfalia, and Hesse. Finally the long cists of South Sweden (p. 245) not only reproduce the Paris plan but also contain splay-footed pots of

SOM form. To the south-east the Horgen culture (p. 346) must be attributed to a similar colonization, though relatively few tombs were built for its spiritual leaders. Even to the south the grave goods from Bougon (Deux Sèvres) unmistakably mark the site of a SOM colony, while a couple of 'porthole dolmens' in the Cevennes and the pottery already mentioned from South France and the Baleares might denote a return of the faith in a barbarized version towards its assumed starting-point.[66]

From this expansion chronological limits for the rise of the SOM culture can be more precisely deduced. Not only have Beaker sherds been found in three tombs in the Paris basin,[67] but also in those of its colonial outposts in Brittany. Thus in the French sequence the culture goes back at least to Chalcolithic II or Pericot's Bronze I. So its arrival in Switzerland initiates Middle Neolithic there. Collared flasks appropriate to Northern Neolithic II occur in the Paris cists of Westfalia and of Brittany,[68] while, judging from a couple of tiny Rössen sherds from their counterparts in Hesse (p. 243), the culture should have arrived there near the beginning of Danubian III if not in Danubian II. The SOM culture must then be among the earliest manifestations of the megalithic religion in temperate Europe. Yet it lasted a long time with no recognizable progress or change. It reached Scandinavia only in Northern Neolithic IV – i.e. Danubian IV, the Early Bronze Age. In its homeland there are no other burials save those in Paris cists and SOM caves to represent the Early and Middle Bronze Ages in the funerary record, while types of these periods are inordinately scarce. The region remained isolated from the great currents of Bronze Age trade, and its population, absorbed in cult practices, was content to subsist in a neolithic stage.

The Armorican Megalithic Culture

In megalithic times the Armorican Peninsula with its extension to the Channel Islands became a goal of pilgrimage so that a bizarre assortment of cultures was superimposed on the primary Western neolithic described on p. 357. Brittany offers the first land-fall on the northward voyage from the Iberian Peninusla to Cornish tin-lodes and Irish goldfields and sets the limit to terrestrial wanderings in search of isles of the blest beneath the setting sun. Moreover, its old rocks contain gold, perhaps also tin and callaïs.[69] The densest and most varied concentration of collective tombs in Europe is to be found round the Gulf of Morbihan,[70] but from this centre the tombs spread coastwise to the mouth of the Loire and to Jersey (still perhaps joined to the Continent in megalithic times) and Guernsey. The diverse tomb plans and the heterogeneous articles constituting the furniture of every sepulchre indicate the varied traditions that went to

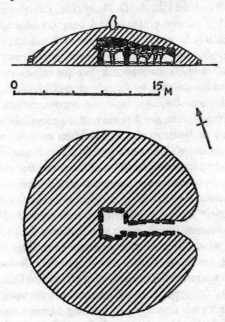

Fig. 148. Passage grave, Kercado, Morbihan.

make up the Armorican culture and the complexity of their interweaving.

Corbelled passage graves are concentrated on the coasts and Islands and are obviously inspired by Iberian, immediately by Portuguese, models. Their counterparts in the orthostatic architecture, more suited to the local rocks, are megalithic passage graves, often P-shaped in plan (Fig. 148), rarely with a lateral cell, as the standard type for Morbihan, while undifferentiated passage graves, like the South Spanish, are commoner in the Channel Islands. The gallery grave,[71] on the other hand, exhibits a more inland distribution and does not cross the sea to Guernsey. Accordingly the idea was brought by land from the Paris basin by migrant pastoralist families. Divergent variations on the exotic models were devised locally. Undifferentiated passage graves with one or two pairs of lateral chambers, arranged like transepts on either side of the principal gallery, may be derived from tholoi with lateral cells, as at Los Millares, and are common to the peninsula [72] and the Islands (La Houge Bie, Jersey,[73] and Déhus, Guernsey [74]). Passage graves with a bent corridor and gallery graves similarly 'angled' are peculiar to Armorica.

Most tombs were covered by a cairn or barrow, generally round and carefully constructed, but sometimes two or even three tombs are covered by a single mound which may then be oblong. Elaborate carvings, including representations of hafted axes and human feet, are a feature of the megaliths of Morbihan.[75] And in Brittany the tombs often contain remains of cremated skeletons. The same heretical rite is associated with other equally novel manifestations of the megalithic cult that are peculiar to the extreme west, but common to Brittany and Britain. Oval or horseshoe settings of megalithic uprights on the islet of Er Lannic,[76] now half submerged, were associated with vase supports decorated with punctured patterns in late Chassey style. But at the feet of the orthostats were little stone cists containing cremated bones almost certainly human; these must be compared to the cremations in pits within British 'henge monuments' (p. 377). So, too, alignments of huge upright stones, one of which runs across one of the long barrows described on p. 357, might be Armorican equivalents of the English cursûs which too are associated with long barrows.

Most tombs have been violated in Roman times and further disturbed in the nineteenth century, so that the grave goods do not contribute as much help as might be expected to unravelling the components of the megalithic complex and establishing the sequence of events. Tombs of most types contain Beaker ware, proving that the Paris galleries had arrived and the local variants been elaborated during the Beaker phase. But the number and variety of the beakers prove that this period was a long one. Z.

le Rouzic [77] and Jacquetta Hawkes [78] assign to a pre-Beaker phase the corbelled passage graves of Morbihan and Jersey; they certainly contain no Beaker ware. That some megaliths are really pre-Beaker is established by the succession of burials in the passage grave (one wall of which was formed of natural rock) at Conguel, [79] Quiberon. There the later interments only were accompanied by beakers, the earlier by vases bearing channelled semicircle patterns as in Portugal and South France (Fig. 146, 2). This fabric is found in other tombs too, and in the fortified settlement at Croh Collé. [80] It links the Pyrenees or Portugal with the Beacharra culture in Scotland.

Chassey pottery, chiefly in the form of vase-supports, is represented in many tombs on the Mainland and in Jersey (Fig. 142). In that island it was found below the Beaker layer in the stratified settlement at le Pinnacle. [81] It was presumably introduced by land from Central France, and the first connections with Grand Pressigny were probably established at the same time. Neither Chassey ware nor Grand Pressigny flint reach Guernsey.

The Beaker-folk seem to have come by sea, like the first megalith-builders from Portugal; they reached even Guernsey, but on land have left only one grave between the Garonne and the Loire, and that not far from the coast. [82] Besides the classic rouletted style, cord ornament is common on Breton beakers, while specifically South French variants are missing. Wrist-guards [83] are represented by a gold strip from Mané Lud, like the South French ones, and a few doubtful stone specimens which may really be whetstones. Two West European daggers have been found in Brittany [84] and one on Guernsey. [85]

From the Paris basin came the SOM gallery grave, the port-hole slab, carvings of a funerary goddess, characteristic splay-footed vases [86] and arc-pendants. [87] Finally, from the North came an amber bead and a boat axe. [88] But 'collared flasks' [89] may be local SOM pots rather than First Northern vessels.

The culture which blended all these foreign elements preserved a rigidly neolithic aspect in Morbihan. Axes with pointed butts were made of fibrolith and greenstone. Large, thin and superbly polished specimens, obviously ceremonial and perhaps late, [90] are surprisingly common and were exported to Portugal and England. Celts with a knob at the butt end found stray in Morbihan seem to copy Egyptian adzes,[91] while double-axes of stone [92] imitated the Minoan metal form or the 'ingot axes' from Vögtland.[93] For arrows, transverse and tanged-and-barbed heads were preferred; leaf-shaped forms are exceptional.[94] In addition to the foreign pottery absorbed, carinated bowls adorned with pairs of vertical ribs are a distinctively Breton variant on the West European tradition, replaced in Jersey by similar shapes decorated with horizontal lines and punctuations.

As charms were worn rather simple beads of talc, callaïs, rock-crystal, or gold, axe-amulets and bracelets of hammered gold. The callaïs and gold may have been obtained locally, but Grand Pressigny flint was certainly imported. Unless the Portuguese and South French callaïs be of Armorican origin, the peninsula's exports must have been immaterial goods. Whatever they were, they were employed to obtain magical rather than practical materials. The whole society was so obsessed with funerary cult that material advancement was neglected.

The chronological criteria applicable to more materialistic societies cannot then be used for dating the megalithic culture in Brittany. Despite its neolithic exterior it may have lasted well into the Bronze Age elsewhere. In fact, in Guernsey some megalithic tombs do contain 'incense cups' and cinerary urns of types appropriate to the mature Bronze Age of England. In Morbihan closed megalithic chambers under gigantic barrows at Tumiac, Mont St Michel and Mané er Hroek are assigned to the Bronze Age by le Rouzic on typological grounds.[95] But they contained ceremonial axes of greenstone, greenstone bracelets and beads of callaïs and rock-crystal that can be matched in more normal megalithic tombs.

The Armorican Bronze Age

Throughout the Atlantic megalithic province, desire for a good burial stimulated production of surplus wealth; the erection of gigantic tombs and the importation of magic substances kept accumulated wealth in circulation. But it was not used to support professional smiths nor to purchase ores. In France, graves furnished with bronze tools and weapons and hoards of bronzes begin in general only during the Middle Bronze Age when Tumulus-builders from Central Europe spread along the Massif Central. Only in Armorica is there a group of graves[96] richly furnished with weapons of Early Bronze Age type.

The tombs in question are closed chambers of dry masonry, sometimes roofed by corbelling and always surmounted by a cairn. The dead were buried in them, generally but not always after cremation, on wooden planks (remains of coffins?), with arms and ornaments. The armament consisted typically of one or two flat or hammer-flanged axes, several daggers and superb arrow-heads with squared barbs and tangs. The daggers are either round-heeled and strengthened with a midrib or triangular with grooves parallel to the edge and sometimes a rudimentary tang. In eight cases the wooden hilts (or scabbards) had been adorned with tiny gold nails forming a pointillé pattern. Ornaments include a ring-head pin[97] and some spiral rings of silver, beads of amber, and one segmented fayence bead.[98] Pottery is represented by biconical urns with two to four handles joining rim and shoulder (Fig. 149).

Fig. 149. Breton Bronze Age vase.

Evidently these graves belong to rich and warlike chiefs. They are concentrated[99] in the north and interior of the peninsula and in general avoid the principal megalithic centres, where the old family vaults were presumably still in use. The Bronze Age warlords can therefore hardly be descendants of the old megalithic chiefs or Beaker-folk, and owe nothing of their equipment to these. Their silver probably came from Almeria or Sardinia. The ring-head pin is a Central European type. The grooved daggers seem related most closely to those of the Saale-Warta culture (p. 248). But the chief source of metal and the dominant inspiration in metal-work must have been in the British Isles, where for instance gold-studded dagger hilts also occur. Relations with Britain were indeed so close that for a while Armorica and Wessex became a continuous cultural province.

Piggott[100] explained this continuity by an invasion of Southern England from Brittany. Cagné and Giot[101] would reverse the process or postulate parallel occupations of both regions by seafarers, coming like the Vikings from farther North. Actually the last-named view is the most likely and the Saale-Warta area the ultimate starting-point. To link the Armorican with the West German Tumulus culture, Hawkes[102] can cite only two isolated 'Bronze Age' barrows between the Rhine and the Atlantic.[103] Relations with the Saale-Warta culture, on the contrary, are clear but direct. While these give a limiting date for the rise of the Armorican Bronze Culture, its strict parallelism with the Wessex culture equates it with Early Bronze Age 2 – Danubian IVb – which, judging by the fayence beads, should last down to 1400 B.C. The conquering aristocrats may have freed the local population from excessive devotion to megalithic rites, but the metal industry that flourished under their patronage failed to develop. The leaders sailed away or were absorbed. No graves in Brittany are furnished with types of my period V, and it is not till the Late Bronze Age – or perhaps even Iron Age I – that large hoards reveal the inclusion of Brittany in a commercial system guaranteeing regular supplies of metal gear.

18   The British Isles

All routes from the South hitherto considered converge on
Britain. It is the northern terminus of the 'megalithic' seaway
along the Atlantic coasts from Portugal; the land route across
France is continued beyond the Channel by the South Downs;
the Danube thoroughfare and the wide corridor formed by the
North European plain converge on the North Sea coasts to be
continued in Kent and East Anglia. And the British Isles offers
to voyagers, migrants, and prospectors inducements to settlement – downs and moors swept bare of trees, excellent flint, copper and gold, and above all tin. But islands they were already in
neolithic times. Would-be colonists embarking in frail craft must
discard unessential equipment and relax the rigid bonds of
tribal custom. Any culture brought to Britain must be insularized
by the very conditions of transportation. Many streams contributed to the formation of British culture, but the blending of
components already insularized inevitably yielded a highly in-
dividualized resultant.

Nor is Britain a unity. The Highland Zone of mountains and
ancient rocks to the West and North is contrasted with a 'Lowland Zone' of more recent formation in the South-East.[1] And
beyond the Highland Zone lies Ireland. It is the Highland Zone
with Ireland that yields tin, copper, and gold. But the megalithic
route alone leads thither directly. Cultures and peoples, desiring
'short sea crossings', must land in the Lowlands and reach the
Highland Zone only after crossing them and absorbing their
already insular cultures.

Cultures arriving from the Continent often preserve their
ancestors' lineaments recognizably in the Lowland Zone; in the
Highlands they assume a mask of stubborn insularity.

Great Britain and Ireland were relatively well populated with mesolithic hunters and fishers. But a neolithic culture[2] of distinctive Western type was first introduced by peasants who crossed to Southern England from North France or Belgium and did not mingle with the pre-existing food-gatherers. In Sussex the latter occupied the greensands, the neolithic peasants colonized the chalk.[3] The neolithic farmers owed hardly an item in their equipment to their mesolithic forerunners and competitors.

Windmill Hill Culture

The oldest neolithic culture is best known from a series of hill-top encampments strung out all along the downs and uplands of Southern England from Eastern Sussex at least to Devon and probably to Cornwall. The classic site where this culture was first really defined – as recently as 1925! – Windmill Hill, near Avebury, Wilts, must serve hereafter as the patent station. The hilltops are girt with a system of three or four flat-bottomed ditches, interrupted at frequent intervals by causeways, as in Michelsberg camps, and supplemented by palisades. The areas thus enclosed are often small: the diameters of the inner ring lie between 250 ft at Windmill Hill and 400 ft at the Trundle, though there is room for settlement beyond it, and Maiden Castle covered 12 acres. It is not yet clear how far the 'camps' should be regarded as permanent villages. Piggott regards them rather as enclosures where cattle were rounded up in the autumn. No houses have been identified inside them, but in Devon, Wales, and Ireland a few isolated neolithic houses are known – most rectangular in plan.[4]

The camps' occupants lived principally by breeding cattle – of a robust breed, perhaps a cross between imported short-horns and native oxen of *Bos primigenius* stock. But they kept a few sheep, goats, and pigs, and cultivated crops – principally wheat (emmer with a small proportion of one-corn), but also a little barley.[5] And naturally they hunted deer and collected nuts and shell-fish. The huntsman used leaf-shaped arrow-heads, Fig. 150, 3. Axes were made of flint where this material is abundant and they include archaic 'picks' as well as polished implements. Elsewhere, in Devon for instance, polished celts of fine-grained stone competed with flint axes. In Southern England and Nor-folk flint was systematically mined by specialized groups of highly skilled miners, who must have lived largely by exporting the products of their industry. But while flint-mining began early in Neolithic times, it flourished more in the subsequent Beaker period. And in Norfolk and even Wiltshire 'Peterborough folk' (p. 383, below) were associated with its exploitation. A textile industry is not clearly attested but flint scrapers and bunched combs of antler emphasize the importance of leather-dressing.

Fig. 150. 1, lop-sided, 2, tanged-and-barbed, 3, leaf-shaped, arrow-heads from Britain ($\frac{1}{2}$).

The earliest Windmill Hill vases (Fig. 151) are leathery round-bottomed pots with simple rims and sometimes vertically pierced lugs. Thickening of the rims by pressing down or rolling over the wet clay is thought by Piggot to mark a later phase in Southern England and is more prominent in the Highland Zone. To an equally late phase should belong incised and channelled decoration and shallow flutings produced by drawing the finger-tips over the moist clay. Trumpet lugs, confined to Dorset and Devon, denote specially close relations with Brittany (p. 357).

A few figurines and phalli, carved in chalk so rudely as to be almost dubious, are all that survives of ritual paraphernalia. Windmill Hill ideology found more durable expression in fun-erary monuments. Most authorities believe that Windmill Hill farmers or their 'chiefs' were buried under 'unchambered long barrows'. These are pear-shaped mounds reaching the extrava-gant length of 300 feet though the interments occupy only a small space near the wide end. The corpses, from one to twenty-five in number, had been interred disarticulated or cremated on chalk platforms or in crematorium-trenches. In two cases a timber revetment at the wide end looks like an attempt to reproduce the forecourt of the chambered long barrows of Highland Britain (p. 378). So it has been suggested that unchambered long barrows are just substitutes for the megalithic tombs of the Atlantic coasts in stoneless regions. However, the extravagantly

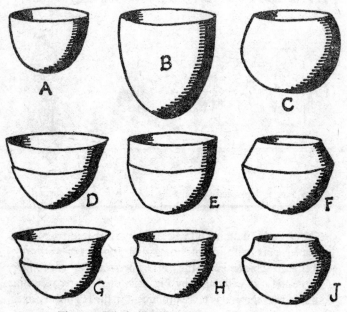

Fig. 151. Windmill Hill pot-forms. After Piggott.

long mounds seem alien to the general megalithic tradition while the plans and the arrangement of the interments within them find surprisingly close parallels in the long dolmens and Kuyavish graves of the German and West Polish tracts of the North European plain of which Lowland England is just the westernmost section.

If such monumental sepulchres were reserved to families of special rank or sanctity, commoners perhaps were buried, after cremation, in pits, arranged in a ring in a cemetery surrounded by a penannular bank and internal ditch. For a few of these so-called 'class I henges' have yielded pure Windmill Hill relics though most contain also 'Secondary Neolithic' types.[6] But even these henges may not have been primarily constructed as cemeteries and to the same periods belong certain non-funerary but ceremonial monuments, traditionally known as 'cursûs',[7] enclosures varying from one to six miles in length and defined by banks and ditches. Association with long barrows justifies their attribution to the Windmill Hill culture.

No causewayed camps have been identified north of the Thames. But judging from pottery finds and long barrows, Windmill Hill farmers colonized East Anglia and the Yorkshire Wolds and spread over Northern England and Eastern Scotland as far as the Moray Firth. In the Highland Zone their culture is known only from megalithic tombs.

Megalithic Tombs in Britain

Apostles of the megalithic faith presumably arrived by the Atlantic seaway; for the tombs they should have introduced fan out from landfalls on the west coasts and round the Irish Sea. More or less close parallels can be found in Western Europe to the plans of these tombs, but their furniture and the long cairns that cover them seem distinctively British. So in Britain the megalith-builders do not appear so much as fresh contingents of neolithic farmers as a spiritual aristocracy who may have led Windmill Hill farmers to the colonization of the rugged coasts of Scotland and Ulster and the adjacent islands. Peculiarities of sepulchral architecture allow of the recognition of at least three groups of missionaries in Great Britain.

The Bristol Channel would have been the entry for the designers of the Cotswold-Severn tombs. All are covered by long cairns with a cuspidal, rather than semicircular, forecourt. Typologically the oldest chambers are long galleries with one or more pairs of transepts or lateral cells opening off them and roofed by corbelling. Cairns, terminating in a dummy portal in the wide end but with small chambers opening on to their sides, twice through porthole slabs, should be later degenerations. Tombs of this family occur on both sides of the Bristol Channel and spread across the Cotswolds to the chalk downs of North Wiltshire and Berkshire. The finest of them all was built under a typically English long barrow at West Kennet near Avebury and Windmill Hill, and the first interments were accompanied by Windmill Hill vases though the tomb remained open till Beaker and Peterborough wares had come into fashion.

Segmented cists characterize the Clyde-Carlingford group of tombs that spread inland from these sea-inlets in South-West Scotland and Northern Ireland but occur also in Man, in Wales, and on the limestone plateau of Derbyshire. Two tombs of this group – in Man and Staffordshire – were entered through port-hole slabs. The tombs contain up to sixteen corpses, normally inhumed but occasionally cremated. In addition to classical Windmill Hill pottery and arrow-heads, the grave goods comprise vases of Beacharra ware, decorated with semicircles arranged in panels and executed by channelling or cord-impression as at Conguel in Brittany (Fig. 146, 2), but also types to be classed as 'Secondary Neolithic'; Beakers accompanied the latest interments in three cases. The sepulchral architecture of the tombs and the semicircular forecourts on to which they open (Fig. 110), but not the long cairns that cover them, seem to be inspired by Pyrenaeic or even Sardinian traditions. Beacharra ware too might have been introduced from the same quarter, but since its decorative technique was used also in the non-megalithic province of Southern England, only the magic semi-circle motive need be regarded as a fresh contribution from the south-west.

Tombs of the Pentland group on the treeless moors and sandy coasts of North Scotland and the adjacent archipelagoes are formally passage graves. But some are covered by extravagantly long cairns with 'horns' framing semicircular forecourts at both ends and the corbelled chambers are normally subdivided into at least three segments by paired jambs projecting from the side walls (Fig. 152). In the stalled cairns of Orkney a multiplication of the same device divided a long corbelled gallery into six to twelve benched stalls (Fig. 153). Round or oval cairns in Orkney, too, cover elongated corbelled chambers with three or more small cells opening off them. In Pentland tombs, too, Beakers accompany only the last interments. The older grave goods include leaf-shaped arrow-heads, developed Windmill Hill ware, a single vase decorated in Beacharra style, and others ornamented with stab-and-drag patterns best represented at Unstan, Orkney, but also Secondary Neolithic types. Here, too,

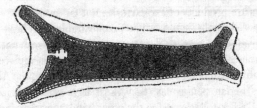

Fig. 152. Passage grave in horned cairn, 240 ft long, Yarrows, Caithness.

cases of cremation have been reported, but inhumation was the normal practice.

Judging from the dispersal of the tombs, each, if it were a communal ossuary, might correspond to a single homestead. But such a unit and the number of burials would be too small to provide the manpower for the erection of such monuments. They

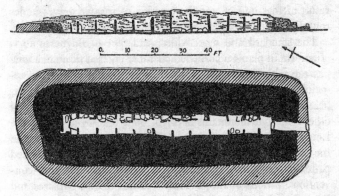

Fig. 153. Long stalled cairn, Midhowe, Rousay.

should rather be, like unchambered long barrows, the family vaults of the leaders of small local groups. These remained simple farmers. The multitude of bones of calves, sheep, and game animals – including horses even in the Cotswolds [8] – imply an

379

economy based primarily on stock-breeding and hunting. But barley (not, however, wheat) was demonstrably cultivated in Orkney and one-corn wheat in Ulster.[9] Metal is totally absent from the grave goods. A few beads of soft stone can be paralleled in the causewayed camps of Southern England. The only imports are products of axe-factories not far away. Chronologically these megalithic tombs had demonstrably been built before the arrival in the province of Beaker-folk and no fresh ones were built thereafter. These round-headed invaders replaced the megalithic aristocracy. If, then, the latter came from the Armorican or Iberian peninsulas, they must have set out before the rise of Beaker-folk there. On the other hand, the secondary neolithic types, so prominent in the Clyde-Carlingford and Pentland tombs, may be little, if at all, older than the Beaker invasion of Southern England; some indeed occur in graves of Early Bronze Age II.

On Ireland a direct impact of megalithic culture from the south-west can be detected only after the island had been colonized from Britain by neolithic farmers of the Clyde-Carlingford and other groups, and hardly before bands of Beaker-folk had established themselves in Limerick and Sligo. The recognizable result of that impact was the erection of passage graves under round cairns that constitute the sole monuments of *Boyne culture*.

The standard and most widespread type of Boyne tomb is cruciform in plan – a corbelled chamber entered through a long passage with three cells grouped symmetrically round the remaining sides. Such tombs, generally located on conspicuous heights, form scattered cemeteries, notably on Carrowkeel and other limestone mountains in Sligo, along the Boyne, and on the Lough Crew hills. The stones walling the tomb and supporting the cairn are often adorned with elaborate incised or pecked patterns, including stylized boats, spirals, and distorted conventionalizations of the funerary goddess of Los Millares and Palmella. Most tombs had been plundered. In the finest, large stone basins alone survive of the original furniture. At Carrowkeel, cremated bones, resting on stone slabs but originally enclosed in hide bags fastened with skewer pins of bone or antler, should represent primary interments while cremations in food-vessels may be intrusive. Of the furniture survive stone balls,

V-perforated buttons and beads, including hammer beads, of hard stone, small scraps of ill-fired pottery, but not a scrap of metal.

It is assumed that these magnificent sepulchres were built for aristocratic lineages. A few decorated tombs in Anglesey and Antrim indicate an extension of their sway to the coasts of Wales and the shores of the North Channel. A spread thence may be denoted by some simpler tombs in Galloway and round the Moray Firth. Most authorities agree that the founders of the Boyne culture came by sea from Portugal and – with less unanimity – that they started after, rather than before, the Beaker phase there.[10] In their wake should have come prospectors and metallurgists who initiated the exploitation of Irish copper and gold and introduced Hispanic types and techniques. In Britain their products – decorated axes and basket-shaped gold earrings – were purchased first by Beaker-folk, while the most significant British parallels to the furniture of the Boyne tombs are hammer-beads from Wessex graves of the succeeding period, but British B Beaker sherds were found in an atypical Boyne tomb at Moytirra, Sligo. Such are the rather slender grounds for believing that the Boyne culture began as early as the Beaker period of England. Raftery has found evidence that at least one decorated tomb at Lough Crew was built as late as Iron Age II!

The Earliest Bronze Age and Secondary Neolithic Phase

The Bronze Age of the British Isles is traditionally considered to begin with the arrival in England and Eastern Scotland of bands of round-headed invaders who buried their dead individually in single graves, generally under round barrows and accompanied by some kind of Beaker. Variations of the latter and of the associated grave goods allow us to distinguish three or even five main groups of invaders. The earliest arrivals used B1 Beakers, decorated with simple zones of rouletted patterns and preserving the profile of Pan-European beakers. They used West European daggers, tanged-and-barbed arrow-heads and stone wrist-guards, as on the Continent, and wore as ornaments basket-shaped earrings (Fig. 154) and sun discs bearing a cruciform pattern of gold.[11] B3 Beakers, of the same shape but decorated with a spiral cord impression, have close analogies in Western Europe (p. 272) and the Rhineland, and may denote a distinct invasion from the latter quarter unless they spread from Britain.[12] A second major group of invaders, coming this time from Holland and landing on the coasts of Northern England and Scotland, introduced the same arrow-heads and wrist-guards, but coarser and more angular Beakers, labelled C. But perhaps the most prominent group of Beaker-folk are characterized by A

Fig. 154. Gold ear-ring ($\frac{2}{3}$).

Beakers, generally decorated with metopic patterns and in profile more like corded than bell-beakers. These vases have no Continental counterparts and are associated with stone battle-axes and flint, or rarely round-heeled bronze daggers. So the A-Beaker culture is believed to be due to a local fusion of intrusive Northern European Battle-axe with established C – and perhaps also B – Beaker traditions.

From their landing-places on the south and east coasts Beaker-folk must have spread rapidly across Britain and even sent out contingents to Ireland.[13] The latter are just as likely as the Boyne megalith-builders to have organized the exploitation and export of Irish copper and gold, but must have been quickly absorbed in the native populations; for they are scarcely represented in the funerary record in which in Britain the Beaker-folk figure so conspicuously. But even in Britain Beaker-folk must have formed a small ruling class, or a succession of ruling classes, among the already heterogeneous Neolithic population, replacing the 'Megalithic aristocracy'. Their advent accelerated a general trend towards pastoralism and promoted the cultivation of barley in preference to wheat.[14] But no pure Beaker settlements are known; Beaker pottery is always mixed with Late Neolithic pottery and flints whether in secondary occupation levels of South English causewayed camps, in coastal encampments in the Highland zone, or in hut-villages in Western Ireland.[15]

The surplus they appropriated enabled them to become the first purchasers of metal gear in Britain. But metal is found in only 5 per cent of the known Beaker graves, and their bronze axes came from Ireland while the round-heeled daggers should be of Central European manufacture. In addition to the metal trade, Beaker-folk may have organized the distribution of axes from flint-mines and from factories at Langdale in the Lake District, Penmaenmawr in North-West Wales, and Tievebulliagh in Antrim,[16] and elsewhere; these factory products were distributed all over England and Scotland, but always turn up in a Secondary Neolithic context.

By displacing the spiritual aristocracy, the invaders liberated farmers and herdsmen in Britain – but not in Ireland – from the Megalithic superstition, but they patronized native cults or gave them a new celestial, rather than chthonic, orientation. Circles of great stones were set up, sometimes in old class I henges or in those of the new class II, with two entrances,[17] that the Beaker-folk had begun to construct. From the Presely Mountains in South-West Wales huge blocks of spotted dolerite (Bluestone) were transported to Salisbury Plain for erection in a Secondary Neolithic class I henge to become Stonehenge II.[18] This fantastic feat, like the construction of the huge class II henge (diameter 1,400 feet!) at Avebury (North Wilts[19]), must illustrate a degree of political unification or a sacred peace guaranteed by the Beaker aristocracy or by the spiritual leaders of the Cotswold-Severn culture before them, and reflects the resources at their disposal but produced by the neolithic farmers of the Wiltshire Downs.

The round-headed invaders did not exterminate the native neolithic population or replace their culture by a new one, brought ready made from the Continent. Yet, while they were establishing themselves as a ruling class, the old Windmill Hill culture changed into, or was replaced by, what Piggott terms 'Secondary Neolithic' cultures. In all these, animal husbandry plays a more prominent part in the subsistence economy than even in the older 'Western' Neolithic, and in sympathy therewith ceramic technique declines. Types of mesolithic ancestry, such as lopsided arrow-heads (Fig. 150, 1), derivatives of the *petit tranchet* (cf. Fig. 3, 6–7), reappear as if the traditions of autochthonous hunter-fishers were being incorporated in those of neolithic societies. Novel types – narrow flint knives with polished edges, antler mace-heads and cushion or pestle-shaped mace-heads of stone, bone pins, some with a lateral loop or bulb, boars'-tusk pendants – came into use. These, though missing from primary Windmill Hill sites in Southern England, are found in long barrows in Northern England, in Clyde-Carlingford and Pentland tombs, and in class I henges, but also alone in single graves under round barrows or at the centre of a ring ditch. Yet none are regular components of the Beaker culture nor of any other assemblage outside Britain. So all may be accepted as insular products of native genius.[20]

Even the new pottery styles were not introduced ready made from the Continent. With Peterborough ware[21] no assemblage of distinctive types is exclusively associated. Three consecutive styles can now be recognized under this head. In the earliest, Ebbsfleet, style the rather ovoid pots have distinct necks but simple rims; they are decorated with a row of pits below the rim supplemented at times with an incised lattice band above the pits or vertical cord impressions. In the derivative Mortlake style the rims are thickened and the pits are supplemented by a lavish decoration of 'maggot' imprints or the impressions of a 'comb' or a bird's leg bone that covers the whole vase surface (Fig. 155). Vases of the still later Fengate style are the immediate forerunners of the Overhanging Rim Urns of the 'Middle Bronze Age'. Ebbsfleet pottery is found, alone or associated with normal Windmill Hill ware, in two causewayed camps in Sussex, in one Cotswold-Severn tomb, and with normal Windmill Hill pottery and arrow-heads in a barrow on the Chilterns.[22] Mortlake pottery recurs repeatedly together with Windmill Hill, and usually also Beaker, wares in causewayed camps, megalithic tombs and around long barrows, but always in strata later than the primary occupational or burial deposits. Hence, despite the really surprising similarity of Peterborough pottery to that of the Swedish 'dwelling-places' and to pit-comb ware beyond the Baltic, no invasion from the Baltic need be postulated to explain it. It may more economically be regarded as the product of the established Windmill Hill farmers, now mixed with descendants of mesolithic stocks and, in the Mortlake stage, subject to the Beaker aristocracy.

Rinyo-Clacton pottery, found in East Anglia in pits submerged by the subsequent 'Lyonesse transgression' and in henge monuments in Wiltshire – sometimes with, never demonstrably before, Beaker ware – does characterize conveniently a distinctive culture,[23] best known from the Orkney Islands,[24] created by a tribe of sheep- and cattle-breeders who had reached

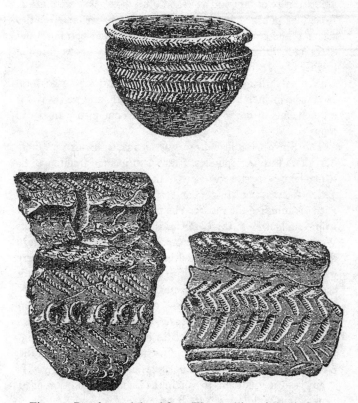

Fig. 155. Peterborough bowl from Thames (⅓), and sherds from West Kennet Long Barrow. By permission of Trustees of British Museum.

Orkney before the first Beaker-folk arrived there. On those wind-swept islands they found ideal pasture for their flocks and herds, but were forced to translate into stone, dwellings and furniture elsewhere made of wood. Their huts, grouped in hamlets of seven or eight, and several times rebuilt on the old site, were some 15 ft square. On either side of the central hearth were

385

fixed beds framed with stone slabs on the edge and covered with canopies of hide. A dresser stood against the back wall, there were cupboards above the beds and tanks let into the floor. As clothing, skins were worn, for the dressing of which innumerable scrapers of flint and awls and other bone tools were made. Adzes, of polished stone, were mounted in perforated antler sleeves. The pots, though badly fired, were flat-bottomed and decorated with grooved or applied ribs and knobs forming lozenges, wavy lines, and even spirals.

Personal ornaments, ingeniously made entirely from local materials, include beads of bone, cows' teeth, and walrus ivory, arc-pendants of boars' tusk laminae and bone pins with lateral loops.

The Rinyo-Clacton culture was an insular British creation, but doubtless incorporates fresh Continental traditions. So Rinyo houses are stone versions of the Horgen huts (p. 347), and antler sleeves and arc-pendants again point to Horgen. The patterns adorning the vases can be paralleled in late Cave pottery from Catalonia,[25] in the Late Chassey ware of Brittany, and its Wessex derivatives and in the carvings on Boyne tombs. But in the earliest habitation level at Rinyo 'Western' Unstan pottery was still current side by side with the local ware as if the latter had grown up out of the former. Though in Essex Rinyo-Clacton ware is older than the Lyonesse transgression and in Orkney than the oldest local Beaker, the similarity of its decoration to that of Wessex incense cups has convinced Scott[26] and others that the Rinyo-Clacton culture need be no older than the Wessex culture in Southern England, i.e. Early Bronze Age II. In any case, its traditions live on in the Encrusted and Cordoned Urns of our Middle and Late Bronze Ages.

The Wessex Culture and International Trade

If the Beaker culture represent the first phase of our Early Bronze Age (E.B.A.I.), that phase ended with the emergence of a new warrior aristocracy in Wessex and Cornwall and of more isolated warrior chieftains in East Anglia, Yorkshire, and Scotland, known exclusively from burials under elaborate barrows. The Wessex chieftains[27] dominated the chalk downs from Sussex to Dorset, but established outposts on both sides of the Bristol Channel. Their bones or ashes were buried, sometimes in coffins hollowed out of a tree-trunk,[28] with extravagantly rich furniture – handled cups of gold, amber or shale, grooved triangular or, later,[29] ogival daggers (some with gold-studded hilts or amber pommels), tanged spear-heads (Fig. 156, 2), flat or low-flanged

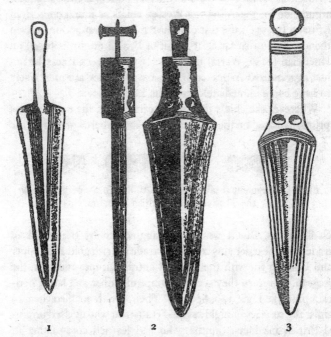

1   2   3

Fig. 156. Evolution of a socketed spear-head in Britain after Greenwell: 1, Hintelsham, Suffolk; 2, Snowshill, Glos.; 3, Arreton Down, I. o. W. (¼).

axes, but also superb flint arrow-heads tanged and barbed in the Breton manner, arrow-shaft straighteners, and stone battle-axes (derivable from the A Beaker type, but absurdly like the Northern Middle Neolithic type of Fig. 95, 4). Their ladies wore gold-bound discs and crescentic necklaces with pattern-bored spacers of amber, halberd pendants of amber, gold, and bronze, double-axe, hammer and other beads of jet and amber and of fayence imported from the Mediterranean.

The vases distinctive of the Wessex graves (domestic pottery is unknown) are 'incense cups' decorated with punctured ribbons or knobs admittedly inspired by the Late Chassey tradition of Brittany, but contemporary Cinerary Urns reflect the Secondary Neolithic traditions of the subject population. Though they are not found in the aristocratic Bronze Age barrows there, the Armorican parallels to Wessex funerary pottery are the strongest arguments for regarding the Wessex chiefs as immigrants from Brittany (p. 371); the rest of their equipment cannot be derived thence, but, in so far as it is not of British origin, is based on Unětician (Saale-Warta) models.[30] If the Wessex rulers be not just aggrandized A-Beaker–Battle-axe folk, they are most likely to have come immediately from the Saale valley.

Wherever the chiefs themselves came from, their wealth was primarily based on the produce of flocks and herds grazed on the

Fig. 157. Segmented fayence beads, Wilts ($\frac{1}{1}$). By permission of the Trustees of the British Museum.

chalk downs. But it was greatly augmented by the profits of trade. For the chieftains controlled trade in Irish gold and copper and Cornish tin with the Baltic, Central Europe, and even the Aegean. In return they secured lumps of amber and late Unětician pins like Fig. 71, 6, 8, and 9. Their wealth enabled them to enlist the services of highly skilled craftsmen who devised original British products. Smiths, who had learned core-casting in Bohemia, developed for instance a distinctively British type of socketed spear-heads (Fig. 156). Jewellers translated Highland crescentic necklaces into amber and bound with Irish gold amber discs. Such products found a market even in the civilized Aegean; the amber disc from Knossos (p. 70) and the necklaces from Mycenae and Kakovatos (pp. 119–20) must rank as 'made in England'. In return, the Wessex chieftains were of course given segmented fayence beads (Fig. 157), trinkets suitable for barbarians. But surely they acquired more enticing rewards. A dagger, carved on a trilithon in Stonehenge III, may represent an imported Mycenaean dirk. The hilt of an actual imported

Mycenaean L.H.IIIb sword (like Fig. 15, 1) was in fact recovered from a barrow at Pelynt near the south coast of Cornwall though not from a typical Wessex grave.[31]

At the same time the Wessex chieftains devoted part of their wealth to sanctifying their power by transforming and enriching the grandest sanctuary of their predecessors. Stonehenge III[32] combines a new arrangement of the holy Bluestones with the trilithon horseshoe and circle of sarsen blocks, dragged some twenty-five miles from Marlborough Downs; the well-dressed uprights are consecrated and dated by carved representations of the axes found in Wessex graves and of a dagger, possibly imported from Greece.

Meanwhile in the Highland Zone of Britain the absorption of the Beaker aristocracy is symbolized by the gradual replacement of their lordly drinking-cups by humble Food Vessels as the appropriate funerary vessels. For these can be derived from Secondary Neolithic vases though sometimes hybridized with Beaker or Battle-axe types. At the same time individual interment finally replaces collective burial in megalithic tombs. But the single graves are often grouped in little cemeteries, as in class I henges, and inhumation slowly gives place to cremation, a change that once more documents a revival of Neolithic rites and ideas. Food Vessels – of the Yorkshire vase form with a sharp, generally grooved shoulder (Fig. 158, 2) – were introduced into Ireland, presumably by a fresh wave of immigrants from Great Britain. As a result, there too collective burial gradually gave way to individual interment; in several Boyne tombs Food-Vessels accompanied intrusive secondary cremations. But in Ireland and Western Scotland[33] developed a bowl type of Food Vessel (Fig. 158, 1) as a substitute for wooden bowls, the form and decoration of which may also be inferred from the Pyrenaean polypod bowls like Fig. 144 and Beaker associates like Fig. 111, 2.

The predominantly pastoral economy favoured by the Beaker-folk was maintained by Food Vessel societies. Though the latter are less obviously stratified than that of Wessex, industry and trade flourished among them too. Halberds and decorated axes made in Ireland[34] were transported across North Britain for shipment to Northern Europe without paying tribute to the chieftains of Wessex. Direct maritime intercourse with the Atlantic coastlands as far as Portugal may be deduced from a cylinder-headed pin, like Fig. 131, found with a Yorkshire Food Vessel in a grave in Galway, from the exact agreement of the cup-and-ring marks, carved on the slabs of such graves with the petro-

Fig. 158. Food Vessels, Argyll and East Lothian ($\frac{1}{3}$): 1, Bowl; 2, Vase.

glyphs of Galicia and Northern Portugal[35] and from the distribution in Brittany and Normandy (and perhaps the imitation in Portugal, p. 335) of gold lunulae like Fig. 159. For the latter, if inspired in the last resort by gold collars worn by Egyptian nobles, are immediately Irish translations into sheet gold of the crescentic jet necklaces, repeatedly associated with Food vessels in Scotland,[36] which were copied in amber in Wessex.

Finally cremationists,[37] of Secondary Neolithic stock, using as Cinerary Urns derivatives of Peterborough vases, were spreading from South-East England into the Highland Zone. They had reached Ireland while segmented fayence beads were still current,[38] while another party, crossing the North Sea, colonized the Low Countries.[39] Burials in Cinerary Urns, like the urns themselves, preserve even more clearly than those with Food Vessels the native neolithic traditions. For they cluster in small cemeteries or urnfields, some enclosed in a penannular bank and

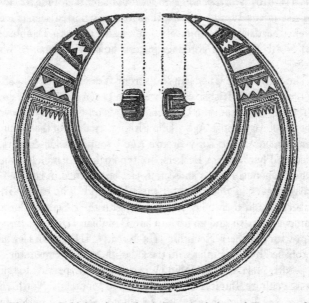

Fig. 159. Gold lunula, Ireland. By permission of Trustees of British Museum.

ditch like a class I henge.[40] They are still poorer and less aristocratic. Nevertheless, contemporary hoards of Middle Bronze Age II show that, though the Wessex chieftains had been expelled or absorbed, the established bronze industry continued to flourish, creating novel types – distinctively British spearheads with a loop at the base of the blade, palstaves, and rapiers, while goldsmiths devised a variety of splendid ornaments, culminating in the superb tippet of sheet gold richly embossed, found in a grave at Mold in Flintshire.[41]

The widespread diffusion of Britannico-Hibernian metalwork, and the variety of products that reached the British Isles in exchange, not only illustrate the leading rôle of these islands at the dawn of the Continental Bronze Age and the diverse influences that fertilized insular culture; they also provide a unique opportunity for correlating several local sequences and assigning to them historical dates. The crescentic amber necklaces from the Shaft Graves of Mycenae and from Kakovatos (pp. 118–19) give a *terminus ante quem* not later than 1600 B.C. for the rise of the Wessex culture, though the imported segmented fayence beads probably indicate that it lasted till 1400. Danubian and North European chronologies can be checked against this dating.

The pins of late Unětician form from Wessex graves (p. 388) on the one hand. Irish axes, halberds, and even a gold ornament of the bar-style from the Unětician hoards on the other[42] prove that our Early Bronze Age 2 falls within period IV of the Danubian sequence. The Early Bronze Age I round-heeled daggers, associated here with A Beakers, are typologically parallel to the earliest Unětician forms and can in fact be matched in late Bellbeaker graves in Bohemia and the Rhineland. The earlier B1 beakers should then be contemporary with their Central European counterparts and go back to late Danubian III. A synchronism with Northern Neolithic IIIa–b (M.N. III) can in fact be established by J. J. Butler with the aid of the sun-disc mentioned on p. 381. Northern Neolithic IV is substantially parallel to our Wessex culture. But it is itself equivalent to Montelius' Northern Bronze Age I, though metal was locally too rare to be buried in its characteristic Long Cist tombs. But one of the earliest Northern graves, furnished with metal gear and so representative of Montelius' Bronze Age IIa at Liesbüttel in Schleswig[43] contained an imported British spear-head of the type distinctive of our Middle Bronze Age 2. In the opposite direction a synchronism between Northern Neolithic II (E.N.C.) and some phase of our Clyde-Carlingford (Megalithic) culture may be deduced from the adoption of the Western semicircle motive, prominent on Beacharra vases, on C funnel-beakers in Denmark and Sweden, and the application of the Northern device of cord impression to the decoration of some Beacharra vases.[44]

Correlations with the Iberian Peninsula are not quite so conclusive. Segmented fayence beads no doubt prove an overlap between the Wessex culture and the El Argar culture of South-Eastern Spain – Spanish Bronze II. But the cylinder-headed pin found with a Food Vessel in Ireland should belong there to Bronze I while the incense cups from Wessex graves and associated with Cinerary Urns have significant parallels in the incised pots and stone vessels of Los Millares and contemporary sites. So, too, daggers with a midrib on one face only, as at Los Millares and Alcalá, have been found with Cinerary Urns in Scotland and Southern Ireland.[45] This phase of the Los Millares culture should then on the British evidence be assigned to Bronze Ib (Los Millares II) and later than the popularity of at least Pan-European Beakers in the Peninsula. These would have to be assigned to Bronze Ia (Los Millares I as Leisner put it), which would be roughly parallel to the Beaker period in England. Even so, the neolithic passage graves of Portugal may be at least as early as the Northern ones of Neolithic III.

19 Retrospect: The Prehistory of European Society

What meaning can be extracted from the intricate details compressed into the foregoing pages? What patterns unify the fragmentary archaeological data? To clarify the issue the abstract results have been schematized into tables and maps. These present the distribution in time and space of cultures, assemblages of archaeological phenomena that should reflect the distinctive behaviour patterns of human societies.

The maps at first sight present a very complicated mosaic of contemporary cultures. But historical reality was certainly more complicated still. So many pieces of the mosaic are missing that even the spatial pattern is blurred. Here it has been deliberately simplified by the omission of a number of assemblages, some of which have been mentioned in the text but most of which in 1956 are little more than pottery styles. This bewildering diversity, though embarrassing to the student and confusing on a map, is yet a significant feature in the pattern of European prehistory. Across it another pattern may be discerned. The first two maps exhibit quite clearly the gradual spread of neolithic farmers, or at least of farming, from the south-east during two consecutive periods of uncertain duration. (But even here there is some doubt as to the right of 'Western cultures' to a place on map II!) Map III should suggest the groups, the complex relations between these and the impact upon them of alien or peripheral cultures in a period not necessarily longer than I or II, but more crowded with archaeologically recognizable events. The main cultures distinguishable at the opening of the period are designated by letters, their boundaries defined by solid lines. Different hatchings denote cultures that subsequently arose from, or were superimposed upon, the foregoing. Finally, map IV displays the main areas that benefited from the Early Bronze Age economy, their interrelation and their dependence on Mycenaean Greece.

The distribution of entries on the several maps is based on the chronological discussions included in all the preceding chapters and summarized in the following tables. In most of the columns the actual order of the entries, the sequence of cultures, is reasonably well-established, though here again a reference to the text will disclose doubts as to the order both in the extreme West and in the East.

But each column is virtually independent and should be regarded as a single scroll hanging freely from its own roller. The lower end is always loose, so that, as far as pure archaeology is concerned, each scroll could be rolled up at least to the 1400 notch – deduced from segmented fayence beads. Nuclear physicists have indeed diffidently offered some provisional radio-carbon dates[1] that might act as pins to keep some scrolls extended. So in column 15 the Windmill Hill culture (at Ehenside Tarn in the Lake District!) might be pinned about 3000 B.C.[2] and the Secondary Neolithic of Stonehenge I at 1850; in column 7 Early Cortaillod about 2740,[3] and in column 14 the earliest, A, funnel-beakers at 2650, while in column 2 Danubian I (in Germany!) might go back before 4000.[4] But radio-carbon dating proves to be infected by so many potential sources of error that European pre-historians accept its results with as much reserve as the physicists offer them. In any case the available dates do not suffice to decide between the competing archaeological chronologies of the European Bronze Age set out on p. 178. The Stonehenge figure perhaps makes the extreme dates for the beginning of the Unětician culture – before 2000 and after 1600 B.C. respectively – less likely, but any year between 1950 and 1650 B.C. would still be equally defensible. Fortunately, for some positive conclusions at least, these uncertainties do not matter.

Whichever chronology be eventually vindicated, the primacy of the Orient remains unchallenged. The Neolithic Revolution was accomplished in South-Western Asia; its fruits – cultivated cereals and domestic stock – were slowly diffused thence through Europe, reaching Denmark only three centuries or so after the

Urban Revolution has been completed in Egypt and Sumer. Ere then the techniques of smelting and casting copper had been discovered and were being intelligently applied in Egypt and Mesopotamia, to be in their turn diffused round the Mediterranean during the third millennium, but north of the Alps only at its close, if not already in the second. The development of industry and commerce in Greece and subsequently in Temperate Europe was as much dependent on Oriental capital as the industrialization of India and Japan was on British and American capital last century.

On the other hand, European societies were never passive recipients of Oriental contributions, but displayed more originality and inventiveness in developing Oriental inventions than had the inventors' more direct heirs in Egypt and Hither Asia. This is most obvious in the Bronze Age of Temperate Europe. In the Near East many metal types persisted unchanged for two thousand years; in Temperate Europe an extraordinarily brisk evolution of tools and weapons and multiplication of types occupied a quarter of that time.

The startling tempo of progress in European prehistory thus documented is not to be explained racially by some mystic property of European blood and soil, nor yet by reference to mere material habitat, but rather in sociological and historical terms. No doubt the Cro-Magnons of Europe created a unique art in the Upper Palaeolithic Age while their mesolithic successors devised and bequeathed to contemporary Europe much ingenious equipment for exploiting their environment (pp. 48–9). No doubt, too, its deeply indented coastline, its propitiously situated mountain ranges and navigable streams, and its resources in tin, copper, and precious metal have conferred on our continent advantages possessed by no other comparable land mass, while the Mediterranean was a unique school for navigators. But the creative utilization of these favours of Nature must be interpreted in sociological terms.

The bounteous water-supply and seemingly unlimited land for cultivation allowed Early Neolithic farmers an unrestricted dispersion of population; dense aggregations had to grow up in the arid cradle of cereal cultivation where settled farming was possible only in a few oases or in narrow zones along the banks of permanent rivers. Hence Jericho, the earliest known neolithic settlement in the Near East, probably contained ten times as many inhabitants as any Early Neolithic village in Europe. But such aggregations require rigid discipline which the scarcity of water enables society to enforce. So from the first the Oriental environment put a premium on conformity. In Europe it was always feasible, however perilous, to escape the restraints of irksome custom by clearing fresh land for tillage; indeed, such an escape was actually imposed on the younger children of a village in historical times, at least in Italy, by the Sacred Spring. But such dispersion under neolithic conditions of self-sufficiency encouraged divergence of traditions and the formation of independent societies. Just that is imperfectly reflected during our period II in the multiplication within a comparatively small area of cultures distinguished by differences in ceramic art, burial rites, equipment, and even economy. Thereby even on our simplified map Europe appears in contrast to Hither Asia where the Halafian and Ubaid cultures are successively but uniformly spread over a vast area. Again in the ideological sphere the variations in megalithic architecture – really far greater than could be indicated here – should be the counterpart of the fission of a single and presumably Oriental orthodoxy into a myriad local sects. It might then be compared to the disruption of Christianity after the Reformation and contrasted with the faithful repetition of temple plans from the Persian Gulf to the Orontes in the third millennium. In short, a multiplicity of neolithic societies, distinguished by divergent traditions but never completely isolated one from the other, offered a European peasant some possibility of comparison and free choice.

The observed diversity was, of course, due not only to the splitting of a few immigrant societies and foreign traditions. Divergence was accelerated and emphasized also on the one hand by the multiplicity of pre-existing mesolithic groups who absorbed the neolithic techniques or were absorbed in the neolithic societies, on the other by the plurality of external stimuli that impinged upon them from Africa, the Levant, Anatolia, and perhaps Central Asia.

Still, material progress was impossible without an accumulation of capital, a concentration of the social surplus. This was effected in Early Aegean times and during period III of the temperate zone by the emergence of chieftains or aristocracies, spiritual or temporal; it made effective a demand for reliable metal weapons promoted by the concomitant intensification of warlike behaviour. Yet the small independent groups of herdsmen, cultivators, and fishers, owing allegiance to such rulers, just could not by themselves accumulate resources sufficient for the development of a metallurgical industry and of an efficient machinery for the distribution of its products. That had demanded the Urban Revolution, the concentration of the surplus produced by thousands of irrigation-farmers in the hands of a tiny minority of priests, kings, and nobles in the valleys of the Nile, the Tigris-Euphrates, and the Indus. Fortunately the effective demands of the masters of this concentrated wealth in Egypt and Mesopotamia enabled Aegean farmers and fishermen to secure a share in the surplus thus accumulated without themselves submitting to the same degree of political unification and class diversion. The archaeological picture of Bronze Age Greece at its most prosperous period corresponds well with Homer's description of many independent but loosely federated principalities, smaller but more numerous than even the Temple States of pre-Sargonic Mesopotamia.

In the sequel, Minoan and Mycenaean demand for tin, gold, and eventually amber, created a reliable market for the peculiar products of Temperate Europe. Thus indirectly the barbarian societies of Central Europe and the British Isles obtained a share in the capital accumulated through the Urban Revolution for the development of their own extractive, manufacturing, and distributive industries without submitting to the repressive discipline of urban civilization or suffering the irrevocable class division it entailed. Specialist craftsmen were liberated from the absorbing preoccupation of food production, but yet were not dependent on a single despot's court, temple, or feudal estate. They must no doubt sell their products and their skill to patrons, but whether these were classless societies, as perhaps in Bohemia and on the Middle Danube, or chieftains, as in the Saale-Warta province and in Wessex, there was plenty of competition for their services. As in Homeric Greece, a craftsman was welcome everywhere. So they had every inducement to display their virtuosity and inventiveness. In the European Bronze Age metal-workers were in fact producing for an international market.

In the ancient East the Urban Revolution had finally divided the societies affected by it into two economically opposed classes and had irretrievably consigned craftsmen, the pioneers of material progress, to the lower class. In prehistoric European and Mycenaean societies the cleavage was never so deep, if only because of their smallness and poverty. Craftsmen at least were not depressed into a class of slaves or serfs.

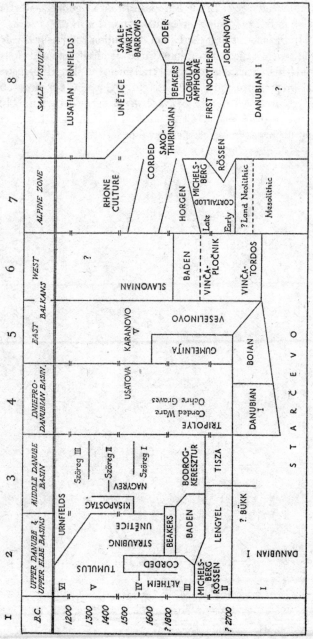

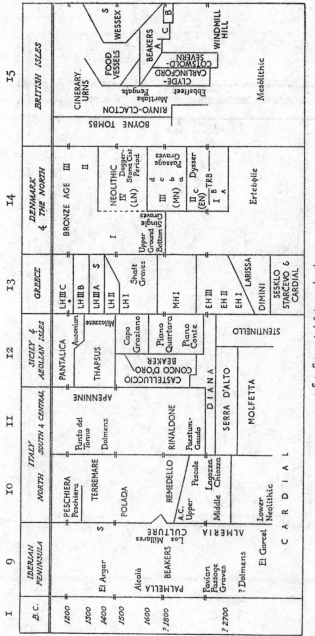

S = Segmented Faience beads

MAP I

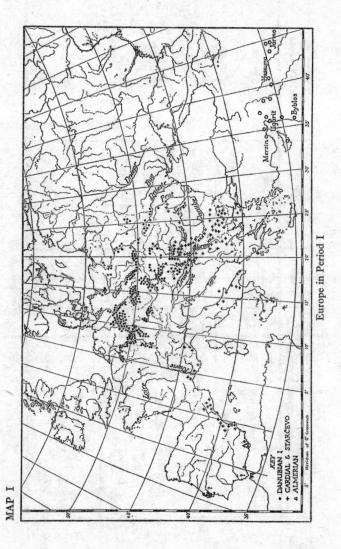

Europe in Period I

KEY
• DANUBIAN I
+ CARDIAL & STARČEVO
▲ ALMERIAN

MAP II

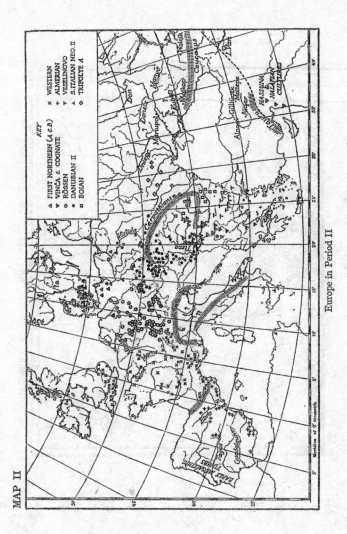

◁ FIRST NORTHERN (A & B)   × WESTERN
▽ VINČA & COGNATE   + ALMERIAN
○ RÖSSEN   ⊤ VESELINOVO
□ DANUBIAN II   ▲ S.ITALIAN NEO. II
⊡ BOIAN   ◇ TRIPOLYE A

Europe in Period II

403

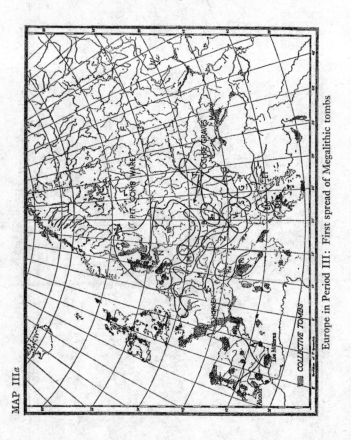

Europe in Period III: First spread of Megalithic tombs

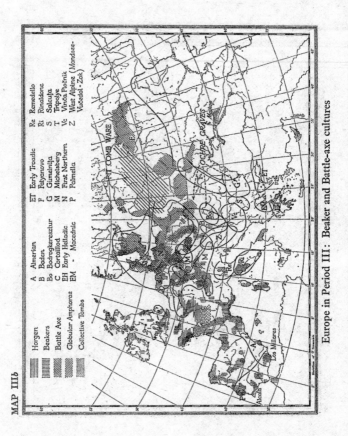

MAP IIIb

| Horgen |
| Beakers |
| Battle Axe |
| Globular Amphorae |
| Collective Tombs |

A Almerian
B Baden
Bo Bodrogkeresztur
C Cortaillod
EH Early Helladic
EM Macednic

ET Early Troadic
F Fatyanovo
G Gumelniţa
M Michelsberg
N First Northern
P Palmella

Re Remedello
Ri Rinaldone
S Salcuţa
T Tripolye
Vc Vinča Ploŝnik
Z West Alpine (Mondsee-
Vučedol-Zók)

Europe in Period III: Beaker and Battle-axe cultures

405

MAP IV

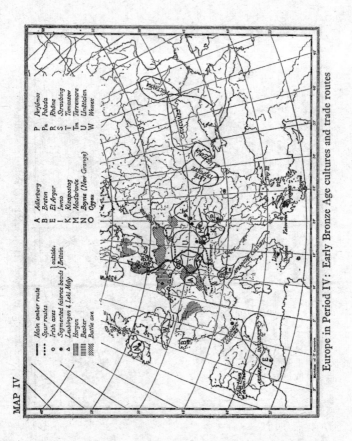

Europe in Period IV: Early Bronze Age cultures and trade routes

Notes on Terminology

Definitions of certain terms, descriptive of *ceramic decoration*, here used in a special or restricted sense.

Cardial decorated with lines executed with a shell edge.

Channelled with relatively wide and shallow incisions, round-bottomed.

Cordoned with applied strips of clay in relief.

Crusted with colours (paints) applied to the vase surface *after* the firing of the vessel.

Excised with regular small triangular or square hollows made by depressing the surface or actually cut out ('fret-work' or 'chip-carving' or 'false relief').

Fluted with flutings separated only by a sharp narrow ridge.

Grooved with broad incisions, not normally round-bottomed.

Incrusted with incised lines filled with white or coloured paste.

Maggot with the impressions of a loop of whipped threads, see Fig. 155.

Particoloured by firing the vessel so that part is reddened by the oxidization of the iron oxides exposed to a free access of air while part is blackened by the reduction of these oxides. (Egyptian black-topped ware is one variety.)

Rusticated by roughening the surface, generally covered with a thick slip, by pinching with the fingers, brushing, etc. ('barbotine').

Rouletted as described on p. 271.

Stab-and-drag decorated with continuous lines formed by jabbing a pointed implement into the soft clay, then drawing the point backwards a short distance and stabbing it in again, and so on.

Celt, a term formerly used to describe chopping implements of stone or metal that could be used as axes, adzes, gouges, chisels, or even hoe-blades. Here we distinguish, where possible, between the several types and in particular describe as

Adze a celt that is asymmetrical about its major axis so that it could not possibly be used as an axe (Fig. 29, D, B). When hafted the handle is perpendicular to the plane of the blade.

Axe   therefore describes a celt that is symmetrical about its major axis even though such a celt could often be used as an adze.

An axe (or adze) provided with a hole for the shaft, like a modern axe-head, is termed a *shaft-hole axe* (or adze), but, if the butt end is elongated and carefully shaped, the term *battle-axe* is conventionally used.

Burials should be described as *contracted* when the knees are drawn up towards the chin so as to make an angle of 90° or less with the spinal column. When the angle is more than a right angle, the term *flexed* should be used. Owing to ambiguities in the authorities followed, it has not been possible to maintain this distinction strictly here.

Abbreviations

Periodicals and Collective Works

AAH. *Acta Archaeologica Hungarica*, Buda-Pest.

'Aamose' 'Stenalderbopladser i Aamosen', by T. Mathiassen, J. Troels-Smith, and M. Degerbøl, *Nordiske Fortidsminder*, iii, 3, Copenhagen, 1943.

Aarbøger *Aarbøger for Nordisk Oldkyndighed og Historie*, Copenhagen.

Acta Arch. *Acta Archaeologica*, Copenhagen.

Act. y Mem. *Actas y Memorias* de la Sociedad Española de Antropología, Etnografía y Preistoría, Madrid.

ΑΔ *Ἀρχαιολικὸν Δελτίον*, Athens.

AE. *Archaeologiai Ertesitö*, Buda-Pest (A Magyar Tudomanyos Akademia).

AfO. *Archiv für Orientforschung*, Vienna.

AfA. *Archiv für Anthropologie*, Brunswick.

Afas. Association française pour l'avancement des Sciences (Reports of congresses).

AJA. *American Journal of Archaeology* (Archaeological Institute of America).

Altschles. *Altschlesien*, Breslau (Schlesische Altertumsverein).

Am. Anthr. *American Anthropologist* (New Haven, Conn.).

AM. *Mitteilungen des archäologischen Instituts des deutschen Reiches, Athenische Abteilung.*

Ampurias *Ampurias*, Barcelona.

Antiquity *Antiquity*, Gloucester.

Ant. J. *Antiquaries' Journal*, London (Society of Antiquaries).

Anuari *Anuari de l'Institut d'Estudis Catalans*, Barcelona.

Arch. *Archaeologia*, London (Society of Antiquaries).

Arch. Camb. *Archaeologia Cambrensis*, Cardiff.

Arch. Ert. See **AE.**

Arch. Hung. *Archaeologia Hungarica*, Buda-Pest.

Arch. J. *Archaeological Journal*, London (R. Archaeological Institute).

AR. *Archeologiské Rozhledy*, Praha (Čeckoslovenská Akademie Věd).

Arh. Vest. *Arheoloski Vestnik*, Ljubljana (Slovenska Akademija Znanosti)

Arkh. Pam. *Arkheolog. Pamyatki U.R.S.R.*, Kiev (Ukrainian Academy of Sciences).

Årsberättelse *Arsberättelse K. Humanistiska Vetenskapssamfundets i Lund.*

APL. *Archivo de Prehistoria Levantina*, Valencia.

AsA. *Anzeiger für schweizerische Altertumskunde*, Zurich.

AsAg. *Archives suisses d'Anthropologie générale*, Geneva.

ASPRB. American School of Prehistoric Research, *Bulletin*, New Haven, Conn.

Bad. Fb. *Badische Fundberichte*, Baden-Baden.

BCH. *Bulletin de correspondance hellénique.*

Belleten *Belleten*, Ankara (Turk Tarih Kurumu).

Bl.f.d.V. *Blätter für deutsche Vorgeschichte*, Königsberg.

Bol.R.Acad.Hist. *Boletín* de la R. Academia de la Historia, Madrid.

BP. *Bullettino di paletnologia italiana*, Parma, Roma.

BRGK. *Bericht der römisch-germanischen Kommission* des arch. Instituts des deutschen Reiches, Frankfurt.

BSA. *Annual* of the British School at Athens.

BSR. *Papers* of the British School at Rome.

BSABrux. *Bulletin et Mémoires* de la Société d'Anthropologie de Bruxelles.

BSAPar. *Bulletin* de la Société d'Anthropologie de Paris.

BSPF. *Bulletin* de la Société préhistorique française, Paris.

CIIA. Institut international d'anthropologie, *Congrès*.

CIPP. Comisión de investigaciones paleontológicas y prehistóricas, Madrid (Junta para Ampliación de estudios científicas).

CISPP. Congrès international des sciences préhistoriques et proto-historiques.

Cuadernos *Cuadernos de Historia Primitiva*, Madrid.

Dacia *Dacia: Recherches et Découvertes archéologiques en Roumanie*, Bucuresti.

Dolg. *Dolgozatok* a m. kir. Ferencz Jószef-tudományegyetem archaeologia intézetéböl, Szeged.

Εφ. 'Αρχ. 'Εφημερὶς 'Αρχαιολογική, Athens.

ESA. *Eurasia septentrionalis antiqua*, Helsinki.

FA. *Folya Archaeologica*, Buda-Pest.

FM. *Finskt Museum*, Helsinki.

FNA. *Fra Nationalmuseets Arbejdsmark*, Copenhagen.

Fv. *Fornvännen*, Stockholm (K. Vitterhets, Historie och Anti-kvitets Akademien).

Gallia *Gallia*, Paris.

Germania Römisch-germanische Kommission des archäologischen Instituts des deutschen Reiches.

IGAIMK. *Izvestiya* Gos. Akademiya Istorii Materialnoi Kultury, Leningrad-Moskva.

Inst. Arch.AR. *Annual Report* of London University Institute of Archaeology, London.

IPEK. *Jahrbuch für prähistorische und ethnographische Kunst*, Köln.

IPH.Mem. Institut de Paléontologie humaine, *Mémoire*, Paris.

Iraq *Iraq*, London (British School of Archaeology in Iraq).

JHS. *Journal of Hellenic Studies*, London (Society for Promotion of Hellenic Studies).

JNES. *Journal of Near Eastern Studies*, Oriental Institute, Chicago.

JRAI. *Journal* of the Royal Anthropological Institute, London.

JRSAI. *Journal* of the Royal Societies of Antiquaries of Ireland, Dublin.

JSEA. Junta superior para excavaciones archeológicas, Madrid.

JST. ⎱ *Jahresschrift für die Vorgeschichte der säshsich-thüringische Länder*, continued as
JMV. ⎰ *Jahresschrift für Mitteldeutsche Vorgeschichte*, Halle.

KS. *Kratkie Soobshcheniya o dokladakh i polevykh issledovaniyakh* Instituta Istorii Materialnoi Kultury, Moskva-Leningrad.

KSU. *Kratkie Sooščeniya*, Arkh. Institut, Ukrainian Academy of Sciences, Kiev.

LAAA. *Annals of Archaeology and Anthropology*, Liverpool.

MA. *Monumenti Antichi*, Rome (Accademia dei Lincei).

MAGW. *Mitteilungen* der anthropologischen Gesellschaft in Wien.

MAGZ. *Mitteilungen* der antiquärischen Gesellschaft in Zürich.

Man *Man*, London (Royal Anthropological Institute).

Mannus *Mannus*, Berlin-Leipzig (Gesellschaft für deutsche Vorgeschichte).

Mat. *Matériaux pour l'histoire primitive et naturelle de l'homme*, Paris.

MIA. *Materialy i Issledovaniya po Arkheologii* SSSR., Institut Istorii Materialnoi Kultury Akademiya Nauk, Moskva-Leningrad.

MDOG. *Mitteilungen* der deutschen Orient-Gesellschaft, Berlin.

MSAN. *Mémoires* de la Société des Antiquaires du Nord, Copenhagen.

MusJ. *Museum Journal*, Philadelphia (University of Pennsylvania Free Museum).

Nbl.f.d.V. *Nachrichtenblatt für deutsche Vorzeit*, Leipzig.

NNU. *Nachrichten aus Niedersächsens Urgeschichte*, Hannover.

Not. Sc. *Notizie degli Scavi di Antichità*, Rome (Accademia dei Lincei).

Obzor *Obzor praehistoricky*, Praha.

OAP. *O Archaeologo Portuguès*, Lisbon.

OIC. Oriental Institute, University of Chicago (*Communications, Publications*, or *Studies in Oriental Civilization*).

Oudh. Med. *Oudheidkundige Mededeelingen* uit 's Rijksmuseum van Oudheden te Leiden.

PA. *Pamātky archeologiské a mistopisné*, Praha.

PDAES. *Proceedings* of the Devon Archaeological Exploration Society, Exeter.

PGAIMK. *Problemy Istorii Mat. Kult.*, Leningrad.

PPS. *Proceedings* of the Prehistoric Society, Cambridge.

Préhist. *Préhistoire*, Paris.

PRIA. *Proceedings* of the Royal Irish Academy, Dublin.

Przeg.A. *Przeglad Archeologiczny*, Poznan.

PSAS. *Proceedings* of the Society of Antiquaries of Scotland, Edinburgh.

PSEA. *Proceedings* of the Prehistoric Society of East Anglia, Ipswich (continued as **PPS**).

PZ. *Praehistorische Zeitschrift*, Berlin.

RAZ. *Russ. Antropologicheskii Zhurnal*, Moskva.

Raz. i. Pro. Razkopki i Proučvaniya Sofia (Naroden Arkheologičeski Muzeĭ).

Rév. Anthr. *Révue Anthropologique*, Paris.

Rév. Arch. *Révue Archéologique*, Paris.

Rév. Ec. Anthr. *Révue de l'École d'Anthropologie de Paris* (continued Rév. Anthr.).

REG. *Révue des Études grecques*, Paris.

Real. *Reallexikon der Vorgeschichte*, edited by Max Ebert, Berlin.

Rev. Guim. *Revista Guimarães*, Guimarães.

Rivista *Rivista di Antropologia*, Rome.

Riv. Sc. Pr. *Rivista di Scienze preistoriche*, Florence.

Riv. St. Lig. *Rivista di Studi liguri*, Bordighera.

RQS. *Révue des Questions scientifiques*, Bruxelles.

SA. *Sovietskaya Arkheologiya*, Moskva-Leningrad.

SAC. *Sussex Archaeological Collections*, Lewes.

SGAIMK. *Soobshcheniya GAIMK.*, Leningrad.

Slov. Arch. *Slovenská Archeológia*, Bratislava (Slovenská Akadémia Vied).

Slov. Dej. *Slovenské Dejiny*, Bratislava (Slov. Akad. Vied) 1947.

SM. *Suomen Museo*, Helsinki.

SMYA. *Suomen Muinaismuistoyhdistyksen Aikakauskirja=Finska Fornminnesföreningens Tidskrift*, Helsinki.

St. s. Çerc. *Studii si Çercetări de Istorie Veche*, Bucuresti.

Swiatowit *Swiatowit*, Warsaw.

TGIM. *Trudy Gosudarstvennogo Istoricheskogo Muzeya*, Moskva.

TSA. *Trudy Setksii Arkhelogii RANION*, Moskva.

UJA. *Ulster Journal of Archaeology* (3rd ser.,) Belfast.

WA. *Wiadomości archeologiczne*, Warsaw.

WPZ. *Wiener Prähistorische Zeitschrift*, Vienna.

ZfE. *Zeitschrift für Ethnologie*, Berlin.

Books

(Only books mentioned in more than one chapter are mentioned here.)

Åberg, N. *Bronzezeitliche und früheisenzeitliche Chronologie*, Stockholm, 1930–35.

Alaca. See Arik and Kosay.

Arik, Remzi Oğuz. *Les Fouilles d'Alaca Höyük*, Ankara, 1937.

Bagge and Kjellmark. *Stenåldersboplatserna vid Siretorp i Blekinge* (K. Vitterhets, Historie och Antikvitets Akademien), Stockholm, 1939.

Bailloud, C., and Mieg de Boofzheim, P. *Les Civilisations néolithiques de la France*, Paris, 1955.

Banner, J. *Das Tisza-Maros-Körös-gebeit*, Szeged, 1942.

Berciu, D. *Arheologia preistorică a Olteniei*, Craiova, 1939.

Bernabo Brea, L. *Gli Scavi nella Caverna degli Arene Candide*, Bordighera, 1946, 1956.

Blegen, Caskey, et al. *Troy*, Princeton, 1950, 1951, 1953.

Böhm. J, *Kronika Objeveného Věku*, Praha, 1941.

Bosch-Gimpera, P. *Etnología de la Península Ibérica*, Barcelona, 1932.

Brøndsted, J. *Danmarks Oldtid*, Copenhagen, 1938–9.

Brinton, G. *The Badarian Civilization*, London, 1928.

Briusov, A. *Očerki po istorii̇̆ plemen evropaĭskoĭ časti SSSR. v neolitčiesku epokhu*, Moskva, 1952.

Buttler, W. *Der donauländische und der westische Kulturkreis der jüngeren Steinzeit* (Handbuch der Urgeschichte Deutschlands, 2), Berlin, 1938.

Castillo Yurrita, A. del. *La Cultura del Vaso campaniforme*, Barcelona, 1928.

Caton-Thompson, G. *The Desert Fayum*, London, 1935.

Childe, V. G. *The Danube in Prehistory*, Oxford, 1929.

—— *New Light on the Most Ancient East*, London, 1954.

—— *Prehistoric Communities of the British Isles*, Edinburgh, 1940.

Clark, G. *The Mesolithic Age in Britain*, Cambridge, 1932.

—— *Prehistoric Europe: The Economic Basis*, London, 1952.

413

—— *The Mesolithic Settlement of Northern Europe*, Cambridge, 1936.

Coon, C. S. *The Races of Europe*, New York, 1939.

Correia, V. *El Neolítico de Pavia*, Madrid, 1921 (*CIPP. Mem.* 27).

Déchelette, J. *Manuel d'Archéologie préhistorique, celtique et gallo-romaine*, Paris, 1908–14.

Ehrich, R. W. (ed.). *Relative Chronologies in Old World Archaeology*, Chicago, 1954.

Engberg and Shipton. 'The Chalcolithic Pottery of Megiddo', *Oriental Institute Studies*, 10, Chicago.

Evans, Arthur. *The Palace of Minos and Knossos*, London, 1921–8.

Forssander, J. E. *Die schwedische Bootaxtkultur*, Lund, 1933.

—— *Der ostskandinavische Norden während der ältesten Metallzeit Europas*, Lund, 1936 (Skrifter av K. Humanistiska Vetenskapssamfundet, XXII).

Frankfort, H. *Studies in the Early Pottery of the Near East*, London, 1925–7 (R. Anthrop. Institute, *Occasional Papers*, 6 and 8).

Garrod, D. *The Stone Age of Mount Carmel*, I, Oxford, 1937.

Gerasimov, M. M. *Vosstanovlenie Litsa po Čerepu*, Moskva (Trudy Instit. Etnografiĭ, XXVIII), 1955.

Giffen, A. E. van. *Die Bauart der Einzelgräber*, Leipzig, 1930 (Mannus-Bibliothek, 44).

Hančar, F. *Urgeschichte Kaukasiens*, Vienna, 1937. *Das Pferd im prähistorischer und früher historischer Zeit*, Vienna, 1956.

Hawkes, C. F. C. *The Prehistoric Foundations of Europe*, London, 1940.

Heurtley, A. W. *Prehistoric Macedonia*, Cambridge, 1939.

Kosay, Hamit Zubeyr. *Ausgrabungen von Alaca Höyük*, Ankara, 1944, *Alaca Höyük Kazisi*, Ankara, 1951.

Kostrzewski, J. *Prehistoria Ziem Polskisch*, Poznan, 1948.

Loë, A. de. *La Belgique ancienne*, Brussels (Musées du Cinquantenaire), 1928.

Laviosa-Zambotti, *Le più antiche Culture agricole Europee*, Milano, 1943.

Leisner, G. and V., *Die Megalithgräber der iberischen Halbinsel, I., Der Süden*. (Römisch-germanische Forschungen, 17) Berlin, 1943.

MacWhite, Eoin, 'Estudios sobre las relaciones atlánticas de la península hispánica' (*Dissertationes Matritenses*, II), Madrid, 1951.

Mariën, M. E., *Oud-België*, Antwerp, 1952.

Milojčić, V. *Chronologie der jüngeren Steinzeit Mittel- und Südosteuropas*, Berlin, 1949.

Nordmann, C. A. 'The Megalithic Culture of Northern Europe', Helsinki, 1935 (*SMYA.*, XXXIX, 3).

Osten, H. H. van der. *The Alishar Hüyük*, Chicago, 1929–37 (Oriental Institute Publications, XIX–XX, XXVIII–XXX).

Patay, P. 'Frühbronzezeitliche Kulturen in Ungarn', *Dissertationes Pannonicae*, S. II, no. 13) Buda-Pest, 1939.

Pendlebury, A. *The Archaeology of Crete*, London, 1939.

Pericot, L. *España primitiva e romana* (*Historia de España*, I), Madrid, 1947.

—— *Los Sepulcros Megalíticos Catalanes y la Cultura Pirenaica*, Barcelona, 1950.

Pittioni, R. *Urgeschichte des österreichischen Raumes*, Vienna, 1954.

Schaeffer, C. F. A. *Missions en Chypre*, Paris, 1936.

—— *Stratigraphie comparée de l'Asie occidentale*, Oxford, 1948.

Schmidt, E. *Excavations at Tépé Hissar, Damghan*, Philadelphia, 1937.

Schmidt, R. R. *Die Burg Vučedol*, Zagreb, 1945.

Sprockhoff, G. *Die nordische Megalithkultur* (Handbücher der Urgeschichte Deutschlands, 3), Berlin, 1938.

—— *Die Kulturen der jüngeren Steinzeit in der Mark Brandenburg* (*Vorgeschichtliche Forschungen*, I, 4), Berlin, 1926.

Stocký, A. *La Bohème préhistorique*, Praha, 1929.

Vaufrey, R. *Préhistoire de l'Afrique*, I, *Maghreb*, Paris, 1955.

Wace, A. J. B., and Thompson, M. *Prehistoric Thessaly*, Cambridge, 1912.

Xanthudides, S. *The Vaulted Tombs of the Mesará*, Liverpool, 1924.

Zeuner, F. E. *Dating the Past*, London, 1952.

Notes

Chapter 1   Survivals of Food-gatherers

1. Zeuner, F. E., *Dating the Past* (London, 1954), summarizes the evidence conveniently.

2. 'Aamosen' (1943), 162; *Årsberättelse* (1937–8), 39–96; cf. *New Phytologist*, XLIV (1944), 64.

3. Confined effectively to the woodland zone; *KS.*, XXXI (1950), 96–110; LIX, 7–9; cf. Clark (1936), 62.

4. Obermaier, *Fossil Man in Spain* (1925), 340 f.; *PPS.*, XX (1954), 193–210.

5. E.g. in Ariège, *L'Anthr.*, XXXVIII (1928), 235.

6. See C. S. Coon, *Races of Europe* (1939), 35–6, 67–8.

7. *Germania*, XVIII (1934), 81–8.

8. *Jb. Bernischen Hist. Mus.*, XXXIV (1954), 197–8.

9. Movius, H., *The Irish Stone Age* (Cambridge, 1942), 180 ff.

10. Hančar, *Kaukasiens*, 116–26, 148–50, 194–206; *SA.* ,I, 195–212; V, 160–75, 299; for the fauna *MIA.*, XXXIX (1953), 460–62.

11. *SA.*, V, 97–100; *KS.*, IV (1940), 29.

12. Clark, *Meso. Britain*, 97–103.

13. *PPS.*, XXI (1955), 14–19.

14. Clark (1936), 190–94.

15. Clark (1936), 198; *Antiquity*, XI (1937), 477; Gumpert, *Fränk. Mesolithikum* (*Mannus Bibliothek*, 40), 14–27.

16. Obermaier, op. cit., p. 234; Breuil and Zbyszewski, 'Revision des industries de Muge', *Communicações dos Servicios geologicos*, XXVIII (Lisbon, 1947); Roche, J., *L'Industrie du Cabeço d'Amoreira* (*Muge*) (Porto, 1951).

17. Pequart, Boule, and Vallois, *Teviec, IPH., Mem.* 18 (1937), with important section on mesolithic races; Pequart, M. and St J., *Hoëdic* (Anvers, 1954).

18. *Riv. St. Lig.*, XII (1946), 36–7.

19. *L'Anthr.*, XLIX (1938–40), 702; *Riv. St. Lig.* XIV (1948), 16–19.

20. Pericot, *La Cueva del Parpalló* (Madrid, 1942), 67, 92.

21. Vaufrey, *L'Afrique*, 413.

22. Clark (1936), 211–13.

23. ibid., 217; 1932, 51.

24. E.g. at Sauveterre (Lot-et-Garonne) Tardenoisian microliths were associated with finger-tipped cordoned pottery and tanged and barbed arrowheads, Coulanges, IPH.*Mem.* 14 (1935), 26.

25. Childe, *Danube*, 18.

26. Sherds of decorated 'cave' pottery were found at least in the upper levels of the midden.

27. Lacam, et al., *Le Gisement mésolithique du Cuzoul*, IPH.*Mem.* 21 (1944), 11; Pequart, et al., *Teviec*, IPH.*Mem.* 18 (1937), 101. At Mas d'Azil even *un tas de blé* was once mentioned.

28. Obermaier, op cit., 349–58; Pericot, *Hist. España*.

29. Rust, A., *Die alt- und mittelsteinzeitliche Funde von Stellmoor* (Neumünster, 1943).

30. In the Magdalenian levels of the Pekarna cave and in the contemporary camp of Pavlovce near Dolni Věstonice.

31. *Dacia*, V–VI (1934–5), 12, pl. III; cf., *Antiquity*, XVI (1942), 259.

32. At Kostienki I; *KS.*, XXXI (1950), 168.

33. Clark, G., *Star Carr* (Cambridge, 1954).

34. *APL.*, IV (1955), 195 f.

35. Clark, *Northern Europe* (1936); cf. Childe, *PCBI.*, 26–8.

36. Indreko, 'Die mittlere Steinzeit in Estland', K. V. H. A. Akademiens, *Handlingar*, LXVI (Stockholm, 1948); *SMYA.*, LVII (1956) (the Askola culture).

37. *FNA.* (1945), 63–5.

38. *Årsberättelse* (1951), 123–36.

39. Clark, *Preh. Eur.*, 42–8.

40. A runner was recovered from a Boreal peat in Finland, *SM.*, XXXVIII–XXXIX (1931–2), 60; XLI, 121; XLII, 22.

41. *Očerki*, 146–8, 168–9; he would derive the Kunda culture from the east but not the west Baltic Maglemosian.

42. Bøe and Nummedal, *Le Finnmarkien* (Oslo, 1936).

43. Freundt, 'Komsa, Fosna, Sandarna', *Acta Arch.*, XIX (1948), 4–55, but cf. *SMYA.*, LVII.

44. Clark, *Northern Europe*, 138–56, but cf. now *Acta Arch.*, VIII (1937), 278–94; Mathiassen, 'Bopladsen Dyrholmen', K. Dansk. Videns. Selskabs, *Ark.-Kunsthist. Skrifter*, I, 1 (1942); Bagge and Kjellmark, *Siretorp.*; 'Aamose', 136–44; and Althin, *Scania*.

45. These 'axes' and the earlier 'adzes' would not be much good for chopping, since the shafts actually preserved are hazel stems not over 2 cm thick though as much as 50 cm long; Mathiassen, 'Dyrholmen', 24.

46. Brøndsted, *Danmarks*, i, 115; round heads exceeded long heads in the ratio of 3 to 2, ibid., 123.

47. *FNA.* (1945), 6.

48. *Søllerød Bogen* (1946), 33.

49. Degerbøl, in Mathiassen, 'Dyrholmen', 118–20.

50. *Aarbøger* (1953), 5–62.

51. Mathiassen, *Aarbøger* (1937).

52. Althin, *Scania*, 159; *Fv.* (1944), 257–79.

53. *WA.*, XX (1954), 23–66; at Janislavice (Skierniewice Dist.) a sitting skeleton showing Lapponoid features is assigned to this phase.

54. Clark, *Northern Europe*, 158.

55. Childe, *PCBI.*, 28.

56. Clark, *Preh. Eur.*, 65.

57. But cf. Nougier, *Les Civilisations campigniennes* (Paris, 1950).

58. Clark, *Preh. Eur.*, 208–9.

59. Peyrony, *Préhist.*, III, 17.

Chapter 2 The Orient and Crete

1. On the cereals see Helbaek, Inst. Arch. *AR.*, IX (1953), 44–52.
2. Braidwood, R. *Antiquity*, XXIV (1950), 190–96.
3. Childe, *NLMAE.*, 28–30.
4. *Antiquity*, XXX (1956), 196.
5. Pendlebury, *Archaeology of Crete* (London, 1939), 35–41.
6. *BSA.*, XLVIII (1953), 94–134.
7. *BSA.*, XXXVI, 30.
8. *BSA.*, XXXVIII, 15.
9. Engberg and Shipton, 'The Chalcolithic Pottery of Megiddo' (O.I.C. *Studies*, 10), 61.
10. Childe, *NLMAE.*, 218.
11. Childe, *NLMAE.*, 39.
12. Childe, *NLMAE.*, fig. 36.
13. Evans, *P. of M.*, II, fig. 20; cf. Childe, *NLMAE.*, 94, 142, 163.
14. Matz, *Frühkretische Siegel*, 88.
15. Schmidt, *Excavations at Tépé Hissar* (1931–3), and *Mus J.*, XXIII, p. CXVI; cf. Frankfort, 'Archaeology and the Sumerian Problem' (O.I.C. *Studies*, 4), 57–64. In Anatolia kindred forms were popular under the Hittite Empires (1950–1200 B.C.); *MDOG.*, 75 (1937), 38. cf. Gordon, *Iraq*, XIII (1951), 40–46.
16. Childe, *NLMAE.*, fig. 105, 3.
17. E.g. by Sidney Smith, *Alalakh and Chronology* (London, 1940).
18. Åberg, *Chron.*, IV, 201 ff.; Pendlebury, *Crete*, XXXI, 300–302; Demargne, *Fouilles à Mallia: Nécropoles (Études Crétoises*, VII, Paris, 1945), 65–9.
19. Smith, *AJA.*, XLIX (1945), 23–4.
20. Hutchinson, *Antiquity*, XXII (1948), 61–3.
21. A diorite amphora, bearing the cartouche of Thothmes III (1500–1447) from a L.M.II tomb near Herakleion, gives new precision to this dating; *Kretika Chronika*, VI (1953), 11.
22. Hazzadakis, *Tylissos à l'époque minoenne* (1921), 77.
23. Described in Boyd Hawes, *Gournia*.
24. Evans, *P. of M.*, I, 147.
25. Garrod, *The Stone Age of Mount Carmel*, I, 14.
26. Xanthudides and Droop, *Vaulted Tombs of the Mesará*.
27. *AΔ* (1929), 103.
28. *Iraq*, II, 20, figs. 13–14.
29. *BSA.*, XXVIII (1926–7), 263–96.
30. 'Archaeology in Greece', *Supplement to JHS.* (1955).
31. *Man*, XXIX (1929), 18.
32. Koumása, tholos X.
33. Mochlos, E.M.I. (*P. of M.*, I, 57).
34. Mochlos (ibid., 102); cf. *Iraq*, II, fig. 51, 7.
35. Mochlos (*P. of M.*, I, 101).
36. *Essays in Aegean Archaeology, presented to Sir Arthur Evans* (Oxford, 1927), 111–28.
37. *BSA.*, Supplementary Volume, *Palaikastro* (1923), 17.
38. *Arch.*, LIX, and LXV, 1–94; Pendlebury, *Crete*, 195, 242, 306.
39. *P. of M.*, II, 14.
40. Mosso, *Dawn of Mediterranean Civilization* (1910), 290.

41. *P. of M.*, II, 619, fig. 392.

42. *P. of M.*, I, 193, n. 3.

43. From Hagia Triada and Prisos.

44. *P. of M.*, IV, 2, 797.

45. *BSA., Palaikastro*, pl. XXV; *JRAI.*, LXXIV, 17.

46. Xanthudides and Droop, pls. XXIII, LIV.

47. *P. of M.*, II, 272; cf. Childe, *NLMAE.*, pl. XXVIa.

48. *Arch.*, LIX, 105 ff.

49. *P. of M.*, I., fig. 72.

50. Evans, *P. of M.*, IV, 867 ff.; cf. Lorimer, *Homer and the Monuments* (1950), 211 ff.; *BCH.* (1953), 57.

51. Hood, *BSA.*, XLVII (1952), 256–61; infra, p. 132.

52. Evans, *Arch.*, LIX, 117; Hood, loc. cit., 262.

53. Evans, *P. of M.*, I, 59.

54. ibid., fig. 22.

55. Frankfort, *Studies*, II, 90.

56. Dikaios, *Khirokitia* (London, 1953); so also at Jarmo, Kurdistan.

57. *P. of M.*, I, fig. 139a; cf. van der Osten, *The Alishar Hüyük* (1928–9), Chicago O.I.C. *Publication* XIX, pl. XI.

58. *P. of M.*, II, 175.

59. Xanthudides and Droop, 69.

60. *Arch.*, LXV, 42.

61. *U. of Penns.*, *Anthrop. Publs.*, III, 3, 184.

62. Xanthudides and Droop, pl. XXXII, 548.

Chapter 3   Anatolia the Royal Road to the Aegean

1. Tahsim Ozgüç, *Kültepe Hafriyati* (Ankara), 19; id., *Belleten, passim*.

2. Remzi Ogiz Arik, *Les fouilles d'Alaca Höyük* (Istanbul, 1937); H. Z. Kosay, *Ausgrabungen von A. H.* (Ankara, 1944); id., *Alaca Höyük Kazisi* (Ankara, 1951).

3. van der Osten, *Alishar Hüyük* (1930–33), OIP, XXIX. Chicago.

4. *Belleten*, XII (1948), 475–6.

5. *Belleten*, XI (1947), 659 ff.

6. Götze, *Proc. Amer. Phil. Soc.*, XCVII (1953), 215–20.

7. Libby, *Radio Carbon Dating* (Chicago, 1950), 71.

8. *AJA.*, XXXIX, 33.

9. *Jahrb. d. Inst.*, LII; *Arch. Anz.* (1937), 167–70; Bernabo Brea, *PPS.* XXI (1955), 144–55.

10. Lamb, W., *Excavations at Thermi* (Cambridge, 1936).

11. Blegen, Caskey, etc., *Troy*, I (1950); II (1951); III (1953), Princeton.

12. On bothroi in general, see *JHS.*, LV (1935), 1–19.

13. One-corn is attested, through perhaps later at Troy and Kusura (*Arch.*, LXXXVI, 10), emmer only at Thermi, where there are some traces of vines.

14. Prausnitz, *Inst. Arch. AR.*, XI (1955), 20 ff.

15. The same device is seen in the Copper Age township of Ahlatlibel near Ankara, Turk Tarih Arkeologya ve Etnografya *Dergisi*, II (Ankara), 1934.

16. Childe, *NLMAE.*, fig. 60.

17. Prausnitz, *Inst. Arch. AR.*, XI (1955), 23 and 28; cf. Childe, *NLMAE.*, 231–7.

18. Blegen, *Troy*, I, 65; cf. Frankfort, *Studies*, ii. 86, n. 1.

19. *Arch.*, LXXXVI, 35, fig. 15; *Alishar*, fig. 30.

20. Very similar figurines turn up sporadically as if imported in Mesopotamia about 2750 B.C.; Speiser, *Tepe Gawra*, pl. LIII, b. Frankfort, 'Iraq Excavations'. *OIC. Communication*, 19, fig. 24.

21. Childe, *NLMAE.*, 162; cf. *Iraq*, IX (1947), 171-6.

22. Childe, *NLMAE.*, fig. 98.

23. Childe, *NLMAE.*, 63, 196.

24. ibid., 196; *LAAA.*, XXIII, 119; *Alaca* (1951), pl. CXII.

25. *Alaca* (1937), pl. CCLXXV; Schaeffer, *Stratigraphie*, 38.

26. Åberg, *Chron.*, IV, 11.

27. Blegen, *Troy*, I, 376, and fig. 357, 37,528.

28. *Antiquity*, XXX, 80-93.

29. Schliemann, *Ilion*, figs. 500-503; cf. *PPS.*, XXI, pl. XVII.

30. Blegen et al., *Troy*, II.

31. ibid., 9.

32. ibid., 107.

33. ibid., 229.

34. Blegen et al., *Troy*, III.

35. Childe, 'The Balanced Sickle', in *Aspects of Archaeology* (ed. Grimes; London, 1951), 145-6.

36. *OIP.*, XXIX, fig. 289; this was, of course, the method used for providing spear-heads with sockets in Crete earlier (p. 66) and in Sumer in the Third millennium.

Chapter 4   Maritime Civilization in the Cyclades

1. For Phylakopi see *Excavations at Phylakopi in Melos* (Society for Promotion of Hellenic Studies, Supplementary Volume, IV, 1904).

2. For tombs on Amorgos and Paros, see Tsountas, Κυκλαδικά, in 'Εφ. 'Αρχ., 1898; for Syros and Siphnos, ibid., 1899.

3. *AM.*, XLIII (1917), 10 ff.

4. *Chronologie*, IV, 71, 84.

5. Frankfort, *Studies*, II, 103.

6. Frankfort, *Cylinder Seals* (London, 1939), 232, 301; the tomb group is in the Ashmolean Museum, Oxford.

7. One dagger from Amorgos was of unalloyed copper, but a ring contained 13·5 per cent tin.

8. On Aegean ships see Marinatos in *BCH.*, LVII (1933), 170 ff.

9. Åberg. *Chronologie*, IV, 59 f.

10. *Phylakopi*, 234-8.

11. Pelos in Melos, *BSA.*, III, 40; Antiparos, *JHS.*, V, 48.

12. 'Εφ. 'Αρχ. (1899); cf. p. 59, above.

13. Papavasileiou, Περὶ τῶν ἐν Εὐβοίᾳ ἀρχαιῶν ταφῶν (Athens, 1910).

14. Goldman, *Eutresis*, 182.

15. Åberg, *Chron.*, IV, 102, nos. 13, 15; in both graves the 'frying-pans' were decorated with concentric circles so that those with running spirals may be earlier.

16. Åberg, *Chron.*, IV, 86; *Congrès Int. Arch. Athens* (1905), 221.

17. Evans, *P. of M.*, II, 26.

18. These palettes, perforated at the four corners, resemble, but only superficially, the wrist-guards of the Beaker complex; cf. *BSA.*, III, 67.

19. B.M., *Bronze*, fig. 174.

20. Evans, *P. of M.*, I, 97; Woolley, *Ur Excavations: The Royal Tombs*, 139.

21. Åberg, *Chron.*, IV, 62–3.

22. Cf. Childe, *NLMAE.*, fig. 36 (Gerzean).

23. Garrod, *Stone Age of Mt Carmel*, I, p. XV, 2.

24. Åberg, *Chron.*, IV, 13, 87; *AJA.*, XXXVIII (1934), 229, 231.

25. Hâmit Zübeyr Kosay, *Ausgrabungen von Alaca Höyük* (Ankara, 1944) pl. LXXXIII, 60.

26. In Ehrich, *Relative Chronologies in Old World Archaeology* (1954), 95.

27. *PZ.*, XXXIV (1950), 196.

28. *Festschrift P. Goessler* (Stuttgart, 1954), 26–34.

29. See Åberg, *Chron.*, IV, 127–37.

Chapter 5   From Village to City in Greece

1. Dörpfeld, *Alt-Ithaka*, R. 7 and R. 24.

2. *AJA.*, LI (1947), 172; Milojčic, *Chron.*, 39.

3. *Hesperia*, VI (1937), 487–97.

4. *Jhb. d. Inst.*, LXIX. (*AA.*, 1954), 11–23.

5. Dörpfeld, *Alt-Ithaka*, 335.

6. Childe, *NLMAE.*, 218; Godman, *Tarsus*, II (1956), 66.

7. Mylonas, Ἡ νεολιθικὴ Ἐποχὴ ἐν Ἑλλάδι (Athens, 1928). Cf. Weinberg, *AJA.*, LI (1947), 167–85, and Schachermeyr, *Die ältesten Kulturen Griechenlands* (1955).

8. Barley is attested for period A at Tsani, wheat, barley, figs, pears, and peas for period B at Sesklo and Dimini, *vulgare* wheat from Rakhmani IV (D). *Triticum durum* from Servia I in Macedonia.

9. *BRGK.*, 36 (1955), 1–50.

10. Forsdyke, British Museum, *Catalogue of Greek and Etruscan Vases*, I, pp. xvi and 23.

11. The surface colour is determined by the firing, an oxidizing atmosphere yielding red, a reducing black. See Blegen, *Prosymna*, 368–9; *Hesperia*, VI, 491–6.

12. Wace and Thompson, 241.

13. Childe, *NLMAE.*, 112, 120, 139, 195, 219, but at Byblos clay stamps are neolithic.

14. Mylonas, op. cit., fig. 64.

15. Dikaios, *Khirokitia* (London, 1953), 314–24; Schaeffer, *Missions en Chypre*, 110. The chalcolithic and proto-chalcolithic of Mersin in Cilicia provide even better analogies, Garstang, *Prehistoric Mersin* (Oxford, 1953), 54–124.

16. *AM.*, LVII (1932).

17. *Dacia*, VII–VIII (1940), 97.

18. It is possible that the fortifications and megara at both sites are Middle Helladic and so unconnected with the Dimini culture.

19. At Gonia and the Argive Heraeum.

20. Cf. Schachermeyr, *MAGW.*, LXXXI–LXXXIII (1953–4), 1–39; below, p. 155.

21. True handles are attached to jugs at Olynthus and a few other Macedonian sites, but Heurtley believes they are influenced by Early Aegean models and not truly 'neolithic'.

22. *Hesperia*, VI, b, c.; *AJA.*, LI, 174.

23. *Studies*, II, 40–5.
24. *AM.*, LVII (1932), 102 ff., LXII, 56–69.
25. *PM.*, 115–20.
26. *Anatolian Studies*, IV. (1954), 202–5.
27. Childe, *BSA.*, XXXVII (1936–7), 31–5.
28. *AJA.*, LI (1947), 170–74.
29. *Razkopki i Proučvaniya*, I, Naroden Arkh. Muzei (Sofia, 1948), 8–20; cf., *Anatolian Studies*, VI (1956), 45–8.
30. Frödin and Persson, *Asine*, 204.
31. Heurtley, *BSA.*, XXXV (1934–5), 39.
32. Marinatos, *BCH.*, LXX (1946), 337 ff.
33. *Hesperia*, XXIII (1954), 21–4.
34. *JHS.*, XLIX (1929), 93–4.
35. Vardaroftsa and Saratse, Heurtley, *PM.*
36. Two copper battle-axes found stray in peninsular Greece and now at the British School in Athens may well be Early Helladic.
37. Blegen, *Zygouries* (Cambridge, Mass., 1928).
38. *AJA.*, XXXVIII (1934), 259 ff.
39. Goldman, *Excavations at Eutresis in Boeotia* (1931).
40. Frödin and Persson, *Asine*, 433.
41. *JHS.*, XLIV (1924), 163.
42. This form resembles the Corded Ware amphora, Fig. 84 (cf. Fuchs, *Die griechische Fundgruppen der frühen Bronzezeit*, 1937), but also good Anatolian forms (*Germania*, XXIII, 62)
43. So Fuchs, *Die griechische Fundgruppender frühen Bronzezeit* (1937).
44. Milojčić, *Germania*, XXXIII (1955), 151–4.
45. Listed by Weinberg, *AJA.*, LI, p. 168, n. 26; add Mikhalic and Rafina.
46. Coon, *Races*, 144.
47. Dörpfeld, *Alt-Ithaka*, 229 (R. 7), 237 (R. 17), 241 (R. 24).
48. *BSA.*, XXVIII (1926–7), 180–94.
49. *AJA.*, XLVIII (1944), 342.
50. *Jhb. d. Inst.*, LII, *AA.* (1937), 20–25.
51. Persson, *New Tombs at Dendra* (Lund, 1942), 87.
52. Frödin and Persson, *Asine*, 286; cf. van der Osten, *Alishar*, 1928–9, *OIP.*, XIX, pl. IV, b 1671.
53. *BSA.*, XXVIII (1926–7), 179 ff.
54. *Hesperia*, XXIII (1954), 21; xxv, 160.
55. *JHS.* (1955), Suppl., p. 11.
56. *JHS.*, XXXIV, 126.
57. Arne, *Excavations at Shah-tepe*; cf. p. 20, n. 1.
58. Frödin and Persson, *Asine*, 433.
59. G. Mylonas, *Ancient Mycenae, the Capital of Agamemnon* (Princeton, 1956).
60. The identification of another blade from this grave as a halberd is incorrect, Blegen, in Ἐπιτύμβιον Χ. Τσουντας (Athens, 1951), 423 ff.; cf. *PPS.*, XIX, 231.
61. *Germania*, XXXIII (1955), 316–18.
62. Schachermeyr, *Archiv Orientalni*, XVII (Praha, 1949), 331–50, suggests that the Mycenaeans learned to build and use chariots while helping Ahmose to expel the Hyksos!
63. Wace, *BSA.*, XXV, 387; the contrary theory of Evans, making 'Atreus'

the oldest tholos (*PM.*, IV, 236 f.), has been refuted by the discovery of the new grave circle.

64. *Hesperia*, XXIII (1954), 158–62.

65. *AM.*, XXXIV, 255; Fürümark, *Chronology of the Mycenaean Pottery* (1941), 4.

66. Persson, *The Royal Tombs at Dendra* (Lund, 1931).

67. So at Kakovatos, Bodia (Messenia), etc.; *Corolla Archaeologica Gustavo Adolpho dedicata* (Lund, 1932), 217 ff.

68. Cf. Piggott in *Antiquity*, XXVII (1953), 141–3.

69. *Arch.*, LXXXII (1932).

70. *AJA.*, LII (1948), 145 ff.; Schaeffer, *Stratigraphie*, 9–12; Stubbings, *Mycenaean Pottery from the Levant* (Cambridge, 1951).

71. *AJA.*, LII (1948), 109–14.

72. Found in a tomb near Patras, *AJA.*, LVIII (1954), 235; cf. Lorimer, *Homer and the Monuments*.

73. Evans, *Arch.*, LIX (1905), 501; cf. Benton, *PPS.*, XVII (1952), 237.

74. Hood, *BSA.*, XLVIII (1953), 85.

75. Childe, *PPS.*, XIV (1948), 185 f.

76. *BSA.*, XLVIII, 15; the actual mould was found.

77. Schaeffer, *Enkomi-Alasia*, I (Paris, 1952), 237–42.

78. Blinkenberg, *Fibules grecques et mycéniennes* (*Lindiaka* V), (Copenhagen, 1926).

Chapter 6   Farming Villages in the Balkans

1. *Godošnik Plovdiv*, II (1950), 4–20.

2. *SA.*, XXIV. (1955), 125; cf. *IzbBAI.*, XVII (1950), 210–12.

3. *Jhrb. d. Inst.*, LVIII, *AA.* (1943), 74–92.

4. *IzbBAI.*, XIII (1939), 195–227.

5. *Antiquity*, XIII (1939), 345–9; Gaul, *BASPR.*, XVI (1948), 43–5.

6. *Preistorijskaya Vinca* (Belgrad, 1930–36), 4 volumes, cited *P.V.*

7. *WPZ.*, XXVI (1939), 1 ff.

8. *Chronologie*, 71–81; *BSA.*, XLIV (1949), 258–82.

9. *Hronologija Vinčanske Gruppe* (Ljubliana, 1951).

10. Kutzian, I., *The Körös Culture* (*Dissertationes Pannonicae*, s. II, no. 23) (Buda-Pest, 1944–7); Garašanin, Arandeljović-, *Starčevačka Kultura* (Univerz v. Ljubljani, 1954); Gaul, 'West Bulgarian Painted', *ASPRB.*, XVI (1948); 'Banyata', *God. Plov.*, II (1950), 4–12; *St. s. Čerc.*, II (1951), 57–64.

11. Banner, *TMK.*, 17; *Dolg.*, IX–X, 75.

12. Garašanin, *Starčevač. Kult.*, 134.

13. *Antiquity*, XIII, 345.

14. Fewkes, *ASPRB.*, IX (1933), 44–6.

15. *BSA.*, XLIV (1949), 261–6.

16. *Starčevačka Kultura* (Ljubljana, 1954), 62–80, 134.

17. *Relative Chronologies in Old World Archaeology* (Chicago, 1954), 112.

18. Heurtley, *PM.*, 116.

19. *AE.* (n.s.), VII–IX (1946–48), 19–41.

20. But probably no sheep or goats, *BRGK.*, XXXVI (1955), 21–5.

21. The 'unfired pottery' reported by Grbic from Subotica is really the clay lining to bottle-shaped silos on a sandy site. Normal Starčevo pottery was found in the silos.

22. *BSA.*, XLIV (1949), 258–306.

23. *Hronologia Vinčanska Gruppe* (1951).

24. *Starinar* (n.s.), III–IV (1953) 107–26.

25. *AE.*, VII–IX, 19–41.

26. Roska, M., *Die Sammlung Zsofia Torma* (Cluj-Koloszvar, 1941).

27. Grbic, *Pločnik* (Beograd, Narodni Muzeum, 1929).

28. Vassits, *PV.*, II, 9, pls. 8–17.

29. *Arh. Vest.*, Ljubljana, V (1954), 229–32.

30. The few sherds of crusted ware reported from Vinča (Vassits, *PV.*, II, p. 134) come mostly from late Vinča II levels.

31. Roska, *Torma-Sammlung*, pl. CXV, 12–21; cf. *St. s. Çerc.*, V (1954), 61, pl. V.

32. Milojčić, *Chron.*, p. 64, writing before the Romanian data were available, equated Gumelniţa as well as Boian with Vinča I.

33. *Chron.*, 77.

34. Fragmentary 'Minyan' and 'Early Helladic' vases from Humska Cuka, quoted by Garašanin (*Arch. Iugoslav.*, I (1954), 19 f.) and Milojčić (*Chron.*, 55–6), are not really much help. Their Aegean provenance is not at all likely and their relation to the Vinča sequence debated.

35. Benac, A., *Prehistorijsko naselje Nebo i problem Butmirske Kulture* (Univerzav Ljubljana), 1952.

36. Information from the excavator.

37. *Godišnik Plovdiv*, II (1950), 4–30.

38. *God, Plovdiv*, I (1948), 160–64; *Razkopki i Proučvaniya* (Sofia, Naroden Muzei, 1948), 75–81.

39. *IzbBAI.*, XIII (1939).

40. The stratigraphical position of the horses' bones—and of the battle-axes – is still uncertain. Neither have been yet found *in situ* at Karanovo.

41. *Belleten*, XII (1948), 475 ff.

42. von der Osten, *Alishar Hüyük*, 1930–32, *OIP.*, XXIX, fig. 93, 2393.

43. *IzvBAI.*, XVII (1950), 171 ff.

44. *Godišnik Plovdiv*, 1927–9 (1940), 55 ff.

45. Gaul, *ASPRB.*, XVI (1948), s.v.

46. *St. s. Çerc.*, V (1954), 395 ff.

47. Rosetti, *Publicat. Muzeului Municip Bucuresti*, I (1934).

48. Berciu, *Bul. Muzeului Judet. Vlasca T. Antonescu*, I (Bucurest, 1935).

49. *Bul. Muzeu, Jud. Vlasca T. Antonescu*, II (1937), fig. 3.

50. Gaul, *BASPR.*, XVI (1948).

51. One from Çunesti, Moldavia, *Dacia*, V–VI (1938), 117.

52. *BRGK.*, XXII, Taf. 7. Maps in Gaul, loc. cit.

53. O. Davis, *Man.*, XXXVI (1936), 119, describes prehistoric mines near Burgas; cf. Gaul, *AJA.*, LXVI, 400.

54. *PZ.*, XIX (1928), 131.

55. *Izv. Bulg. Arch. Inst.*, VIII (1934), 209.

56. But cf. Milojčić, *Chron.*, 61–2.

57. *Izv. Bulg. Inst.*, III (1925), 91–101; XIX, 1–13.

58. *Dacia*, VII–VIII, 97.

59. *IzbBAI.*, II (1924), 187 ff. In *IzbBAI.*, XIX (1952), 182–9, thirty-six further burials – at relatively high levels – are reported.

60. Berciu, *Arheologia preistorica a Olteniei* (Craiova, 1939, 50–68).

61. E.g. at Krivodol, *Raz. i Pro.* (1948), 26–57.

62. *MPK.* (1940), IV B, 1–2.

63. *Raz. i Pro.* (1948), fig. 43.

64. At Yasatepe, Plovdiv (*God. Plovdiv*, I (1948), 4–11, fig. 12), and Banyata III (ibid., II (1950), fig. 30).

65. *Dacia*, VII–VIII, 90 ff.; *St. s. Çerc.*, V (1954), 540–48.

66. *Godišnik Plovdiv* (1940), 55–70; Milojčić, *Chron.*, 50–52.

67. *IzbBAI*, XVII (1950), 171–87, with list of other sites on 187.

68. Berciu, *Arheol. preistorica a Olteniei*, figs. 136–8.

69. Milojčić, *Chron.*, 55, and fig. 2.

70. *IzvBAI.*, XIX (1952), 121–8.

Chapter 7   Danubian Civilization

1. For points not otherwise documented see Childe, *Danube*.

2. For the distribution in Hungary, *BRGK.*, XXIV–XXV, 30–32; *AE.*, XLIV, 30 ff.; in Poland and East Germany, *Przeg A.*, VIII (1949), 315–17; for the rest of Germany, Buttler, *Donau*; for Bohemia, Stocký, *Boh. Préh.*; for Belgium, Mariën, *Oud-Belgie*, 13–47; for Austria, Pittioni, *Österreich*, 125–40.

3. Emmer is reported only from the Rhineland and Belgium, bread wheat from Poland alone; both might have been borrowed from other populations. Cf. *BRGK.*, XX (1930), 30.

4. *BRGK.*, XXXIII (1943–50), 66–82; *AR.*, II (1950), 208; VII (1955), 5–10.

5. *PA.*, XLV (1954), 81–5.

6. *BRGK.*, XXXIII, 90–109.

7. Buttler and Habery, *Das bandkeramische Dorf Köln-Lindenthal* (*Römisch-Germanische Forschungen* 11) (Berlin, 1936).

8. Stocký, *Boh. Préh.*, 62.

9. *IPEK.*, XI (1936–7), 16 f.; *PA.*, XL (1934–5), 3.

10. Buttler, *Donau.*, 32.

11. Buttler, *Donau.*, 36; *Marburger Studien*, I, 27–9.

12. *JST.*, XXIII (1935), 73; *Bl. f. d. Vorg.*, VII, 51; Buttler, *Donau.*, 21.

13. Listed in *AR.*, VIII, 697 ff.

14. *Germania*, XXVI (1942), 177–81.

15. Radiocarbon date, Schachermeyr, *Die ält. Kulturen Griechenlands*, 98.

16. *PA.*, XLV (1954), 81 ff.

17. *SA.*, XX, 100; *KSU.*, IV (1955), 142–5 (Nezviska, stratified below Tripolye B1); *St. s. Çerc.*, II (1951), 54.

18. *Anthropozöikum*, III (Praha, 1953), 207–22.

19. Tompa, *Arch. Hung.*, V–VI (1929), 9–38; *BRGK.*, XXIV–XXV, 32–9; *Slov. Dej.*, 58.

20. *AE.*, XLIV (1930), 301; cf., *AE.* (1943), 22.

21. *Arch. Hung.*, V–VI, pls. XVIII, 5, XXIV, 13.

22. *AR.*, VIII, 637; *AE.*, XLIX, 86 and 70.

23. *Folya Arch.*, III (1941), 1–27; VII (1955), 42–4.

24. ibid., pl. V, 1–3.

25. Banner, *MTK.*, 31–8; *Dolg.*, VI (1930), 50–150; *AE.* (1943), 22.

26. *Dolg.*, VI, pls. III, VI; *BRGK.*, XXIV–XXV, 43.

27. *AE.*, XLV (1931), 253.

28. Csalog, *FA.*, III–IV (1941), 1 ff.; VII (1955), 37–41.

29. *FA.*, VII, 27–36; *Germania*, XXIII (1939), 145 ff.; *Dalg.*, XIX, 130.

30. *MAGW.*, LXXXIII (1953–4), 21–34.

31. Mylonas, *Excavations at Olynthos* (Johns Hopkins University, *Studies in Archaeology*, 6) (1929), fig. 59.

32. Buttler, *Donau.*, 38–43; *Arch. Hung.*, XXIII (1939); Slovenské Dejiny, 58–61; *Obzor*, VIII (1929), 1–53; XIV (1950), 163–72; *Przeg.A.*, VIII (1949), 318–21; Böhm, *Kronika*, 136–49; Pittioni, *Österreich*, 143–67.

33. Tompa's extension to this of the name 'Tisza' (*BRGK.*, XXIV–XXV, 70) has caused confusion with the quite different assemblage just described; cf., Milojčić, *Chron.*, 80, and Csalog, *FA.*, VII, 24–6.

34. *AR.*, II (1950), 52–6; III, 136–9.

35. *WA.*, XIX (1953), 7–53.

36. Schránil, *Böhmen*, 50; cf. p. 55 here.

37. *PA.*, XXXIX (1933), 50–53.

38. Vildomec in *Obzor*, VIII, 1–43.

39. *Arch. Hung.*, XXIII (1939).

40. *Obzor*, XIV (1950), 335.

41. *AR.*, VIII, 1956, 773–4.

42. Buttler, *Donau.*, 29, 45; *Anthropozoïkum*, III (1953), 207; IV, 411.

43. E.g. at Lobec, Bohemia, *AR.*, III, 130.

44. *PA.*, XXXIX (1933), 50–53.

45. *AR.*, VIII (1956), 710–18.

46. *Altschles.*, III (1931), 153; Buttler, *Donau.*, 60.

47. *Obzor*, XIV (1950), 330.

48. The theory of its derivation from 'the North-West German Megalith Culture', once dominant in Germany, was refuted by Stocký, *Boh. Préh.*, 161, and more conclusively by Engel, *Mannus*, XXXII (1940), 57–81.

49. See Buttler, *Donau.*, 40 ff., and Kimmig, *Bad. Fb.* (1948–50), 47–62.

50. *Germania*, XX (1936), 229–34; see Fig. 137 here.

51. Buttler, *Donau.*, 47, pls. 10, 12; 12, 1; cf. Blegen, *Troy*, I, form D 28. The Rössen and Troadic 'barrels' could both be derived from geomorphic vases of the Lengyel culture like Stocký, *Boh, Préh.*, pl. LIX, 11, or *WPZ.*, XXVIII (1941), 39.

52. *Germania*, XXVI (1942), 177–81.

53. Buttler, *Donau.*, 62.

54. Buttler, *Donau.*, 31.

55. E.g. Homolka in Bohemia, *Proc. Am. Phil. Soc.*, LXXI (1932), 357–92.

56. *Nbl. f. d. V.*, XV (1939), 114–17.

57. *Arch. Hung.*, IV; *AE.*, XLI (1927), 50–57; *BRGK.*, XXIV–XXV, 53.

58. Report by Kutzian to the 'Conférence Archéologique de l'Académie hongroise des Sciences' (Buda-Pest, 1955); cf. *AE.* (1946–8), 42–62.

59. *PZ.*, XXII, 111; *AE.* (1944–5), 1 ff.

60. *Dolg.*, XIX (1943), 135–9.

61. *Dacia*, III–IV, 352–5; cf. *Közlemények*, Cluj, II (1942), 15 ff.

62. *Archaeologia Geographica*, III (1952), 1–5.

63. *Inst. Arch. AR.*, VII (1951), 44–5.

64. What looks like a typical milk-jug was found at Maltepe near Sivas in northern Anatolia, *Belleten*, XI (1937), 659 ff.

65. *J. Indian Oriental Soc.*, IV (1936), 1–30.

66. *Obzor*, XIV (1950), 163–257.

67. Buttler, *Donau.*, 43.

68. *WA.*, XV (1938), 1–105; the graves have disturbed foundations of Danubian I long houses.

69. Pittioni, *Österreich*, 189–208.

70. Bayer, *Die Eiszeit*, V (Vienna, 1928), 60 ff.

71. Banner, 'Die Péceler Kultur', *Arch. Hung.*, XXXV (1956).

72. Stocký, *Boh. Préh.*, 115 ff.; Böhm, *Kronika*, 134–49; cf. *Slovenské Dejiny*, 61–4.

73. *WA.*, XII (1933), 140–67.

74. Bayer, *Die Eiszeit*, V (Vienna, 1928), 60 ff.

75. *AAH.*, I (1951), 49, 75.

76. Bayer, *Die Eiszeit*, V (Vienna, 1928), 60 ff.

77. *Dolg.*, XV (1939), 166; the attribution of an antler cheek-piece from a bit to the Pécel culture is dubious.

78. *Folya Arch.*, VI (1952), 29–35; Banner, loc. cit., 127.

79. *AAH.*, I (1951), 38–40.

80. Measuring 4·5 by 3·4 m at Palotabazsok (Banner, 'Péceler Kultur', 214), 8·0 by 5·5 m at Praha-Bubenic (Böhm, *Kronika*, 198).

81. *Vučedol*, 10–15.

82. *Österreich.*, 204.

83. *WPZ.*, XXIV (1937) 15–21.

84. *AR.*, IV (1952), 244; V, 733–6.

85. Banner, 'Péceler Kultur', 200–204.

86. *PZ.*, XXII (1931), 111–15.

87. *Arch. Hung.*, XXXV, 293–309.

88. Maier in *Germania* XXXIII (1955), 159–73.

89. Garstang, *LAAA.*, XXV, p. XXVIII, 22.

90. Turk Tarih Arkeologya ve Etnografya, *Dergisi*, II (1934), 90.

91. *PPS.*, XVII (1951), 178 ff.

92. Otto-Witter, *Handbuch der ältesten Metallurgie in Mitteleuropa* (Leipzig, 1952).

93. Only in graves 2 and 211 at Szöreg and 14 at Deszk; *Dolg.*, XVII (1941); cf. Milojčić, *CISPP.* (Zurich, 1950), 268.

94. *AJA.*, XLIII (1939), 17; Banner, *Dolg.*, XVII.

95. Especially at Vyčapy-Opatovce near Nitra, unpublished.

96. In Kisapostag graves at Dunapentele, *AAH.*, II (1952), 66.

97. *Germania*, XXI (1937), 89.

98. At Nemčice and Jirikovice, Mus. Brno.

99. Schaeffer, *Ugaritica*, II (1949), 49, calls these metallurgists 'Torque-Bearers'.

100. *Syria*, VI (1925), 18.

101. Childe, *NLMAE.*, 161–2.

102. ibid., 53, 63.

103. Milojčić, *Germania*, XXXIII (1955), 405–7, points out that the 'Asiatic' types do not all appear simultaneously at the beginning of period IV, but severally during phases A1, A2, and B respectively.

104. *PA.*, XLIV (1953), 203; *Arch. Aust.*, VII (1950), 1–8.

105. Derived through the Caucasus, or Crete; cf. *PZ.*, XXVII (1936), 150; *Folya Arch.*, VIII, 43.

106. *PZ.*, XXXIV (1949–50), 232–8; *JMV.*, XXXV (1951), 65.

107. *Iraq*, XI (1949), 118.

108. *PZ.*, XXV, 130–42; *Arch.*, LXXXVI (1937), 222–5.

109. Banner, *Dolgozatok*, VII (1931), 1–53; XVII, 70–82; Patay, *Frühbronzezeitliche Kulturen in Ungarn*; Nestor, *BRGK.*, XXII, 84–8; *CISPP.* (1950), 267–77.

110. The culture from the lowest levels in the Tószeg tell is termed Nagy-

rév.; cf. Patay, *Frühbronzezeitliche Kulturen in Ungarn* (1939); Mozsolic, *AAH.*, II (1952); Banner, *PPS.*, XXI, 127.

111. Mozsolic, *Arch. Hung.*, XXVI (1942); Patay, op. cit.; in Slovakia Kisapostag and Unětice types occur with inhumations, *AR.*, VI (1954), 297–300.

112. *PZ.*, XXII (1931), 33.

113. Cf. e.g. Schaeffer, *Stratigraphie comparée*, fig. 183, 36.

114. *Essays in Aegean Archaeology*, ed. Casson, pp. 1–4; cf. Petrie, *Ancient Gaza*, III, pl. XIV, 29–33.

115. Four hundred at Hainberg-Teichtal (*MAGW.*, LX (1930), 65 ff.); 255 at Gemeinlebarn (Szombathy) *Flachgräber bie Gemeinlebarn*, *R.-G. Forsch.* 3, Berlin, 1929.

116. *AR.*, V (1953), 308–18.

117. 'Beitsch and Knossos', *PPS.*, XVIII (1952), 36–47, cf. p. 66 above.

118. Formerly attributed to a distinct 'Marschwitz culture' and period III.

119. *PZ.*, XX (1929), 70–128.

120. cf. p. 123; even violin-bow fibulae are first reliably attested in urnfields of period VI. A fragment from an Unětice grave at Polepy in Bohemia (Schránil, *Bohmen*, 101; Böhm, *CISPP.* (London, 1932), 242; cf. *AR.*, VI (1954), 533, where the fragment is accepted as an Unětician fibula) is too small for reliable diagnosis; another from Gemeinlebarn is just as likely to belong to the urnfield at that site as to the late Unětician cemetery.

Chapter 8   The Peasants of the Black Earth

1. Passek, *Periodizatsiya Tripolskikh Poselenil* (*MA.*, X, 1949), though written in 1946, documents facts unless another reference be given.

2. Kričevskiĭ, *KS.*, VIII (1940), 53.

3. *KSU.*, IV (1955), 142–6.

4. Schmidt, H., *Cucuteni in der oberen Moldau* (Berlin, 1932).

5. Vulpe, *ESA.*, XI (1937), 134–46.

6. *St. s. Çerc.*, V (1954), 36–54.

7. Passek, *La Céramique tripolienne* (*GAIMK.*, Leningrad, 1935).

8. Bibikov, *Ranne-tripolskoe poselenie Luka-Vrublevetska*, *MIA.*, XXXVIII (1953).

9. Hančar, *Das Pferd*, 65 ff.; *KS.*, LI (1953), 53.

10. Pidoplička in Passek, note 1, 146.

11. Childe, *Danube*, 98–104.

12. *Hăbăşeşti*, *Monografie Arheologica* (Acad. Repub. Pop. Romine, Bucuresti, 1954).

13. Kričevskiĭ, 'Tripolskie Ploščadki', *SA.*, VI (1940), argued that the floors were baked by fires kindled upon them before the house was roofed over.

14. F. Vovk in *Antropologiya*, 1927 (Kiev, 1928), 20–25, pl. III, 9.

15. See p. 181, n. 12.

16. *Arkheolog. Pamat. Ukrain. S.S.R.*, IV (Kiev, 1952), 78–83; a clay copy of a Scythian cauldron, allegedly from the same horizon, prompts doubts as to the reliability of the excavation report.

17. See p. 181, n. 11.

18. Page 181, n. 12, pp. 235 ff., fig. 9.

19. At Luka-Vrublevetska (p. 180, n. 8); Ariuşd; Sabatinovka, etc.

20. Especially at Traian on the Seret, *Dacia*, IX–X (1941–4), 11 ff.

21. *MIA.*, XXXVIII, p. 338, tab. 46.
22. *BRGK.*, XXII, 45 and 51, n. 80.
23. Page 181, n. 12, 414.
24. Page 181, n. 13, 468.
25. *St. s. Çerc.* (1954), V, 36.
26. Page 180, n. 6, 436; the disc is very like that from the Danubian III grave at Brześć Kujawski, p. 165 above.
27. Sulimirski, *PPS.*, XVI (1950), 45–52.
28. Full summary by Passek in *MIA.*, X, 190–200.
29. *SA.*, V. 258; *Naukove Zapiski IIMK.*, II (Ukrain. Akad. Nauk, Kiev, 1937), 116.
30. For these barrows see also *SA.*, V (1940), 240–56.
31. Figured in Mongaït, *Arkheologiya v SSSR.* (Moskva, 1955), 109.
32. Rosenberg, *Kulturströmungen in Europa zur Steinzeit* (Copenhagen).
33. Passek, loc. cit.; *Arkheologiya*, VIII (Kiev, 1953), 95–107.
34. *KSU.*, IV (1955), 119–23; V, 13–17.
35. *MIA.*, II (1941), 251–3.
36. *Očerki*, 240 ff. Note distribution map on p. 234.
37. Tallgren, *ESA.*, II.
38. Kostrzewski, J., *Prehistoria Ziem Polskich* (Kraków, 1939–48), pl. LXII, 18.

Chapter 9   Culture Transmission over the Eurasian Plain?

1. Briusov, *Očerki*, 181–203.
2. *Antropologiya*, II (Kiev, 1928), 190–91.
3. *KS.*, XXXI (1950), 110–16; *SA.*, V (1940), 97–100; cf. Gerasimov, *Litsa*, 263–5.
4. *SA.*, XII (1950), 157–85.
5. *ESA.*, IV, 1–19.
6. Degen-Kovalevskiǐ (*KS.*, II (1939), 14–16) and Artamonov (*SA.*, X (1948), 161–81) proposed much later dates for the Early Kuban barrows.
7. *KSU.*, IV (1955), 147–9; cf. *Arkheologiya*, V (Kiev, 1951), 163, for a similar burial farther down the Dniepr, and Gerasimov, *Litsa*, 260–80, for others; the skulls are 'Cromagnonoid'.
8. Makarenko, *Mariupilski Mogilnik* (Kiev, Vse-Ukrainska Akad. Nauk, 1933); Stolyar (*SA.*, XXIII, 16) distributes the burials over four successive phases.
9. *MIA.*, III (1940), 69 ff.
10. Near Nalčik, *MIA.*, III (1940), 192; Mikhaǐlovka on the Lower Dniepr, *KSU.*, IV (1955), 119–22.
11. *IGAIMK.*, 100 (1933), 105.
12. Rau, *Hockergräber der Wolgasteppe* (Marxstadt, 1928); *SA.*, IV (1937), 93 ff.; *MIA.*, XLVI, 12 ff.
13. *KSU.*, I (1952), 21; V (1955), 75–8.
14. Though found in graves that are typologically 'yamno', most common from 'catacombs'.
15. Found from the Dniepr to as far east as Stalingrad.
16. *KS.*, XXXVII (1951), 117; *Arkheologiya*, V (Kiev, 1951), 183–8.
17. Hančar, 248.
18. *LAAA.*, XXIII (1936), 114–15.
19. Yessen, *IGAIMK.*, 120, 81.

20. Hančar, 244.

21. *Mus J.*, XXIII (1933), pls. CXIX, CXX.

22. Vozdvizhenskaya, Hančar, 253; Letniskoe, Yessen, *SA.*, XII.

23. Ulski aul, Hančar, loc. cit.

24. 'Iz Istorii drevnei Metallurgiya Kavkaza', *IGAIMK.*, 120 (1935).

25. *IGAIMK.*, 120, 99.

26. *SA.*, XII, Plate, Col. III, 3; Rau, *Hockergräber*, pl. III, 3.

27. Hooked metal sickles were being made in Yessen's phase IV.

28. Artsikovskiï, *Osnovy Arkheologiï* (1954), 75.

29. *SA.*, IV, 122; XI (1949), 327; *KS.*, VIII, 86; cf. Dingwall, *Artificial Cranial Deformation*.

30. *ESA.*, VIII, 61; in Cis-Caucasia Yessen attributes these to phase IV.

31. Popova, *SA.*, XXII (1955), 20–60 distinguishes six local varieties, some not represented in catacomb tombs at all.

32. *SA.*, X (1948), 147–56.

33. Angell in Dikaios, *Khirokitia* (London, 1953).

34. *ESA.*, II (1932).

35. Childe, *NLMAE.*, 159.

36. Arne, *Excavations at Shah Tepé* (Sino–Swedish Expedition, Pub. 27, Stockholm, 1945), 258.

37. Schmidt, *Excavations at Tepe Hissar, 1931–3* (Philadelphia, 1937), 185; actual axe-adzes of this precise type are known from Uzbekistan (*KS.*, XXXIII, 1950, 152) and the Indus valley.

38. Schmidt, op. cit.

39. Hamit Zubeyr Kosay, *Alaca Höyük Kazisi, 1937–9* (Ankara, 1951), pl. 135, 68–9; cf. *Germania*, XXXIII (1955), 240–42, and pp. 44, 183 here.

40. *Dacia*, VII–VIII (1937–40), 81–91.

41. *KS.*, XLVI (1952), 48–53.

42. *Slovenské Dejiny*, 64–6.

43. *Księga Pamietkowa*, 141–95; *Swiatowit*, XVI (1934–5), 117–34.

44. Shaft graves under barrows without pottery may, however, be earlier even in Saxo-Thuringia. *Festchr. d. Röm-Germ. Zentralmuseums*, III (Mainz, 1953), 168.

45. Kiselev, *Drevnaya Istoriya Yuzhnoi Sibiri* (Moskva, 1951).

46. Save for occasional satî burials of a male and female.

47. Äyräpää, *ESA.*, VIII (1933), 5; Glob, *Aarbøger* (1944), 18; Forssander, *Bootaxt.*, 56.

48. Childe, *ESA.*, IX (1934), 156–67.

49. Troels-Smith, *Aarbøger* (1953), p. 225, below.

50. Troels-Smith in Mathiassen, *Dyrholmen* (1942), 175–6.

51. Brøndsted, *Danmarks*, I, 215 ff.; *Aarbøger* (1944).

52. Sometimes encircled by an annular ditch, *Aarbøger* (1944), 170.

53. Glob, *Aarbøger* (1944), 207, implicitly dates the beginning to M.N.IIb (IIIa), Becker, *Acta. Arch.*, XXV (1954), 114, 127, explicitly to M.N.III (IIIc).

54. Forssander, *Die schwedische Bootaxtkultur* (Lund, 1933).

55. Hinsch, 'Yngre steinalders stridsøkskulturer i Norge', Bergen Universitets *Årbok* (1954), No. 1.

56. *SM.* (1952), 22–5; cf. *SMYA.*, XXXII, 1, 152 ff. For Esthonia, see Gerasimov, *Litsa*, 396–9; the skulls closely resemble those from Pontic *yamno* graves.

57. van Giffen, *Die Bauart der Einzelgräber*; Stampfuss, *Jungneol. Kul-*

turen; *NNU.*, II (1928), 20; Albrecht, 'Die Hügelgräber der jüngeren Steinzeit in Westfalen', *Westfalen*, XIX (1934), 122 ff.; Glasbergen, *Palaeohistoria*, V, VI.

58. See e.g. *Offa*, I (1936), 62–77.

59. *Kiel-Festschrift* (1936), 79.

60. *Aarboger* (1936), 145 ff., for parallels from Holstein, see *Mannus*, XXVII (1935), 60; cf. Brøndsted, *Danmarks*, I, 269–75, and *Acta Arch.*, XXV, 74–6.

61. *JST.*, XIV, 30; XXIV, 115.

62. Forssander, *Bootaxtkultur*, 146.

63. *Mannus*, XXV (1933), 271–82.

64. E.g. *Danube*, fig. 92.

65. *Nbl. f. d. V.*, X (1934), 146; XIV, 73; Witter, *Die älteste Erzgewinnung in nordgerman. Lebenskreis*.

66. *PA.*, XL (1934–5), 21.

67. Behrens, *JMV.*, XXXVI (1952), 52–65.

68. *Mannus*, XXVIII (1936), 363; *Nbl. f. d. V.*, IX (1933), 93.

69. Forssander, *Bootaxtkultur*, 164; *Årsberät.* (1937–8), 38.

70. *Germania*, VI (1922), 110 (Haldorf near Cassel); *Mannus*, VI, Erg.-Bd., 214 (Sarmenstorf, Switzerland).

71. *Altschles.*, V (1934), 37; *Mannus*, XXVIII, 376.

72. Killian, *Die Haffküstenkultur* (Bonn, 1955).

73. *Altschles.*, V, 62.

74. Childe, *Danube*, 152; Kozłowski, *Młodsa*, 66; *WA.*, VIII, 98; IX, 34.

75. *Pravek*, V (1909), 56–130; Real., s.v. *Drevohostice*.

76. *Księga Pamietkowa*, 141–9; *Swiatowit*, XVI (1934–5), 117–44; Sulimirski, 'Die schnurkeramischen Kulturen', 3–5.

77. Kostrzewski, *Prehistoria*, 183; *Swiatowit*, XIX (1946–7), 105 ff.

78. Material from 300 graves at Nitra, unpublished.

79. Briusov, *Očerki*, 215–20; *KS.*, XVI (1947).

80. *Arkh. Pam.*, IV (1952), 112–21; *Arkheologiya*, Kiev, VIII (1953), 94–101.

81. Sprockhoff, *Mark-Brandenburg*, 60 ff., 160; *Mannus*, XXVIII, 374.

82. Forssander, *Ostskandinav.*, 60; Böhm, *Bronzezeit Mark-Brandenburg*, 30.

83. *PrzegA.*, VIII (1949), 256.

84. Tretyakov, *IGAIMK.*, 106, 126–8; *SA.*, II 32; cf. *FM.* (1924), 1 ff. Häusler, *Wissenschaftliche Zts. d Martin-Luther Universität*, Halle-Wittenberg, V (1955–6), H. 1 (*Arbeiten aus d. Inst. f. Vor- u. Frühgeschichte*, 5) gives a convenient German summary of the Russian literature.

85. *KS.*, XVI (1947), 22–32.

86. *Problemy GAIMK.* (1934), Nos. 11–12.

87. *SA.*, II, 33–5.

88. *TGIM.*, XII (1941), 125.

89. As by Äyräpää, *ESA.*, VIII, 16–23.

90. *SA.*, IV, 302.

91. *SA.*, XXII, 120.

92. *TGIM.*, VIII, 63. Showing that the models from Mikhalic and Tripolye sites are not necessarily ritual objects!

93. *TGIM.*, XII, 132.

94. *SA.*, VI, 79.

95. *TGIM.*, VIII, 70.

96. *TGIM.*, XII (1941), 119, 135–7.
97. *KS.*, XVI, 30.
98. *ESA.*, II, 137 ff.
99. *SA.*, II, 30 ff.; III, 38; *IGAIMK.*, 106, 100 ff.
100. *Sovietskaya Etnografiya* (1949), 3, 72; (1950), 3, 37.
101. *Očerki*, 94.
102. e.g. Äyräpää, *ESA.*, VIII, 101–10.
103. Sulimirksi, *PPS.*, XXI, 118–22.
104. 'Ursprung und Verbreitung der Urfinnen und Urindogermanen', *Mannus*, I–II.
105. *Das nordische Kulturgebiet* (1918).
106. Most recently by Killian, *Die Haffküstenkultur* (Bonn, 1955), who relies, in addition to battle-axes, on the skeuomorphic pattern impressed or painted on amphorae.
107. 'Snurova keramika na Ukrajine,' *Obzor* IX (1930), cf. *PA.* (1933).
108. *Bootaxtkultur*, 174, 213.
109. *PPS.*, XXI (1955), 108 ff.
110. 'Indogermanskiĭ vopros arkheologičeski razrešennyĭ', *IGAIMK.*, 100 (1933), 158 ff.

Chapter 10   The Northern Cultures

1. cf. P. V. Glob, *Danske Oldsager*, II (Copenhagen, 1952).
2. e.g. N. Åberg in *Das nordische Kulturgebiet*, and Reinerth, *Chronologie der jüngeren Steinzeit*.
3. Helbaek in *Aarbøger* (1954), 202–4.
4. *Aarbøger* (1953), 5–62.
5. Becker, *Aarbøger* (1954, published in 1956), 127–97.
6. *Aarbøger* (1953), 16–21.
7. *Aarbøger* (1947), 205 ff.; (1954), 168–9.
8. Iversen, 'Landnam i Danmarks Stenalder', *Dansk. Geol. Undersog.*, R. II, No. 66 (1941).
9. Mathiassen, *Aarbøger*, 1940, 3–16.
10. Bagge and Kjellmark, *Stenålders Boplatserna* (1939); but cf. *Acta Arch.*, XXII (1951), 88 ff., where the first occupation is attributed to Northern II= E.N.C.
11. Brøndsted, *Danmarks*, I, 130, 338.
12. Florin, 'Vrå-Kulturen', *Kulturhistoriska Studier tillägnade N. Åberg* (Stockholm, 1938).
13. *FNA.* (1949).
14. Nordmann, 'Megalithic Culture', fig. 63.
15. *Aarbøger* (1947), 250–55.
16. ibid., 141 ff.
17. *Aarbøger* (1941), 63–8; (1947), 266.
18. Nordmann, 'Megalithic Culture', 26.
19. *Aarbøger* (1936), (1936), 1–8.
20. Forssander (1935–6), 2 ff.; *NNU.*, X (1936), 22 f.; *Aarbøger* (1936),15; (1947), 141 ff.; Brøndsted, *Danmarks*, I, 162, 344.
21. Nordmann, 'Megalithic Culture', 28.
22. Mathiassen, *Acta Arch.*, XV, 88; cf. Becker, ibid., XXV, 50–66.
23. Winther, *Trøldebjerg* (Rudkøbing), 1935, and Tillaeg, 1938.
24. Nomardnn,'Megalithic Culture', 131, fig. 60.

25. Forssander, *Ostskandinavische*, 10, 51, etc., Kersten, *Zur älteren nordischen Bronzezeit*, 72, 98.

26. *Arch.*, LXXXVI (1936), 277.

27. *Aarbøger* (1929), 204.

28. I follow the division established on the basis of settlement finds by Mathiassen in *Acta Arch.*, XV (1944), 89–97, rather than that of Eckholm, *Real.*, IX, 42; cf. now Lili Kaelas, *Fv.* (1951), 352–7.

29. These ceramic types, though proper to Danubian II in Hungary and Moravia, may have reached Denmark indirectly from the Upper Elbe-Oder region and, if so, would not justify a synchronism between Northern IIIa and Danubian II as suggested by Schwabedessin, *Offa*, XII (1953), 58–64; cf., Milojčić, *Germania*, XXXIII (1955), 401–4.

30. Winther, *Blandebjerg* (Rudkøbing, 1940).

31. Forssander, 'Gropornerad Megalithkeramik', *Årsberättelse* (1930–31), 10–30.

32. Becker, *Acta Arch.*, XXV (1954), 22–5.

33. Kaelas, *Fv.* (1951), 352–7; Bagge and Kaelas, *Acta Arch.*, XXII (1951), 118; Becker, *Acta Arch.*, XXV 55–66; Berg, 'Klintebakken', *Medd. Langelands Mus.* (Rudkøbing, 1951).

34. Becker, *Aarbøger* (1950), 155–251.

35. Nordmann, 'Megalithic', 122; Glob, *Danske Oldsager*, II, 119, 196; cf. *Acta Arch.*, XXV, 80.

36. Childe, *NLMAE.*, pl. XVI, a.

37. *Z Otchłani Wieków*, XVIII (1949), 184; *WA.*, XVII, 120.

38. *WA.*, XVII (1950), 228; cf. *Germanenerbe*, IV (1939), 240; Hančar, *Das Pferd*, 34–7.

39. *WA.*, XVII, pl. XXXV, 1.

40. *WA.*, VII, 53–4; Krukowski, *Krzemionki Opatowskie* (Warszawa, 1939), *Dawna Kultura*, IV (Wroclaw, 1955) 204.

41. *WA.*, XVII, 143.

42. Jazdrzewski, 'Kultura Puharów Lejkowatych w Polsce' (*Bibliotheka Prehist.*, 2 (Poznan, 1936), 365–8.

43. cf. also *WA.*, XVII, pls. XXXVII–XLI.

44. Jazdrzewski, op. cit.; for Holland, van Giffen in *Drenthe* (1943), 435.

45. W. Chmielewski, 'Zagadanie Grobowców Kujawskich' (*Biblioteka Muz. Archeol.*, (2), Lódz, 1952. He regards them as collective tombs, but the maximum number of interments recorded was ten and the skeletons were not buried together in a single chamber.

46. Sprockhoff, *Megalithkultur*, 25–31.

47. ibid., 59 ff.; van Giffen, *Hunebedden*.

48. The flint celts too are thin-butted, but diverge from the Danish forms, Sprockhoff, *NNU.*, IV (1930), 36.

49. Sprockhoff, *Megalithkultur*, 59 f.; cf. *Westfalen*, XIX (1934), 150–57.

50. *Mannus*, XXV (1933), 131–2; Kuhn, *Die Felsbilder Europas* (1952), 153–4.

51. Sangmeister, *Die Glockenbecher* . . . (*Die Jungsteinzeit in Nordmainischen Hessen*, III), Melsingen, 1951, p. 73 and n. 246.

52. *Universitets Oldsaksamling Årbok* (Oslo, 1951–3), 140–60.

53. *Aarbøger* (1947), 262.

54. ibid., (1953), 61.

55. *Acta Arch.*, XXIV (1953), 174–86.

56. *Aarbøger* (1954).

57. *Antiquity*, XXIII (1949), 130–35; *PPS.*, XXI, 96–101.

58. Potratz *NNU.*, XV (1941), quoted by Milojčić, *Chron.*, 97.

59. Glob, *Acta Arch.*, X (1939), 132–9.

60. Sprockhoff, *Megalithkultur*, 10, emphasizes the similarity of such a long barrow to a 'house with low-pitched gabled roof'.

61. *NNU.*, VII 50; X (1936), 22.

62. Childe, *Danube*, 133–9; Sprockhoff, *Megalithkultur*, 106–16.

63. Grimm, *Mannus*, XXIX (1937), 186 ff.

64. *JST.*, XXIX (1938), 20 ff. For the culture sequence in Central Germany, see Mildenberger, *Studien zum Mitteldeutschen Neolithikum* (Leipzig, 1951); Behrans, *JMV.* (1953), 105; Fischer, *Festschr, d. Röm-Germ. Zentralmuseums*, III (Mainz, 1953), 175.

65. Sprockhoff, *Megalithkultur*, 120–30; *Mark-Brandenburg*, 108; *JST.*, XXVIII (1938).

66. Stocký, *Bohème préhist.*, 128; *Proc. Amer. Philos. Soc.*, LXXXI (1932), 380.

67. Levitskiï, *Antropolgiya*, II (Kiev, 1928); *Zapiski Vse-Ukrainskogo Arkh. Komitetu*, I (Kiev, 1931); Briusov, *Očerki*, 220–23.

68. *Offa*, XII (1953), 8–9.

69. *Germania*, XXXIII (1955), 239.

70. *Bootaxtkultur*, 174.

71. *AR.*, VI (1954), 652–8.

72. Böhm, *Die ältere Bronzezeit in der Mark-Brandenburg*, 32.

73. Forssander, *Ostskandinavishce*, 162.

74. ibid., 118, fig. 23; Brøndsted, *Danmarks*, I, fig. 251.

75. Forssander, 95 f., 116 ff.; Kersten, *Nordischen Bronzezeit*, 98; Broholm, *Danmarks Bronzealder*, 2 (1944), 30 ff.

76. Nordmann, 'Megalithic Culture', 44.

77. Forssander, *Ostskandinavische*, 114, 140, 156; Brøndsted, *Danmarks*, 290.

78. *AsA.*, XL (1938), 14.

79. Forssander, *Ostskandinavische*, 176, 196; Kersten, *Nordischen Bronzezeit*, 100.

80. Kersten, *Zur älteren nordischen Bronzezeit*, 65.

81. Broholm, *Danmarks Bronzealder*, 1, 224; M81.

82. *Acta Arch.*, XXV, 241.

83. Hawkes, *BSA.*, XXXVII, 144–51.

84. *PZ.*, XX (1929), 128 ff.

85. e.g. Irish axes from Dieskau and Leubingen, *Arch.*, LXXXVI, 303; *PPS.*, IV, 272 ff. Note that the Irish axe from Dieskau is rich in tin, the other 'bronzes' from the hoard contain none! *JMV.*, XXXIV (1950), 90 ff.

86. *JST.*, V, 1–59; *Arch.*, LXXXVI (1936), 205; cf. also *JST.*, VI (Helmsdorf); I (Baalberg), and perhaps Kuttlau, Silesia (*Götze-Fest.*, 84–9), and Anderlingen, Hanover, *Jb. Prov Mus. Hannover*, 1907–8, 242–4, and *Arch.*, LXXXVI, 225.

87. Kowiańska-Piaszykowa and Kurnatowski, 'Kurhan Kultury Unietyckiej', *Fontes Archaeol. Posnanienses*, IV (Poznan, 1954), 1–34 (with analyses of bronzes, and English résumé).

88. Childe, *Danube*, 242–4.

89. *Götze-Fest.*, 93, and *PZ.*, XVI, 205; cf. p. 387 below.

90. *PZ.*, XXXIV (1949–50), 238, Taf. 15, 1; cf. Childe, *NLMAE.*, fig. 91; Jahn in *JMV.*, XXXV (1951), 65–70.

91. See for halberds O'Riordain's map, *Arch.*, LXXXVI, 277, and for narrow double-axes, Sturm's *Die Bronzezeit im Ostbaltikum* (Berlin, 1936), 32.

92. cf. Childe, *Danube*, 313.

93. One bronze-shafted halberd of Saale-Warta type is said to have been found with a socketed celt, *Mannus*, XIII (1923), 42–55.

94. So the characteristic Wessex and Armorican daggers seem to be derived from the Elbe-Oder type, the Anglo-Armorican gold-studded hilts were copied in the Saale region, Wessex amber pendants copy bronze-hilted halberds.

Chapter 11   Survivals of the Forest Culture

1. E.g. at Panfilovo in Central Russia, *IGAIMK.*, 106 (1935), 125.

2. M. Stenberger, *Das Grabfeld von Västerbjers auf Gotland* (Stockholm, 1943).

3. *SA.*, VI (1940), 46–62; cf. Gerasimov, *Litsa*, 296–320; physically the population was mixed Europeoid and Mongoloid.

4. The techniques have been admirably described by Voyevodskiǐ, *SA.*, I (1935), 51–78.

5. Made at first with the curved and notched edge of a flat pebble, later with short-toothed bone combs figured by Voyevodskiǐ, loc. cit.

6. Bagge, *Acta Arch.*, XXII (1951), 56–88.

7. Äyräpää, *Acta Arch.*, I, 165–90, 205 ff.; he discusses correlations with Sweden in *FM.*, LXII (1955), 26–50.

8. *MIA.*, XX (1951), 77–140.

9. e.g. Foss, *MIA.*, XXIX (1952); Briusov, *Očerki*.

10. Wrongly since good comb-ware is cited in *SM.*, LVII (1950), 5–22.

11. Also transverse arrow heads; *SM.*, LIV (1947–8), 1–18; LVII(1950), 9.

12. Lower Veretye (Foss, *MIA.*, XXIX), Pogostišče, 1 (ibid., XX, 46), cf. Briusov, *Očerki*, 28–31.

13. Mapped by Gurina, *MIA.*, XX, 95.

14. *MIA.*, XX (1951), 110 ,Gurina's group 3; *SM.*, LX (1953), 33–44 – F.III!

15. *SA.*, III, 101; V, 44; cf. Clark, *Ant. J.*, XXVIII (1928), 67–8.

16. Imprints of nets are often found on pit-comb ware, *IGAIMK.*, 106, 118.

17. Finds listed and mapped by Foss, *MIA.*, XXIX (1952), 46; cf. *TGIM.*, XXIX, 108 f.

18. *FM.*, LXII, 30–33; Briusov, *Očerki*, 58, 69.

19. Aïlio, *Wohnplatzfunde*, 29, 33; *SGAIMK.* (1931), No. 6, 7, found with contracted skeleton in an 'ochre grave'.

20. Veretye and Kubenino, *MIA.*, XXIX; Lyalovo, near Moscow, *RAZ.*, XIV (1925), 37.

21. *Fv.* (1924), 298; *RAZ.*, XIV, loc cit.

22. *SM.*, LVI (1949), 1–26.

23. *SM.*, XLI, 1–10.

24. Clark, *Preh. Europe*, 283, pl. IV, b.

25. *Acta Arch.*, I, 210.

26. *Real.*, VI, 222.

27. Brøgger, *Den arktiske Stenålder*, 185; *Real.*, I, 436; *IGAIMK.*, 106, 132.

28. *Aarbøger* (1950), 155–245.

29. *Preh. Europe*, 88, 256.

30. North Russian burials are described and listed by Gerasimov, *Vosta-novlenie litsa po čerepu* (*Trudy Inst. Etnografiya*, XXVIII), Moscow, 1955, 328–65. Stenberger, *Das Grabfeld* . . .; the cemetery should be Northern III, D, or F.III.

31. *SA.*, VI (1940), 46–62; Ravdonikas dates the cemetery to F.III or IV, but Briusov (*Očerki*, 108) to the Atlantic phase, i.e. F.O.! See also Gerasimov, op. cit.

32. Foss, *MIA.*, XXIX, 35 ff.; Äyräpää, *SM.*, XLVIII (1941), 82–119. Save perhaps for the bone figurine from Deer I., all seem late.

33. Bøe, *Felsenzeichnungen in westlichen Norwegen* (Bergen, 1932).

34. Ravdonikas, *Les Gravures rupestres des bords du lac Onega et de la Mer Blanche* (*Trudy Inst. Etnografiya*), Moscow, 1936, 1938.

35. Zamiatnin, 'Miniatiurnye kremnevye skulptury', *SA.*, X (1948); Hausler, *Wiss. Zts. d. Martin-Luther Universität*, Halle-Wittenberg, III (1954), 767–82.

36. Briusov, *Očerki*, 35–6; *KS. Inst. Etnografiya*, XVIII (1953), 55–65; Gerasimov, *Vostanovlenie litsa* (1955), 296–395.

37. *Aarbøger* (1950), 251.

38. *Očerki*, 30–40, 164–74, 147–9; Äyräpää, too, seems to favour a south-east origin for pit-comb ware, *FM.*, LXII, 32.

39. *TGIM.*, XXIX (1956), 70.

40. e.g. *MIA.*, XVIII, 169 ff.; but some pots in addition to pits bear net impressions.

41. Hančar, *Kaukasiens*, pl. XXIX.

42. A. Rosenberg, *Kulturströmungen in Europa zur Steinzeit* (Copenhagen, 1931).

43. Okladnikov, *MIA.*, XVIII (1950), 220.

44. *SM.*, LIX (1952), 6–24.

45. *ESA.*, XI (1937), 16–30; *MIA.*, XX (1951), 133.

46. Tallgren, 'Ett viktigt fornfynd', *FM.* (1915), 73 ff., and *ESA.*, II (1926), 137, remains the best publication of this 'hoard'.

47. Childe, *Inst. Arch.*, *AR.*, X (1954), 11–25.

48. Clark, *Northern Europe*, 186; *SM.*, XXXV (1928), 36–43.

For further details consult in addition to works mentioned in the footnotes:
On Norway: 'Vistefundet', *Stavanger Museums Årsheft*, 1907; Gjessing, *Norges Stenälder* (Oslo, 1945).
On Latvia; Balodis, *Det äldsta Lettland* (Uppsala, 1940).
On Estonia: Moora, *Die Vorzeit Estlands* (Tartu, 1932).
On Finland: Ailio, *Steinzeitliche Wohnplatzfunde in Finland* (Helsinki, 1909).
On the whole region: Gjessing, 'The Circum-Polar Stone Age', *Acta Arctica*, II (Copenhagen, 1944).

Chapter 12   Megalith Builders and Beaker-folk

1. V. Correia, 'El Neolitico de Pavia', *Mem. CIPP.*, XXVII (1921), 63 f.; cf. Forde, *Am. Anthr.*, XXXII (1930), 41.

2. Elliot Smith, 'The Evolution of the Rock-cut Tomb and Dolmen', in *Essays and Studies presented to Sir William Ridgeway* (Cambridge, 1913), was a pioneer in this interpretation.

3. cf. Daniel, *PPS.*, VII (1941), 1–49.

4. *Antiquity*, XIII, 376.

5. Crawford, *Long Barrows of the Cotswolds*, 21; Daniel, *Antiquity*, XI (1937), 183–200.

6. For instance Adam's Grave near Dunoon is just a segmented cist reduced to a single segment.

7. *Marburger Studien*, I (1938), 147–55.

8. *Arch.*, LXVIII, 266.

9. Kendrick, *Axe Age*, 48.

10. *BP.*, XLIII, 17, fig. 6.

11. *Arch.*, LXXXVI, 132; *PPS.*, IV (1938), 201.

12. *BP.*, XVIII, 75; *Ausonia*, I, 7; *Not. Sc.* (1920), 304; Correia, 'Pavia', 72; Childe, *Prehistory of Scotland*, 26, 33. Vestiges of such a forecourt can be seen in Balearic navétas (*CIPMO.*, 26), and with timber revetment in English unchambered long-barrows (p. 375, below).

13. Nordmann, *Megalithic*, figs. 36–9.

14. *Arch. Camb.* (1927), 13, 17.

15. Childe, *Scotland*, 43; Nordmann, *Megalithic*, 28.

16. *PPS.*, IV, 147; *Aarboger* (1915), 319; Nordmann, *Megalithic*, 30.

17. Hemp, in *PPS.*, I (1935), 110.

18. In Eyre, *European Civilization*, II, 182.

19. Perry, *The Growth of Civilization*.

20. *L'Anthr.*, XLIII (1933), 248; Childe, *Scotland*, 43; Nordmann, 'Megalithic', 122; Leisner, *Megalithgräber*, 554.

21. *Arch.*, LXX, 215 ff.; 'El Dolmen de Matarubilla' (*CIPP.*, 26); *Real.*, X, 358; *Rev. Anthr.*, XL (1930), 244 ff.; *Préhistoire*, II (1933), 189 f.

22. *BSR.*, V (1910), 87–137; VI, 127–70.

23. *Am. Anthr.*, XXXII, 16.

24. *Antiquity*, XIII (1939), 376–7.

25. Brøndsted, *Danmarks*, 198, 345.

26. *CIAA.*, 1930 (Portugal), 356.

27. *Časopis vlastenického spolku museijniho v Olomouci*, XLI (1929), T. 11; Forssander, *Ostskand. Norden*, 70.

28. *Germania*, XXXIII (1955), 13–22.

29. General review in A. del Castillo, *La Cultura del Vaso campaniforme* (Barcelona, 1928), and 'Cronologia de la cultura del vaso campaniforme', *Arquivo Español de Archeologia*, LIII (1943), 388–435; (1944), 1–67; add for Belgium, Mariën, *Bul. Musées roy. d'Art et d'Hist.* (Brussels, 1948), 16–48; for Poland, Żurowski, *Wiad. Arch.*, XI (1932), 116–56; for Central Germany, Neumann, *PZ.*, XX (1929), 35 ff.; for North Germany, *NNU.*, II (1928), 25 ff.; X, 20; for Holland, Bursch, *Oudh. Med.*, XIV (1933), 39–122.

30. Savory, *Revista Guimarães*, LX (1950), 363 ff.

31. e.g. Castillo, pls. VII, 4 (Andalusia); L, 2 (Portugal); LXI (Castellon); LXXVI, 1 (Catalonia); LXXXIV (Galicia); XCIV (Hautes Pyrenées); CIII (Brittany); CXIX, 2 (Sicily); CXXIII (Po valley); CL, 7 (Bohemia); CLII, 8 (Moravia); CLXXXII, 2 (Middle Rhine).

32. Nordmann, 'Megalithic', 100; *Actas y Mem.*, XIV (1935), Noticiario, 5; Bosch-Gimpera, *Man*, XL (1940), 2; but the stratigraphy of Somaen on which the latter relies does not, as published, afford any clue as to the relations between my 'classic' and 'grand' styles; Savory, loc. cit., 169.

33. Childe, *Scotland*, 83; *PCBI.*, 93.

34. *Corona d'Estudis dedica a sus Martires* (Madrid, 1941), 128.

35. *Mat.*, 1881, 552; Cazalis de Fondouce, *Les Allées couvertes de Provence*; *L'Anthr.* XLIV, 507; Childe, *Danube*, 191, 193.

36. *PA.*, XXXIX (1933), 50–53; cf. pp. 102, 106.

37. e.g. Villafrati in Sicily, commonly in the caves of Monges, near Narbonne, in Central and Northern Spain and in Portugal.

38. e.g. Anghelu Ruju, Sardinia; Palmella and Alapraia (Portugal).

39. e.g. at Los Millares and other Almerian sites, and in Var.

40. e.g. in Brittany and Portugal.

41. e.g. in Brittany and in the Paris basin.

42. Puig Rodo (Catalonia) and La Halliade (Hautes Pyrénées).

43. Childe, *Danube*, 192; cf. *Mannus*, XXXI (1939), 467 ff., for a cemetery of twenty-four graves in Swabia.

44. *PZ.*, XX, 45.

45. *Oudh. Med.* (1933), 120.

46. *Bol. R. Acad.* Madrid, LXXI, 22 ff.

47. Gerhardt, *Die Glockenbecherleute in Mittel- und West-Deutschland* (Stuttgart, 1953).

48. Schuchhardt, *PZ.*, I (1909), 43.

49. Childe, *NLMAE.*, 34, fig. 10; cf. pl. XVIIIb for Mesopotamian analogies.

50. Mond and Myres, *Cemeteries of Armant*, 268 ff., Arkell, *Early Khartoum*, pl. 89; Vaufrey, *Inst. Pal. Hum.*, *Mem.*, 20 (1939), 72 ff.

51. *Germania*, XXXIII (1955), 13–22.

52. Childe, *NLMAE.*, 98, fig. 39.

53. Castillo, op. cit., Bosch-Gimpera, *Real.*, X, 356; *PPS.*, XXIX, 95 ff.

54. Forssander, *Ostskand. Norden*, 37; Childe, *Am. Anthr.*, XXXIX (1937), 10.

55. Childe, *Danube*, 190; Forssander, *Ostskand. Norden*, 72; *Mannus*, XXXI, 478, fig. 17.

56. *PZ.*, XXV, 137.

Chapter 13   Farmers and Traders in Italy and Sicily

1. *The Stone and Bronze Ages in Italy and Sicily* (Oxford, 1909). No equally comprehensive survey has superseded this work save for Sicily, where Bernabo Brea, 'La Sicilia prehistorica', *Ampurias*, XV–XVI (1954), has replaced Orsi's system.

2. Bernabo Brea, *Gli Scavi nella Caverna delle Arene Candide*, II (Bordighera, 1956) (cited *AC.*, II), 155–292.

3. Perhaps at Coppa Nevigata, *MA.*, XIX (1909), 340–45; cf. *AC.*, II, 162–6.

4. Bradford, in *Antiquity*, XX (1946), 191; XXIII, 60–65; XXIV, 86–8.

5. *BP.*, XLIV (1924), 107–21; *MA.*, XX, 238 ff.

6. *BP.*, XLV, 92.

7. But on Lipari the querns are saucer- or even trough-shaped.

8. Stevenson, *PPS.*, XIII (1947), 88–92.

9. Rellini, *La più antica Ceramica dipinta in Italia* (Rome, 1935), 56–62.

10. Rellini, op. cit. The style of painting represented on Capri, Lipari, and Sicily diverges substantially from the Apulian.

11. Bernabo Brea, *APL.*, III (1952); *BP.*, n.s., X (1956), 18–24.

12. e.g., at Molfetta, *MA.*, XX, 251–8; Mosso mistook the ruined wall for a street!

13. *BP.* (1956), 25–8.

14. *MA.*, XX, 255–8; Rellini, *Ceramica*, 67; Mayer, *Matera und Molfetta*, Leipzig (1924), 20–30.

15. Mayer, *Matera*, 67, pl. IX, 19; *BP.* (1956), 27; analogies to the Italian *pintadere* come from early Aegean levels at Gözlu Kale (Tarsus) in Cilicia, *AJA.*, XLII (1938), 39 – and from Neolithic Byblos.

16. *Riv. Sc. Pr.*, VIII (1953), 86–93.

17. *BP.* (1956), 31.

18. *BP.*, XXXII (1906), 36–48.

19. *BP.*, XLV, 113.

20. *BP.*, XXV (1898), 53; XXXIV (1908), 119; XLV, 62.

21. *Ampurias* (1954), 158–60.

22. *MA.*, XL (1944), 1–170.

23. *Annales de Géol. et Paléontol.* (Palermo, 1900), No. 28.

24. *APL.*, III, 85–7; *BP.* (1956), 51.

25. Arias in *MA.*, XXXVI (1937), 695–838.

26. *Ampurias* (1954), 181–2; *APL.*, III (1952), 78–9.

27. von Duhn, *Italische Gräberkunde*, 71–9.

28. *Antiquity*, XXX (1956), 80–94.

29. *BP.*, XLIII, pl. II, 6.

30. von Duhn, pls. 4, 18; 6, 22 and 7, 23; *BP.*, XVIII, 75; *Not. Sc.* (1920), 304; *Ausonia*, I, 7.

31. *BP.*, XXIV, 202.

32. *MA.*, XVIII, 643; *BP.*, XXXVI, pl. 12.

33. *Ampurias* (1954),177–8.

34. *BP.* (1956), 43–52.

35. Not in the same tomb as the Beaker, though with the same local variety of pottery.

36. Fullest list by Levi in *Paoli Orsi a cura dell'Archivio Storico per Calabria* (Rome, 1935); cf. *BP.* (1936–7), 57 ff.

37. Evans, *Arch.*, LIX, 1906, 108 ff.

38. *P. of M.*, I, 3.

39. Buchner, *BP.*, n.s., I (1936–7), 65.

40. *Ampurias* (1954), 184; *BP.* (1956), 56–7.

41. *APL.*, III, 71–4, 80; *BP.* (1956), 53–63.

42. At a different place to the pithos cemetery; *Ampurias* (1954), 203–5; *BP.* (1956), 78.

43. *Ampurias* (1954), 203–5.

44. E.g., Punto del Tonno, Taranto, Säflund in *Dragma Martino P. Nilsson* (Skrifter Svensk. Intsī), Rome, 1939, 458 ff.

45. *Riv. Sc. Pre.*, VIII (1953), 89–93.

46. *BP.*, XXI (1905), 153; Quagliati, *La Puglia preistorica* (Trani, 1936); *MA.*, XXVI (1921), 494.

47. *LAAA.*, II, 80; *BP.*, XLIV, 116; ibid., n.s. (1938), 42; *Riv. Sc. Pre.*, V (1950), 126; von Duhn, 72–4.

48. Gervasio, *I Dolmen* (Bari, 1913).

49. ibid., p. 63.

50. ibid., p. 68.

51. *Riv. Antr.*, LXI (1954), 1–31.

52. Stevenson, *PPS.*, XIII, 197.

53. *Riv. Sc. Pr.*, I (1946), 249, 257; II, 284–92.

54. *St. Et.*, XIII (1939), 58.

55. A sepulchral cave at Sasso near Civitavecchia containing a hundred skeletons (one with trepanned skull), sling bullets but no arrow-heads is assigned by the excavator (*BP.*, VIII (1953), 43–8; *Riv. d'Antr.*, XLI (1954), 40–50) to 'Middle Neolithic', but a cup with elongated handle would seem more appropriate to an Upper Neo. or even Apennine context.

56. To Peet's list add *BP.*, XL, 53; XLIII, 97; n.s. VIII (1951), 109; *Atti* I₀. *Con. Preh. Med.* (Firenze, 1950), 334–40; *Riv. Sc. Pr.*, V (1950), 122; VI, 3, 151.

57. *Archivio per Antrop. ed Etnog.*, XLII (1912), 263; *BP.*, XXXVIII (1923), 132.

58. Puglisi, *Riv. Antrop.*, LXI, 1–22.

59. Especially Belleverde (Cetona), *Not. Sc.* (1933), 50 ff.; *St. Et.*, X (1936), 330–38; XII, 227 ff.; and Manacore (Gargano), *BSR.*, XIX (1951), 23–38; XXI, 1–31.

60. According to Bernabo Brea, *AC.*, II, 259, Belleverde does in fact go back to the Rinaldone phase.

61. *BP.*, XXVI (1900), T.I., but cf. ibid., n.s. (1938), 64.

62. Säflund, *Dragma Martino P. Nilsson*, 458 ff.; *Not. Sc.* (1900), 440–64.

63. *Gli Scavi nella Caverna delle Arene Candide*, Bordighera, I (1946), II, 1956.

64. Escalon de Fonton 'Les stratigraphies du néolithique', *Bull. Musée d'Anthropologie préhistorique de Monaco*, II (1955), 245–52.

65. *Riv. St. Lig.*, XV (1949), 28; *AC.*, II, 218.

66. Found in M.N. layers 21, 23, and 24, but also in L.N. layers 25 and 27, *AC.*, II, 65; cf. Vogt, *CISPP.*, 3 (Zurich, 1950), 33.

67. *AC.*, II, 91–5.

68. *BP.*, XLIII, 110.

69. Antler sleeves and other types in bone and horn, so prominent in the Swiss lake-dwellings, are totally absent from the Lagozzian collections in the museums of Como and Varese, and pan-pipe lugs are euqally missing, cf. *Sibrium*, II, Centro di Studi Preistorici (Varese, 1955), 99.

70. *Appunti per una cronologia relativa neo-eneolitico emiliano*, Centro Emiliano di Studi preistorici (Modena, 1953); cf. *St. Et.*, XVII (1943), 3–19; *BP.* (1952), 13–38.

71. Found also in a cemetery of contracted burials at Quinzano near Verona.

72. cf. recent lists, Åberg, *Chronologie*, iii, 8, and van Duhn in *Real.*, s.v. *Italien*.

73. *BP.*, LII, 9 f.; Forssander, *Ostskandinavische*, fig. 10.

74. *BP.*, XLI (1915), pl. 1.

75. *MAGW.*, LXI (1931), 74–80; p. 299 below.

76. Relation to cemetery uncertain, Castillo, *Campaniforme*, 133.

77. Laviosa Zambotti, *St. Et.*, XIII, 50 ff.; *BP.* (1940), 120 ff.

78. *BP.*, (1940) 69–79.

79. Battaglia, 'La palafitta di Lago di Ledro', *Mem. del Museo di Storia Naturale della Venezia Tridentana*, VII (Trento, 1943).

80. *BP.*, XVII (1891), 1–12.

81. Bicknell, *Rock Engravings in the Maritime Alps* (Bordighera).

82. At Ledro *Triticum monococcum* and *dicoccum*, *Hordeum hexastichon*, *Panicum miliacum*.

83. Lorimer, *JHS.*, XXIII (1903), 132–51.

84. Säflund, *Le Terremare* (Rome, Svenska Institut, 1939).

85. cf. Bernabo Brea, *A.C.*, II, 276.

86. J. Sundwall, *Die ältere italischer Fibeln* (Stockholm, 1943).

87. Säflund, *Le Terremare*, 157, n. 1, considers that a sword, bearing the cartouche of Seti II who died in 1198, is of *terramara* type.

88. Montelius, *CPI.*, 200.

89. *St. Et.*, XII (1938), 18–22.

90. Bicknell, *Prehistoric Rock Engraving in the Italian Maritime Alps* (Bordighera), 1913.

91. M. O. Acanfora, 'Le Statue antropomorfe dell'Alto Adige', Università di Padova, *Studi sulla Regione Trentino-Alto Adige* (Bolzano, 1953).

Chapter 14   Island Civilizations in the Western Mediterranean

1. L. Hogben, *Science for the Citizen*, 106.

2. The best collection of illustrations and plans of Maltese monuments and relics is L. M. Ugolini, *Malta : Origini della Civiltà Mediterranea* (Rome, 1934), but the views expressed there are scarcely plausible.

3. The culture sequence has been established on an objective basis by John Evans, *PPS.*, XIX (1953), 45–89.

4. cf. T. Zammit, *Prehistoric Malta ; the Tarcsien Temples* (Oxford, 1930).

5. Noted first by Leeds, *LAAA.*, IX (1922), 35 ff.

6. T. Zammit, *The Neolithic Temples of Hajar Kim and Mnaidra* (Valetta, 1927), 9 and 28.

7. ibid., 13; the resultant effect is that of the alternating buttresses and recesses that adorn the façades of early Egyptian mastabas and Sumerian temples; cf. Childe, *NLMAE.*, 85 and 125.

8. *BSR.*, XXII (1954), 1–21.

9. *JRAI.*, LIV, 67 ff., *IPEK.* (1927), 131.

10. *BSR.*, XXII, 13, pl. III.

11. ibid., 11.

12. *LAAA.*, III (1910), 1–22.

13. *PPS.*, XIX, 44–62.

14. ibid., 55.

15. Evans, *P. of M.*, II, 182–9.

16. The best illustrations of the cemetery furniture are given by M. A. Murray, *Corpus of Bronze Age Pottery of Malta* (London, 1934).

17. Curiously like some figurines from Middle Bronze Age sites near the Iron Gates on the Danube, e.g. Hoernes-Menghin, *Urgeschichte der bildenden Kunst* (Vienna, 1925), 411.

18. e.g. *MA.*, XXV, pl. VIII; *Not. Sc.* (1888), pl. XV, 2; *St. Et.*, III (1929), 21 ff.

19. Evans, *PPS.*, XIX, 85; Bernabo Brea, *BP.* (1956), 51.

20. Clavijo (*Embassy to Tamerlane*, London, 1928) *en route* from Cadiz to Constantinople in 1403 sailed from Minorca through the Straits of Bonifacio to the Tyrrhenian coast but was forced to shelter off Lipari before passing the Straits of Messina.

21. *PPS.*, XIX, 69, 88.

22. *BP.*, n.s., X (1956), 60.

23. *BP.*, XXIV (1898), 253 ff.

24. *BP.*, XLI, 102 ff.

25. *Not. Sc.* (1904), 305 ff.; *MA.*, XIX, 409 ff.

26. *Antiquity*, XIII (1939), 461–3.

27. *BSR.*, V (1910), 103, fig. 5.

28. Taramelli, *Il Convegno archeologico sardo*, fig. 65.

29. Taramelli, *Il Convegno archeologico sardo*, fig. 66; *BSR.*, V, pl. IX, 1.

30. *BSR.*, VI (1913), 167; *BP.*, XLI, 15.

31. *Antiquity*, XIII (1939), 376–7.

32. *Rivista*, XX, 6 ff.; *BSR.*, V, 135.

33. *MA.*, XI, 268; *Not. Sc.*, 1933, 360.

34. Quoted by Giuffridi-Ruggieri in *Archivio per Antrop. ed Etnogr.*, XLVI, 18.

35. Nordmann, 'Megalithic', p. 122.

36. *Not. Sc.* (1909), 103.

37. So Hall, *Cambridge Ancient History*, II, 282.

38. *BP.*, XXXIX, 100; *MA.*, XXV, 896; *Archivio*, XLVI (1916), 9; *RM.*, XIII (1928), 74.

39. Bosch-Gimpera, *Etnologia*, 194.

40. e.g. at Monte Sa'Idda, *MA.*, XXVII, 14 ff.

41. At Monte Sa'Idda and Alà dei Sardi, *Not. Sc.* (1925), 466.

42. *Not. Sc.* (1922), 293; (1926), 374; cf. Bosch-Gimpera in *CIPMO.*, 30 f.; *Studi Etruschi*, III, 20.

43. *Arch.*, LXXVI, 121 ff.; *Ant. J.*, XIII (1933), 33 f.; *CAS.*, 113.

44. *CIPMO.*, 26.

45. Castillo, *Campaniforme*, 125; *CIPMO.*, pl. II.

46. In museum at Palma unpublished before the rebellion.

47. *Ant. J.*, XIII, 35, 39; *CIPMO.*, pl. III.

48. So the axes of the Talayot culture include both flat and socketed forms, *CIPMO*, 21.

49. *PPS.*, I (1935), 110.

Chapter 15   The Iberian Peninsula

1. Pericot, *Historia de España*, I (Madrid, 1947); *La España Primitiva* (Barcelona, 1950), 355.

2. *Rev. Anthr.*, XLI (1931), 158; A. Ruhlmann, *La Grotte préhistorique de Dar es-Sultan* (Paris, Col. Hesperies), 1951.

3. Pericot, *Historia*, 121; *Act. y Mem.*, XVII, 1942, 88–108.

4. *Riv. St. Lig.*, XV (1949), 22–5; Bailloud and Mieg, 58–71; *AC.*, II.

5. San Valero Aparisi, *La Cueva de la Sarsa*, Servicio de Investigacion Prehistorica (Valencia, 1950), pl. II.

6. ibid., pl. I.

7. Bailloud and Mieg, 71 (Châteauneuf-lez-Martigues), but in *Préhistoire*, XII (1956), 89, this is classed as 'néolithique cardial'.

8. Sereni, 'Il sistema agricola del debbio nella Liguria antica,' *Mem. della Acad. Lunigianese*, XXV (La Spezia, 1955).

9. San Valero, op. cit., 37–46, argues that these are weights for digging-sticks. Similar objects are widespread in the North African Capsian, cf. Vaufrey, *Préhistoire de l'Afrique*, I, 413–15. They are too light for digging-sticks.

10. *Riv. St. Lig.*, XVII (1951), 132.

11. cf. Arkell, *Shaheinab* (London, 1953), 69.

12. cf. Milojčić, *Germania*, XXX, 314–18; Bernabo Brea, *A.C.*, II, 192–8.

13. *Anuari*, VIII (1936), 19 ff.; *Ampurias*, V, 190.

14. Siret, *RQS.*, XXXIV (1893), 489 ff., and *Les premiers Âges du métal dans le sud-est de l'Espagne;* Gossé, *Ampurias,* III (1941), 63–84.

15. Siret, *Questions de chronologie et d'ethnographie ibériques,* Paris, 1913.

16. *BSPF.*, XXXIII, 633; *Rev. Anthr.*, XLI (1931), 158, fig. 1, 4.

17. Caton-Thompson, *The Desert Fayum;* Childe, *NLMAE.*, 58.

18. Siret, *Âges du métal,* pl. 3; segmented bone heads, a clay plaque perforated at the four corners and a heap of ore suggest that this site should be assigned rather to the Copper Age.

19. Siret, *Questions,* 38; *APL.*, I (1928), 25.

20. Leisner, *Megalithgräber,* 390–404.

21. *Préhistoire de l'Afrique, I, Maghreb* (Paris, 1955), 412.

22. ibid., 415.

23. Leisner, *Antas do Concelho de Reguengos de Monsarraz* (Lisbon, 1951), 177.

24. Maluquer de Motes, 'La Cultura neolitica del Valles,' *Arrahona,* 1–2 (Sabadell, 1950), 4–13.

25. *Ampurias,* VI (1944), 43–58.

26. *AJA.*, LIII (1949), 150, figs. 1–4.

27. Cf. e.g. Graziosi, *L'Arte rupestre della Libia* (Napoli, n.d.), 275–85.

28. Breuil, *Les Peintures rupestres schématiques de la Péninsule ibérique* (Paris, 1936).

29. *BSPF.*, XLI (1944), 168.

30. Siret, *RQS.* (1893); Leisner, *Megalithgräber,* 19–64.

31. Leisner, ibid., 10, 13, 73.

32. *T. dicoccum* and *compactum, H. hexastichon;* Telles and Ciferri, *Trigos arqueologicos de España,* Madrid (Inst. nac. de Investigaciones Agronomicas), 1954; *Cuadernos,* I (1946), 38 f.

33. *Cuadernos,* III (1948), 117–24.

34. From Tres Cabezos (neolithic), Velez Blanco, Mas de Menente (Alicante, Bronze Age!).

35. Leisner, *Megalithgräber,* 289–328.

36. Leisner, *Megalithgräber,* 84–168.

37. ibid., 174–85.

38. ibid., 194–213.

39. S. Gimenez Reyna, 'Mem. arqueol. de Prov. Malaga hasta 1946', *Informes y Memorias* (Madrid, Junta para Excavaciones, 1946).

40. *Acta Arqueol. Hispanica,* III (1945), 37; Bonsor, 'Les Colonies agricoles préromaines de la vallée du Bétis,' *Rev. Arch.*, XXXV (1899), 111.

41. op. cit., 36–9, 105–10, fig. 41–2.

42. Estacio de Veiga, *Antiguidades monumentaes do Algarve* (Lisbon, 1886–91).

43. Peña (*OAP.*, XIV, 354), and Barro, with semicircular forecourt; V. Correia, *CIPP.*, *Mem.* 27 (1931), 72, relics at Belem.

44. Cartailhac, op. cit.; *OAP.*, II, 211.

45. *OAP.*, XII (1907), 210, 320.

46. Afonso do Paço, 'As Grutas de Alapraia', *Broteria,* XXI (Lisbon, 1935); *Anaïs* IV (Lisbon, 1941).

47. *Alapraiá e S. Pedro,* Junta de Turismo de Cascais, 1946; Congresso Luso.-Espanhol. do Porto, T. VIII, 1943.

48. Leisner, *Antas do Concelho de Reguengos* (Lisbon, 1951), 284–9.

49. ibid., 212 and 310.

50. Correia, *CIPP.*, *Mem.* 27.

51. *Marburger Studien*, 1, 150.

52. Afonso do Paço, *Act. y Mem.*, XX (1945).

53. *Id. Broteria*, LIV (1952), 7–16.

54. *Anaïs*, V (1954), 280–356, *T. sphaerococcum*; cereals from other sites are described here.

55. *Zephyrus*, III (Salamanca, 1952), 32–9.

56. Childe, *Revista Guimarães*, LX (1950), 7–12.

57. One such 'point' was found sticking in a skull at Valdenabi, Leon; *Corona d'Estudis dedica a sus Martires* (Madrid, 1941), 128.

58. *Ethnos*, II (Lisbon, 1942), 449–58.

59. Afonso do Paço, *Anaïs*, IV, 122, compares these to Irish gold lunulae, but the perforations, if any, are near the centre, not the ends; comparison with the clay arcs might be equally legitimate.

60. Leisner, *As Antas de Monsarraz* (Lisbon, 1952), 145.

61. Breuil, *Les Peintures rupestres schématiques*, IV (1936), 148.

62. Blanquires de Labor, Murcia, *Cuadernos*, III, 5–30; Cami Real and Barranc de Castellet, Alicante (*Arch. Preh. Levant.*, I, 31–72); Monte de Barsella, Alicante, *JSEA.*, *Mem.* 112 (1930); *APL.*, II, 115–40.

63. The alleged stratigraphical evidence for Bosch-Gimpera's view (*Man*, XL (1940), 6–10) making the Palmella style older than the Pan-European, has been demolished by Castillo, *APL.*, IV (1953), 135 ff.; cf. also Savory, *Revista Guimarães*, LX, 363–6; Leisner, *As Antas nas Herdades da Casa de Bragança* (Lisbon, 1955), 20–27.

64. 'Colonies agricoles' (*Rev. Arch.*, XXXV), 88–90, 116–23, 132.

65. *PPS.*, XIX (1953), 95–107.

66. Xanthudides, *Vaulted Tombs*, pls. XI, 1850 (stone birds' nest vases), XXXI, 687 (clay tumbler), XXX, 4982 (stud-ornament), M.M.I.

67. *Act. y Mem. Soc. Españ. Anthropologia*, XIX (1944), 135.

68. Schliemann, *Ilion*, fig. 536; van der Osten, 'The Alishar Hüyük, 1928–29,' *OIC. Pubs.*, XIX, fig. 85; for arcs, see p. 40, n. 1.

69. As described in the late Latin poem, *Ora Maritima*, by Avienus; cf. Hawkes in *Ampurias*, XIV (1952), 81–95.

70. MacWhite, *Estudios sobre las relaciones atlánticas de la península hispánica* (*Dissertationes Matritenses*, II, Madrid, 1951).

71. *The Prehistoric Foundations of Europe* (London, 1940), 159.

72. Siret, *Les premiers âges* is the principal source.

73. *Arch.*, LXXXVI (1936), 288, 298.

74. Institut d'Estudis Valencians: Servei d'Investigacio Prehistórica, No. 5 (1928), *Collecció de Treballs del P. J. Fergus*, IV, lam. I, 2.

75. Coon, *Races*, 151, insists on contrast with 'Copper Age' population.

76. So Bosch-Gimpera, *Archivo Español de Arqueologia* (1954), 48.

77. *Bol. R. Acad. Hist.*, LIV, 357; *APL.*, II, 151–63.

78. *JSEA.*, *Mem.* 94 (1927).

79. *A.P.L.*, I, 101–12.

80. Gimenez Reyna, 'Mem. Arqueol. de Malaga', *Informes y Mems.*, 12 (Comisario gen. de Excavaciones, Madrid, 1946), 49 ff.

81. *Archivo Español de Arq.*, XXII (1949), 310.

82. *OAP.*, XI (1906), 108; *Act. y Mem.*, XXII (1947), 158.

83. Savory, 'The Atlantic Bronze Age', *PPS.*, XV (1949), 128 ff.

84. cf. MacWhite, *Estudios*, 48–64.

85. Hawkes, *Ampurias*, XIV, 81 ff.

86. Piggott, *Revista Guimarães*, LVII (1948), 10 ff. Sir Lindsay Scott

(*PSAS.*, LXXXII (1950), 44) has pointed out the close resemblances between British Middle Bronze Age 'incense cups' and stone and pottery vases from Los Millares and cognate Copper Age sites.

Chapter 16   Western Culture in the Alpine Zone

1. J. Hawkes, *Antiquity*, VIII, 26–40; Piggott, *L'Anthr.*, LVII (1953), 413–42.
2. Piggot, loc. cit., 426; Bailloud and Mieg, 100.
3. *Riv. Sc. Pr.*, VI (1951), 130–37; Heléna, *Les Origines de Narbonne* (Paris-Toulouse, 1937).
4. Vogt, *CIPPS*. (Zurich, 1950), 33; Piggott, loc. cit., 430.
5. *Germania*, XVIII (1934), 91 ff.
6. Welten, in *Das Pfahlbauproblem* (*Monographien zur Ur- und Frühgeschichte der Schweiz*, XI), (Basel, 1955), 78.
7. Vouga, 'Le Néolithique lacustre ancien' (Université de Neuchâtel, *Recueil de Travaux, Faculté de Lettres*, 1934); *Antiquity*, II (1928), 388–92; von Gonzeobach, *Die Cortaillodkultur in der Schweiz* (*Monographien zur Ur- und Frühgeschichte*, 1949).
8. Vogt, Guyan, Welten in *Das Pfahlbauproblem*; but Tschumi, *Urgeschichte der Schweiz* (1948) adhered to the classical theory of pile-dwellings formulated by Keller in 1854.
9. *Urgeschichte der Schweiz*, 597; cf. Beck, Rytz, Steklen, and Tschumi, 'Der neol. Pfahlbau Thun', *Mitt naturforschenden Gesellschaft* (Bern, 1930).
10. The proportions are: oxen 39 per cent, swine 21 per cent, sheep and goats each 18·5 per cent of food animals; game only 30 per cent of total animal bones; Vouga, op. cit. Bones of wild horse are reported from Port; Tschumi, *Die ur- und frühgeschichtliche Fundstelle von Port, im Amt Nidau* (Biel, 1940), 73.
11. Troels-Smith, *Pfahlbauproblem*, 49–52; Guyan, ibid., 262.
12. Ischer, *Pfahlbauten des Bielersees* (Biel, 1928), 43, pl. VII.
13 Such actually survive with wooden handles: von Gonzenbach, *Cortaillodkultur*, 51.
14. von Gonzenbach, 25; Vogt, *PPS.*, XV (1949), 50–52.
15. *Sibrium*, II (1955), 133–8.
16. Tschumi, 'Dis steinzeitliche Hockergräber der Schweiz', *AsA.*, XXII–XXIII (1920–21); *Altschles.*, V, 96 ff.
17. von Gonzenbach, 68–76; Kimmig, *Bad. Fb.* (1948–50), 58–64.
18. von Gonzenbach, 47; Vogt, *Acta Arch.*, XXIV (1953), 180, Abb. 2, 2.
19. *Das Pfahlbauproblem*, 113.
20. The culture of this (Vogt, *Ztschr. f. schweiz. Altertum. u. Kunst*, XII (1951), 205–15) and other villages in Middle Switzerland diverges from that familiar on Lake Neuchâtel; it might be Cortaillod still quite uninfluenced by Rössen (von Gonzenbach, op. cit., 21).
21. Buttler, *Donauländische*, 79–91; Baer, A., *Die Michelsberger Kultur in der Schweiz. Monographie zur Ur- und Frühgeschichte*, Bâle.
22. See also R. R. Schmidt, *Jungsteinzeitliche Siedelungen in Federseemoor*, Tübingen, 1930 ff.; Paret, *Das Steinzeitdorf Ehrenstein bei Ulm* (Stuttgart, 1955).
23. Paret, op. cit., 60.
24. *Pfahlbauproblem*, 269.
25. ibid., 261.

26. Paret, op. cit., 20.

27. ibid., 66.

28. Loë, *La Belgique ancienne*, I, 190 ff.; and Mariën, *Oud-België*, 59–79.

29. Kimmig, *JSGU.*, XL (1950), 150, regards it as a Michelsberg-Rössen hybrid.

30. Loë, *La Belgique ancienne*, 235, 241; Mariën, *Oud-België*, 55–83; *L'Anthr.*, LVII, 410.

31. von Gonzenbach, 35, 76; Vogt, *CISPP*. (Zurich); *Acta Arch.*, XXIV, 185.

32. *Germania*, XX (1936), 230.

33. E.g. *JSGU*. (1944), 32.

34. *Germania*, XXXIII (1955), 166–9.

35. *JSGU.*, XL, 149.

36. Childe, *Danube*, 171–3; Vouga, *AsA.*, XXXI (1929), 167–70; Vogt, ibid., XL, 1938, 1–14.

37. *Germania*, XVIII, 92–4; *AsA.*, XL, 2–4.

38. *Germania*, XXI, 155–8; Buttler, *Donauländische*, 76.

39. *AsA.*, XL, 2–14.

40. *Germania*, XXI (1937), 149; cf. von Gonzenbach, *Cortaillodkultur*, 76.

41. *Antiquity*, II, 398; *AsA.*, XXXI, 171.

42. *Germania*, XVIII, 94.

43. *Antiquity*, II, 401; VIII, 38; Childe, *Danube*, 175–6.

44. *Altschles.*, V (1934), 102.

45. *Altschles.*, V., pl. XVIII, 5.

46. *AsAg.*, IV, 2 ff., Viollier in *Opuscula archaeologica O. Montelio dicata*, 126 ff.; *MAGZ.*, XXIX, 200.

47. Kraft, *AsA.*, XXIX (1927), 5 ff.

48. Vogt in *Tschumi Festschrift* (Frauenfeld, 1948), 54–68.

49. *ZfsAK.*, VI (1944), 65 ff.

50. Burkart, *Crestaulta* (*Monographien zur Ur- und Frühgeschichte*, V), Basel, 1946; *JSGU*. (1947), 42.

51. The Early Bronze Age village succeeded Horgen and Michelsberg settlements, all stratified; D. Beck in Vols. 47 and 48 of *Jahrbuch des historischen Vereins für das Fürstentum Liechtenstein*.

52. The bones of 22 bovids, 22 sheep, 22 pigs, 10 goats, and 71 horses were recognized at Crestaulta.

53. *Bayerische Urgeschichtsfreund*, IV (Munich, 1924), 13 ff.; Childe. *Danube*, 125–8.

54. Franz, 'Die Funde aus den prähistorischen Pfahlbauten im Mondsee' (*Materialien zur Urgeschichte Österreichs*, III), Vienna, 1927; Willvonseder, *Oberösterreich in der Vorzeit*, Vienna, 1933, 20–28; (Attersee); *WPZ.*, XXVI (1939), 135; Pittioni, *Urgeschichte*.

55. Childe, *Danube*, 210–12; Schmidt, *Vučedol*; Patay, 'Korai Bronzkori', 24–8 ('Zok' culture).

56. Childe, *Danube*, loc. cit.

57. *MAGW.*, LXI, 75–80.

58. Franz, 'Mondsee', 11–12.

59. *WPZ.*, V, 19.

60. Schmidt, *Vučedol*.

61. Schmidt, *Vučedol*.

62. Patay, 'Korai Bronzkori', 24–8.

63. *WPZ.*, XXVI (1939), 135–47.

64. Novotny, *Slov. Arch.*, III (1955), 7–22, lists and maps 15 sites in Bohemia, 3 in Moravia and 22 in Slovakia.

65. ibid., 16.

66. As far as the shape is concerned, both groups could be derived independently from the Starčevo types of period I, but the decoration of the Slavonian and the Catacomb lamps is also very similar.

67. The porterage (from the Adige to the Inn) is much shorter on the Brenner route than on that across the Julian Alps which replaced it when the Romans had built a road to Nauportus.

Chapter 17   Megalith Builders in Atlantic Europe

1. Déchelette, *Manuel*, I, 559; Bailloud and Mieg, 97 ff.; Piggott, *L'Anthr.*, LVII (1953), 410–32.

2. Many authors thus describe all plain Western pottery from France; Arnal and Benazet distinguish therefrom 'Chasséen decoré' which they consider earlier than the plain ware; *BSPF.*, XLVIII (1951), 552–5.

3. *BSPF.*, XLVIII, 555.

4. *BSPF.*, XXVII (1930), 268–76.

5. This is the truth underlying Bosch-Gimpera's thesis of the existence in North France of a 'culture de silex' – just another way of saying that in this area rich in flint but poor in fine-grained rocks, flint was the normal material even for axes, cf. *Rev. Anthr.*, XXXVI (1926), 320.

6. At Nermont, Danubian pottery seems to precede Western, Bailloud and Mieg, 50.

7. Philippe, 'Cinq années de fouilles au Fort Harrouard' (Société normande d'études préhistoriques, XXV bis), Rouen, 1927.

8. The actual proportions are: cattle 68 per cent, swine 18 per cent, sheep 10 per cent, goats 1·5 per cent, game 2·5 per cent; *L'Anthr.*, XLVII (1937), 292.

9. *L'Anthr.*, XLVI, 270–71.

10. *L'Anthr.*, XLVI, 559.

11. *L'Anthr.*, XLVI, 604.

12. *L'Anthr.*, XLVI, 541 f.

13. *L'Anthr.*, XII (1901), 359 and 354; LVII, 441–2.

14. But besides Late Bronze Age pins the crutch-head type occurs, as in the Copper Age lake-dwellings, Philippe, 'Cinq Années', pls. XI, 11, and XVIII, 19.

15. *L'Anthr.*, XLIV (1934), 486–9.

16. *Antiquity*, XI (1937), 441–52.

17. Cazalis de Fondouce, *Les Allées couvertes de la Provence* (1878), describes the 'grottes' de Bounias, Castellet, and des Fées; cf. Hemp., *Arch.*, LXXVI, 150.

18. Pericot, *Sepulcros megaliticos* (1950), gives a comprehensive survey of tombs and grave goods from South France as well as from Spain.

19. *Mat.* (1881), 522.

20. *BSPF.*, XXVII (1930), 536–9; the tomb contained '300' skeletons, at least 7 beakers, 12 palettes, gold beads, tanged arrow-heads.

21. Goby 'Les Dolmens de Provence', *Rodania: Congrès de Cannes-Grasse* (1929).

22. Arnal, *Ampurias*, XI (1949), 29–44.

23. *Les Origines de Narbonne* (1937). To Bernabo Brea (*A.C.* II, 232) only

some sherds from the Arles tombs might be (Upper) Neolithic; the pottery from all other tombs should be Chalcolithic – in the Ligurian sequence.

24. Bailloud and Mieg (1955), 163–79; Pericot, *Sepulcros megal.*; Piggott, *L'Anthr.*, LVIII (1954), 7–22.

25. Louis, Peyrolle, Arnal, *Gallia*, V (1947), 235–57.

26. *L'Anthr.*, XXII (1911), 413.

27. Listed by Sandars, *Inst. Arch., AR.*, VI (1950), 44 ff.

28. Morel, 'Sépultures tumulaires de la Region de Freyssinel', *Bul.* Soc. des Lettres, Sci., Art. du Lozère (1936), 17–23.

29. *L'Anthr.*, LVIII, 7 and 27.

30. *Rev. Ét. Anc.*, XIII, 435.

31. Heléna, *Origines*, fig. 64.

32. *Mat.* (1869), 328.

33. *Sepulcros megal.*, 122, 131.

34. Heléna, *Les Grottes sépulchrales de Monges* (Toulouse, 1925), pl. V, 49; wrongly termed 'stone'; a segmented bone bead from the 'dolmen' of Cabut, Gironde, may be a copy, Bailloud and Mieg, 190.

35. *Cuadernos*, III, 37–42; *Préhistoire*, II (1933), 37.

36. ibid.

37. ibid.; cf. Hawkes, *Ampurias*, XIV, 90 ff.

38. Bailloud and Mieg, 190; *BSPF.*, XLIX (1952), 158; (1953), 60.

39. At La Halliade and other sites in Acquitaine, Fabre, *Les civilisations protohistoriques de l'Acquitaine* (Paris, 1952); a similar bowl was found in a Hallstatt grave in Côte d'Or.

40. *Act. y Mem.*, XXI (1946), 196; *L'Anthr.*, LVIII, 6.

41. Pericot, *Sepulcros*, 190.

42. *L'Anthr.*, XLVIII, 8–10; *BSPF.*, XLVIII, 557.

43. *Riv. St. Lig.*, XV (1949), 42–4; Pericot, *Sepulcros meg.*, 125–6, and map 84.

44. Maluquer de Motes, 'Yacimientos postpaleoliticos', *Monografias de la Estacion de Estudios Pyrenaicos*, I (Zaragoza, 1948), 22 and n. 1.

45. *BSPF.*, LI (1954), 255–66.

46. *Ampurias*, XI (1949), 29.

47. Heléna, *Origines*, 80.

48. See p. 359, n. 28.

49. MacWhite (*CauDernos*, I (1946), 61–9) enumerates 15 trepanned skulls from this region.

50. In Lozère 52 cases come from 'dolmens', 105 from caves, Déchelette, *Manuel*, I, 474 f.; cf. *AsAg.*, XI (1945), 56; E. Guiard, *La Trépanation cranienne chez les néolithiques et chez les primitifs modernes* (Paris), 1930.

51. *Rev. Anthr.*, XLI (1931), 300 ff.

52. *Afas.*, 1890, 629; *Rev. Anthr.*, XLI, 362; the usual plans are wrong.

53. General review Childe and Sandars, *L'Anthr.*, LIV (1950), 1 ff., and Bailloud and Mieg, 190–99.

54. E.g. Vaucelles, Namur, Loë, *La Belgique ancienne*, I, 144.

55. In Marne and also Oise, *Mem. Soc. académique d'Archéol. du Dép. de l'Oise*, IV (Beauvais, 1860), 465.

56. J. de Baye, *L'Archéologie préhistorique* (Paris, 1884); cf. also *BSPF.*, VIII (1911), 669; *Gallia*, I (1943), 20–25.

57. *Rev. Anthr.*, XLI, 371–3.

58. Déchelette, *Manuel*, I, 397 ff.; *Rev. Arch.*, XXVII (1928), 1–13; Forde, *Am. Anthr.*, XXXII, 63–6; *AsA.*, XL (1938), 1–14.

59. *Rev. Anthr.*, XLI, 371–3.
60. Breuil in *Afas.* (1899), 590.
61. See also *BSPF.* (1934), 282–5; (1951), 558; *L'Anthr.*, LVIII, 18–20.
62. *Gallia*, I (1943), 24.
63. Bailloud and Mieg, 48.
64. E.g. Tregastel, *BSPF.*, XLIII (1946), 305.
65. Mariën, *Oud-Belgie*, 142–5; 152 ff.
66. But if the megalithic religion were introduced into the Seine-Marne basins from the Loire, from the coasts of Normandy (Piggott, *L'Anthr.*, LVIII, 20), or from the Caucasus via Hesse, the Paris cists and the Marne carvings must represent the germs from which evolved the rock-cut tombs and statue-menhirs of South France!
67. Sievekng, Inst. Arch. *AR.*, IX (1953), 60–67; *L'Anthr.*, LVIII, 20.
68. *BSPF.*, XLIII, 307.
69. Forde, *Am. Anthr.*, XXXII, 85.
70. Types summarized by le Rouzic, *L'Anthr.*, XLIII (1933), 233–48; for Guernsey, T. D. Kendrick, *Archaeology of the Channel Islands*, I (1928), for Jersey, J. Hawkes, *Archaeology of the Channel Islands*, II (1939).
71. Forde, *Man*, XXIX, 80; *Am. Anthr.*, XXXII, 74.
72. *L'Anthr.*, XLIII, 242; *Antiquity*, XI, 455.
73. Société Jersiaise, *Bulletin* (St Helier, 1925).
74. V. C. C. Collum, 'Re-excavation of Déhus', *Trans. Soc. Guernesiaise* (1933).
75. Pecquart et le Rouzic, *Corpus des signes, gravés*, Paris, 1927; *Préhistoire*, VI (1938), 1–48.
76. Z. le Rouzic, *Les Cromlechs de Er Lannic* (Vannes, 1930).
77. *L'Anthr.*, XLIII, 233–5; XLIV, 490–2, so Breuil, *Préhistoire*, VI, 47.
78. *CISPP.* (Oslo, 1936); *Archaeol. Channel Islands*, II, 90, 248.
79. *BSA.* (Paris, 1892), 41.
80. *L'Anthr.*, XLIV (1934), 496, fig. 9, numbers 8, and 12–16.
81. *CISPP.* (London, 1932), 140; Hawkes, *Channel Islands*, 7, 162.
82. In a 'small dolmen' near Trizay, Charente Inférieure, with a West European dagger, tanged-and-barbed arrow-heads and gold ribbon; *BSPF.*, XXXVIII (1941), 45; cf. *L'Anthr.*, LVIII, 26.
83. *L'Anthr.*, XLIV, fig. 19, 11; *Rev. Arch.* (1883), pl. XIV.
84. Inst. Arch., *AR.* VI (1950), 49.
85. V. C. C. Collum, 'Re-excavation of Déhus', *Trans. Soc. Guernesiaise* (1933).
86. Kendrick, *Axe Age*, 34.
87. Jersey, Kendrick, *Channel Islands*, 94.
88. *L'Anthr.*, XLIV, 504, figs. 14, 5 and 15.
89. From an angled passage grave at Lann Blaen (Morb.) and a SOM gallery at Trégastel (Côtes du Nord); *BSPF.*, XLIII (1946), 306.
90. Some have expanded blades imitating copper axes, *Am. Anthr.*, XXXII, 87.
91. Petrie, *Tools and Weapons*, Z., pl. XVII.
92. *L'Anthr.*, XLIV, figs 14, 11, and 16, 1; *Ant. J.*, VII, 17.
93. Copper double-axes with a hole too small to take a shaft occur in Central France, Switzerland, and Southern Germany, *ZfE.*, XXXVII, 525; Childe, *Danube*, 177, 193; *BSA.*, XXXVII, 152–6.
94. *L'Anthr.*, XLIV, 500.

95. *L'Anthr.*, XLIII, 251–3; Forde, *Am. Anthr.*, XXXII, 76–9, notes that the supports are sculptured like those of normal collective tombs.

96. *L'Anthr.*, XI, 159; XLIV, 511; LV, 425–43; *Bul. Soc. Arch. Finistère*, XXXIV (1907), 125; *Ant. J.*, VII, 18; *Les Trésors archéologiques de l'Armorique occidentale.*

97. *Bul. Soc. Arch. Fin.*, XXXIV.

98. From the tholos of Parc Guérin which had been converted into a single grave of Bronze Age type, *L'Anthr.*, LV (1952), 427.

99. See maps in *PPS.*, IV (1938), 65, and *L'Anthr.*, LV, 428.

100. *PPS.*, IV (1938), 64 ff.

101. *L'Anthr.*, LV (1952), 442–3.

102. *Foundations*, 312–14.

103. Apart from these barrow graves in Allier and Dordogne (Déchelette, II, 142, 147), the poor non-megalithic cists in Vienne, Charente, and Lozère (de Mortillet, *Origine du culte des morts* (Paris, 1921), 79 f.) might be 'Bronze Age' though only one contained any metal. East of the Saône, of course, there are Early Bronze Age graves, related to the Swiss though several contained polished flint or greenstone axes (Déchelette, II, 136 ff.).

Chapter 18   The British Isles

1. Fox, *The Personality of Britain* (Cardiff, 1938).

2. For Neolithic Britain see Piggott, *The Neolithic Cultures of the British Isles* (1954), unless other reference is given. But on relations with Northern Europe see now *PPS.*, XXI (1955), 96–101.

3. Clark, *Mesolithic Britain*, 90.

4. Piggott, op. cit.; cf. *PRIA.*, LVI (1956), 300–306, 447–7; *Arch. Camb.*, CII (1953), 24–9.

5. Jessen and Helbaek, *Det kong. danske Videns. Selskab, Biol. Skrifter*, III, 2; *PPS.*, XVIII, 194–200.

6. Atkinson et al., *Excavations at Dorchester, Oxon.* (Oxford, 1951).

7. Atkinson in *Antiquity*, XXIX (1955), 4–10.

8. Crawford, *Long Barrows of the Cotswolds* (Gloucester, 1925), 26; *Ant J.*, XV, 435.

9. Jessen and Helbaek, see p. 374, n. 5.

10. The sole probable Hispanic import found in a Boyne tomb is matched in a Spanish sepulchral cave, *JSEA.* (1929), pl. VII, 11–12; *Rev. Guim.* (1948), 12.

11. Childe, *PCBI.*, 92–4; add *Arch. Aeliana* (1936), 210, and *Oxoniensia*, XIII (1948), 1–9; the earrings are associated with B3 rather than B1 beakers.

12. Childe, *Act. y Mem.*, XXI (1946), 196; Piggott, *L'Anthr.*, LVIII, 6; Fox, *Arch.*, LXXXIX (1943), 100–104.

13. To Co. Limerick from the Bristol Channel (*PRIA.*, XLVIII (1942), 260–69); LIV. (1951), 56–9, 70–72; to Ulster from Southern Scotland (*UJA.*, II, 264; III, 79).

14. *PPS.*, XVIII, 204.

15. *PRIA.*, LVI (1954), 343, 379; *PPS.*, XVII, 53.

16. *PPS.*, XVII, 1951, 100–159; *UJA.*, XV, 1952, 32–48.

17. Atkinson, *Excavations at Dorchester*, I, 84 ff.

18. Atkinson, *Stonehenge* (London, 1956), 63 ff.

19. Childe, *PCBI.*, 102–4.

20. Bone pins with lateral loops occur in a boat-axe grave in Sweden and in

another in Estonia (*Fv.* (1956), 196–207); all may be copies of – rare – metal Unětician pins of like form.

21. Piggott, op. cit., 315, must be revised in the light of Isobel Smith's researches.

22. Smith, *PPS.*, XX (1954), 227.

23. Piggott, op. cit., 321–40.

24. Childe, *Skara Brae* (London, 1931); *PSAS.*, LXXIII, 6–31 (Rinyo).

25. *PSAS.*, LXIII (1929), 273.

26. *PSAS.*, LXXXII (1950), 44 ff.

27. Piggott, *PPS.*, IV (1938), 52–106; cf. ibid., 107–21; *Inst. Arch. AR.*, X, 107–21.

28. *PPS.*, XV (1949), 101–6.

29. Ap Simon, *Inst. Arch. AR.*, X (1954), 107–10.

30. For instance, the earlier Wessex daggers seem derivable from the Elbe-Oder type; the halberd pendants reproduce the Saale-Warta bronze-shafted type.

31. Childe, *PPS.*, XVII (1951), 95.

32. Atkinson, *Stonehenge*, 68–77.

33. Childe, *PCBI.*, 119–34; *SBS.*, 8–10, 51–62, 105–18.

34. *PPS.*, IV, 272–82; *Arch.*, LXXXVI, 305 ff.; Childe, *PCBI.*, 115–17.

35. MacWhite, *Estudios*, 42–3; Sobrino Buhigas, *Corpus Petroglyphorum Gallaeciae* (Compostella, 1945).

36. Childe, *PCBI.*, 123–4. Note that the gold lunulae found in Northern Europe are not of Irish manufacture.

37. Childe, *PCBI.*, 145–59.

38. Such a bead was discovered in a secondary grave in the Mound of the Hostages at Tara by Prof. O'Riordain in 1955.

39. Glasbergen, 'Excavations in the Eight Beatitudes' (*Palaeohistoria*, II–III), Groningen, 1954, esp. pp. 127–31; 168–70.

40. Childe, *PCBI.*, 151–3.

41. *PPS.*, XIX (1953), 161 ff.

42. *Germania*, XXII (1938), 7–11.

43. Kersten, *Zur älteren nordischen Bronzezeit* (Neumünster, n.d.), 65; cf. also Broholm, *Danmarks Bronzealder*, I (Copenhagen, 1944), 223.

44. Childe in *Corolla archaeologica in honorem C. A. Nordmann* (Helsinki, 1952), 8.

45. Childe, *APL.*, IV (1953), 182–4.

Chapter 19   Retrospect: The Prehistory of European Society

1. The method is explained by Zeuner, *Dating the Past* (1952), pp. 341 ff.

2. Libby, *Radio Carbon Dating* (Chicago, 1953), 75. British prehistorians unanimously reject this date.

3. See p. 341, n. 19.

4. These figures have frequently been mentioned by archaeologists, but not formally published by the responsible physicists.

Index

459